Teaching and the Case Method

Teaching

C. Roland Christensen
with ABBY J. HANSEN

and the Case Method

Text, Cases, and Readings

HARVARD BUSINESS SCHOOL

Boston, Massachusetts

92-840

This book is available from Harvard Business School Publishing Division, Harvard Business School, Boston, Mass. 02163. Order No. 9-387-001.

Fourth Printing

Library of Congress Cataloging-in-Publication Data

Christensen, C. Roland (Carl Roland), 1919–
   Teaching and the case method.

   Rev. ed. of: Teaching by the case method. 1981.
   Bibliography: p.
   1. Business education—Teacher training—United
States. 2. Case method. I. Hansen, Abby J., 1945–
II. Christensen, C. Roland (Carl Roland), 1919–
Teaching by the case method. III. Title.
HF1131.C48 1986   650'.07'12   86-22732
ISBN 0-87584-178-3

Printed in the United States of America.

To Edmund P. Learned
Master Teacher

He has given so much
To so many
In his multiple career worlds—
Academia, business, and government.

Contents

*Distributed by the instructor
(and also found in the Instructor's Guide)

Contents

*Distributed by the instructor
(and also found in the Instructor's Guide)

Contents

*Distributed by the instructor
(and also found in the Instructor's Guide)

IV
Supplementary Materials for Seminar Participants · 233

Section 1. Reappraisal and Reflection

The Art of Leading a Discussion · 235
ADENA ROSMARIN

The Crisis of Professional Knowledge and the Pursuit of an Epistemology of Practice · 241
DONALD A. SCHÖN

Have You Done Your Best? · 254
PAUL HAMILTON

Section 2. Planning Next Steps

The Uses of Videotape Replay · 256
CATHERINE G. KRUPNICK

Reflections of a Casewriter: Writing Teaching Cases · 264

We're Just Wasting Our Time: Case and Teaching Note · 271
GALE MERSETH
JAMES MOORE

Bibliography · 287
CYNTHIA INGOLS
KAREN MALONEY

Acknowledgments

This book is the result of the imagination and effort of a great number of people. We wish to take this opportunity to thank, all too briefly, those whose contributions have made its development possible. We are in their debt, as will be the instructors who use this volume to improve discussion teaching at their own institutions.

In addition to the material that we ourselves created, the cases in this edition are the product of the hard work and creativity of our colleagues, past and present, as well as participants in about 25 seminars in which this material has been tested.

We would like to record our thanks to Tamara Gilman for "Henry Jasper," Gale Merseth for "We're Just Wasting Our Time," and Joy Renjilian-Burgy for "I Felt as if My World Had Just Collapsed!" Our sincere appreciation goes to the following colleagues, all of whom contributed case material to this book: Douglas Anderson, Carliss Baldwin, Kathleen Curley, Heather Dubrow, David Garvin, Nancy Kane, Janice McCormick, Brian Scott, and Richard Tedlow.

We are grateful to the following authors and/or publishers for the use of their articles, included in the reading sections of our seminar outlines: Lane Cooper for "Louis Agassiz as a Teacher," used with permission from the Cornell University Press; Peter Frederick for "The Dreaded Discussion: Ten Ways to Start," reproduced with permission from *College Teaching*; Maryellen Gleason for "Why Teach?", reprinted with permission from *Change* magazine; Robert Goheen for "In Defense of Teaching" reprinted with permission from *Princeton Alumni Weekly*; the late Charles I. Gragg for "Teachers Also Must Learn," used with permission of the *Harvard Educational Review*; also Haim G. Ginott for excerpts from "Teacher and Child," reproduced with permission from the Macmillan Publishing Co.; Sophie Freud for excerpts from "The Passion and Challenge of Teaching," reprinted with permission from the *Harvard Educational Review*; and Neil Postman for excerpts from "Teaching," reprinted with permission from the *Wall Street Journal*—all included in "Teaching and Teachers: Three Views." In addition, our thanks go to Robert G. Kraft for "Bike Riding and the Art of Learning," reprinted with permission from *Change* magazine; James Laney for "The Education of the Heart," reproduced with permission of *Harvard Magazine, Inc.*; Steve McFadden for "Ana Roje," reproduced with his permission; Yuri Nagiben for "Winter Oak," reproduced with the permission of the Am-Rus Literary Agency; Laura Nash for "Seven Questions for Testing My Teaching," reprinted with permission from the author and the Harvard-Danforth Center for Teaching and Learning; Carl Rogers for "Personal Thoughts on Teaching and Learning," from his *On Becoming a Person*, reprinted with permission from the Houghton Mifflin Company; Carl Rogers and Richard Farson for "Active Listening," reproduced with permission from the Industrial Relations Center of the University of Chicago; Selma Wassermann for "How I Taught Myself How to Teach" and "The Gifted Can't Weigh That Giraffe," the former with permission from *Teacher Education* (University of Toronto), and the latter with permission of the *New York Times*; Marcia Yudkin for "The Professor-Student Barrier to Growth," reprinted with permission of the *New York Times*; and Jeffrey Zax for "Hybrids Are Successful Adaptations," reprinted with permission of the author, the Harvard-Danforth Center for Teaching and Learning, and the *Harvard Crimson*.

Our collective efforts to develop a seminar on case method teaching have received the long-term, enthusiastic support of Dean John H. McArthur. Professor E. Raymond Corey, former director of the Division of Research, marshaled the resources of that division to help produce this book. Florence Lathrop, curator of the Manuscripts and Archives Department, provided valuable archival support. Special thanks go to Dyanne Holdman, who with efficiency and good humor managed the edition's planning and production process and who was an active contributor to its organizational design.

Dean W. Currie, associate dean for Administration and Policy Planning, provided major contributions to this effort. His wise counsel, his belief in the worthwhileness of our work, and his unfailing support are deeply appreciated.

Within the wider university scene, President Derek Bok has been instrumental in integrating the efforts of his program to improve ·teaching effectiveness throughout Harvard College with our similar effort at the Harvard Business School. Instrumental to his linkage has been the work of the Harvard-Danforth Center for Teaching and Learning and Dean Whitla, its director, as well as his associates. We were pleased to be associated with Dr. Margaret Morganroth Gullette's *The Art and Craft of Teaching*, a publication of the Harvard University Press.

Another university colleague, Professor David Riesman, Henry Ford II Professor of Social Sciences

Emeritus, provided us with both the inspiration of dedicated professional teaching practice and personal support for our adventure into teaching teachers.

From the wider academic scene, we are appreciative of the contributions of many colleagues: Professors Albert Schrieber and William Newell of the Graduate School of Business, the University of Washington; Thomas R. Williams, dean of the Faculty of Education, and John R. M. Gordon, dean of the School of Business, Queens University, Kingston, Ontario; William R. Boulton and Frederick J. Stephenson, Jr., College of Business Administration, the University of Georgia; Professor Miguel Ochoa Torres of I.P.A.D.E. in Mexico City; Michael R. Leenders of the School of Business Administration, University of Western Ontario, London, Ontario—all have experimented with these materials in their own academic settings and we have learned from their experiences. Cherie Bottum, managing editor of *College Teaching*, and Robert Jacobson, assistant editor of the *Chronicle of Higher Education*, have been constructive advisors.

We acknowledge our significant debt to the tradition of superlative teaching which has been an integral part of the Harvard Business School milieu for more than 75 years. Our former colleagues, all now deceased—Charles Bliss, Melvin Copeland, Franklin E. Folts, Charles I. Gragg, John D. Glover, Malcolm P. McNair, Elton Mayo, Fritz J. Roethlisberger, Benjamin M. Selekman, George Albert Smith, Jr., and Joseph L. Snider—were the teaching giants of their times.

We are in special debt to three colleagues—David Garvin, Andrew R. Towl, former director of Case Development, and Kenneth R. Andrews. Professor Andrews, building on the pioneering work of Cecil Fraser (*The Case Method of Instruction*), edited *Teaching Human Relations by the Case Method*. That book, along with Professor McNair's *The Case Method at the Harvard Business School* and Professor Towl's *To Study Administration by Cases*, became academic beacons for instructors interested in case teaching. The Andrews-Towl tradition of inquiry into the case method of instruction is being continued by colleague David Garvin, whose intellectual contribution to this edition has been major.

We express our gratitude to the over 800 participants who played such an active role in the development of our seminar concepts and cases; we learned a great deal from them. We owe special mention to colleagues Derek Abell, Norman Berg,

Louis Barnes, Colleen Burke, Bart van Dissell, Thomas W. Dunn, John Hennessey, Patrick Kaufman, Habib Ladjevardi, Gordon Marshall, John Matthews, Marina McCarthy, David Rikert, Michael Roberts, William A. Sahlman, Malcolm Salter, Robert Simons, Ann Sweet, Howard H. Stevenson, Robert B. Stobaugh, Michael Y. Yoshino, and Abraham Zaleznik. From other departments at Harvard we are grateful for the support of Patricia A. Graham, dean of the Graduate School of Education; Edith M. Stokey, lecturer in Public Policy and Secretary of the J. F. Kennedy School of Government; and Myra Bergman Ramos, assistant dean for Educational Planning at the Harvard Medical School. From other academic institutions, Selma Wassermann, professor of Education, Simon Fraser University, Burnaby, British Columbia, has been a long-time collaborator and mentor; we have learned much from her insights into teacher development.

Our gratitude also goes to associates who have contributed articles and notes to this edition. James Sloan Allen, director of Liberal Arts and Academic Administration, The Juilliard School; Adena Rosmarin, University of Texas–Austin; Anne Harlan and John Gabarro of the Harvard Business School; Donald A. Schön, Massachusetts Institute of Technology; Catherine G. Krupnick, deputy director of Harvard's BRIDGES and former director of the Video Laboratory at the Harvard-Danforth Center for Teaching and Learning; and Paul Hamilton, as well as Cynthia Ingols and Karen Maloney of the Harvard Graduate School of Education.

Dr. James F. Moore, formerly of our faculty, has earned special thanks for his contributions to the *Instructor's Guide*, which is available as a supplement to this book; his creativeness brought new insights to the development of teacher-support materials.

This program to learn more about the complexities of case teaching has benefited enormously from the contributions of a dedicated group of Harvard Business School faculty—James Austin, David Garvin, James Heskett, and William Poorvu. Their leadership of seminars throughout Harvard University and at sister institutions has enabled us to gain additional knowledge and insight. We owe them so much.

Dr. Abby J. Hansen, coauthor and colleague, richly deserves special recognition for her contribution, not only to this book but to the Harvard Business School's ongoing program on discussion teaching. Her clinical research skills are matched by an ability to create cases which bring reality into the seminar room. She is the author of "Suggestions for Seminar Participants" and "Reflections of a Case Writer," and has written many of the teaching cases included in this edition; she is also the architect for the liberal arts seminar program. Her contributions have been major and are deeply appreciated.

A hug and kiss for my wife "Smitty." For over forty-two years, her zest for life, her love of the artistic, and her belief in the power of goodness have been my life's beacon. She has helped me to persevere, to soften competition with compassion, and to see beauty, grace and "mystery" in everyday routines. This dream would not have been realized without her wonderfulness.

We acknowledge our major debt to Dr. Edmund P. Learned, to whom this book is dedicated. By reading his introductory piece, "Reflections of a Case Method Teacher," one gains an appreciation of the evolution of case method teaching and research at the Harvard Business School.

Ed Learned's contribution to that evolution—forty years of teaching and research and the leadership of nine course areas—is noted in this article. What is less obvious is the creative nature of many of his assignments. He was key, for example, in the development of three critical management-oriented courses that still, in 1986, form the backbone of our MBA curriculum. And he was a pioneer in the field of executive education at the Business School and programs throughout the world. Not only a teacher but a practitioner, he puts his administrative concepts and philosophy to work in a variety of undertakings, ranging from assignments with the senior leadership group of the United States Air Force to private service as a consultant to presidents of numerous large American corporations.

While Ed worked with the leaders of our nation—private and public—his first academic priority was always the development of young faculty members. For dozens of students who were coached by Ed, he was the Master Teacher. His reservoirs of patience were great, his belief in the potential of his younger staff group was unlimited, and his tutorial skills were superior. His graduates have become leaders in education, business, and government. So many owe Ed so much. We hope that the dedication of this book to him indicates in a small way our great affection and respect.

Finally, we all know that even master teachers are students. Ed's teacher for many decades was a great and wonderful lady—Zella Rankin Learned. We honor her memory.

Introduction

This book—text, cases, and readings—is a revision of one originally published in 1981. That first edition, entitled *Teaching by the Case Method*, overviewed a decade-long experiment conducted at the Harvard Business School. Our goals had been twofold: to learn more about the skills and knowledge essential to case method teaching and to develop better ways of helping instructors lead case discussions. Robert Frost once remarked that "education is hanging around till you've caught on." Too often, we believed, the same methodology was used to prepare instructors for discussion teaching. The typical sink-or-swim initiation into this complex pedagogy was economically inefficient and, far worse, exacted major human costs. In response to this problem, we developed a seminar program to help case method instructors become more adept in their craft. Not surprisingly, the seminar itself is based on cases reporting actual classroom situations.

This new edition reviews another phase of our continuing efforts to learn more about the artistry of case teaching. Since our first report, we have made modest progress accompanied, of course, by the usual blunders of any exploratory effort. We would like to share the current status of the project with you, and we hope that many readers will experiment with one of the teaching modules found in Parts II and III of this edition. Your comments and suggestions will be appreciated, for we plan to move forward with this program—refining existing modules and developing new ones, generating cases especially relevant to beginning instructors and female instructors, and continuing our research.

A Growing Concern about Teaching

Interest in teaching and in teachers has increased dramatically since our earlier report, fueled in part by a dozen or more private and governmental study commission reports on the current state of academe.[1] A major conclusion of most of these reports is that teaching needs to be improved. The Association of American Colleges sums up the point: "The faculty should concern itself with the quality of

1. See also Robert N. Shapiro, "Excellence: What Every School Seeks and No One Defines," *Independent Schools*, February, 1982, pp. 12–15; Holmes Group, Inc., *Tomorrow's Teachers: A Report of the Holmes Group* (East Lansing, Michigan); and Peter Elbow, *Embracing Contraries: Explorations in Learning and Teaching* (New York: Oxford University Press, 1980).

college teaching on which, after all, the effectiveness of any curriculum depends. We must assure that future college teachers are better prepared to teach."[2]

Claude Mathis, director of the Center for the Teaching Professions at Northwestern University, reminds us that the teacher is central to any such revitalization process:

> In a recent editorial in the *New York Times*, Fred Hechinger points out that "education is the teachers you remember after you've forgotten the others." Changing the way schools are organized and introducing technology to provide much of the instruction may increase the chances for serendipity to provide what is missing in schools, but the ultimate reform must come through the person of the teacher.[3]

These pleas for more attention to teaching have been accompanied by a questioning of higher education's traditional dependence on lecturing. Both users (students) and producers (teachers) are demanding greater use of active, student-involved teaching methods.[4] Interest in discussion teaching is clearly on the rise throughout the academic community. For example, a special panel convened by the Association of American Medical Colleges (AAMC) urged medical schools to provide more active learning experiences by reducing lecture time, emphasizing independent learning skills, and requiring less factual memorization. Specifically the report recommended that

> medical schools should establish programs to assist members of the faculty to expand their teaching capabilities. . . . Faculty members who guide students in independent learning must do more than merely transmit information. They must challenge medical students to be involved actively in their own education rather than being passive recipients of prepack-

aged information. To create such a learning environment, faculty members will require assistance in developing the skills they need to be effective and stimulating guides and mentors.[5]

Under the leadership of Dean Daniel Tosteson, the faculty of the Harvard Medical School has instituted the New Pathway Program, which meets many of the needs outlined in the AAMC report. This innovative experiment promises to have a major influence on American medical education.

Other professional fields are also reviewing their instructional modes. The Trustees of the Pew Charitable Trust of Philadelphia, for example, have announced an Initiative in Diplomatic Training "to strengthen and broaden the curriculum at schools of international affairs through the development and use of case studies for instructional purposes." The Education Development Center (EDC), the League for Innovation in Community Colleges, and the Fund for the Improvement of Postsecondary Education are sponsoring a program to develop case studies tailored to community college classrooms. Led by Cynthia Lang of EDC and David Garvin of the Harvard Business School faculty, this program will develop cases in both written and videotaped form.

The Teaching Seminars

Harvard Business School's efforts to improve case method instruction through a formal program of teaching seminars mirrors these broader trends. It has contributed, in minor measure, to the emergence within this University of a vibrant and growing community of discussion-oriented instructors. In these seminars committed teachers gather to share common challenges, learn from colleagues in different disciplines, and experiment with case-based, problem-solving teaching. As one participant said, "Working with these dedicated teachers has reaffirmed my faith in the worth of teaching, its tremendous contributive potential, and its centrality to the complete academic life. It has given me impetus for career rededication."

Our early seminars focused on the needs of the Business School's faculty and candidates for its doc-

2. Association of American Colleges, "Report of the Project on Redefining the Meaning and Purpose of Baccalaureate Degrees," *Chronicle of Higher Education*, February 13, 1985, p. 13.
3. B. Claude Mathis, "Faculty Disdain and Poor Schools," *Improving College and University Teaching*, Spring 1984, p. 148.
4. Alexander W. Astiv, "Involvement: The Cornerstone of Excellence," *Change*, July/August 1985, pp. 35–39, and Alvin M. White, "Teaching Mathematics as Though Students Mattered," *Teaching as Though Students Mattered: New Directions for Teaching and Learning* (San Francisco: Jossey-Bass, 1985), pp. 39–48.
5. *Physicians for the Twenty-First Century: The GPEP Report*, Association of American Medical Colleges, Washington, D.C., September 1984; see also Peter Houts and Thomas Leamon, *Case Studies in Primary Medical Care* (University Park: Pennsylvania State University Press, 1983).

torate in business administration. Over the years we were joined by faculty from many departments in arts and sciences—history, literature, music, philosophy, economics, zoology, and physics—as well as most of the University's professional schools—medicine, government, education, public health, and architecture and design. Despite their diverse backgrounds, seminar participants readily became engaged in cases based on business school classroom situations. The challenges of discussing a sonnet, an opera, a proposed legislative act, or a curriculum change have much in common with the fundamental teaching issues raised, for example, in the "Assistant Professor Graham and Ms. Macomber" case.

We owe a great deal to these seminar colleagues from other disciplines. They have been our teachers. We appreciate their contribution, their interest, and their insistence that we share this academic adventure with the wider academic community.

This new edition called *Teaching and the Case Method* remains an interim report, for our work continues to move ahead, slowly but certainly aided by the contributions of colleagues from many universities and colleges. To encourage more widespread experimentation, we provide seminar outlines, cases, and readings for two academic audiences: a prototype module for teachers in liberal arts departments, and a well-tested module for instructors in professional schools. Although our program of case research and development is broadening to include more nonbusiness settings, the "tried and true" cases included in this edition are drawn predominantly from a graduate school of business administration identified alternatively as Metropolitan, New Dominion, Charles River, and the Bay Area Graduate School of Management. (Some of you may be able to penetrate the disguise.)

An Instructor's Guide for each module is also available from the HBS Publishing Division. Its case commentaries and detailed case teaching plans are designed to support an instructor who would like to experiment with either one of these modules at her or his own institution.

Four theses are central to an understanding of our efforts to help instructors work more effectively in case discussion classes. They are, perhaps, more articles of faith than hypotheses capable of validation. But, is it reasonable to hope for scientific proof when the object of our inquiry is the elusive essence of the fundamental teaching-learning process? We

put these propositions directly. At best they will help the reader identify the assumptions and philosophy behind these modules; they offer inward windows to the authors' teaching credo. At a minimum they alert you to our biases.

First, we believe that when educational objectives focus on qualities of mind (curiosity, judgment, wisdom), qualities of person (character, sensitivity, integrity, responsibility), and the ability to apply general concepts and knowledge to specific situations, discussion pedagogy may well be the most effective approach. Lectures about judgment typically have limited impact. Reading about problems or memorizing principles does little to prepare the practitioner—architect, doctor, or manager—to apply concepts and knowledge to the complexity of real-life problems. Discussion teaching achieves these objectives better than alternative pedagogies. It puts the students in an active learning mode, challenges them to accept substantial responsibility for their own education, and gives them first-hand appreciation of, and experience with, the application of knowledge to practice.

Second, as our explorations indicated, the artistry of discussion leadership can be abstracted, articulated, and taught. John Dewey recognized the value of trying to capture the massive unused potential of gifted teachers:

> The successes of such individuals tend to be born and to die with them. . . . The only way by which we can prevent such waste in the future is by methods which enable us to make an analysis of what the gifted teacher does intuitively, so that something accruing from his work can be communicated to others.[6]

Our experience is that instructors can improve their classroom competency modestly through participation in formal programs such as those described in this book.

Third, the knowledge, skills, and attitudes associated with discussion teaching are universally relevant. The capacity to ask appropriate questions, to deal with student uncertainty, to reward and punish, to create learning environments of openness and trust are common to any discussion class,

6. John Dewey, *Sources of a Science of Education* (New York: Liverwright, 1929), pp. 10–11.

whether the substantive topic be Elizabethan poetry or national military policy.

Finally there is "scholarship in teaching," to borrow the phrase of Harvard Medical School's assistant dean for educational planning, Myra Bergman Ramos. Too often academics draw a sharp contrast between scholarly research and teaching assignments. But teaching offers many opportunities to use scholarly skills. Evidence of scholarly accomplishment is evident in what Rippey calls "the corpus of artifacts or products developed in connection with instruction"[7]—course syllabi, case analyses, teaching plans, lecture notes, case histories, and examinations. A course syllabus provides opportunities for the exploration and evaluation of the literature of a field or course. A case analysis offers opportunities for systematic inquiry and rigorous reasoning about the substantive issues in that statement. A teaching plan evidences the instructor's creativity in the process of planning for the discussion, in the use of supplementary readings and exercises, and his or her understanding of what is known and what remains to be discovered about the substantive issues raised by the case.

Equally important is the instructor's attitude toward his or her teaching responsibilities. A teacher who views the classroom as a laboratory gains both knowledge and insight. Students, in their naivete, pose wonderful research questions. Opportunities for experimentation abound. A teacher may use different opening and closure procedures in two sections of the same course or explore different combinations of readings and cases, and various patterns of questioning and responding. So often, effective teachers are clinical researchers of the classroom scene.

This Volume

This book includes text, cases, and readings for two seminar programs—one aimed at liberal arts instructors, the other at educators in professional schools. These materials will aid readers to experiment with conducting some of these seminars in their own institutions.

The materials presented in Part I, "Teaching with Cases: Opportunities, Dilemmas, and Risks," will be useful for participants as they prepare for this academic adventure. The text section leads off with

Emeritus Professor E. P. Learned's reflections on four decades of practice as a case teacher at the Harvard Business School. The second text section describes the case method of instruction as it is practiced at the Business School, and presents operational suggestions for a case teacher. It also briefly overviews the experimental liberal arts seminar presented in Part II and comments in some detail on the professional school program presented in Part III. James Sloan Allen's essay on the relationship between humanistic education and action is an intriguing and sensitive statement—an article to be savored. The final text section concludes with some remarks about the experience of participating in a case-based teaching seminar.

The readings associated with Part I are both insightful and delightful. The first essay by Charles Gragg explores the instructional philosophy fundamental to the conduct of case discussions. We suggest that participants read it before the seminar begins and again at its conclusion. Each rereading brings new insights and additional questions for one's reflective moments.

The next two statements are a paean to the teacher's vocation—a calling honored more in public relations releases than in the hard currency of promotion and institutional support. Professor Maryellen Gleason gives us personal insights into the responsibilities, opportunities, and joys of the profession. Robert Goheen, a former president of Princeton, reaffirms that superior teaching is critical not only to academia but to our nation.

The final readings bring us close to the presence of some special teachers, any one of whom might be ranked with Joseph Epstein's "master teachers" and Ken Macrorie's "distinguished enablers."[8] Their styles range from the hands-on instruction of Madame Ana Roje's ballet practice room to Professor Louis Agassiz's laissez-faire "wait and watch—let the students learn" mode in his laboratory to the humanistic approach of Haim Ginott, Sophie Freud, and Neil Postman. Despite differences, we suspect these master teachers share common beliefs: respect for, and devotion to, their practice or field of study; a sense of high expectation for any student's contribution; and a recognition that superlative teach-

7. Robert Rippey, *The Evaluation of Teaching in Medical Schools* (New York: Springer, 1981), p. 99.

8. Joseph Epstein, *Masters, Portraits of Great Teachers* (New York: Basic Books, 1981); Ken Macrorie, *Twenty Teachers* (New York: Oxford University Press, 1984); see also Jacques Barzun, Chapter 1, "Profession: Teacher," *Teacher in America* (Indianapolis: Liberty Press, 1981), pp. 1–15.

ing, as Sophie Freud puts it so beautifully, involves a delicate blending of discipline and caring. We are certain they would agree with Martin Buber's remark that all education is the education of character—that teachers are engaged in the architecture of the human soul.

Parts II and III of this volume present teaching seminar programs for liberal arts and professional school audiences. Part III, the professional school seminar, will be the key section of the book for many of our readers. This program has gone through numerous iterations over a period of years as we have modified topic outlines and added new text, cases, and readings.

Part IV offers materials of possible interest to participants in a teaching seminar and information potentially helpful to participants who might want to try their hand at leading a seminar. For reflective moments, participants may wish to read Adena Rosmarin's "The Art of Leading a Discussion." It is a former participant's interpretation of this experience and provides a backdrop for your own critique of the program.

Donald A. Schön's seminal paper, "The Crisis of Professional Knowledge and the Pursuit of an Epistemology of Practice," was delivered at the Harvard Business School's 75th Anniversary Colloquium on Teaching by the Case Method. Schön overviews the situation confronting all professional education and outlines the fundamental dilemmas of teaching and practice that derive from those circumstances. His detailing of a process of "reflection in action" (found on pages 247 to 253) approximates the practice of a skilled case method instructor. He joins with the authors in urging new approaches to the traditional problems of our vocation. Our selection of readings for reflection concludes with Paul Hamilton's moving vignette of Miss Evelyn Forbes, teacher of mathematics at Stadium High School. Thus we come full circle in our celebration of the gift of teaching, from Madame Ana Roje to Professor Louis Agassiz to Miss Evelyn Forbes.

For participants who want to develop their own seminar, we offer several practical suggestions. Catherine G. Krupnick, former director of the Video Laboratory at the Harvard-Danforth Center, reviews videotaping as a technique through which instructors can improve their teaching skills. The next ar-

ticle offers suggestions on how to write a teaching case; and James Moore, working with Gale Merseth's classic case "We're Just Wasting Our Time," shows how teaching notes can help instructors use case studies effectively. Lastly, we include a bibliography of relevant literature prepared by Cynthia Ingols and Karen Maloney.

To augment these materials, a bank of additional cases is available. Abstracts of most of these cases are included in the Instructor's Guide. Individual cases may be ordered from the HBS Publishing Division. One can design experimental modules for a range of specific audiences, such as beginning instructors, female teachers working in a male-dominated institution, or those who face special instructional challenges of foreign and physically handicapped students, as well as for the perennial instructional concerns of grading and discipline.

The authors and contributors to this book, joined by dedicated teachers in many other institutions, invite you to join our effort to improve the effectiveness of discussion teaching. In a very fundamental sense, we are in your hands, for as Alfred North Whitehead puts it so persuasively:

The word "education" means, literally, the process of leading out. Thus we are talking of the way in which all your faculties and capacities should be encouraged to expand and unfold themselves. Consider how nature generally sets to work to educate the living organisms which teem on this earth. You cannot begin to understand nature's method unless you grasp the fact that the essential spring of all growth is within you. All that you can get from without is some food—material or spiritual—with which to build your own organism, and some stimulus to spur you to activity. What is really essential in your development you must do for yourselves.[9]

Our dearest wish is that we might all return to our discussion classes with increased knowledge and skill, a rededication to the importance of our vocation, and greater awareness of its complexity, beauty, and power.

9. Alfred North Whitehead, *Essays in Science and Philosophy* (New York: Philosophical Library, Inc., 1947), p. 179.

PART I

Teaching with Cases: Opportunities, Dilemmas, and Risks

Reflections of a Case Method Teacher

What highlights of the learning-teaching process by the case discussion method should I share with readers of this casebook? My practice of it began in 1922 and included three years at the University of Kansas, two years as an MBA candidate at Harvard, and 40 years on the faculty of the Harvard Business School. In addition, in the late 1970s I observed discussion teaching at the School of Management of John F. Kennedy University in California. Students were undergraduates, MBA candidates, doctoral candidates, executives in middle- or advanced-management training programs, and Air Force officers with duty assignments. All told, nine course areas were involved. In all classes there was a diversity in students' personal backgrounds, experience, and intellectual abilities. Such diversity is both a challenge and an opportunity for the instructor in charge.

Most of the comments that follow are based on my experience in my most recent teaching interest—business policy. A few remarks about work in marketing, statistics, management control, and administrative practices, however, reveal something of the evolution of teaching cases at the Harvard Business School.

I was trained as a teacher and casewriter by the early pioneers in marketing. They gave carefully thought out specifications for case material to the field agents; they insisted that agents talk with various people involved in marketing decisions and urged field persons to learn how the decisions were made, who differed with whom about choices among possible "sizeups" of the situation and solutions. Agents also recorded for the files how the decisions worked out. Professors asked key questions in class and cross-examined students vigorously.

Instructors in marketing realized that classifications of consumer and industrial goods and analyses of buying motives of customers at various points in the distribution process were important. Professors established theories on the meaning of events and were prepared to revise these inductive conclusions as new evidence was obtained from comparative case studies. As early as 1934, professors asked students to list currently useful generalizations and to test them out in ongoing cases. The more sophisticated scientific methods of modern marketing were not then available, but at least we sensed a need for guiding principles and better methods.

Formerly Charles Edward Wilson Professor of Business Administration at Harvard Business School, Professor E. P. Learned is now retired and lives in Walnut Creek, California.

The year I was made a professor of marketing at HBS, I was asked to help revise the Statistics course. Students did not like the first term, which was devoted to statistical methods; they preferred the second half, devoted to forecasting business conditions. Instructors decided to increase methods work in the laboratory periods and to devote class time to cases involving application. On the assumption that our students might become interested in the statistical problem of how clothing manufacturers determine sizes, we prepared an excellent case on that subject. Our hunch proved correct and no doubt helped these students appreciate other application problems involving such things as measurement of risk, comparative studies of costs of distribution, and choice of proper types of average, dispersion, or index numbers.

Management Control was established as a wartime course and was designed to merge cost controls with human aspects of administration. It was offered to MBAs and to the War Retraining Program for executives. We asked these businessmen to write up an experience of their own and to make an analysis of it in terms of what they had learned in the course. Many of the early cases in Administrative Practices (now Organizational Behavior) were based upon these thorough and quite self-critical accounts of their reactions and the reactions of other executives.

The development of Administrative Practices was a fascinating experience. We always went to class with a list of 10 men—there were no women in our classes in those days—we planned to ask to participate. In the late 1940s, recently discharged officer students were eager to participate. Volunteering was the norm, in contrast to the marketing classes mentioned earlier. With few exceptions, the professors teaching the course had established their own interest in management and were learning about human beings in organizations under the guidance, principally, of Elton Mayo, Fritz Roethlisberger, and George Lombard. As head of the course I had an active role in obtaining case material and in leading faculty discussions before and after our class experiences with them. Two incidents from class indicate the challenges our instructors faced.

One morning in Ad Prac I called on a student in the back row to start discussion. He made a perfect analysis, if there be such. I wondered if I should say so and dismiss the class. I decided, however, to ask a man in the front row to describe what he heard man #1 say. Number 2 obviously had heard nothing. I asked #3 on the right of the room what he had heard #1 say. After #3's recital, #1 shouted, "I did not say that." Then the class was off for a full period of heated and animated interpretation. In the last 10 minutes I tried to synthesize the meaning of the need for "listening with an open mind." One's preconceptions and experiences limit, so much, the capacity to hear and understand. It often takes a long time to really hear and understand another's spoken or implied words or feelings.

In Ad Prac, as in other courses, there was often a midsemester slump in class morale, when students wondered what they were learning. I asked one section to list five principles about people in organizations about which they were reasonably sure. I also suggested they list points about which they were uncertain and therefore would regard as hypotheses subject to further investigation. I told the class that it might be possible for them to distinguish between those things they accepted because they must, even though their sentiments were offended, and those which they accepted because they coincided with their sentiments. I urged them not to make these distinctions in their list, but I was definitely planting "seeds" about the wisdom of distinguishing between themselves and the situation which they were analyzing. I also asked the class to make notes on what they had learned about the art of administration in Ad Prac. We had students collect the papers, turn them upside down on my desk, shuffle them around in order to disguise whose papers they were and then I drew at random. The first draw produced a superb statement.

I did not want to grade these papers and planned to return them to the class immediately, but it was voted to have a committee summarize them for the benefit of the group. Thirty-one men out of 109 volunteered to serve on a review committee and 14 men prepared summaries which were further audited for sense and accuracy by another group of men. This exercise increased the self-confidence of the men in their learning abilities. There is also no doubt in my mind that it contributed ultimately to the formulation of leadership principles, better listening, and team work from bottom-up, top-down, and among peers for the section. This section produced many business leaders of consequence. Some men told me years later they had kept this list as a reminder and as a tool of self-discipline.

The remainder of this paper is based upon my

final teaching interest, Business Policy—known as BP—a required second-year course. I taught sections or conducted research in this field for 14 years; half of this time, I was active chairman of this group. The group met regularly to plan the course work and to discuss its classroom experience. Mixing strong-minded men having experience and individual teaching styles with junior men having little experience, much potential ability, and great self-confidence had its hazards. Because the faculty intended to be student-oriented in the best sense, it sought student opinion through the chairman of the Student Educational Committee, and by means of carefully planned questionnaires about the course, cases, methods of class conduct by the instructors, and grading. In December 1957, the instructors asked students to rate several aspects of teaching performance on a grading scale ranging from Distinction to Unsatisfactory. Students were frank and honest; they did not spare their professors.

The materials assembled in this collection, no doubt, would have been of use to the pioneering teachers in the field of business policy and should benefit current instructor-leaders and their students in a variety of other academic areas. In a partnership of teachers and students, each has responsibilities and expectations of the other. Some suggestions made by students in 1954 follow:

1. Professors should take responsibility for classroom leadership. They should not run massive nondirective interviews.
2. Don't let a class "beat a dead horse." When students pursue a sideline, nip it in the bud.
3. If a sideline is potentially important, let it be developed if there is time.
4. Professors should insist that students state their positions or conclusions. Students do not want to nail each other down.
5. Rules of attendance should be stated and enforced vigorously the first time the rule is violated.
6. Professors should give direct or indirect signals that student analysis is moving in the right direction. Any way of expressing satisfaction or dissatisfaction is better than no response at all. "One professor appeared bored. We fought him. We want more than a poker-faced response."
7. Professors should serve as sounding boards for the class, but need not enter actively into the class discussion. Students want to know "what we

have done well, what we have done poorly." Such comments should be given after the middle or near the end of the class period.
8. Asking students to list major topics for discussion and writing them on the blackboard is useful for the first ten minutes. Thereafter, the instructor should help ensure their coverage.
9. Professors should state the objectives of the course sufficiently and show their enthusiasm for those objectives.

In response to the last point, the following catalogue announcement was bound into the casebook for 1955–56:

The Business Policy course covers the fields of policy-making and administration, building upon and integrating the other work of the School. The viewpoint is at the level of top management, where company-wide objectives are set and departmental policies and activities are coordinated.

The course emphasizes sizing up a company's situation in the light of general conditions, and of conditions within the company itself; determining objectives; developing sound and consistent policies and plans for achieving objectives; organizing administrative personnel to carry out the plans; guiding, developing, and maintaining an administrative organization; continually reappraising and, when necessary, altering objectives, policies, and organization on the basis of new developments.

During the course the student deals with the problems of a large number of companies in widely diversified industries. He thereby acquires an understanding of the nature of such problems and of the responsibilities of company managements, including directors. He also develops his own ability to deal realistically with matters involving policy formulation and requiring administrative skill.

A major objective of the course is to develop the general management point of view about business problems in order that the graduate, throughout his business career and whatever his management level, may guide his activities in such a way as to make the most effective contribution to the business as a whole.

The course provides students with an opportunity to bring to bear on business problems an unlimited variety of knowledge and skills acquired in all their previous academic and practical experience. The course also provides the student with additional opportunity to develop further his personal zest, as well as his professional competence, for imaginative, creative, risk-taking, profitable, responsible business enterprise.

In December 1956, I issued a statement on objectives of the Business Policy course. Some paragraphs from its statement were intended to provide a framework for application of course concepts to a specific case study; they also helped in a review of skills partly learned or fully accomplished. Two paragraphs follow:

A major objective of the course is to develop in students a general management point of view that can be helpful in the *first positions held after graduation* and other jobs thereafter. This course does not train general managers nor departmental vice presidents. As subordinates to men who perform such tasks, or as subordinates to those subordinates, or as members of cross-departmental teams working on policies, plans or programs, you are likely to have early opportunities to show talents that contribute to general management types of diagnoses or solutions. Consequently, acquiring a conceptual framework of the interrelatedness of parts of the business should aid in comprehending the manifold implications of a particular problem or proposal.

A general management point of view involves these components:

a. A recognition of the relationship between the individual enterprise and its social environment. The firm influences and is influenced by this external system. These relationships must be considered in making general management decisions.
b. The concept that general management decisions involve a blend of variables from traditional functions. Such decisions should be broader and better balanced than one approached from the point of view of a single function.
c. The assumptions that (1) general management decisions should have as their objective the long-run good of the business and, (2) general management should not sacrifice, if at all avoidable, the long-run good for present gain.
d. The recognition that the timing of decisions is an important factor in the decisions.
e. The recognition that human considerations and human resources do enter into decisions and their implementation.

There were two paragraphs on the development of personal skills: one was on analytical skills, and the other was on skills of listening, asking questions of various technical experts, and integrating suggestions into well-rounded programs of action.

My remaining comments on pedagogy are based on the relation of written reports to class work, grades, or personal development of students. In my active years at Harvard, reports in Business Policy were always an important part of the course. They were a burden to students, to be sure. Learning to write succinctly and effectively to some specified person such as the executive or executives in the case, the professor, or to fellow students prepared students for their future business positions. One former alumnus gave a series of cases to the School because he wanted to benefit from both class discussions of it and the reports written to him. Executives who attended class or responded to student questions after reports were handed in spoke openly to students of the value of their analyses and recommendations. Sometimes the visitor received very critical recommendations. One businessman on a year's leave of absence from his firm chose to visit MBA classes rather than Advanced Management classes because MBA candidates were not inhibited by their past experiences.

Students were urged to form discussion groups. If possible, such groups included majors in marketing, finance, control, and organizational behavior. Each fall students gave us a list of courses and any special topics or industries of special interest to them. Such background information provided an inventory of potential expertise in the section and served as a basis for starting a call list or for volunteer recognition at crucial points in class discussion.

In the academic year 1954–55, the teaching staff requested that students write the shortest cogent report they could on assigned cases. Comments, rather than grades, were to be written on reports. A review of these comments with the student at his request, and by the professor at the end of the year, revealed the personal progress of students.

One interesting, two-part assignment was on the Linton Company, a wholesale grocery firm. For Tuesday at 10 A.M., students were to prepare a one-page outline or summary of the points they wanted to make in discussion with the Corbett brothers, owners. No argument in support of points was required. On Thursday, the two executives arrived to answer questions and talk about the further development of their business. Simultaneously four student reports from the previous year were given to students. The assignment was: "In terms of your own understanding of the situation of the company, write as succinct a report as you can, describing and evaluating the possible usefulness to Robert and/or Frank Corbett of these four student papers."

The fourth report of the first term was to be written to Mr. Ditmars, president of the Gray Manufacturing Company. Students were to recommend one important change in policy or one important program of action to be implemented in the next five years. They were to indicate the position within or without the company from which they wrote. The assignment was deliberately limited in scope so that an in-depth analysis or prognosis might be accomplished. Instructors hoped students would realize that a great deal of thorough analysis must precede any final short report. They also hoped that students would capture the notion that most policy or program reports are presented in several stages to management.

In the second term four reports with limited formal guidelines were assigned. The teaching staff, however, limited the reports to 750 words and stated that the following questions provided good leads for approaching a Business Policy case:

> What, in your opinion, is the most fundamental, crucial or urgent issues or problems—or issues and problems—before the company? Why do you think so?
> What, accordingly, if anything, should anyone do? Who? When? How? Why do you think so?
> How will you communicate your ideas to the top management of the company? Why?

The assignment for the final report of the year gave students several options:

1. Write upon some topic or question which you see involved in several or all of the cases which have been taken up in Business Policy this academic year. Document your ideas by reference to these cases. If there are cases from other courses or from your own experience which you think provide illuminating documentation of your ideas or

instances of what you are talking about, feel free to make reference to such cases.
2. Write a report dealing with one of the topics listed below:
   a. The relationship between the basic policies of a specified company of your selection and the suitability of its common stock as an investment for a specified investor.
   b. The relationship you have discerned between ideas, ways of thinking, skills, etc., you have come by or enhanced in the Business Policy course and in some other course or courses at the Harvard Business School.
   c. Some other topic of your own choosing, with the concurrence of your instructor.

It was hoped that these would permit students to reflect on the year's work in Business Policy and what it meant to them. The customary 750-word limit did not apply to this assignment. The range of creative responses both pleased and surprised professors.

In the 1955–56 academic year an experiment in group report writing was conducted. It was sufficiently successful to justify its use in later years. In my section, we had 12 study groups. Students from two or three groups at a time were asked to write on each classroom case, and everyone had to write at least three reports during the term. For instance, groups reporting on the La Plant–Choate case were to play the role of advisor to Mr. Choate and to consider his key policy issues. Students were encouraged to meet and discuss the cases; each student, however, was expected to write his own report not to exceed 750 words. Benefits of this plan were summarized at the time as follows:

> The members of each group would provide a nucleus especially well prepared for class discussion. The members could be used to conduct the class for the first half of the discussion or they could be available to the professor if he wished to refer questions to them at any time.
> Good preparation of this sort should spark student enthusiasm. The men will have taken positions which they need to defend. Inasmuch as the class as a whole will not have taken positions, however, the entire discussion will not fall into a position-defending condition which has occasionally reduced interest in the past.

If report writers were asked to lead the discussion, many students who seldom enter into class discussion would be forced to take an active part several times a term. Furthermore, such activity might lead a significant proportion of them to continue to enter into discussion on days when others were leading. It would be extremely useful to discover whether this procedure would substantially increase class participation.

As a direct benefit from writing the reports, the writers would obtain in addition to readers' comments the class views on their positions as a result of their presentation and defense against class attack. There is some likelihood that with the discussion groups formally established for the reports, their members might decide to come together for class case discussions as well. Such a consequence would be of material benefit to the students in their day-to-day progress.

The faculty also tried a group report program where only a single, joint report of the group was submitted. For example, one group was asked to write a report on Pilgrim Life Insurance to the president of that company. The report had no length limit; if it exceeded five pages, however, a summary of one page or less on the principal conclusions or recommendations was to be provided. Choosing a leader for writing the report bothered some groups. Some men wrote excellent sections assigned to them. Others neglected their obligations to fellow students. Some reports had varying styles because no one had tried to convert the parts from each student into a unified whole.

Each group was invited to make an appointment of from one to two hours to obtain my reactions to their report. During my first reading of it, in their presence, I provided an oral commentary as I read. I tried to combine the role of a "receiving" executive with that of a professor trying to lead a discussion on report writing to executives. Sometimes I immediately summarized the report; sometimes I read nearly through the report, marking places I wanted to discuss. More than once, there was a single section that seemed weak. The student responsible for that (unknown to me) invariably said: "I am responsible for that," or "I let my classmates down because I had some other report pressing me." I pointed out strong sentences supporting an argument. I sometimes asked, "What do you mean by this sentence? I can't tell." If an individual would

rephrase it, I often replied: "Had the new phrasing been in the report, its impact on the executive would have been greater."

Group oral reports to the class on a lengthy, in-depth series of cases on the Hilton Hotel Corporation were used with good results. Students did more work than normal preparing the cases and running the class (while the professor sat on a bench); they wanted to make a good showing before their peers. This technique was also used in the Advanced Management Program. There, groups competed in presentations and were judged both by their colleagues and their professors. The best groups made a final presentation to the executives of the company. Some of these reports ran from 800 to 1,100 pages.

Reports were also assigned on cases involving the experience of graduates on their first job. Students might elect to discuss their reports with the professor. Eighty-five percent of my last class in Business Policy either discussed reports or some aspect of their own job interviews with me. The most extreme case I recall was of a student whom I expected to grade Unsatisfactory. He came to me with a job opportunity and asked if I could give him a recommendation. An in-depth discussion revealed that he knew exactly what he wanted out of a job in the shipping industry. He had realistic beliefs about his skills and how far he might go up the management ladder. In transportation courses and others germane to his job objective, he had done well. I concluded that he had high chances of making good on the job he had been offered. But I was unwilling to write a bland letter of endorsement, as I had respect for employers and a desire to have my recommendations regarded highly. I told the student that I would write a letter, deliver it to him signed with stamped envelope enclosed, and leave it up to him to decide whether to mail it. My only regret is that he did not report back his decision. This letter made clear his aptitudes and his limitations. I had no doubt that the man would perform satisfactorily on this initial job, but I expected him to learn from the company and develop other capabilities.

I concluded my last class in MBA Business Policy in 1961 with these words:

We have placed a premium on the ability to reach conclusions and to make and defend recommendations and decisions. Yet today's answers do not necessarily fit tomorrow's problems. What have you acquired for your effort, your money, and your debt? I predict a large fund of knowledge, a bundle of personal skills, and a variety of methods for analyzing and solving problems and for understanding organizations at work. In addition you have made progress in formulating your personal goals and have begun to develop your management philosophy and leadership skills. Even though you may never be able to control your boss's behavior, within limits you may be able to influence the administrative climate of your subordinates and peers.

There is a great need for business leaders of ability, integrity, and character. There must be higher ethical standards sponsored and practiced by these executives. They must recognize their obligations to the communities in which they operate, and they must accept their role in creating jobs and maintaining employment. Such leaders cannot forget their stockholders and the sources of capital that facilitate dealing with change.

Great business leaders will be required to deal with the vast technological changes that continually appear and with the shifts in power between labor, management, states or nation, and have and have-not nations. They now live in a world society—a world in revolution. Above all else they must not forget man himself.

You men and women have a rare chance to serve your fellows and assist in releasing creative talent. Be humble as you begin but be self-confident about the path ahead to achieve the foregoing goals and objectives.

Alumni feedback varying in time from a few years after graduation to memorable encounters after the passage of 15, 27, 29, and 52 years lead me to assert that professors who read, discuss, and profit from the materials in this book will make a difference in the lives and work of their students.

Teaching with Cases at the Harvard Business School

In business education, the case method has been closely identified with the Harvard Business School. Though the approach was not invented on the banks of the Charles River—witness the long Talmudic tradition—the Business School is well known for its commitment to an active, discussion-oriented learning mode, disciplined by case problems drawn from the complexity of real life. It is a pedagogy that supports our fundamental objective: to train women and men for professional business practice.

Together with colleagues in other professional schools, we urge the university to "mate" knowledge and action, as Alfred North Whitehead puts it:

> What the faculty have to cultivate is activity in the presence of knowledge. What the students have to learn is activity in the presence of knowledge.
>
> This discussion rejects the doctrine that students should first learn passively, and then, having learned, should apply knowledge. It is a psychological error. In the process of learning there should be present, in some sense or other, a subordinate activity of application. In fact, the applications are part of the knowledge. For the very meaning of the things known is wrapped up in their relationships beyond themselves. Thus unapplied knowledge is knowledge shorn of its meaning.
>
> The careful shielding of a university from the activities of the world around it is the best way to chill interest and to defeat progress. Celibacy does not suit a university. It must mate itself with action.[1]

The Business School's commitment to linking knowledge and application is supported by a number of programs designed to assist instructors in the effective use of cases. One is the teaching seminar presented later in this volume. The faculty has appreciated noted educator James Harvey's admonition that teaching may hasten learning but it may also block it or kill it outright, or sometimes just render it comatose for years. The faculty has recognized that a tradition of teaching excellence is essential to the School's accomplishments. Harvard Business School Dean John H. McArthur puts it succinctly: "How we teach is what we teach."

---

1. Alfred North Whitehead, *Essays in Science and Philosophy* (New York: Philosophical Library, Inc., 1947), pp. 218–219.

Before detailing the objectives and organization of our case method teaching seminars, it may be helpful to review their historical development and to present a general overview of the case method of instruction—its origins and evolution at the Harvard Business School, the reasons for its educational success, the changing nature of cases and their classroom use, and the basic pedagogical elements of the method. At a more operational level, we will describe how an instructor evaluates and prepares for a case discussion. Finally, we will overview our two current seminar programs—one designed primarily for use in liberal arts teaching, the other for professional education.

Much of what the Harvard Business School represents has never been interpreted in words: our practice, values, and traditions remain oral.[2] Focusing on one individual's observations may involve a possibility of substantial misinterpretation. The risk is especially great when one attempts to interpret the School's intellectual core—the case method of instruction—the still point in our rapidly changing academic world. We acknowledge that danger.

Evolution of the Seminar

Phase I: The Seminar Begins

Forward thinking sometimes starts with a backward glance. On February 1, 1968, Thomas Graves, then assistant dean of Harvard Business School, now (1986) director of the H. F. Du Pont Winterthur Museum, and Andrew R. Towl, then director of case development at HBS, convened a group of research assistants and instructors interested in learning about teaching with cases. Experienced faculty members were asked to talk about leading the case discussions.

During the next several years, these sessions were repeated several times. They enjoyed modest participant acceptance, and the instructors gained from the discipline of preparation and the process of answering questions. We soon knew, however, that our format was inappropriate and that our impact on teaching practice was limited.

The first problem was that we simply could not accomplish our mission in a one- or two-session program. Teaching is a complex activity, requiring

considerable skill on the part of the instructor. A lecture can be a work of art, extremely difficult to create and deliver. Discussion teaching is an even more complicated instructional task. We needed time to carry out our mission.

Second, we found we knew little, in any systematic sense, about the dynamics of leading a case discussion. We could not specify precisely what we wanted "old pros" to talk about with their "apprentice" audience. It soon became obvious that good teachers could not necessarily abstract and articulate the skills and techniques they employed in their daily classroom practice.

Critics correctly pointed out that we should have anticipated this age-old problem of the artist as teacher. The dilemma is well illustrated by a story told of Anna Pavlova, the great classical star of the Imperial Ballet. A young ballerina once asked her, "What was the meaning of your dance?" Pavlova's response was that if she could *tell* the meaning, she wouldn't have needed to dance. Artists are often inarticulate about both meaning and method.

Finally, we found but a modest amount of helpful literature. Though a great deal of research has been conducted at early childhood, elementary, and high school levels, less had been done to explore the dynamics of large-scale section teaching in professional schools. Much of the research had been directed at developing new theory rather than improving day-to-day teaching.[3] The Harvard Business School had addressed the "why" of case teaching, but said little about how instructors carried out such a complex educational assignment.

While we encountered many a doubting Thomas, other colleagues urged us to continue our efforts. Dean George P. Baker gave us both psychological and financial sustenance at a critical juncture. Andrew Towl, who led a pioneering broad-scale effort involving case teaching and research activities with the Visiting Professor's Case Method Program and with the Southern Case Writer's group, was especially supportive.[4]

2. Professor Melvin T. Copeland's history of the school, *And Mark an Era* (Boston: Little, Brown & Co., 1958), is a valuable reference. In particular, Chapter IX, "The Case Method of Instruction," is a rich resource.

3. For an excellent review of research on teaching, see Arthur S. Bolster, Jr., "Toward a More Effective Model of Research on Teaching," *Harvard Educational Review*, August 1983, pp. 294–308.

4. The results of Professor Towl's exploration and experiments are reported in his book *To Study Administration by Cases* (Boston, Mass.: Harvard Business School, 1969). It contains a wealth of information essential to understanding a total case method curriculum.

Phase II: Investigation

Our efforts to resolve the problems of the early seminar program led us in two major directions. First, in 1973, we developed a multisession seminar on case method teaching for doctoral candidates in Business Policy. Simply having more time enabled us to explore a wider range of topics related to case teaching—for example, the development of teaching notes and class teaching plans, the creation of a course syllabus, evaluation of students' classroom contributions, and the use of cases for exams and report-writing programs. We still asked "master teachers" to talk about their craft, but this became just one part of a wider-ranging program.

A second initiative was an attempt to analyze the dynamics of the in-class discussion process. We needed to understand how an instructor could use a specific case situation to stimulate individual students, as well as the overall section, to engage in constructive educational dialogue. Our focus was on the knowledge, skill, and attitudinal requirements of the discussion leader. We sought to compare the discussion process in classes that seemed to have gone particularly well or badly. Toward these ends, we observed more than 70 case discussion classes over several years and informally interviewed dozens of students and instructors about their experiences with this methodology.

Our attempts to learn more about this teaching-learning process mirrored those of Henry Miller, who noted in "Reflections on Writing":

> My whole work has come to resemble a terrain of which I have made a thorough geodetic survey, not from my desk with pen and ruler, but by touch, by getting down on all fours, on my stomach, and crawling over the ground inch by inch, and this over an endless period of time in all conditions of weather.[5]

As students of teaching, we found this a joyful research experience; it gave us a chance to explore familiar, yet unknown, territory. Over the years we became increasingly interested in the specific instructor decision points that recur over and over again in any discussion situation. For example:

How does the instructor select a student to start off the class?

How does the instructor select one student to answer a question when many others with hands raised are asking for recognition?

What kinds of questions can be used by the instructor? What type of question is most appropriate at what specific time in class?

How does an instructor decide whether or not to respond personally to a student's comment, ignore it, or refer it to another student for comment?

When does one put a comment on the chalkboard?

How does an instructor obtain high levels of student involvement in a case discussion? Deal with apathy? Work with an angry student?

What should an instructor "know" about a student? How can such information be obtained?

In this observational universe—section, student, and instructor engaged in a case discussion—we observed a beautiful and infinitely complex educational endeavor, one that we could not hope to capture in its totality, but could understand in part. Our goal was to learn a bit about this discussion dynamic and the instructor's contribution to its productive outcome.

As our investigative phase moved forward, we turned to Professor Nathaniel Cantor's framework for observing and understanding the discussion process. He asks three fundamental questions: What is happening to the student(s)? What is happening to the instructor? What happens between them?[6] Given the complexity of the territory, the simplicity of this framework was both powerful and helpful.

Our explorations, although rough cut, reinforced our sense of the power of a pedagogy that emphasized student discovery rather than instructor revelation and, to borrow Professor Charles Gragg's phraseology, those "attitudes of mind" that engendered mutual respect between teacher and student. This research effort allowed us to identify both the everyday decisions an instructor must make and the basic recurring problems encountered throughout a

5. Henry Miller, "Reflections on Writing," *The Henry Miller Reader*, ed. Lawrence Durrell (New York: New Directions, 1959), p. 249.

6. Nathaniel Cantor, speech to the Visiting Professors Case Method Program, cited in Andrew R. Towl, *To Study Administration by Cases*, p. 153.

semester. It enabled us to define some of the skills and techniques used by sensitive instructors in leading case discussions—a process whose success depends on an intricate integration of course objectives (substantive knowledge as well as analytic and clinical skills), case problems, and student and section learning needs. Most important, we gained additional appreciation for the complexities of the discussion leader's task and the way those complexities help unleash learning power.

Phase III: Experimentation and Case Development

At the end of our investigation, we summarized our findings in three integrated propositions that became the basis for the seminar's philosophy, organization, and operations:

1. A critical responsibility of the instructor is the leadership of the case discussion *process*. It is not enough to be in command of the substantive knowledge of one's field or the specifics of the case problem. The instructor also must be able to lead the process by which individual students and the overall group explore the complexity of a specific case situation.

2. The key to effective discussion leadership is the instructor's artistry, which consists primarily of mastering detail. The effective instructor, for example, expands the entire section's opportunities for learning by asking the appropriate question of a specific student at the best time during the discussion.

3. The pertinent details (skills and techniques) can be observed, abstracted, and taught. Case discussion leaders can be helped to learn their craft.

Having identified the basic challenges confronting a discussion teacher and the skills and techniques that can be helpful, we could now move forward with a case research program. We began building a bank of teaching cases which numbered over 60 by 1986. Some of the first cases were based on our own teaching experience; others were joint efforts developed with the help of former participants. Most of these early cases were snapshots of a classroom incident that had occurred some time in the past. Later we began to develop longitudinal case studies that involved detailed study of a student group's activities over a period of time, such as the "Ernie Budding" series of cases. In building our case collection, we aimed to explore important

teaching issues in depth and to address some specific kinds of problems we thought should be covered in a basic seminar program.

Simultaneously we began an iterative curriculum development program. We worked through various combinations of topics, cases, and readings with seminar groups that were increasingly catholic in composition. With the support of the Harvard-Danforth Center for Teaching and Learning, we began to include participants from other departments of the university. These newcomers contributed to the substantive development of our seminar, sharing experience gained in a wide range of academic disciplines and professional schools, and helped us clarify the assumptions on which the seminar was based.

Because we wished to focus on the process of discussion leadership, we assumed the instructor had intellectual command of his or her professional field or academic discipline, and of particular theories and knowledge relevant to the specific course. We also assumed the instructor had a framework for organizing those constructs so as to encourage student learning. Clearly, knowledge and conceptual understanding lie at the heart of any academic effort. But we were convinced that an important stimulus to learning can be the way in which a class is conducted.

Taking mastery of content for granted, we developed what we called process-dominant cases. They focused primarily on the dynamics of individual and group interaction, but included enough data on the knowledge requirements of the course that one could appreciate the academic circumstances in which the teaching problem had developed.

Another critical assumption was that student growth, not instructor ego gratification, was the instructional goal. There is a bit of the actor in most teachers. In the intensity of the classroom drama, they may seek to play center stage, with the class as but their supporting cast. Emotional electricity must be harnessed to power student learning, not to spotlight an instructor's dreams of glory. We assumed that the instructor had a sincere interest in helping students to learn.

During Phase III we also began to sort out the circumstances under which the Harvard Business School's version of discussion teaching might best be used by other institutions. Unlike James Garfield's belief that true teaching required only a simple log hut with a simple wooden bench, he at one end and the great American educator Mark Hopkins at the other, the Business School believes that physical facilities are extremely important to the success of case teaching. The traditional academic classroom, with its podium and rows of chairs in military formation, severely limits group discussion. A U-shaped amphitheater classroom can help make any instructor a more effective discussion leader. Scale is also important. Much of our pedagogical approach seems most appropriate in groups of roughly 20 to 80. Group continuity is essential: with stable membership, the class develops a social organization and a group dynamic that can be very helpful.

A central consideration, of course, is the intellectual character and instructional needs of the discipline or applied field of study. Thomas Clough, a seminar participant, observed that case discussion methodology is best applied in certain circumstances.

> Where truth is relative, where reality is probabilistic, and where structural relationships are contingent, teaching and learning are most effectively accomplished through discussion rather than exploration. With intrinsically complex phenomena and the limited usefulness of simple theoretical relationships, little of value can be communicated directly from teacher to student. The learning process must emphasize the development of understanding, judgment, and even intuition.[7]

Discussion teaching requires a major change in an instructor's role and classroom responsibilities. Traditional teaching, and the lecture mode with which it is so often associated, gives primacy to the instructor. Classroom activity derives from the teacher's presentation of subject matter and follows his or her class plan. The student's role is clearly subordinate.

Discussion teaching proceeds from a quite different perception of teacher-student relationships and responsibilities, emphasizing student involvement and self-teaching. As Professor Nathaniel Cantor put it:

> A skilled teacher recognizes that all significant learning can only come from the creative efforts of

the learner. That's another way of saying learning is personal. You cannot learn for anybody. . . . Essentially the student must be the one to raise the significant problem for you to help him find the answer.[8]

Discussion teaching works best when the instructor gives up the relative certitude of a planned lecture and an instructor-dominated question period for the ambiguity of a hard-to-plan, free-flowing discussion driven by student ideas, which may well follow unusual paths and come to unexpected end points. For teachers who like to be in charge, discussion teaching is a most uncomfortable assignment.

Phase IV: Testing and Reappraisal

In 1981, we prepared an interim report on teaching by the case method.[9] Since the publication of our first report, we have continued to test and refine seminar objectives, concepts, and case studies. More faculty members have become involved, giving us opportunities to hold sessions at other universities, domestic and foreign, to meet with groups of educational specialists, and to conduct a colloquium that brought together 80 experienced participants representing all major professional fields, liberal arts and science faculties, and training specialists from industry. The colloquium gave us a chance to test a "compressed" two-and-one-half-day version of our standard twelve-session, three-month format. In all these ventures, we experimented with different participant combinations (varying age, experience, and pedagogical interest), the use of team teaching, and a variety of topic and case outlines.

Aided by suggestions from participants, we gained a better understanding of seminar strengths, weaknesses, and opportunities. A liberal arts seminar program was developed by Dr. Abby Hansen. Support materials for seminar leaders were also given high priority. For the most frequently used cases, we have prepared teaching notes (emphasizing the process by which a case might be taught) and researcher perspectives (presenting the casewriter's personal analysis and interpretation of the situation).

Many of our cases focus on difficult classroom situations. Looking forward, we plan to give more

7. From a report on Discussion Leadership prepared by Thomas Clough for the Fall 1979 Teaching by the Case Method Seminar.

8. Nathaniel Cantor speech, in Towl, p. 157.
9. C. Roland Christensen, *Teaching by the Case Method* (Boston: Harvard Business School, Division of Research, 1981).

attention to situations in which instructor and students have achieved maximum learning opportunities. Just as physicians often find it easier to define "disease" than "health," we began by looking at problems. Now we need to learn more about how a skillful teacher develops and nurtures a healthy classroom milieu. We hope to develop better ways of relating readings and cases—a very complicated process.[10] Other opportunities abound in the combined use of cases and film,[11] videotaping of instructors as they teach a class, and the development of short two- or three-case modules on specialized topics. Finally, we need to learn more about the skills of lecturing,[12] especially when a question-and-answer period is also involved.

Much remains to be done; our adventure has but begun.

The Case Method of Instruction

Before turning to the seminars themselves, it may be useful to review the historical development of the case method of instruction at the Harvard Business School.[13] First, a brief look at the founding and early years of the School will suggest some reasons for the initial adoption of case instruction. Then we ask why this approach remains the essence of the School's educational efforts in both teaching and research as well.[14] Finally, we focus on cases themselves and their continuing evolution in concept, format, and classroom use.

The Historical Origins of Case Instruction at the Harvard Business School

Like many other Harvard endeavors, the Business School originated in a pragmatic marriage of intellectual challenge, societal need, and practical ad-

10. For a first-hand description of the use of a seminar reading, "Louis Agassiz as a Teacher," see Professor E. Raymond Corey's "Note on Case Method Teaching," HBS Case No. 9-581-058. Professor Corey's article, in addition, provides us with an excellent overview of the case method of instruction.
11. Professor Selma Wassermann of Simon Fraser University offers a seminar on "Critical Incidents in Teaching," a fascinating example of this approach.
12. For an excellent statement on the complexity of creating and delivering lectures, read Professor Michael Mandelbaum's "Notes of a First-Year Teacher," HBS Case No. 9-377-043.
13. See also "The Genesis of the Case Method in Business Administration," The Case Method at the Harvard Business School, ed. Malcolm P. McNair (New York: McGraw-Hill, 1954), pp. 25–33.
14. Lawrence E. Fouraker, Dean's Report, Harvard University, Graduate School of Business Administration, 1978–1979.

vantage. President Eliot described the new undertaking to the University Club of Indianapolis on May 6, 1908.

We are just establishing a school of business administration which is to be for graduates only. That is to say, admission to the school of business administration is to be on the same footing as admission to our Schools of Divinity, Law, and Medicine. No one can enter it unless he already possesses a preliminary degree. We start that school next October. It is our last contribution to the list of professions for which Harvard prepares.

What does that development mean? It means that the universities propose to supply, in the end, the leaders in business. We do not imagine that the University will be able to produce, through teaching, the peculiar instinct for profitable trade which characterizes some men who have had defective education, and who nevertheless arrive at the height of business success. That class of men will arise in our country independently of all institutional education. We do propose to train systematically in the universities a large class of men who will make a probable success in business, because they know all the administrative methods therein used. . . . The motives which determined us to establish this school at Harvard are plain; we observed last June that more than half of our Senior class, then graduating, went into business, and we have also observed for a good many years past that a large proportion of our graduates who have gone into business have attained high place.

With a bit of "tongue in cheek," President Eliot presumably intended *defective education* to signify non-Harvard. His distinction between professional men and business leaders was probably applauded by those in his community who did not accept business as an appropriate academic field. One such purist is said to have objected to "Sully[ing] the robes of Chaucer and Shakespeare with seekers of gold. Why should a great university concern itself with the mundane of commercial life, with the way of the trader, with the training of men for business and wealth?" But even without a marketing background, the president knew something about meeting consumer needs; Harvard men were business bound.

The magnificence of President Eliot's vision for a new school was matched only by the boldness of his decision to require a bachelor's degree for admission to a two-year course of study, culminating with the award of a master's degree in business administration. In 1908 only 5% of the nation's 18- to 21-year-old age group enrolled in colleges, and fewer than 4,000 master's degrees were awarded by the entire educational system in 1909–1910. Business practice was rudimentary, in some respects approximating the level of medical practice when showmen traveled the West dispensing advice and elixirs from a wagon tailgate. *Safe Methods of Business*, a guidebook popular in 1908, covered topics such as spelling and penmanship, methods of bookkeeping (including a better way to add long columns), a guide to law, and such miscellaneous information as a treatise on the uselessness of lightning rods.[15] Typical preparation for business simply involved going to work for a company or signing on as an apprentice. Some studied law as a background for management; others took secretarial training courses.

Academic studies in commerce, as business education was then often designated, were limited. Pioneering efforts included the undergraduate program of the Wharton School of Commerce and Finance, established in 1891, and undergraduate and graduate programs of the Amos Tuck School of Administration and Finance (1900).[16] Courses in accounting, finance, commercial geography, and law, along with the emerging field of industrial management, provided an instructional base, but in many respects there just wasn't much to be taught about business education during the early twentieth century! President Eliot's decision was ahead of its time; his vision guided business education for decades to come.

Lacking traditional academic building materials— theory, concepts, an epistemology of practice,[17] faculty trained in specialties, programs of research— the new school faced monumental challenges. It had difficulty even in stating what preparatory work its incoming students should have mastered—sug-

gesting only that applicants should have a command of good English and a reading knowledge of at least one modern foreign language, and that "some knowledge of mechanical drawing is highly useful in almost all branches of business."

The early curriculum was a potpourri of courses— some borrowed from other departments of the university, others specifically constructed for the new venture. There were three required courses: Principles of Accounting, Commercial Contracts, and Economic Resources. Other offerings were Commercial Correspondence, Fire Insurance, Economic Resources of Eastern Asia, and Railroad Operations (in which, the course description noted, "there will be studied in detail the arrangements of freight and passenger stations, the operations of yards and terminals and the organization of train service"). A surveying course was listed as a useful adjunct.

To convert President Eliot's vision into an operational reality, Dean Edwin Gay gathered an academic faculty of seven and recruited a considerable number of visiting lecturers, including F. W. Taylor, father of scientific management, and Henry L. Gantt, a pioneer in the field of industrial engineering. Catholic in composition, divided by background and field of study or practice, the faculty seemed to agree on only one point: that business administration was *not* the study of applied economics. Apart from this negative definition, they were less articulate about just what business administration was. Unable to define their field of study or a logic for curriculum design, the faculty was paradoxically precise in its statement of educational purpose, proposing "to give each individual student a practical and professional training suitable to the particular business he plans to enter." The key words, *practical* and *professional*, remain central to the Business School's mission.

Dean Gay was clearly determined to achieve that objective with an emphasis on a pedagogy that linked the classroom to the realities of business and engaged the MBA student in a practice-oriented, problem-solving instructional mode. In the first school catalogue, he stated:

> In the courses on Commercial Law the case method will be used. In other courses an analogous method, emphasizing classroom discussion in connection with

15. J. L. Nichols, *Safe Methods of Business* (Naperville, Ill.: J. L. Nichols & Co., 1899).

16. Copeland, *And Mark an Era*, pp. 15–16.

17. This topic is covered generally in Donald A. Schön, *The Reflective Practitioner* (New York: Basic Books, 1983) and more specifically for the field of business administration in Dr. Schön's paper "The Crisis of Professional Knowledge and the Pursuit of an Epistemology of Practice," presented at the colloquium on Teaching by the Case Method held at the

Harvard Business School, April 1–4, 1984, and included in Part IV of this book.

lectures and frequent reports on assigned topics—
what may be called the "problem method"—will be
introduced as far as practicable. Visits of inspection
will be made under competent guidance to various
commercial establishments in Boston and in the
neighborhood manufacturing centres of New England. Similar field work of a more specialized character will form a feature of the advanced work of the
second year.[18]

He encouraged faculty to explore not only *what* they
taught but *how* they taught—a tradition that persists
to this day.

The setting was hospitable to Dean Gay's dream:
a vocation struggling to take small steps toward
formalizing its practice to meet the needs of an increasingly complicated industrial society; an absence of interest on the part of traditional academia
in meeting these needs; a great university willing
to experiment; and a new school committed to creating new ways of educating young people "for the
oldest of the arts," to use President Lowell's words,
"and the newest of the professions." We underscore
the importance of its being "new," for, as Business
School Professor Kenneth Andrews reminds us,
freedom from traditional academic dogma encouraged major experimentation.

So did the maverick, almost antiacademic nature
of the School's early faculty. For example, Professor
William James Cunningham, one of the School's
first chaired professors, had obtained his academic
preparation from the International Correspondence
School of Scranton, Pennsylvania. As the late Professor George Albert Smith, Jr., often observed,
these pioneers were convinced that traditional
means of preparing men for a career in business
were ineffective; they were eager to apply new insights to old problems.

Why the Success of the Case Method Approach?

"No question," said George Bernard Shaw, "is so
difficult to answer as that to which the answer is
obvious." Why has the case method played such an
important role in our institution's accomplishments? Why its success?

First and foremost, this pedagogy suits the Business School's mission of training men and women
not only to know, but to act. One of the School's

early professors, Arthur Stone Dewing, philosoph-
ically compared the lecture method with the case
method of teaching. Referring first to the more typical teaching method, he said:

This method [lectures] has great advantages. Above
all, it is efficient, it is also economical of the time,
energy, and the patience of instructor and student.
Further, this method produces brilliant results. A student trained under it seems to possess a sureness, a
precision, a firming of grasp remarkable for the relatively short time which he is compelled to spend on
acquiring his knowledge. . . .

The other method starts with an entirely different
purpose and ends with an entirely different result.
. . . [Businesspeople must be able] to meet in action
the problems arising out of new situations of an everchanging environment. Education, accordingly,
would consist of acquiring facility to act in the presence of new experience. It asks not how a man may
be trained to know, but how a man be trained to
act.[19]

In a more pragmatic vein, President A. Lawrence
Lowell underscored the relationship between classroom discussions and the day-to-day work of a businessman.

The case method of business training is deemed the
best preparation for business life, because the discussion of questions by the banker, the manufacturer,
the merchant or the transporter consists of discerning
the essential elements in a situation and applying to
them the principles of organization and trade. His
most important work consists of solving problems
and for this he must have the faculty of rapid analysis and synthesis.[20]

Professor Bertrand Fox, writing some 35 years
later, emphasized the individual learning opportunities in a group's discussion process.

With so many practical business problems the final
decisions are reached only after discussion among

18. Copeland, *And Mark an Era*, p. 27.

19. Arthur Stone Dewing, "An Introduction to the Use of Cases,"
The Case Method of Instruction, ed. Cecil E. Fraser (New York:
McGraw-Hill, 1931).

20. Exact citation not available. Believed to have been quoted in
the foreword to a Harvard business problem book in the
early 1920s.

smaller or larger groups. I have felt that each class is in essence a practical experience in group behavior and in the benefits of group discussions in arriving at business decisions. As a part of this process, but in part distinct from it, each class provides an experience in learning to listen to the views of one's peers and in learning how to express one's self and perhaps to persuade others to one's point of view. The method provides an opportunity to gain confidence in one's own judgment, but also a degree of humility as well. It also provides a most invaluable opportunity to learn how far one can go by rigorous logical analysis of one or another dimension of the problem and the extent to which judgment comes into play when many factors which have no common denominator must be weighed.[21]

Columbia's John Dewey would have given strong support to the Dewing-Fox position, for his theories of learning support a discussion-oriented teaching methodology. As Jonas Soltes notes, Dewey believed the learner is like an explorer who maps in unknown territory:

The explorer, like the learner, does not know what terrain and adventures his journey holds in store for him. He has yet to discover mountains, deserts, and water holes and to suffer fever, starvation, and other hardships. Finally, when the explorer returns from his journey, he will have a hard-won knowledge of the country he has traversed. Then, and only then, can he produce a map of the region. The map, like a textbook, is an abstraction which omits his thirst, his courage, his despairs and triumphs—the experiences which made his journey personally meaningful. The map records only the relationships between landmarks and terrain, the logic of the features without the psychological revelations of the journey itself.

To give the map to others (as a teacher might) is to give the results of an experience, not the experience by which the map was produced and became personally meaningful to the producer. Although the logical organization of subject matter is the proper goal of learning, the logic of the subject cannot be truly meaningful to the learner without his psychological and personal involvement in exploration. [Dewey:] "Only by wrestling with the conditions of the prob-

lem at hand, seeking and finding his own way out, does he think. . . . If he cannot devise his own solution (not, of course, in isolation but in correspondence with the teacher and other pupils) and find his own way out he will not learn, not even if he can recite some correct answer with one hundred percent accuracy."

Although learning experiences may be described in isolation, education for Dewey consisted of the cumulative and unending acquisition, combination, and reordering of such experiences. Just as a tree does not grow by having new branches and leaves wired to it each spring, so educational growth does not consist of mechanically adding information, skills, or even educative experiences to students in grade after grade. Rather, educational growth consists of combining past experiences with present experiences in order to receive and understand future experiences. To grow, the individual must continually reorganize and reformulate past experiences in the light of new experiences in a cohesive fashion.[22]

The case method enables students to discover and develop their own unique framework for approaching, understanding, and dealing with business problems.[23] To the extent that one can learn business practice in a classroom—and the limits are substantial—it achieves its goal efficiently.

Equally important, case method teaching is intellectually stimulating for the faculty. In current jargon, it is teacher friendly, affording the instructor opportunities for continuous self-education. In this respect, what's good for the faculty is good for the students—paralleling John Dewey's observation that if teaching becomes neither very interesting nor exciting to teachers, how can we expect teachers to make learning very exciting to students?

Every class provides opportunity for new intellectual adventure, for risk taking, for new learning. One may have taught the case before, but last year's notes have limited current value. With a new group of students, the unfolding dynamic of a unique section, and different time circumstances, familiar material is revitalized. Class discussions typically leave the instructor with new questions about enduring challenges.

21. Copeland, *And Mark an Era*, pp. 264–65.

22. Jonas Soltes, *Encyclopedia of Education*, 5th ed., s.v. "Dewey, John."
23. See Pearson Hunt, "The Case Method of Instruction," *Harvard Educational Review*, Summer 1951, pp. 175–192.

The case method also meets a faculty's teaching and research needs.[24] The development of new field cases links instructors to the world of practice. It encourages them to be in touch with their professional counterparts, maintaining a dialogue that explores current problems and anticipates future issues. Clinical field work provides a faculty with rich data from which to extract new hypotheses and modify current working generalizations.

Also, the case method is supportive of a culture that places high value on review and innovation. Too often, faculties teach change—but practice the status quo. Individual course and overall curriculum reviews often depend on the personal initiative of an instructor or the work of faculty committees. But when faculty must prepare teaching cases, their continuing contact with the world of practice provides the institution with an external force for change. Suggestions that a familiar framework be reviewed or new concepts developed are often received more sympathetically when they derive from the impersonal demands of practice rather than from colleagues or departments, with their personal agendas. The case method encourages an adaptive culture.

Finally, the case method as practiced at the Harvard Business School is economically efficient. A distinguished Harvard dean once said that discussion teaching "is not operative in groups larger than seven." Similarly, Professor Theodore Sizer had argued that a questioning (discussion) group approach "requires a seminar format, a circle of fewer than twenty people."[25] But case method teaching does work well with much larger groups—given well-crafted cases, instructors trained in large-scale discussion teaching techniques, and physical facilities designed to support this method.

Harvard Business School classrooms have been architecturally designed to minimize physical distance and to maximize psychological togetherness between teacher and student, and to encourage student-to-student rather than instructor-to-student interactions. An 80-person class has an obvious economic advantage over a traditional small discussion group. Spreading instructional fixed costs over a larger group makes it possible to finance a very expensive case development program.

Skilled teachers are a scarce resource. If they can work with larger student groups, instructional efficiency increases. Moreover, in a large section, the instructor can draw on a wider range of student interest and experience. The need to limit the "air time" of each student encourages the instructor to find ways of helping the class practice the skills of listening, observing, synthesizing, and summarizing. Thus, scale can be an asset, not a liability, in discussion teaching.

Heralded by Dean Gay, and infused with intellectual substance and organizational support by Dean Donham, the case method succeeded because of its educational effectiveness for both students and faculty, its economic efficiency, and its nurturing of an adaptive institutional milieu. First tentatively identified as the "laboratory method," then as the "problem method," the Business School's distinctive pedagogy has undergone substantial changes over the years. Our ideas have changed as to just what constitutes a case, how cases are developed, and how they are taught in the classroom.

The Evolution of the Case Method of Instruction

Originally, cases were just about anything the new faculty could find to provide a basis for provocative classroom discussion: a legal document, a business report, or a business problem with which the teacher was familiar. Instructors preferred the latter for they intuitively saw these problems as a bridge between academia and business. Businessmen had to deal with a daily succession of problems (cases). Why not bring those problems to the classroom for apprentice managers' use? At first businessmen were asked to write up their own company problems and then to lead class discussions of their situation. Later the School dispatched researchers into the field. By 1924 the Bureau of Business Research had 20 recent MBA graduates at work preparing cases.

These early efforts are well illustrated by the Badger Manufacturing Company and the Ajax Manufacturing Company cases, shown here:

BADGER MANUFACTURING COMPANY:
BUYING HABITS OF CONSUMERS

The Badger Manufacturing Company produces enamelware for kitchen use in a wide variety of

24. Professor E. P. Learned wrote an unpublished history of the Business Policy course which provides an in-depth study of this phenomenon.
25. Theodore Sizer, *Horace's Compromise* (Boston: Houghton Mifflin, 1984), p. 119.

articles and styles of several qualities. The company has recently decided to start an extensive advertising campaign in order to increase its sales.

What are the buying habits and motives of consumers purchasing such products, which the advertising manager of Badger Manufacturing Company should take into account in planning this campaign?

AJAX MANUFACTURING COMPANY: FILING RECEIVING CLERK'S COPY OF PURCHASE ORDER

The Ajax Manufacturing Company has, for the past five years, sent a copy of each purchase order to the receiving clerk. The receiving clerk places these copies on a spindle and when the shipment is received, if it is complete, he attaches his copy of the purchase order to the detailed notification of material received report which he makes out.

When this method of placing the copy of the purchase order on a spindle was started this company was producing approximately eight hundred pairs of men's goodyear welt work shoes per day. During the years 1916–1918, however, it expanded its output to over 3500 pairs per day. This expansion has necessitated the filing of the copies of the purchase orders in the receiving department, in accordance with some systematic scheme.

Mr. Carney, the receiving clerk, has visited several factories and has found that some receiving clerks file their copy of the purchase order by the date the shipment is due; others file them by the name of the commodity or by the name of the vendor.

What method of filing the copy of the purchase order should Mr. Carney establish in his department?

From these rather simplistic problem statements, cases have evolved into complex educational instruments, based on carefully designed research plans and intensive field research.[26] Their content has broadened to include internal company information as well as external industry data, and psychological, sociological, and anthropological observations as well as technical and economic material. Whereas

early cases were essentially snapshots of a company at a single point in time, students now learn from series cases that report company operations at all levels of management over a period of time. One series on NIKE, Inc., consists of 15 teaching cases tracing that company's managerial challenges as it evolved from a small entrepreneurial firm to a billion-dollar organization. Individual cases have been designed so they can be combined into course modules for senior management, middle management, and MBA groups.

The evolving definition of case studies has been marked by both continuity and change.[27] Professor Gragg's classic statement defines the intended role of case studies in the 1930s:

> A case typically is a record of a business issue which actually has been faced by business executives, together with surrounding facts, opinions, and prejudices upon which executive decisions have to depend. These real and particularized cases are presented to students for considered analyses, open discussion, and final discussion as to the type of action which should be taken.[28]

In the 1950s, Professor Paul Lawrence of the Harvard Business School viewed a case history in more operational mode:

> A good case is the vehicle by which a chunk of reality is brought into the classroom to be worked over by the class and the instructor. A good case keeps the class discussion grounded upon some of the stubborn facts that must be faced in real life situations. It is the anchor on academic flights of speculation. It is the record of complex situations that must be literally pulled apart and put together again for the expression of attitudes or ways of thinking brought into the classroom.[29]

For seminar development purposes, we worked with the definition shown on the next page.

26. See E. Raymond Corey, "The Use of Cases in Management Education," HBS Case No. 9-376-240.

27. See also James Erskine, M. R. Leenders, and L. A. Mauffette-Leenders, *Teaching with Cases* (London, Ontario: School of Business, University of Western Ontario, 1981).

28. Charles I. Gragg, "Because Wisdom Can't Be Told," *The Case Method at the Harvard Business School*, p. 6.

29. Paul Lawrence, "The Preparation of Case Material," *The Case Method of Teaching Human Relations and Administration*, ed. Kenneth R. Andrews (Cambridge, Mass.: Harvard University Press, 1953), p. 215.

A case is a partial, historical, clinical study of a situation which has confronted a practicing administrator or managerial group. Presented in narrative form to encourage student involvement, it provides data—substantive and process—essential to an analysis of a specific situation, for the framing of alternative action programs, and for their implementation recognizing the complexity and ambiguity of the practical world.

This definition reaffirms the traditional elements of a case: real-life business problems confronting business managers at a particular moment. It enlarges on Lawrence's theme of the case as a teaching instrument crafted to create a specific discussion opportunity. In addition, it indicates some of the basic limits of all case studies: they are partial in coverage, and historical distortion is a probability. As our field research methodology becomes more sophisticated, as we expand our cases to include a combination of verbal, numerical, and visual data, one can be certain that the case studies of our centennial year, 2008, will be very different from those used in 1986.

The classroom use of cases also underwent an evolutionary change. The limited archival documentation available, supported by interviews with emeriti professors and alumni, makes it clear that the manner in which cases were taught changed substantially in the decade following World War II.

Dean Wallace B. Donham, who led the Business School from 1919 to 1942, often compared its teaching methodology with that of the Harvard Law School. Then as now, however, legal and business cases were quite different. Some faculty members thought the dean's effort to link the two systems publicly was intended to quiet critics by associating the fledgling Business School with one of Harvard's most distinguished professional schools.

Yet there were similarities. At both schools student sections were large, and instruction centered on a professor's disciplined questioning of an individual student, with little if any group dialogue. The objective of that professorial interrogation, however, was quite different in the two schools. Many Law School instructors used the Socratic method,[30] which first required a student to boil

down case facts to their essence—in Law School jargon, to "state the case." Then, through interrogation, they encouraged the student to derive appropriate legal principles from the specific case circumstances. The Business School instructors questioned students on the quality of their analysis, the scope of their proposed action plans, and their sensitivity to the managerial challenges inherent in their proposals. The instructor's objective was to help the student develop a way of understanding and contributing to the solution of a corporation's problems. The development of principles was given only modest attention.

A New Pedagogy Emerges

The years after World War II brought major changes to the Business School. A "re-educated" faculty, a new breed of student, a major curriculum revision emphasizing the teaching of administrative skills, and the introduction of new classroom facilities all contributed to the emergence of a "new" case method of instruction.

During the war many senior faculty held defense-related leadership positions in government or business, thereby gaining firsthand managerial experience. Those remaining at the Soldiers Field campus taught senior managers in newly developed executive education programs and engaged in an intensive review of existing academic programs that culminated in the development of a new curriculum. In the early postwar expansion period, younger faculty members brought additional questions and ideas for pedagogical change.

The needs and interests of the student body also changed. Postwar MBA students were very different from their prewar counterparts. Members of the new breed were older, and many were married and lived off-campus. The academic section, rather than the dormitory, became a crucial element in the educational setting. Most postwar students had had substantial military leadership experience. Questioning traditional authority patterns, impatient and independent, these men were confident of their ability to participate in the give-and-take of a group discussion and eager to assume responsibility for their own education.

In 1946 a first-year curriculum, The Elements of Administration, was introduced; this decision was crucial to the long-term evolution of the School's educational strategy. The curriculum design was powerfully simple: a single, first-year

30. ". . . questioning of another to reveal his hidden ignorance or to elicit a clear expression of a truth supposed to be implicitly known by all rational beings." Webster's New Collegiate Dictionary, 9th ed., s.v. "Socratic."

course integrating all the traditional functional areas into one study program. Three new administratively oriented courses were developed: Public Relations and Responsibilities, Control (a combination of Accounting and Statistics), and Administrative Practices. These courses, particularly Control and Administrative Practices, underscored the faculty's interest in moving the MBA program closer to the practice of management through the development of administrative attitudes and skills and the cultivation of sensitivity to organizational relationships and processes.

This experiment had substantial impact. The day-to-day faculty collaboration required by an integrated curriculum gave instructors firsthand experience with managerial circumstances in functional fields other than their own. The faculty soon discovered that while the tasks of leading a sales department and a production operation differed in substantive knowledge requirements, their managerial dimensions had much in common. One faculty member, Professor James Culliton, summarized this well when he observed that a set of concepts and skills, basic to any functional management position, had been identified, and that more important the faculty were beginning to understand better just what was involved in education for management.

Somewhat paradoxically, increasing knowledge about functional management sparked faculty interest in exploring the functions, roles, and skills of the general manager and ways of researching and teaching them. The School had long identified itself as a "school of general management" without precisely specifying just what was meant by that phrase. Now it was ready to address a question posed by Professor Kenneth Andrews: "Just what is the specialty of being a generalist?" In seeking an answer, the Business Policy course (a second-year required course focusing on general management functions) led to a series of research and teaching programs that resulted in the adoption of the concept of corporate strategy as the unifying theme for that course and later for the entire MBA program.

Greater knowledge at both the functional and generalist levels reinforced the faculty's intuitive conviction that management was a field of academic study separate and distinct from its supporting disciplines. In a sense they had answered the 1908 question, What is education for business if it is not applied economics? The key word in the School's name became *administration*, not *business*.

In June of 1953, as these developments were unfolding, Aldrich Hall opened. Its parabola-shaped classrooms were an architectural breakthrough. For the first time, the faculty had facilities designed to support large-scale discussion teaching.

All of the forces for change—faculty, student, curriculum, and facilities—were now in play. While the large-section format remained constant, the instructional scene had changed dramatically. No longer was the student section simply an administrative convenience, an agglomeration of individuals assigned to a course and a room at a designated time. It became the center of the MBA's intellectual and social life, with a powerful dynamic of its own.[31] With process teaching goals becoming more important, the group discussion format provided an excellent way to sensitize students to administrative problems and processes and allow them to practice managerial skills.

The impact on the instructor was significant. His new role was less to question a series of individual students than to direct a process by which the section explored a complex case situation. Symbolically, the older Baker Library classroom had enthroned the professor on a platform, separated from the students he overlooked by a brass railing and curtain. In the new classroom, the professor sat at a desk from which he looked up at the members of his section. The power balance between teacher and student shifted perceptibly; students gained increased opportunity for personal learning and group contribution.

Thus a new case method of teaching was born, quietly, over time, and in some measure without faculty's full appreciation of the magnitude and magnificence of the change.

Basic Pedagogical Elements

A case history provides only the foundation for the learning process we call the case method of instruction—a complicated interaction of case situation, individual student, overall class section, and discussion leader. Education theorists would describe the method as an effort to blend cognitive and affective learning modes. Any attempt to cap-

31. See also Charles D. Orth III, *Social Structures and Learning Climate: The First Year at the Harvard Business School* (Division of Research, Harvard Business School, Boston, Mass.: 1963); and John Van Maanen, "Golden Passports: Managerial Socialization and Graduate Education" in *The Review of Higher Education* 6, no. 4 (Summer 1983): 435–455.

ture this dynamic, the subtle ebb and flow of inter-acting ideas between teacher and student, is diffi-cult at best—perhaps impossible. This may be why the phenomenon of class discussion has so seldom been analyzed or even described.[32]

A few snapshots may give a useful view of this process. Writing about a case class in the late 1920s, Professor Arthur S. Dewing noted that

teaching by the case method is class discussion of possibilities, probabilities, and expedients—the possi-bilities of the combination of very intricate facts, the probabilities of human reactions, and the expedients most likely to bring about the responses in others that lead to a definite end. . . . Cases should be used with clear consciousness that the purpose of business education is not to teach truths—leaving aside for a moment a discussion of whether there are or are not such things as truths—but to teach men to think in the presence of new situations. There should not be a single problem [case] in use which is not capable of at least two intelligent solutions.[33]

Donald R. Schoen and Philip Sprague, reflecting on their personal experience as MBA students dur-ing the early fifties, commented:

The initial atmosphere of the classroom does little to restore a feeling of certainty. The behavior of the professor is strangely disconcerting. There is an ab-sence of professional dicta, a surprising lack of "an-swers" and "cold dope" which the student can record in his notebook; rather he is asked what *he* would do, and what problems *he* feels are important. Similarly he finds that today's problems cannot necessarily be solved by yesterday's solutions. Every time he feels that he has arrived at generalizations or principles which will apply in all cases, he is confronted with a set of variables which will not yield to such analysis. The plea that he has insufficient evidence or data on which to make a decision is more or less ignored; he is told to do the best he can with what is available.

As he airs his views, feelings, reactions, attitudes and prejudices and sees them reinforced or rejected by thinking individuals around him; he has an oppor-

tunity to re-evaluate and re-appraise his own charac-ter and personality. Preconceived notions and handed-down attitudes examined in an atmosphere of reality and with a focus on effectiveness can be seen for what they are.[34]

Robin Hacke described her experience during the 1980s:

I entered the battle of the case method unarmed. The routines and tools that had allowed me to sur-vive years of schooling no longer helped me; my old study habits were useless—counterproductive, in fact. For example, I had always been a diligent student, priding myself on completing the assignments I was given. If I was expected to read pages 220–256 of a book, I read them. As a student in a case class, though, my assignments were open-ended: prepare the case and develop recommendations. I was sup-posed to decide how to approach the material, but it was hard to know how much to do, hard to know where to stop. Was I supposed to consider two alter-natives or six? Was I supposed to consult outside sources (textbooks, classnotes, the business library)? I had always been an outliner, finding that outlining helped me see the structure of the material. But cases by their very nature could not be outlined. They were not books, logically organized by the author to facili-tate my understanding. Just because a particular as-pect of the case situation occupied the first three pages of the case booklet did not mean it was more important than an aspect mentioned in one small par-agraph on page 17. Just because certain data was not provided did not mean it was not necessary.

Like a "real" manager in a "real" business situa-tion, it was now my job to impose a meaningful framework on the unruliness of case facts. I had to search for the key nuggets of data, distinguishing central facts from peripheral ones. I had to sort out the conflicting explanations and alternatives pre-sented to me, and arrive at a reasonable recommen-dation for action.

I understand the importance of these skills in the real world. But that understanding didn't make the skills any easier to develop. When I tried to ignore six pages of a case in order to focus on one crucial ex-hibit, a little voice inside me would ask, Why did

---

32. See Selma Wassermann, *Put Some Thinking in Your Classroom* (Chicago: Benefic Press, 1978) and Clark Bouton and Russell Garth, eds., *Learning in Groups* (San Francisco: Jossey-Bass, 1983).

33. Arthur Stone Dewing, "An Introduction to the Use of Cases," *The Case Method at the Harvard Business School*, pp. 3–4.

34. Donald R. Schoen and Philip R. Sprague, "The Case Method as Seen by Recent Graduates," *The Case Method at the Harvard Business School*, pp. 80–81.

they give you this if it's not important? Every time I needed to make an assumption, particularly one involving numbers, I hesitated and thought, How would I defend my assumption? How could I know what was reasonable? I rarely could walk into class secure in the knowledge that I had "cracked" the case. The uncertainty was frightening.[35]

A review of the fundamental principles underlying case method teaching may help explain its extraordinary power to involve the student in a highly personal learning experience. Keeping Occam's razor in mind, let us note the five we believe to be most important.

1. *The primacy of situational analysis.* For both administrators and students of administration, the primary consideration is "the law of the situation," to use sociologist Mary Parker Follett's pithy phrase.[36] Analyzing a specific situation forces the student to deal with the "as is," not the "might be." He or she must confront the intractability of reality: an absence of needed information, the ever-present conflict of objectives, and the imbalance between needs and resources. The manager must and can act effectively under those circumstances; the intern manager is also expected to do so.

This situational orientation, moreover, insistently reminds the student of the vast gap between simplistic, global prescriptions and what can be said to a specific manager, at a specific time, on a specific issue. The goal of the case discussion is to help students develop the capacity to deal with the situation-specific, not to deliver commentaries on the general. From experience garnered in many case discussions, the student will in fact derive generalizations, but they are stated tentatively, tested frequently, and always used with care.

2. *The imperative of relating analysis and action.* The traditional academic accomplishment has been to know; the practitioner's necessity has been to act. The case method of instruction seeks to combine these two activities. The application of knowledge, always partial, to the complexities of an administra-

tive problem, never capable of complete solution, is the manager's primary task.

A case discussion is a crude mirror of that reality. The class considers action in tandem with analysis whenever possible. The minimum end product of a case discussion is an understanding of what needs to be done and how it can be accomplished. At its best, the case discussion will include an exploration of how a plan can be translated into the committed behavior of a group of managers.

The importance of action influences the entire case discussion, which focuses on the practical and doable, the partial but accomplishable, and the necessity of dealing with first-step accommodations rather than waiting for complete solutions.

3. *The necessity of student involvement.* The active intellectual and emotional involvement of the student is a hallmark of case teaching. That involvement offers the most dramatic visible contrast with a stereotypical lecture class.

In education for management, where knowledge and application skills must be related, student involvement is essential. One does not learn to play golf by reading a book, but by taking club in hand and actually hitting a golf ball—preferably under a pro's watchful eye. A practice green is not a golf game, and a case is not real life. Fortunes, reputations, and careers are not made or lost in the classroom. But case discussion is a useful subset of reality; it presents a microcosm of actual administrative life. It also allows students to practice the application of real-life administrative skills: observing, listening, diagnosing, deciding, and intervening in group processes to achieve desired objectives.

Case discussion demands total participant involvement in a variety of ways, first and foremost in the give-and-take of class discussion—with mind as well as vocal cords. It insists that students practice managerial skills both in class and in all other academic activities, taking responsibility for their own self-education and for the development of their colleagues. Managers are, after all, both teachers and students in their everyday work.

4. *A nontraditional instructor role.* A teacher thoroughly experienced in traditional methodologies may well find case teaching difficult to understand. "As far as I can see, the instructor's job is to give an intelligent grunt of approval or disapproval, ask some questions, and make a summary statement,"

35. Robin Hacke, *The Case Method: A Student Perspective,* unpublished working paper, Harvard Business School, 1986.
36. M. P. Follett, *Creative Experience* (New York: Longmans, Green and Co., 1924), p. 152.

said one. Another commented, "It's a blinking bit of intellectual chaos and so darned inefficient! Why let a class 'muck around' for an hour trying to work through a point when I can explain it in a few minutes. They call that teaching? Just what's the instructor doing?" Guiding a process of discovery, an advocate of the method might reply.

Some instructors, unfortunately, use the case method in masquerade form. While espousing openness and collaboration, they require students to follow their teaching plan point by point, with drumbeat cadence. It may seem as if the students' assignment is to come up with the missing words in an academic crossword puzzle—the instructor's teaching plan. Such pedagogical failures give ammunition to our critics, for a badly executed case discussion can be a disaster: inefficient in use of time and ineffective in student motivation.

Even when the teacher is a master of case method instruction, it is difficult to say just what he or she is doing.[37] We all appreciate the difficulty of describing what an artist "does." Witness the story attributed to symphony orchestra conductor Antal Dorati's three-year-old daughter. After watching her first rehearsal, she explained the mystery of conducting: "Daddy," she said, "you are the only musician who makes no noise."

What conductors or instructors do or don't do, when and how, may be as important as what they know. The artistry of teaching may be arcane, but some of its mystery can be clarified. Professor Kenneth Andrews has thoughtfully described the case instructor's role:

The instructor provides the impromptu services which any group discussion requires. He keeps the proceedings orderly. He should be able to ask questions which invite advance in group thinking and at the same time reveal the relevance of the talk that has gone before. He needs the ability to weave together the threads of individual contribution into a pattern which not only he but his class can perceive. He needs the sense of timing which tells him that a discussion is not moving fast enough to make good use of available time or is racing away from the comprehension of half the class. He knows what to do on such occasions. He exercises control over an essentially "undirected" activity, but at the same time he

keeps out of the way, lest he prevent the class from making discoveries new also to him. Since unpredictable developments always distinguish real learning, he examines his class rather than his subject.[38]

This approach to teaching has its parallels in a variety of fields, as these comments on the teaching of drawing suggest:

The job of the teacher, as I see it, is to teach students, not how to draw but how to learn to draw. They must acquire some real method of finding out facts for themselves lest they be limited for the rest of their lives to facts the instructor relates. They must discover something of the true nature of artistic creation—of the hidden processes by which inspiration works.

My whole method consists of enabling students to have an experience. I try to plan for them things to do, things to think about, contacts to make. When they have had that experience well and deeply, it is possible to point out what it is and why it has brought these results.[39]

The instructor's role in this kind of learning process differs in several respects from traditional practice.[40] First, the task is not so much to *teach* students as to encourage *learning*. This shift in mission affects a wide range of instructor activities, from preparing class material and planning class sessions to measuring what the course has accomplished.

Second, the teacher must be willing to forgo the role and status of a center-stage, intellectually superior authority figure.[41] As a discussion leader, he or she is simply a member of a learning group, albeit one with a unique position. Professor Gragg puts the point well in his classic piece, "Teachers Also Must Learn." In addition to providing information and monitoring the quality of student analysis and presentation, the instructor must facilitate a process of joint inquiry. A primary responsibility, therefore,

37. See Pearson Hunt, "A Professor Looks at Teaching and Himself," *Harvard Business School Bulletin*, January–February 1964.

38. K. R. Andrews, "The Role of the Instructor in the Case Method," in *The Case Method at the Harvard Business School*, pp. 98–99.

39. K. Nicolaides, *Introduction to the Natural Way to Draw* (Boston: Houghton Mifflin, 1941).

40. See also Ronald T. Hyman, *Improving Discussion Leadership* (New York: Teachers College Press, Columbia University, 1980).

41. A delightful sketch of one such an experiment is detailed in Donald W. Thomas, "The Torpedo's Touch," *Harvard Educational Review*, May 1985, pp. 220–222.

is the maintenance of the quality of those paths of inquiry.

Third, the instructor must be both teacher and practitioner. Students will accept that one can legitimately discuss the battle of Waterloo without having the capacity to command a brigade of infantry. But an instructor who tries to develop students' skills of observation, listening, communication, and decision making will be expected to practice what he or she preaches. Failure to do so brings swift retribution.

5. A balance of substantive and process teaching objectives: the development of an administrative point of view. When successful, the case method of instruction produces a manager grounded in theory and abstract knowledge and, more important, able to apply those elements. At the Harvard Business School, that accomplishment has traditionally been summed up as the development of an administrative point of view.

While the faculty has always agreed that the development of professional competence was its primary educational goal, only limited efforts have been made to define and articulate the necessary educational components. A young instructor, many years ago, asked a senior colleague to define the administrative point of view. The curt reply has been long remembered: "If you have to define it, you will never understand what it is. If you know what it is, you don't need to define it. Give your students an opportunity to discover it for themselves."

This advice, whether good or poor, was a bit disquieting. Clearly, however, it reflected the normal operating mode of the school's faculty. The Business School's tradition, then and now, has been to devote its intellectual resources to teaching, to practice, to accomplishment; pedagogical theorizing is given short shrift.

The research of Professor F. J. Roethlisberger, however, made a major contribution to our understanding of the skill components of an administrative point of view. His definition of "skill" underscored the complicated nature of our educational mission:

Skill is the response of a whole organism, acting as a unit, that is adequate to a particular point in a given situation. A skill is always manifested at a particular point as a complex capacity acquired by expe-

rience in responding appropriately to particular, concrete, and whole situations.[42]

That definition, together with his emphasized distinction between "knowledge about" and "knowledge of," pinpointed the skill/competence we hoped our students might achieve:

Although related, we assumed that there were two kinds of knowledge that needed to be different. One is the kind of knowledge that is associated with the scientist who is seeking to make verifiable propositions about a certain class of phenomena. The other is the kind of knowledge that is associated with the practitioner of a skill in relation to a class of phenomena. . . .

The difference between these two kinds of knowledge can be readily seen by contrasting the aim of the scientist with the aim of a practitioner of a skill. The aim of the scientist is to discover and make verifiable propositions about a certain class of phenomena; the aim of the practitioner is the immediate "control" of the phenomena with which he deals. Although the "knowledge of acquaintance" which the practitioner acquires from the practice of skills often remains intuitive and implicit, it serves his immediate purposes well. A skillful carpenter who works with many kinds of woods, for example, has a great deal of "acquaintance with" the properties of different woods. He "knows" what different woods will and will not do for certain conditions—at least sufficient for his purposes of fashioning them into useful objects. He does not have, however, that kind of analytical "knowledge about" phenomena sought by the scientists. He does not "know" about the relative tensile strengths of different kinds of building materials.[43]

Although the faculty may not have been able to define the administrative point of view, it knew that it wanted to train carpenters—albeit carpenters who drove Cadillacs and wore Brooks Brothers' suits—and not to create wood theorists. And it knew how to train these practitioners.

The Administrative Point of View: Its Complexities

As the Harvard Business School approaches its 100th anniversary, the faculty still has not articu-

---

42. F. J. Roethlisberger, *Training for Human Relations* (Boston: Division of Research, Harvard Business School, 1954), p. 8.
43. Ibid., pp. 6–7.

lated a neat definition of the administrative point of view, although all of us have our own working explanations. Perhaps we might think of it as a manager's skill in ordering his or her relationship to an organization, understanding how that organization functions, what its needs are, and how to intervene constructively in its affairs to achieve desired change.

Clearly the administrative point of view is a composite of many elements whose successful application depends on the skill with which they are combined. We can now identify some of the critical elements in that fusion; such a listing may clarify the kinds of in-class experiences we hope to create for our students.

A focus on understanding the specific context. What are the unique circumstances that differentiate this situation from others? Or, as one colleague asked at the beginning of each class, "What's the nature of the beast?" The manager's choice of problems to work on, and the manner and sequence in which he or she deals with these challenges, depend very much on whether the company is a textile converter, a film producer, or an integrated steel operation. Equally important, what are the key challenges facing this manager, at this time, with these resources and limits?

A sense for appropriate boundaries. Problems do not come to the manager in neatly delineated form. Some boundaries are established by external forces, others by organizational structure and financial limits. A key managerial skill is to define the boundaries of any issue so as to balance the need for breadth (to include all essential factors) with the need for sufficient focus (to enhance the probability for constructive improvement).

Sensitivity to interrelationships: the connectedness of all organizational functions and processes. An organization is like a tangle of rubber bands: tugging on one affects all the others. In dealing with a specific issue, the manager must recognize that it will always influence and be influenced by the general situation. How he or she deals with a problem in the sales department, for example, may affect overall company operations. The effective manager must think about the organization holistically and behave accordingly.

Examining and understanding any administrative situation from a multidimensional point of view. The manager must consider not only the present circumstance of any issue but also its historical legacy and future perspective. He or she must accept that any problem may well be understood differently by individuals and groups, and that perceptions change dramatically by organizational level. Presidents and foremen have different agendas. An awareness of this multidimensional context and the capacity to deal with the inevitable conflicts it creates are the hallmarks of a manager.

Accepting personal responsibility for the solution of organizational problems. Much of academic life revolves around the role of commentator and critic. The successful administrator, in contrast, is one who defines problems in ways that encourage their solution and then accepts personal responsibility for the accomplishment of that objective.

An action orientation. The ultimate contribution of any manager is to help the organization deal with problems and exploit opportunities, to move it from an imperfect present to an improved future. Action is the core ingredient in an administrative point of view.

This last point is critical. John Dewey, whose views loom largely behind the Business School's educational philosophy, put it succinctly when he said that it was the saints who engage in introspection while the "burly sinners run the world."

Action: Its Main Ingredients

The manager's primary contribution is to lead the organization—to get things done. We can identify some important ingredients of this action orientation:

- A sense for the possible. A willingness to accept compromise, accommodation, and modest forward motion instead of a fruitless search for the perfect solution. A willingness to view action as a spectrum of potential possibilities, not simply as a few "go" or "no-go" intervention points.
- A willingness to make firm decisions on the basis of imperfect and limited data and, despite omnipresent risk and uncertainty, to have the courage and self-confidence to carry out the proposed action.

33

• A sense for the critical, the jugular. Managers must set the appropriate priorities for attention—select action points essential to their organization's resolution of its crucial problems.

• The ability—marrying analytic discipline with personal creativity—to create a vision of what the undertaking is all about. Such a scenario for the future enables the manager to tie actions taken in a specific context to a larger conception of what is to be accomplished.

• The skill of converting targets into accomplishments. Managers do not confuse intent with impact. They understand the complexity of implementation, the process of converting abstract goals into the committed behavior of the organization's members. Action requires skill in carving out doable tasks and sequencing these initiatives for maximum effectiveness, as well as a sense for when objectives and plans need to be reappraised.

• An understanding that almost all management challenges are grounded in the human and organizational context. Technical, financial, or conceptual issues usually become "people problems" as they move toward the action stage. They can be dealt with only when those human issues are resolved.

• An appreciation of the major limits of managerial action. The complexity of the general manager's problems rules out "solutions" in the conventional sense of that word. Instead, the manager must settle for accommodations, knocking off the rough edges of the problem, knowing that it will never disappear and, even if managed successfully, will recur.

We have identified five basic dimensions of the case method of instruction. It is not the individual elements in isolation that give force to the method, however, but their fusion into an operational gestalt. When this blend of the cognitive and affective is built into the preconscious, it has a unique capacity to prepare a student for continuous learning, growth, and administrative maturity throughout his or her career.

Evaluating Case Discussions

As in many other professional fields, it is difficult to evaluate the overall effectiveness of management education.[44] Our tests measure only partial ele-

---

44. See Martin R. Lip, *The Bitter Pill: Doctors, Patients and Failed*

ments of practice, perhaps the less important ones. Christine McGuire puts the point dramatically: "After thirty years of research we do not have a satisfactory methodology for evaluating professional habits and attitudes. Perhaps a radical new approach is required to achieve any progress in this arena. . . . Work on the development of an acceptable theory or unifying conception of competence is urgent."[45] Grade designations do little more than sort out individuals who perform well and less well in academia. As J. Sterling Livingston and others have pointed out, there is little direct relationship between academic and practical accomplishments.[46] Perhaps Howard Gardner's concept of multiple kinds of intelligence offers us at least a partial answer.[47]

Nathaniel Cantor offers another explanation. Implicitly he asks us to consider whether our curriculum is not shaped by our sense of what we can teach well rather than by the needs of practice:

Logic and mathematics do not begin to exhaust the nature of reality. Yet most of us have grown up in the tradition that the solution to human problems is found in statements, logical propositions. Our formal education is primarily intellectual. We learn answers, general propositions, abstract concepts. We accumulate facts but continue behaving pretty much the same as the generations of biblical times. Knowledge does not seem to make much difference.[48]

Whether or not Professor Livingston is correct, it is undoubtedly difficult to predict long-term results of any educational effort. To paraphrase Amy Lowell, teaching is like dropping ideas into the letterbox of the human unconscious: You know when they are posted but you never know when they will be received or in what form.

Expectations (New York: Harper and Row, 1980) and Greer Williams, *Western Reserve's Experiment in Medical Education and Its Outcome* (New York: Oxford University Press, 1980).

45. Christine H. McGuire, "Evaluation of Student and Practitioner Competence," Chapter 12, in Frank Stritter, ed., "Faculty Evaluation and Development" in *Handbook of Health Professions Education* (San Francisco: Jossey-Bass, 1983).

46. See J. Sterling Livingston, "The Myth of the Well-Educated Manager," *Harvard Business Review*, January–February 1971.

47. Howard Gardner, *Frames of Mind* (New York: Basic Books, 1985).

48. Nathaniel Cantor, *The Learning Process for Managers* (New York: Harper & Brothers, 1958), p. 85.

In the third phase of the seminar development effort, we attempted to learn more about this "posting and delivery" process by comparing classes evaluated as "effective" and "poor" by students, instructor, and researcher. This rough-cut evaluation did not tell us anything about long-term educational results, but did give us some understanding of how students and teachers evaluated short-term case-course efforts. At a minimum it provides instructors with a profile of questions to ask about their current teaching efforts.

One early finding departed somewhat from conventional wisdom. Instructors often judged a class "good" if there were numerous hands in the air, impressive verbal pyrotechnics, and a great deal of student excitement and laughter. Students, however, indicated that those classes, while enjoyable, often were not particularly useful and tended to be forgotten. Our inquiries identified several characteristics of a successful case discussion class and course.

1. *The section functions as a learning group.* Students are usually assigned to a specific section. They may or may not already know their sectionmates. Productive case discussions typically developed only after that agglomeration of individuals had been converted into a cohesive learning group.

In some sections, after weeks of togetherness, the class was still an assemblage of individuals; students sitting next to one another were but distant neighbors. Individual interests dominated the discussion patterns, and the overall group accepted few responsibilities. Other sections, by contrast, had gone through an acculturation process that enhanced the possibilities for effective discussion. Individual students behaved so as to make contributions to the section's learning requirements. The section as a whole was sensitive to the specific learning needs of individual members, and maximized the opportunities for them to contribute. The section took responsibility for the setting of academic standards, for the discovery, exploration, and resolution of case issues, and for the enforcement of appropriate standards of discussion behavior.

Productive case discussions were much more likely to occur in such a cohesive learning group and were typically characterized by a high level of student-to-student discussion. Where instructor-to-student interactions dominated, it was often an indication that the section had not yet made the transition to a learning group.

2. *High levels of student involvement.* Involvement is the hallmark of any case discussion, but in certain class sessions extraordinary levels of involvement developed.

Discussion dialogue can develop at three levels. At the first level, students explore a problem by sorting out relevant facts, developing logical conclusions, and presenting them to fellow students and the instructor. The students discuss someone else's problem; their role is that of a commentator-observer in a traditional, academic sense.

The second level of discussion may be achieved by assigning students roles in the case under discussion. Their comments then tend to reflect a sense for the organizational and personal circumstances of the company managers whose robes they wear. Their analyses and recommendations embrace both academic logic and situational dynamics. When the role-playing session is completed, the section resumes a regular case discussion pattern, but the dialogue usually is more firmly rooted in practical realities. The section has moved away from the external observer's role toward that of an involved insider.

The third discussion level is reached when students, on their own initiative, project themselves into the situation. The classroom and case meld together, with the students vicariously acting as the firm's executive group (albeit an unusually large one). Problems are not discussed as abstract topics, but as issues inextricably bound up in a manager's career and power circumstance. Student comments reflect a personal commitment to the arguments advanced. This level of discussion comes as close to real life as can be achieved in an academic situation. Learning opportunities and risk, however, are high for all.

3. *Instructor direction, not domination, of the discussion.* Instructor direction, as opposed to control, of the class is critical. In classes controlled by instructors, the students' obligations were simple: They had only to follow a predetermined teaching plan, question by question. The instructor decided issues to be discussed and determined when these points had been adequately covered. There was little room for student-initiated exploration or discovery. Students knew that once they had worked through the

instructor's teaching plan, they would be given his or her summary of significant conclusions.

This instructional style may be comfortable for the instructor, but it provides thin educational gruel for a student. Kenneth Eble makes a similar point:

> I once had an intense argument with an English teacher who took me to task for saying offhandedly that a teacher could be too well organized. That seemed to me a simple truth implicit in Melville's remark that "there are some enterprises in which a careful disorderliness is the true method." But to her my statement assailed revealed truth. Organization was on an ascending scale, the highest organization, I presume, approximately of being heaven. For me, organization, like other principles that rule our lives, is more like temperature, offering a range in which humans can live: comfortably but with extremes where discomfort begins. Surely students, from primary school classes to graduate seminars, are familiar with teachers who are simply too organized. It may be a passion for organization distorts the actual relationships among a collection of diverse particulars. Or the organizing power of the teacher may leave too little for the student to do and offer too few possibilities for seeking a structure closer to the student's own understanding. Teachers can be, as one student told me, "beautifully organized but dull as hell."[49]

In other discussion classes we observed a free-flowing, instructor-student collaborative exploration that we categorized as leadership via direction. This "directional" style of leadership was fostered by a complex of factors, of which two seemed most important. First, the instructor provides the students with a path of inquiry—a conceptual framework for understanding the complexities of the problems being studied.[50] Second, he or she develops a teaching plan that considers both what is to be taught and *how* the discussion may unfold.

In the classroom, the instructor shapes and molds the discussion flow so as to make certain that critical case issues are covered in a disciplined way. Direction may take the form of questions, often derived from prior student comments; suggestions of alternative approaches to the problems; the highlighting

of neglected information and its possible consequences; a request for clarification of assumptions; or a strategically timed proposal for a summary by a section member or the exploration of alternative programs of action. In this way, the instructor can achieve discipline and productive discussion with a maximum of student input and freedom.

In summary, our observations suggested that case discussions were most productive when sections functioned as learning groups, students were personally involved in the discussion, and instructors directed the discussion process skillfully. These objectives, difficult to achieve, became the basis for the later development of our teaching seminars.

Some further clues to the personal impact of a well-taught case class emerged as students reviewed case discussion experiences with us. Here are some of their perceptions:

> I learned something about myself; I really uncovered a blind spot in the way I deal with others.

> Learning how to prepare a funds flow statement was a real mystery until Jill James explained it in class. Professor Abbot never could. I may go into banking now.

> I didn't realize there were so many different ways of dealing with this "situation," and there are lots of "situations" in every case. I'm going to get away from "single track" thinking.

> The module on cost accounting taught me a lot. It isn't just that I can understand variance analysis; more importantly, I could stand the pressure of not knowing—not making any progress for weeks. They were hell, but I didn't quit. Funny, I've gotten a lesson in patience and perseverance.

> I went into class with one point of view; it came under attack! In the old days I would have dropped my idea immediately, but I stuck in there, gave ground where I saw I was weak, and came away having convinced most of my section that our plan was right. I can do it!

> I'm now confident that I have a framework of understanding, how to understand and get things done in a company. That case gave me the final know-how on ways of working in complicated production circumstances.

49. Kenneth E. Eble, *The Craft of Teaching* (San Francisco: Jossey-Bass, Inc., 1976), p. 159.
50. See F. J. Roethlisberger, *The Elusive Phenomena*, ed. George F. F. Lombard (Boston: Division of Research, Harvard Business School, 1977), pp. 69–71.

I sure goofed! My plan was a good one and I had spent hours working it through. Yeah—but I ignored the key element: how was I going to convince others that doing it was the best plan?

You'll think it funny, but I came out of that class with a greater respect for Dad. I'd always figured he was nuts to spend his life at the office working his butt off. But business is a challenge; strategy makes a difference for workers too. Business can be done professionally.

These comments illustrate the rich and varied nature of student learning experiences in a case setting. They do not do justice to students' substantive learning experiences, however, emphasizing instead the development of personal insight into individual strengths and weaknesses, reaffirmation of the importance of qualities perhaps not fully appreciated—patience and persuasion, and confidence in one's own capacities to endure stress. Instructors must wonder how much of this can be planned or even predicted. Few of us set out to teach students patience or filial piety. We tend to assume, understandably and appropriately, the primacy of our academic objectives. What and when students learn is often only indirectly related to formal teaching plans.

Instructors commenting on productive discussion experiences believed that in ideal circumstances, students took the conceptual framework of the course, modified it to meet their personal requirements, and then practiced its application until use became intuitive. Their evaluations, however, tended to focus on the group rather than on specific students, and on the course as a whole rather than individual class sessions. A "good" section, with self-discipline, worked through the cases—incorporating individual contributions into a unified discussion that produced not only situational diagnosis but pragmatic action suggestions. When that process unfolded with a maximum of student-to-student interaction and student direction of the dialogue, the class was doubly successful. Instructors gave high marks to sections that understood both the power and the limits of course concepts, that noted not only conclusions but also questions for further reflection.

As the course moved along, instructors evaluated progress by the section's ability to draw on previous sessions in analyzing the case of the day. When

such linkages gradually built up a matrix of concepts and case problems that students could use to formulate summary operating generalizations, instructors believed course objectives had been substantially achieved.

The ultimate class, in their judgment, occurs when section discussion imperceptibly melds academic dialogue with intense student involvement, mirroring the reality of organizational struggle and danger. The student confronts the circumstances of corporate life at close range. Cantor describes this well.

> What one wants to do, however, is not simply a matter of knowledge or analysis. What one *does* occurs in a complicated context of hope, fear, risk, courage, resistance, guilt, rationalization, confusion, ambivalence, and so on (dimensions of norms, ethical beliefs, and personal needs). It is a spectrum of feeling which eventuates in the drive or will or motivation which is the decision. To escape from the discomfort of struggle, to avoid the disagreeable feelings of uncertainty, inadequacy, and self-responsibility, we turn to the expert, the formula, the book, the superior or *the* verbal answer. Thus we think we avoid the heartache and headache of assuming responsibility for our own decision. . . . Answers are, by definition, verbal propositions, statements, abstractions. The application of the answer requires a commitment, a bit of living with its accompanying disturbance, risk, and recognition of feeling.[51]

Amy Lowell was correct; we do not have a good way of understanding or evaluating how people learn. But in our brief excursion into this complicated area, we found a good bit of agreement between teachers and students as to the elements of an effective case class. Both felt the ultimate teaching objective was the student's development of a personally tested, intuitive pattern of understanding and acting in complex administrative situations.

While all of us hope for that ultimate case discussion, a more practical challenge is to improve our everyday teaching contribution. A central theme of these teaching seminars is that case instruction calls for a dual competency: command of the basic conceptual and knowledge component of one's field, and an ability to lead the class discussion process.

51. Nathaniel Cantor, *The Learning Process for Managers*, pp. 86–87.

To emphasize the importance of process is not to denigrate the value of knowledge. It is the relationship of knowledge to practice that is critical for any practitioner. Sir William Osler, the great physician, makes the point well:

To study the phenomena of disease without books
Is to sail an uncharted sea
While to study books without patients
Is not to go to sea at all.[52]

For a teacher of management, the interplay of knowledge and the discussion process is critical. Like two scissor blades, both elements must work together for incisive learning. Not all instructors appreciate that reality; most students do.

Preparing for Class

It is easier to declare the need for this "dual competency" than to provide practical, detailed support for instructors wishing to improve their proficiency as discussion leaders. How does the need for mastery of both knowledge and process affect preparation for a class? What are the consequences for a teacher's leadership of the case dialogue? An experienced seminar participant stated the problem poignantly. She asked, "How do I plan for a discussion session yet to be born? How do I ready myself for the minute-by-minute job of running the class—to be able to understand, organize, and guide the free-flowing give-and-take of a case class? As soon as I ask the first question, everything is up for grabs. It is a frightening process—traditional approaches just don't seem to work for me. What's the answer?" We empathize with our colleague; there are no simple solutions.

We have developed a method of preparing for a discussion class that we would like to share with you. (Obviously our approach is just one of many possibilities.) Our first step is to evaluate the progress that has been made toward fulfilling course-teaching objectives. We review the substantive material covered to date and that to be introduced in upcoming classes. We note the critical issues that have been raised in previous sessions and try to pinpoint where further examination should be encouraged. What topics remain to be raised, and

what upcoming cases offer the best possibilities for their exploration? Detailed instructor summary notes, made after each class session, provide the data for much of this exercise. Postclass commentaries are also invaluable as one prepares for summary sessions, examinations, and eventually a review of course strengths and weaknesses.

Next, we begin an in-depth preparation of the case. Our objective is to prepare a detailed analysis of the organization's situation, state the conclusions that might be derived from that analysis, and outline a spectrum of action recommendations that might be appropriate to suggest to company management. Superior command of substantive information and the discipline of a rigorous intellectual analysis are basic to any preparation, but offer special benefits to a discussion leader. Command of the substantive gives the instructor additional opportunities to concentrate on understanding and managing the discussion process, the only first-hand data with which he or she has to work.

Professor Roethlisberger put this point well: "For me the important 'facts' existed in the discussion of the case and not in the written case per se. It could be said that they [other instructors] were teaching the written case, whereas I was teaching the discussion of it."[53] Our personal preference is to try to use both data banks.

Once this analytic exercise is complete, preparation shifts to a more complex task: trying to predict and prepare for the process by which students and instructor will discuss the case. Without attempting to draw up a formal statement, we aim to develop an internalized appreciation and command of the complexities that may influence the section dynamic during a specific class. First and foremost is an understanding of each student's academic strengths and weaknesses, and a reading of the section's current academic standing and group dynamic. The instructor needs to anticipate approximately where in the discussion opportunities may arise to meet individual student and group learning needs. Where are the danger spots? As we develop teaching questions, we try to predict alternative responses the section might make to each question and to plan for constructive replies on the part of the instructor.

Specifically, we work through a simple six-step process review before each class discussion. First

52. Sir William Osler, "Books and Men, Remarks," *Boston Medical and Surgical Journal* 144 (January 17, 1901): 60–61. Reprinted with permission.

53. F. J. Roethlisberger, *The Elusive Phenomena*, p. 141.

we assess the status of the section. How far and well has it progressed in terms of academic objectives? Where has it made the most progress, where the least? What is the capacity of the section to work together as a learning group? What is its mood? Are students having fun, or are they glum? What is happening in the overall academic program that might affect our discussion (e.g., exams, reports, or conferences)? What is the overall university scene? What's the leading editorial topic in the student newspaper?

Second, we review each individual student's history and performance. Who might have the most to learn from this particular case problem? Who might contribute most? Will the case offer special learning opportunities for students who have experience, or perhaps career interests, in this company and/or industry? Does the case contain data that might be offensive to some students? Which quiet students might find this case a useful entry point into section give-and-take?

Third, we recognize and try to deal with our own mood. Is this a case we like or dislike? Is this a fun section of the course or an academic chore? Are there some sour apples in the section—students we just plain don't like? Where might our personal biases and prejudices affect our leadership of the discussion? All these considerations, as well as family and personal concerns, influence one's behavior in the classroom. It is helpful to acknowledge and examine the potential impact of these factors on your leadership of the case.

Fourth, we review the case as a discussion instrument. What are its faults, if any—factual or editorial errors, missing basic data, or inadequate description of the situation? Where are the best opportunities to practice needed analytic and administrative skills? What will be the students' attitude toward the case? How well will they prepare? What questions will they bring to the discussion? What issues have high potential for involvement and conflict? How does this case connect with past and future cases?

Fifth, we work up a series of operational guidelines. How active a role do we wish to play as instructors: should we intervene on numerous occasions or merely enter the discussion when changes in direction or summary statements are needed? What will be the mode of the class: is it to be a drill in technique or an exploration of questions for reflection? How should class time be divided

between diagnosis and action? How should the chalkboard be used: what would we hope to have on the board at the beginning and end of class? How should the class be paced: where would we hope for the high-involvement points?[54]

Finally, we think about ways to open and close the class. The opening minutes of a session present the instructor with a series of decisions that, if made appropriately, can do much to ensure a productive discussion. Do you ask for volunteers or select one or two lead-off students? If the latter, how do you choose those individuals? Do you begin with a specific prepared question or simply invite a student to "open up the case"? If you pose the first question, is it to be a specific, directed question or a general request for an overall appraisal of the company's position? What possible responses might a student make to those questions, and how might you best work with his or her comments? What opening comments, if any, should you make about the course, the prior class, or expectations for the current class?

A similar set of complex decisions confronts the teacher at the end of the class. Should you, for example, offer a prepared general summary or let the summary evolve extemporaneously—or both? What "mind benders"—basic questions—do you want to leave with the section for reflection? What suggestions, if any, for tomorrow's class?

Though there is no way to predict precisely what will happen in an upcoming class, this preparation regime is usually helpful. Systematically previewing the major process dimensions—the group dynamic, student needs and ambitions, instructor interests and biases, and the interplay of specific case and course concepts—helps you to predict the general paths of inquiry a section might want to explore and to anticipate where in those discussion flows might be the most opportune times to deal with important section and individual student learning needs. At a minimum, such planning helps instructors avoid some errors and capitalize on learning opportunities. At best it may help them appreciate the power and complexity of a teaching approach that deals with both content and process.

54. See Laura Nash, "The Rhythms of the Semester: Overall Preparation, Evolving Roles, and Special Classes," *The Art and Craft of Teaching*, ed. Margaret Morganroth Gullette (Cambridge, Mass.: Harvard-Danforth Center for Teaching and Learning, 1982).

A still more complicated challenge is to ready oneself for the minute-by-minute leadership of a discussion class. In writing about another complex skill development challenge—the improvisation of jazz—David Sudnow offers a valuable perspective: the artist (or the teacher) must have a capacity for "the organization of improvised conduct."[55]

An instructor must be able to instantaneously organize and influence the ongoing case discussion. Success involves balancing the needs for student freedom of inquiry—the encouragement of questioning, the willingness to explore the unexpected—with a disciplined direction that ensures the achievement of the class and course objectives. Failure opens up the possibility of chaos as students with widely diverging agendas attempt to discuss a case problem.

How does one become adept at this minute-by-minute direction of a case discussion? Clearly there is no simple solution: no instructional patent medicines, no set of tricks, no equivalent of the how-to paperback. We all recognize that much of discussion leadership is intuitive, the instantaneous application of past experience to present challenges. Intuition—a sensing that precedes knowing—enables an instructor to understand and exploit the unspoken words and the latent feelings of the section. It encourages confidence in the face of awesome complexity.

Instructors' effectiveness is closely related to their fundamental attitudes toward individual students and the section. If that attitude communicates respect for each student as a very special person and a belief in his or her potential for contribution and growth, trust is an almost inevitable reciprocal. Students then accept personal responsibility for the success of their class and make a commitment to supporting your efforts. One suspects that this "quality of attitude" was a primary reason for the success of master teachers Neil Postman, Haim Ginott, and Jinks Harbison.

Our investigations indicated that successful discussion leadership involves certain concepts, skills, and techniques. Effective discussion teachers have a highly developed capacity to observe and are accomplished in framing appropriate questions, listening to the explicit, detecting the latent, and responding constructively. They are sensitive to the

need for developing learning contracts between teacher and student, and deft in their ability to guide rather than control the discussion flow.

Rather than bemoaning our limited ability to deal with the intuitive, we have focused our seminar efforts on the doable. To help others ready themselves for "the organization of improvised conduct," we adopted a threefold approach. Our first objective has been to alert instructors to the need for a command of both course content and discussion process. Second, we encourage all instructors to work through the preclass-preparation protocol just outlined. Such a drill sensitizes teachers to the complexities of process planning and offers them firsthand evidence that such efforts can enhance section learning opportunities. Finally, and most important, the seminar programs detailed in Parts II and III provide a chance for personal skill development. While it may not be possible to *teach* very much about discussion teaching, a great deal can be *learned*. Critically observing a seminar leader at work is beneficial. Developing one's analysis of a specific teaching problem, testing its accuracy and completeness and the utility of your "solution" against peer judgment, is both exciting and humbling. Monitoring the types of questions and responses made by your fellow teacher-students offers new insights into old classroom problems. Seminars are learning laboratories. Adena Rosmarin has described such an experience in "The Art of Leading a Discussion," found in Part IV of this book.

The Seminar Programs

Under ideal circumstances, there are substantial advantages to be gained by including both professional and liberal arts instructors in a case-teaching seminar. However, not every college is associated with a professional school, so practical considerations often make the ideal impossible.

Part II presents a syllabus for a liberal arts faculty. We will describe the program in only modest detail, for it is still under development. We plan further testing during the coming academic years, but preliminary results have been most encouraging. Part III describes the seminar for instructors in professional schools in more detail; we have more extensive experience with that material.

Both seminars assume that the instructor is in command of her or his professional field or academic discipline. All cases, and the associated case discussion, dramatically downplay content and

55. David Sudnow, *Ways of the Hand* (Cambridge, Mass.: Harvard University Press, 1978).

overemphasize process. In most classroom circumstances, of course, instructors must work with both dimensions.

Both seminars are ongoing. Like any creative educational experiment, they are inevitably unfinished. Alan Gregg, the great medical educator, once lightheartedly noted that a good education should leave much to be desired. Clearly we need to develop new cases and concepts, and to do additional research on the classroom discussion process.

Both seminars are case based. "All that is profound wears a mask," Nietzsche observed. The "mask" here is recurring classroom challenge, sometimes as dramatic as the section rebellion described in "The Section Just Took Over," sometimes as routine as those ever-present problems of poor attendance, declining participation, and lack of student involvement that confronted Professor Rowe in "We're Just Wasting Our Time."

A good case looks at a deceptively simple moment and describes its complexity. They are rich in what Jerome Bruner calls predicaments: puzzles without neat and tidy answers. Classic cases provide ample opportunity for a participant to confront, explore, and learn from the stubbornness of practice. They give life to James Russell Lowell's aphorism, "One thorn of experience is worth a whole wilderness of warning."[56] Beyond immediate problems, they pose fundamental issues for continuing reflection. Margaret Morganroth Gullette, assistant director of the Harvard-Danforth Center for Teaching and Learning, describes cases as "a form of educational drama." They are stories, she emphasizes.

> People get some of their best learning from stories. Great novelists know this, parents know it, and of course great teachers do too. Naturally, for the learning to work, the stories have to be good ones. They have to be about absorbing situations that grip and puzzle. Teaching cases are real stories of this kind: they contain challenging and perilous moments that teachers have actually experienced.[57]

Both seminars provide a number of provocative cases from which we may learn.

56. James Russell Lowell,"Shakespeare Once More," *Among My Books* (Boston: Fields, Osgood & Co., 1870).
57. Margaret Morganroth Gullette, "Introduction to a Case Discussion," a speech delivered at Wesleyan University, May 1980.

The cases included in the two seminars differ somewhat in terms of design, data, and institutional source. Most of the teaching problems found in Part III came from graduate business schools. Those in Part II often involve the traditional academic small seminar setting, without the social dynamic of large sections common to many professional schools. Happily these cases also tend to be shorter than their counterparts in Part III.

Both seminars share the major goals of helping instructors become more skillful and professional in their discussion leadership assignments and winning additional respect for the complexity and creativity involved in case discussion teaching. These objectives, however, are only a means to the ultimate goal of any teacher: the development of educated, creative men and women who will contribute their talents to society's needs. We subscribe enthusiastically to Sir Richard Livingstone's statement of an educator's fundamental mission.

> For the teacher to have clearly in his mind this distinction of means and ends, and the need for higher ends, to feel that he is training his pupils to live a life that is a symphony and not a series of disconnected noises—even if they are beautiful noises—to see that while they acquire the means which they need for the practical purpose of life, they should also form an idea of the end at which they should aim. If that could be done we should have cured the chief disease of our times. If you want a description of our age, here is one: The civilization of means without ends; rich in means beyond any other epoch, and almost beyond human needs; squandering and misusing them because it has no overruling ideal; an ample body with a meager soul.[58]

The conversion of these lofty goals into day-to-day practice is the ultimate goal of our teaching seminars. To give you a better understanding of seminar objectives and materials, the following sections review their teaching themes and describe how we work with these materials.

Seminar for Liberal Arts Instructors

This Liberal Arts seminar is largely the creation of co-author Abby J. Hansen. The following, abstracted from her course description found in the

58. Sir Richard Livingstone, *On Education* (New York: Cambridge University Press, 1956), p. 99.

Instructor's Guide (which is available as a supplement to this book), overviews the rationale for its development and summarizes the educational objectives for each of the program's four sub-modules.

All discussion leaders wish to encourage participants to apply their emotions as well as their intellects to the material, to cooperate with each other and challenge each other's positions helpfully, and to take perplexing questions home to ponder. Nonetheless, certain aspects of liberal arts teaching do seem unique. For one thing, liberal arts students tend to be younger and less experienced than those in professional schools. For another, their institutional cultures are different. Undergraduates in a Renaissance French literature course will probably have goals, styles, expectations, and preconceptions unlike those of students in an MBA course. Accordingly, the cases in the liberal arts module have been selected to highlight the challenges typically encountered by arts and sciences instructors. The seminar does include professional school cases whose basic issues seem to be universal.

I have organized the liberal arts teaching seminar into four general units. These topics roughly parallel the way a group develops over the course of a semester, but the issues with which a teacher must deal can vary widely from this pattern: problems common to the beginning of most classes can crop up at the end, and vice versa. Nonetheless, in the interest of bringing order from chaos, let us consider these rubrics and explore some of the reasons I have organized the cases in this particular order.

SECTION 1. EARLY CLASS SESSIONS. This start-up unit includes cases particularly likely to raise issues germane to meeting new people and beginning to help them form a learning group. Any teacher has to establish authority without appearing lax on the one hand, or stuffy and dictatorial on the other. He or she must set a workable contract swiftly, or it will set itself. What do you want to accomplish with this group? What do they want to do? The seminar leader must also begin to create an environment conducive to the sort of discussions that can actually help expand and deepen participants' appreciation of teaching even though they may have been teaching for years, possibly with diminishing enjoyment and effectiveness.

SECTION 2. LEADING THE CLASS. Classroom dialogue is the crux of discussion teaching. A teacher who attempts to control classroom proceedings too tightly falls into the classic trap of trying to play ventriloquist. This almost invariably produces bilateral frustration. The students fail to perform the dummy's role satisfactorily, and the teacher strikes them as a martinet with no imagination. *Directing* the proceedings is quite another matter; it requires more subtlety, greater attunement to the participants' thoughts and feelings, and a shift in focus away from the teacher to the students. It also requires listening.

SECTION 3. RESPONSIBILITIES OF LEADERSHIP. All teachers should be protectors by virtue of their *de facto* authority. But the true nature of protection—whom to protect, how, when, and how to recognize genuine weakness—is by no means obvious. This unit deals with 'problem' students, and helps focus the teacher's attention on various ways to spot them, appreciate their impact upon the rest of the class, and begin to think creatively and usefully about ways to offer real assistance.

SECTION 4. OPERATIONS: DAY-TO-DAY CLASSROOM PRACTICE. This section takes up issues that schools of management classify under *Operations*. How does one move, speak, question, respond, give assignments, behave in the classroom? What are the overtones of these actions and words? How can teachers begin to appraise and manage these often unconscious procedures? This is the section in which we consider details. We end with it because it is the most subtle. It should demand the greatest sophistication in the group's abilities to perceive and analyze intricacies in classroom interaction. We also end with it because it highlights implications that we consider absolutely crucial to discussion teaching. The cases in this group describe situations that seem to damage students, yet the teachers are by no means malicious. On the contrary, both are experienced, successful instructors whose philosophies of teaching include humanitarian goals. Why, then, do they encounter precisely the sort of problems they would most like to avoid? Participants will find that the implications of these teachers' classroom behavior summarize most of the issues the seminar has considered from the beginning. We end intentionally on this note of complexity in the hopes of raising more questions—more *personal* questions for each participant—than we answer.

Seminar for Professional School Instructors

SECTION 1. INTRODUCTION. The first section of this seminar offers an instructor the opportunity to cover usual first-day tasks, reviewing institutional protocol and course administration. When we conduct the seminar, we comment, in considerable detail, on the outline of cases and readings and give advance warning about cases whose length or complexity will require special preparation.

The first of our two key objectives in this section is to "romance" the seminar; we highlight the unique learning opportunities it presents. To be a superior instructor one must be continually relearning what it is like to be a student. Seminar participants learn a great deal from watching skilled colleagues explore and deal with familiar problems in innovative ways, and from noticing how the session leader meets the familiar challenge of directing the discussion process.

In addition, we begin our efforts to change a gathering of individuals into a cohesive, supportive learning group. We personally welcome each participant to the seminar room. In the first session we ask each member to share a bit of his or her background and future career interests with the group. We address each participant by name and make certain that participants do likewise. An instructional philosophy of openness and trust must be behaved to be believed. Professors Glover and Hower put the point well.

> Clearly, if the students are to take responsibility for analyzing and discussing cases, they need a favorable climate for doing so. This means a permissive atmosphere in which they feel free to put forth their ideas and their questions without the instructor reacting in the form of rejection, derision, blame, or authoritarian injunctions to think along certain other lines preferred by the instructor at that moment. This free atmosphere will be fostered if the instructor makes up his mind to hear and to try to understand what students have to say, and encourages others to do the same. At times he may have to ask for amplification or restatement, and certainly what students say will often seem wrong or absurd; but in any event, he

will try to grasp and respect whatever views the student tries to express.

> Behind such behavior will be a feeling of equals collaborating in the struggle for enlightenment. Whether or not the instructor agrees with what the student has said, he will want to explore further in a joint effort to find out where such views lead. And he will want to hear what other students think, too. On occasion (usually when asked) he will put forth ideas of his own; but he will do so with the explicit understanding that his ideas are to be scrutinized, discussed, criticized, accepted, or rejected with the same freedom that is accorded those of anyone else in the class. Even the wisest instructor has no monopoly on ideas. In short, he will regard, and therefore treat, his students as adults, with the respect, tolerance, and will to understand which goes with mature relationships.[59]

Operationally we start with short cases presenting apparently simple problems that are really extremely complex; they allow us to raise the key issues covered by the entire seminar. We prepare only a "bare-bones" teaching plan with just a few questions, for we want to allow maximum opportunity for the participants to follow lines of inquiry important to them. Our summary focuses on questions raised and points not explored by the participants, as well as suggestions on how they might want to work with the next case.

SECTION 2. THE EARLY CLASS SESSIONS: ESTABLISHING THE INSTRUCTOR-STUDENT LEARNING CONTRACT. The second section has four teaching themes. Initially we focus on the challenges of the early weeks of the semester, when the perennial problems of instructor uncertainty and "section building" are at their peak. Someone once said that academic communities do not commit homicide with new instructors, they simply induce suicide. How does a novice instructor survive in the present, and yet plan for the future—the remainder of the semester?[60] How does an experienced instructor avoid a faltering start-up, from which tiny errors

---

59. John D. Glover and Ralph M. Hower, *Some Notes on the Use of the Administrator* (Homewood, Ill.: Richard D. Irwin, 1950), p. 5.
60. See Kevin Ryan, *Don't Smile Until Christmas* (Chicago: University of Chicago Press, 1970).

may cumulate later into major problems for the section?

We highlight preparation requirements for those early meetings: what crucial observations about section behavior need to be made? What information about students might be useful and how can it be obtained? How does a section of students "read" the instructor in those beginning sessions? How might those "readings" affect the instructor's behavior in early classes? What personal information, if any, should instructors offer the group: their academic credentials and interests, their personal background, their likes and dislikes?

The first day of class is critical, and the name of the game is detail. For example, being in the classroom early allows you to enact David Reisman's concept of the teacher as host, personally welcoming members to the section. Beyond such practical advantages as a chance to make simple equipment checks (avoiding the frustration of a projector that won't work), you will have an opportunity to interpret the subtle signals being sent by students who arrive very early for class. "Early birds" sing important songs! Almost always the early arrivals have a personal message they want to give you in a private moment. A sensitive instructor will try to hear and understand those important songs.

The second theme, crucial to the attainment of seminar goals, is the importance of establishing a constructive instructor-student learning contract. We urge instructors to work out a section operating charter specifying the "rules of the game"—the responsibilities of both teacher and student. Although some things can be stated explicitly about how the section is to run, other aspects of the contract can only be communicated by attitude and behavior. It is the latter dimension that creates complications. For if the contract is partially—some would say primarily—set by the unconscious behavior of the instructor, how can he or she know if it has been abrogated? We explore the consequences of instructor domination of that contract, and the reverse issue: to what degree and on what matters is it useful to have students determine the rules of the game? Finally—and here the "Ernie Budding" case series provides us with fascinating data—we explore the instructional challenge of changing an established contract. If instructional needs shift in midsemester, how does the instructor modify existing patterns of operation to meet the changed circumstance?

The third theme contrasts the roles, responsibilities, knowledge, and skill requirements of a discussion leader with those of a lecturer or laboratory teacher. We invite the participants to explore the implications of these differences for their day-to-day classroom practice. The questions raised are predictable: What happens to my "power" when I move away from more traditional instructional modes? How do I prepare for a class where I must be expert in process leadership as well as course content? How do I evaluate both student and section performance? What is a good class?

Finally, we probe the complexities of an academic rite of passage—the transformation of doctoral candidate into full-fledged instructor. This change in role and status is difficult for any instructor; it seems to be especially complicated for a case discussion teacher who lacks the traditional academic trappings of power. If many seminar members are in the middle of this career complication, involvement is intense! Older, experienced instructors find these sessions useful for coaching purposes.

It may be helpful to alert the discussion leader—whether the seminar is oriented toward liberal arts or professional school instructors—to the complexity of using multipart cases effectively. Each section of such a case ends at a critical decision point or at least a point at which the concerned instructor might want to pause for self-questioning. We typically hand out the (A) section of the case for preclass preparation, while the (B) and (C) units are distributed at the session. Although the latter sections are usually quite short, they do put slow readers at a disadvantage and break the flow of discussion. With limited time (90 minutes with our format), careful advance planning is essential.

SECTION 3. QUESTIONS, LISTENING, AND RESPONSE: THE KEY SKILL DIMENSION. Central to the effectiveness of any discussion leader is the ability to ask questions, listen, and respond.[61] Unfortunately, relatively little research has been done on just what goes on in the crucial black box of professional education—the classroom.[62] The pioneering

61. See Theodore Sizer, Chapter 3, "Skills: The Importance of Coaching" and Chapter 5, "Understanding: The Importance of Questions," *Horace's Compromise* (Boston: Houghton Mifflin, 1984).
62. Two overviews of research on teaching effectiveness are: David C. Berliner, "The Half Full Glass: A Review of Research on Teaching," in *Using What We Know About Teaching*, edited

investigations of Dwight Allen, formerly University Professor at the Darden School of Education, Old Dominion University, and Don Oliver's work[63] have been most helpful. Some very practical advice can be found in Margaret Morganroth Gullette's *The Art and Craft of Teaching*.[64]

Questions, listening, and response is a topic we explore throughout the entire seminar as well as in these designated cases. We attempt to demonstrate this skill in our own teaching, and we encourage participants to critique this dimension in the seminar and in their regular classes. Simple of design but difficult of execution, our teaching plan for this section takes a two-step approach.

First, we encourage participants to identify and categorize question-and-response patterns: to develop their own typologies. Instructors are typically intrigued when they realize there are six or eight basic types of questions and dozens of subsets of questions available for their use—a whole armament, in fact. They can ask, for example, questions of fact, of interpretation, of extension, or they can create hypothetical questions. Designing questions for maximum student learning opportunities is an essential ingredient in the artistry of case teaching. John Ciardi puts it succinctly:

A good question is never answered;
It is not a bolt to be tightened into place
But a seed to be planted and to bear more seed
Toward the hope of greening the landscape of idea.[65]

Once participants have established their own first-cut typology, we seek to make these categories operational. When, for example, would you use a very general, interpretive question—"What is your appraisal of this company?"—versus a very specific, factual question—"What is the current ratio of the company?" When do you personalize a question—for example, "Janet, how did you react to that con-

clusion?" When do you make your questions more, or less, abstract? In what ways is the first class question unique? What questions are most appropriate in the early part of class as opposed to the later part?

We explore the complexities of response. Should the instructor respond verbally to a speaker or simply shift to another participant? If you respond to the first student, do you express personal approval or disapproval of those comments? Do you restate the comment and ask for elaboration of one or more of its component ideas? Do you demand defense? Ask for clarification? Suggest how the current point could be combined with a comment made by an earlier contributor? Do you respond to the technical content of the comment or to latent feelings of the speaker?

We emphasize related operational decisions. How does one decide which student to recognize? Do you make a random selection? Do you call on the student whose hand has been raised longest? (Our experience suggests not; thinking often stops when the hand is raised, and if the patient student is recognized, his or her comment usually will not fit into the current discussion flow.) How does one determine a student's involvement level?

Sensitive listening is the bridge that links questioning and responding. In *Teachers Also Must Learn*, Charles Gragg puts the point well: "Teaching is not only the art of thinking and speaking. It is also the art of listening and understanding. Nor by listening is meant just the act of keeping still. Keeping still is a technique; listening is an art."[66] Our objective is to make each class session a laboratory to explore the barriers and gateways to "active listening"—to use Carl Rogers's phraseology. Our approach highlights five principles. First, we ask numerous "checking questions" during these sessions—for example, "Is that what you said, Ms. James? Did Ms. Young hear your point?" When miscommunication occurs—and the first law of communication is to expect miscommunication—we explore the reasons for the breakdown. These interchanges serve as a continuing reminder that listening is hard work and that miscommunication is all too easy.

Second, we emphasize the fundamental distinction between listening for content and listening for latent feelings—the hidden agenda. Instructors

by P. Hasford, Association for Supervisor and Curriculum Development, 1984, and N. L. Gage, "What Do We Know About Teaching Effectiveness?", *Phi Delta Kappan*, October 1984, pp. 87–93.

63. "Discussion with Direction," by Donald W. Oliver in *Changing Public Controversy: An Approach to Teaching Social Studies*, by Fred M. Newmann with the assistance of Donald W. Oliver (Boston: Little, Brown & Co., 1970), pp. 71–84.

64. Margaret Morganroth Gullette, editor, *The Art and Craft of Teaching* (Cambridge, Mass.: Harvard University Press, 1984).

65. Reprinted by permission of the author.

66. Charles I. Gragg, "Teachers Also Must Learn," *Harvard Educational Review* 10 (1940): 30–47.

must continually make decisions about which level they should respond on. Our third principle is closely related: effective listening is most difficult unless one knows each participant as a unique human being. Knowing a person helps the instructor hear what that person is really saying, especially when that person's latent feelings are critical to the subject being discussed.

Fourth, constructive listening asks that one understand not only what the other person has said but also what that person might have been expected to say and did not. We need to keep in mind what the section has been talking about and what it may be talking about in the next few minutes, in the next few classes.

Our final working proposition can be expressed in an old Swiss proverb: "When one shuts one eye one does not hear everything." Observations of the entire classroom scene—its hot and quiet spots, the speaker's manner in putting the point, and the reaction of the other person to whom the message is being sent—all contribute to one's understanding.

Two operational topics typically arise in these discussions. First, how does one evaluate a classroom contribution? What is a useful comment; what is a poor one? Does one reward a student for an excellent process contribution to the group's deliberation? Or punish a student for a clumsy process intervention? How does an instructor remember, for evaluation purposes, the 30 or 40 comments made in each class session?[67]

The crafting of questions, sensitive listening, and constructive response are the key skill requirements for effective discussion teaching. Our ability to stimulate meaningful classroom dialogue, to multiply individual insights and points of view, and to create circumstances in which individual students may practice seminar skills and gain in knowledge, maturity, and wisdom depends in large measure on our ability to carry out these critical tasks.

SECTION 4. LEADING THE DISCUSSION PROCESS: THE CRITICAL INSTRUCTIONAL CHOICE—DIRECTION VS. CONTROL. In this part of the seminar we examine the problem of reaching instructional targets while maintaining a delicate balance between *controlling* classes—putting students through a series of questions usually based on the instructor's

analysis of the case and following his bent and logic—and *directing* classes—allowing participants substantial leeway to explore ideas of significance to them at a pace appropriate to the needs of most section members.

We put the challenge directly: The discussion teacher in a professional school seminar or workshop such as this must learn to relinquish some control over the content of the discussion and try to orchestrate participants' comments. This is a deceptively straightforward task, for merely stepping aside and letting the group chat will produce chaos and accelerating frustration. The discussion leader *is*, in the final analysis, responsible for the proceedings. But he or she must endeavor to help the group succeed, and give their comments shape and direction, without being either dictatorial or irritatingly manipulative—no small task. A tightly controlled seminar is an anomaly, neither as efficient as a lecture nor as involving as an open discussion.

Cases in this section cover both philosophical and operational issues. Most important, these discussions provide participants with a friendly and open forum to state their own instructional philosophy for peer comment and criticism. Operationally the group examines the implications of a "directing" philosophy for one's day-to-day teaching practice. Clearly it affects the preparation of a teaching plan, discouraging a "paint by numbers" approach and encouraging the use of a framework of key questions with alternative plans for dealing with anticipated student responses. We are always ready in our own classes to make major changes in that teaching plan if student interests move in dramatically unplanned directions.

SECTION 5. LEADING THE DISCUSSION PROCESS: SOME BASIC OPERATING ISSUES. Here we highlight a number of operating issues, rather than focusing on one specific topic. We attempt to tailor this portfolio of issues to meet the interests and needs of the specific participants. Because the seminar group is now more experienced, we attempt more complicated teaching objectives. Priority is given to issues that cut across many of the cases we previously discussed and that highlight key course concepts. We explore, at the participants' initiative and in the depth they believe appropriate, some of the fundamental dilemmas of their vocation: relating content and process, balancing in-class student freedom with instructor control, simultaneously help-

67. Derek Rowntree, *Assessing Students: How Shall We Know Them?* (London: Harper & Row Ltd., 1977).

ing and evaluating students. It is the participants' weaving together of individual cases and basic themes that produces the seminar's working generalizations. We intrigue with small truths and larger lessons.

"Trevor Jones" and "The Case of the Handicapped Heckler (A)" provide fascinating opportunities to probe a complex of issues: working with special-needs students, the ethical complexities of high-involvement teaching strategies, the challenges and opportunities of working with foreign students in a discussion setting, and career needs versus institutional demands. In previous iterations the classic case for this section has been "We're Just Wasting Our Time," found in Part IV of this book. Our handling of that case suggests what we hope to achieve in these concluding sessions.

In the case, Professor Rowe had a problem of poor attendance, declining participation, and across-the-board lack of student involvement. The situation deteriorated to a point at which Professor Rowe became angry and walked out of class—quite unusual professorial behavior given the norms of his school.

Our approach is summarized by four basic discussion questions:

(1) How did this situation develop, from Professor Rowe's point of view? From the section's point of view?
(2) What is your appraisal of Professor Rowe's action? What alternatives were open to him?
(3) What should Rowe do, if anything, that afternoon? Before the next class? At the beginning of the next class?
(4) How does an instructor energize an apathetic section? What general guidelines could you suggest that might be useful in dealing with a similar situation?

Our typical classroom operating pattern is to consider diagnosis first, followed by an exploration of what needs to be done. In the diagnostic section of this discussion we focus on the dramatic differences between the perceptions of professor and students. What was apathy to Professor Rowe was perceived by students as a complex set of circumstances. In the action portion of our discussion, we stress the importance of an instructor's learning about the "state of the section." We detail the possible steps Professor Rowe might take before he returned to

the classroom, and outline alternative ways of opening up his next class session. We explore questions such as how an instructor can acknowledge a mistake and when it may be appropriate to devote a class meeting to exploring the instructor's and section's way of working together. Encouraging participants to develop their own plans for dealing with this type of problem, we emphasize techniques for keeping in contact with a section's student leaders and ways of obtaining help from a variety of academic and administrative sources.

The cases in this section allow the seminar leader to test the group's accomplishments. As Gide observed, "We wholly conquer only what we assimilate." The seminar leader will know whether the participants have conquered seminar objectives by their handling of these case problems.

SECTION 6. SUMMARY. This section affords us the opportunity to meet traditional closure protocol and to outline a bit of our own teaching philosophy. In addition, the "Class on World Hunger" cases are symbolically appropriate for a final session. Rich in detail, they offer an opportunity to observe an instructor constructively defuse and convert a potentially destructive classroom prank into a useful learning experience. And Professor Clarkson's description of the evolution of his own teaching philosophy offers participants a final opportunity to share views on that complex topic. Clearly Clarkson has empathy for both the intellectual and emotional dimensions of teaching.

Case teaching places a heavy emotional burden on both student and teacher. From the student's point of view, it requires an extraordinary degree of openness: a willingness to state and publicly defend personal positions, often on controversial issues; to expose one's own feelings and uncertainties to peer scrutiny; to attempt to practice publicly some very complicated techniques and skills.

Section openness is possible only in a climate of mutual trust and support. The creation of that trusting relationship depends very much on the instructor's willingness and ability to be open and honest about himself with his students. Hugh Prather put it well in Notes to Myself: "In order to see I have to be willing to be seen."[68] As a discussion leader you must be willing to cast aside your traditional aca-

---

68. Hugh Prather, Notes to Myself (Moab, Utah: Real People Press, 1970).

demic armor, the certitude of platform and podium, of knowing the right answers, to take on the role of teacher-student, to learn from your students.[69]

This "willingness to be seen" is particularly difficult for many young people starting out in their teaching careers carrying the normal baggage of skill and career uncertainty. But maintaining a milieu of openness is a major challenge for experienced instructors, too—particularly when complex educational goals are pursued. At Harvard Business School, to use a musical analogy, we try to teach students to play—not simply to tune—their instruments. That is a complicated objective, and we must be content with major defeats and measured progress—learning to rejoice at small victories.

Some Next Steps

Whether your current academic interest is music or marketing, some of you may want to continue with this experiment after completing your current seminar program. Three suggestions are in order. First, why not develop teaching cases based on your own classroom experience, or on a colleague's? It's fun and at a minimum will deepen your appreciation of both the possibilities and the limits of methodology.

Second, why not try your hand at teaching a module selected from one of the seminar programs? Each module has been designed so that it can be taught independently. Readings are suggested, though you may wish to substitute others more appropriate to your own interests. We suggest teaching a module (e.g., Operations: Day-to-Day Classroom Practice) rather than a single case. Our experience has been that setting educational objectives for too narrow a case base may force you into stating points rather than letting them emerge from the give-and-take of a discussion. Give yourself maneuvering room; don't fill up every space in your discussion outline. Another operational suggestion may be of use. Compare the class preparation notes you made as a "student" participant in your seminar with the plans you develop later to "teach" the same case. This simple procedure offers new insights into the teacher-student relationship. And if teaching a module proves rewarding, try your hand at design-

ing and teaching a seminar for your department or institution. It is exciting.

Finally, see if you can find a colleague who might be willing to observe and offer you feedback on your classroom practice in return for similar assistance. A sensitive observer, genuinely interested in helping rather than "grading" your classroom leadership, can provide invaluable assistance. You will learn not only from suggestions received but also from the discipline of having to design and implement a scheme for observing and analyzing the classroom instructional dynamic.

Conclusion: Independent Ideas out of Actual Experience

So much of teaching is the artistry of encouraging personal discovery. This concept is central to the educational philosophy that underlies the case method of instruction. Discussion teaching, in contrast to the lecture mode, assigns both student and teacher nontraditional roles and relationships. Students are asked to assume primary responsibility for their own learning and for the education of others. The instructor must provide not only necessary theory and knowledge, but also an appropriate learning milieu and pedagogical skills that maximize the student's opportunities for personal discovery and learning.

We share this educational philosophy with colleagues in other professional schools and academic disciplines. This often provides us with an opportunity to participate directly in the birth of learning. A most magnificent example of this process was Helen Keller's experience in learning about the relationship between reality, W-A-T-E-R, and language systems.

You will recall that Miss Keller was deaf and blind. Through the genius of her teacher, Annie Sullivan Macy, she became not only an educated person but a scholar and leader of her times. With the assistance of Michael Anagnos, director of the Perkins Institute for the Blind, the two women influenced the then current practices for teaching blind students.

Helen Keller reports "her lesson" with beauty:

As the cool stream gushed over one hand, she, Annie, spelled into the other the word *water*, first slowly, then rapidly. I stood still, my whole attention fixed upon the motions of her fingers. Suddenly I felt a misty consciousness as of something forgotten—a

---

69. This blending of roles is well described in Yuri Nagibin, "Winter Oak," a suggested reading for this part of the seminar.

thrill of returning thought; and somehow the mystery of language was revealed to me. I knew then that W-A-T-E-R meant that wonderful cool something that was flowing over my hand. . . . I left the well-house eager to learn. Everything had a name, and each name gave birth to a new thought. As we returned to the house every object which I touched seemed to quiver with life.[70]

Annie Sullivan Macy summarized her philosophy in a letter to Michael Anagnos:

If the child is left to himself, he will think more and better, if less showily. Let him go freely, let him touch real things and combine his impressions for himself instead of sitting indoors at a little round table while a sweet-voiced teacher suggests that he build a stone wall with his wooden blocks or make a rainbow out of strips of colored paper or plant straw trees in bead flower pots. Such teaching fills the mind with artificial associations that must be got rid of before the child can develop independent ideas out of actual experiences.[71]

All teachers will be moved by these vignettes; they enable us to share in the joy of student discovery, in the victory of our philosophy of teaching under circumstances far more difficult than we encounter in our daily classroom routines. We applaud both Helen Keller and Annie Sullivan Macy; we can learn from both!

Teachers at the Harvard Business School and other schools have a community of interest with these two remarkable women; we too try to provide an academic setting in which our students can develop "independent ideas out of actual experiences." Our academic circumstances, however, are a bit different. We cannot bring the spring, well-house, and water into our classroom. Much as we applaud the "reality" of our cases, they are second-order reporting, not first-hand experience.

Even more challenging is the nature of our teaching goals. Helen Keller could touch and feel water, and when her teacher spelled out W-A-T-E-R, she suddenly experienced the joy of learning. Our students cannot touch and feel decisions. Instructors cannot give immediate feedback when the hoped-for educational output is student maturity, wisdom, and judgment.

Yet it is the imperfectness of what we are doing that promises such an exciting future. The challenges confronting business education are major; we note only a few areas for preferential attention. We need, of course, to continue to improve the quality of our teaching and to find better ways of researching the artistry of discussion leadership. We resist John Dewey's pessimistic dictum that the success of gifted teachers is inclined to be born and die with them.[72]

At the Harvard Business School, we are increasingly coming to recognize that classroom teaching cannot convey all that is important to management practice. Accordingly, the Business Policy course, building on the work of others, is taking the first steps to abstract, systematize, and teach the key skills of clinical practice in the field. Perhaps we should consider internship and residency programs for business students, as for medical students. Finally, we need to rethink present methods of evaluating students' work to provide them with useful feedback. Traditional academic grading arrangements give the comfort of order and rationality to teacher and student, but they serve little constructive purpose during the academic program and are poor predictors of future career accomplishments.

While new dimensions of professional education unfold, there is much to be done to improve our present ways of teaching with cases. These seminar programs attempt to make a small contribution to that undertaking. We hope you will want to participate in this adventure by experimenting with them in ways meaningful to you and your institution.

70. Joseph P. Lash, *Helen and Teacher* (New York: Delacorte Press/ Seymour Lawrence, 1980). An excellent review of this book in the Radcliffe Biography Series is by L. A. Waltch, *Radcliffe Quarterly*, June 1980.
71. Ibid.
72. For an overview of the challenges of teaching in the American high school system, see Patrick Welsh, *Tales out of School* (New York: Viking Penguin, Inc., 1986).

The Use and Abuse of Humanistic Education

JAMES SLOAN ALLEN

James Sloan Allen is director of Liberal Arts and Academic Administration at the Juilliard School.

In the famed Renaissance book *The Courtier* by Baldassare Castiglione, a count describes the ways of courtly life. The secret of the courtier's success, he says, is grace. But, he quickly adds: "I am not bound to teach you how to acquire grace or anything else, but only to tell you what a perfect courtier ought to be."

Here Castiglione puts his finger on a troubling truth of teaching: it is one thing to describe the end of education; it is another to prescribe the means. This truth points to another, possibly even more troubling truth: some things can be learned but cannot, strictly speaking, be taught. Long before Castiglione, Aristotle had identified moral virtue as such a thing. Castiglione's grace is a form of virtue. And any parent who has tried to teach virtue to a child knows that Aristotle and Castiglione were onto something.

When we ask why the likes of grace or any virtue can be learned but not taught, we must answer that this is because they are not matters of intellectual knowledge or even of technical skill, but of *right action*. Although the rules of right action might be learned intellectually, right action itself can only be mastered by will and repeated doing.

The impossibility—or at any rate the difficulty—of teaching right action does not, to be sure, keep us from trying. And those attempts disclose many clues to the limitations and possibilities, failures and successes, of teaching.

The case method of teaching is, in its way, one such attempt. Within the curriculum of general education the subjects most closely associated with right action, or the value judgments underlying it, are the humanities—especially philosophy, literature, and history. Yet few who study the humanities, and fewer who teach them nowadays, would likely identify right action as the end of humanistic education. Among those who do, even fewer could say with conviction just how humanistic education is related to action, or how teaching shapes that relation.

There are many reasons why teachers deny, neglect, or fail to advance the relation between education and action. Of these, three stand out as pedagogical fallacies that illuminate both bad teaching and good—as well as the use and abuse of humanistic education in general.

The first of these fallacies is Sentimentalism. By Sentimentalism I mean the tendency to identify learning with the subjective pleasures of mind and emotion, or "spirit," aroused by encounters with art and ideas. Most of us have had teachers of this type at one time or another. They summon us to read literature, listen to music, study philosophy, eye the sunset, and so on, in order to be moved and elated, to weep and to yearn. And they do so on the assumption that to be so moved is to be awakened to one's elemental and exalted humanness and thereby taught the humanistic meaning of life.

There is some justice in this summons. Education should disclose states of mind and feeling that lend value and direction to our lives, and should help us cultivate the means of achieving those states. But there is folly in identifying learning entirely with the subjective satisfactions aroused by art and ideas. That folly is to equate such subjective satisfactions with intellectual or moral truth. The teacher who encourages students to derive all their truths from experiences that *feel good* is encouraging them to neglect the kind of analytical thought that helps determine which experiences should be pursued and when and for what reasons. Thus, although Sentimentalism has sources in experience, it obscures rather than clarifies the relation of education to experience and action.

It is no wonder that the fallacy of Sentimentalism should have its antithesis in the fallacy of Scientism. For science has the virtues that Sentimentalism lacks: it provides objective knowledge and curbs the sway of subjectivity. But teachers who adopt this value-free ethos of science undermine humanistic education no less than do those who steep themselves in Sentimentalism. For they pursue technical knowledge irrespective of its relation to lived experience and action. Those who, for example, make the study of literature a cerebral inquiry into structural patterns, or those who turn philosophy into a technical analysis of linguistic and logical intricacies are not really engaged in humanistic learning at all. For whatever science-like discoveries they produce, these discoveries do not cast much light on either the nature or the proper use of human experience. As the familiar humanistic saying goes, science can tell us how to make a bomb or save a life, but it cannot tell us whether we should do either.

Closely related to Scientism, and probably the most widely practiced of the three fallacies, is Academicism. This is the fallacy of valuing knowledge for its own sake, whether that knowledge lays claim to scientific certainty or simply to the understanding of images, ideas, aesthetic forms, and so forth. A mind well-stocked with such knowledge—so this fallacy asserts—has the advantage over lesser minds of being able to acquire more knowledge faster: if you know a little Shakespeare, you can the more readily know more; if you understand the metric structure of poetry, you can analyze poems; if you grasp Plato's metaphysics, you can explain how Aristotle's differs; if you can define the Renaissance, you can fit Machiavelli into it; if you can recognize Impressionism, you can label Monet. Thus is learning added to learning, with no discernible end beyond itself.

This is not to say no ends lie beyond such learning. There are many such ends. But unless they shape the experience of learning, students cannot help but ask: Why all of this? Where is it going? Or, as Jean-Jacques Rousseau had young Emile question his tutor at every instruction: "What is the use of that?" If they get no satisfactory answers, if teachers can do no more than commend learning as an end in itself, those students are likely to foresake humanistic education as merely "academic" and embrace vocational or professional studies, in which practical ends stand clearly in view. In this way, the fallacy of Academicism, as surely as the fallacies of Sentimentalism and Scientism, robs humanistic education of its uses to human life. And in robbing it of those uses, these fallacies commit an error fatal to all education: communicating the idea that we live in order to learn, we do not learn in order to live.

Here we encounter the proper use of humanistic education. Humanistic education has to do not simply with states of mind or feeling, or scientific truth, or bodies of knowledge. It has to do with action. For by virtue of its subject matter, which is human experience—intellectual, emotional, social, cultural—it implicitly addresses the questions that underlie action: "How should one act?" "How should one live."

To assert an inherent relation between education and action is to raise anew the question put at the outset: Can right action be taught? As noted above, strictly speaking, it cannot, because it consists in willed doing, not passive knowing. But if we cannot teach right action itself, we can nevertheless lead students toward it. The means of doing this are known to adroit teachers of the humanities and the professions alike—an affinity more teachers of the humanities would do well to heed. For these means are none other than instruction in how to think about action and in how to translate those thoughts into action.

But how do you teach students how to think about right action? A simple answer is supplied by dogmatism. Teach them absolutes, says the dogmatist; then they will know not only how to think, but what to think and what to do. George Orwell coined the term "Goodthink" for this way of thinking, and to its practitioners in the novel *1984* it meant the official "truths" irresistibly accepted because they admitted of no alternatives.

But dogmatism is not actually thought at all. It is a memorized creed that precedes experience, precludes thinking, and prevents learning. Voltaire's Pangloss in *Candide* may be the archetypal professor of dogmatism in just this sense (of which more below).

Thinking about right action is quite the opposite of embracing dogmatism. For such thinking is complicated, not simple; difficult, not easy; active, not passive—requiring the careful examination of all facts, ideas, experiences, and choices in the light of value judgment. One must examine, for example, the ideal ends of action, the relative goods in human experience, the costs and rewards of obligation, the effects of actions on both the actor and others, the relation of thought to feeling, the merits of disparate claims to truth.

Anyone accustomed to asking such questions is thinking about right action. This is not to say that all who ask will agree on the answers. Nor is it to say that anyone who asks will act on the answers given. Yet without asking such questions, no one can be counted on to act properly. Thinking about right action is, therefore, a necessary but not a sufficient cause of acting properly, i.e., thinking doesn't by itself cause the action, but the action could not occur without it.

But beyond this training in thinking by means of value-charged questions, can teachers lead students from thinking to acting? If this is possible, it is only by demonstrating the uses and benefits of such thinking in experience.

The case method of teaching does this by placing challenges to thought in the context of practical experience. Whether the case be drawn from law, business, ethics, or teaching, the assumption is the same: experience is the matrix of thought, and the end of thought is action. To satisfy the demands of a case is to decide what should be *done*.

Humanistic education should openly share this

rootedness in actuality and directedness toward it. Nowhere is this more appropriate than in the study of the classics of Western thought.

Taking their cue from the use of cases in the professional schools, teachers of the classics could use those works to prompt thought about experience and action and to demonstrate the uses of thought in experience. The range of experience addressed by a classic work of philosophy or fiction is, of course, far wider than that addressed by examples in a case book. Yet taken as a whole, or by chapters, or even by paragraphs, such books are analyses and dramatizations of experience. As such, they should automatically prompt the kinds of questions that bear on experience and right action.

Take, for example, the dialogues of Plato dealing with the trial and death of Socrates, or the *Ethics* of Aristotle. These works are full of abstract philosophizing, but they also ask the value-charged questions: What is the difference between belief and knowledge, and what difference does this difference make? What are the moral consequences of wrongdoing? To what extent are we responsible for our actions and for our own characters? Is there a human nature, and if so, what are its implications for right action? To what ends should one dedicate a life? What is the relation between material and moral or spiritual well-being? What is the proper relation between self-interest and social obligation? Is it ever right to break a law? These questions directly address the relations among education, experience, and action. And the mind attuned to them is both analytically alert and ready to initiate action.

Or take Dante's *Inferno*. It can be read in a number of ways, but as a case study in right action it is an exploration of the moral landscape that we all inhabit. It asks, most generally, What are the nature and consequences of wrongdoing? In pursuing an answer during his journey through hell, Dante discloses the psychology of wrongdoing and its cultural consequences by compelling us to ask, above all, Why does Dante deem fraud—including flattery, hypocrisy, and theft—worse than murder, and treason the worst evil of all? To answer this question is not simply to become conversant with Dante; it is to see the indispensability of trust to the social bond, and to understand the moral psychology of deception. With this knowledge in mind, who could thoughtlessly deceive others, much less betray them?

Or Machiavelli. Arguably the first political "how-to" book, *The Prince* also asks: How do we succeed at anything? Machiavelli presents many historical cases of political success and failure to demonstrate his point that success always requires (a) clear perception of ends, (b) comprehensive understanding of circumstances, and (c) willingness to employ any means within those circumstances to achieve those ends. Although applied by Machiavelli particularly to politics, Machiavelli's rules apply equally to any other pursuit—teaching among them. *The Prince* is, therefore, not just a book about *realpolitik*; it is a casebook in how to think about ends and means and how to act on the means.

Voltaire's *Candide* and Rousseau's *Emile* can also be read as cases in right action. They both address the question: How does one learn? Candide's misadventures under the tutelage of Pangloss repeatedly draw the reader, along with Candide, into the gulf between dogmatism and experience. The dogmatism of Pangloss, expressed in the creed "this is the best of all possible worlds," enables him to "explain" every experience, but to understand none. For to understand experience is to learn from it, to be changed by it, to be able to master it. Pangloss and Candide can do none of these, to their persistent detriment. Eventually Candide discards Pangloss's empty reasoning for practical knowledge born of experience—specifically the knowledge that hard work brings greater mastery of experience than does any philosophizing.

In *Emile*, the barrier to learning from experience is not an individual's dogmatism but the mistaken assumptions and misguided practices of society at large. To disclose those errors, Rousseau follows Emile from childhood to adulthood under the tutelage of a teacher who accepts no common assumptions and practices but asks of everything: What is the difference between the natural and the artificial, the necessary and the accidental, the beneficial and the detrimental, the actual and seeming uses of things? No parental practice, schooling demand, or social manner escapes scrutiny under this question. This scrutiny reveals how parents, teachers, and society have repeatedly supplied the wrong answers, with the results that children are usually educated to be learned but ignorant, moralistic but dishonest, self-indulgent but miserable, selfish but enslaved. We all learn from experience, Rousseau is saying, but we too often learn the wrong things from it, because we fail to examine closely enough exactly how that learning occurs. In short, we don't learn how to learn. If we did, we would act more responsibly toward others and ourselves. No one who reads *Emile* carefully in this way can fail to think and even to act a little differently as parent, teacher, student.

The list could go on and on: e.g., Moliere's *The Misanthrope* and Virginia Woolf's *Mrs. Dalloway* as studies in the uses of politeness and dinner parties; Wordsworth and Dickens as explorers of the terrain where emotions and intellect meet and experiences acquire their disparate meanings in human life; Marx, Nietzsche, and Freud as detectives of self-deception and physicians of its cure.

By so treating the classics as something like casebooks in thinking and right action, teachers could avoid the fallacies that diminish the authority and value of humanistic education; and they could transform that education into the study of lived experience and the preparation for right action that it should be. Then humanistic education could gain the compelling authority of the *useful*, its worth confirmed by the rewards of experience.

So, even if we cannot strictly speaking teach people to act properly, we can prepare minds to think about action and to see the uses in experience of acting one way rather than another. When a person habitually, or even regularly, thinks about the ends and means of action and accordingly acts to achieve the best ends, that person can be said to have learned virtue, or grace, or how to win at law or make a profit or teach a class, or how to live well, or any other form of right action. Such a person has truly learned how to learn from experience and how to act on that learning. And the teacher has made this possible.

Suggestions for Seminar Participants

ABBY J. HANSEN

1. What Is a Case-based Teaching Seminar?

Any seminar is a gathering—usually with a leader—of people who apply their collective wisdom and energy to a subject that perplexes, intrigues, and touches all in some way. At the Harvard Business School seminars, our special subject is the process of teaching by holding discussions (as opposed, for example, to labs or lectures). One source of the uniqueness of our approach is that seminar discussions reproduce, in concentrated form, the process they study. They are conducted by groups of teachers analyzing other teachers' classroom experiences, probably under the guidance of yet other teachers. The effect can be prismatic: our discussions are tinted by the reality they analyze.

A second unusual characteristic of our approach is the use of *teaching cases* to help focus discussions that might otherwise degenerate into bull sessions. Teaching cases are condensed accounts of thought-provoking events in the professional lives of real instructors. As the seminar—or workshop group—tackles each set of occurrences, designations of role may begin to blur. It is often difficult to say precisely who is teaching and who is learning in case method instruction, because teacher and students form a conversational continuum whose organic structure stems from the teacher's questions—only some of which are prepared. Much of the discussion's momentum often springs directly from the students' responses. Both teacher and students actively participate. Furthermore, our approach encourages students not only to generate their own questions but to address them to each other. If the discussion leader inadvertently starts playing "what's on teacher's mind?" we believe the class is failing. When skill and sophistication distinguish true case method discussion, the leader's interventions may be so subtle as to challenge detection.

In an academic group where all involved are likely to be colleagues, it seems inappropriate to call the person who moderates the discussion "teacher" and all the rest "students." All have gathered to study in each other's company. Yet, despite the intrinsic equality of all members of the seminar, we recommend that one person assume responsibility for leadership, attend to the continuing details of the group's organization, oversee the distribution of reading materials, and guide the discussions with the twofold goal of encouraging analytical thoroughness and the participation of as many group members as possible. Chaos—even cheerful chaos—is not among our goals. Our preferred designation for the person who undertakes these guiding tasks is "discussion leader." We refer to the rest of the group as "participants," aware that these roles are flexible. The leader will always participate; at times participants may lead. And this is another unusual aspect inherent in our approach: as long as the spirit of cooperation informs the proceedings, even a neophyte discussion leader may shepherd a group of experienced colleagues through a case discussion—given that the leader focuses primarily on the process of discussion while the participants worry about the case, the leader's questions, and each other's comments. (In teaching notes that we make available to the discussion leaders, our heaviest emphasis falls upon ways to manage the discussion process, because we consider classroom interaction to be both the prime matrix of teaching and learning and the aspect of intellectual growth most susceptible to influence.)

Consider a moment—any moment— of a classroom discussion. Someone is probably talking; others are listening; but all are reacting intellectually and emotionally, emitting subtle, almost subliminal signals—facial expressions, changes in posture, small nonverbal sounds. Furthermore, all are in some way absorbing what has gone before and projecting what may come. Learning begins somewhere in this tapestry of thought and feeling. We offer our materials as a means to improve one's own weaving techniques by unraveling others' webs.

Given our dynamic approach to the discussion process, we recommend that participants view case discussions as voyages of exploration. Primed by our teaching notes and other supporting materials, the discussion leader may be expected to offer each class a battery of questions rather than a rigid agenda of points to make and memorize. As a rule, discussions should be fluid, cordial, collaborative, and fun. Participants should read and study each case before class (using our appended Study Questions for convenience if they wish), with an eye to presenting and defending opinions and helpfully criticizing those of their colleagues. Each participant's deepest allegiance will, of course, be to his or her own professional needs. As a participant, you should determine what each case says to you. But we also hope that, as the group meshes its strengths, your loyalty to the other members will grow along with your ability to help them, and their ability to help you.

Some people have assumed that the purpose of a case-based seminar must be to prepare case method teachers. Not so. Because our materials encourage emphasis upon process, the insights our teaching cases can trigger apply to almost the whole spectrum of teaching disciplines. Professors of Chinese History, Fine Arts, Musicology, Law, Medicine, Sociology, Economics, Business, Government, and some branches of Mathematics have refined their skills in each other's company by means of our case discussions.

2. Why Join a Case-based Teaching Seminar?

The prevailing philosophy during the 1980s could be described as follows: Most teaching beyond the secondary school level is still a sink-or-swim affair. Quite a few graduate students simply become teachers the day they find themselves facing undergraduates in a classroom because their fellowships require it. Sometimes serendipity results from the confrontation: a natural teacher emerges, to everyone's delight and profit. At other times the encounter causes pain for all concerned. Many teachers experience both at various times. When things go well, they sigh and dive into the next day's preparation. When things go wrong, they may corral a sympathetic pal for a few teaching tips, but just as often they muffle their misery for fear of seeming incompetent. Once a discussion group has reached a solid rapport, instances of gloom and glee may surface and provide substance for objective, constructive analysis. In teaching, the difference between success and maladroitness often resides in some deceptively small detail. Extraordinary power lurks, for example, in the way a teacher moves in the classroom. Some teachers persistently frustrate fully half of each class by failing to make eye contact with students on one side of the room during discussions. Others intimidate students by speaking too fast, or too loudly. Still others overprotect students with condescending questions that effectively obstruct the students' progress. Small failings, perhaps—yet potentially devastating, and fairly easily corrected. Our cases deal with issues like these, and the teaching notes we offer discussion leaders suggest ways to focus the group's attention upon just such practical details along with more general and theoretical formulations of policy.

Our basic mission is to familiarize teachers with

the potentially vast array of choices open to them in order to produce insights that lead to practical improvements. The case discussions are meant to provide a safe testing ground for the participants' evolving ideas, because our emphasis on cooperation stresses the value of all contributions to the process. Not that we consider all opinions equally "correct." On the contrary; most of our discussions tend toward a consensus that finds some approaches to be "righter" than others, but few worthwhile goals can be reached without the exploration of a blind alley or two along the way.

Prospective participants often challenge our stress upon the discussion process, raising the issue of content. Our answer—"For present purposes, we shall assume that the teacher has mastered the course material"—sometimes inspires skepticism. We tend to avoid discussions of content, not because we consider it unimportant, but because it is too specialized to yield useful, broadly applicable insights that will cut across disciplines. When the issue is the selection of a textbook, even a very experienced teacher of Urban Real Estate Development will have little useful advice for an instructor of French Romantic Poetry. But these two may very well enlighten each other about ways to encourage shy students or probe overly dogmatic opinions in class without giving offense. Content imbues the teaching and learning process with significance. Issues such as the choice of primary readings, design of research assignments, and the timing and phrasing of examination questions (to mention a few topics we do not generally discuss) make huge differences. But the breadth of our intended public forces us to concentrate on the few virtually universal factors of discussion teaching: the discussion process, its preparation and evaluation, and the teacher's power to influence it. We hope to reveal the amplitude of choices available to teachers on every level and the rich possibilities in activities often considered mundane: preparation, questioning and responding to participants' answers, selecting students to speak in class, judging their work, and many more.

3. What, Exactly, Is a Case?

A good case is a condensation of some real event, or sequence of events, that contains enough perplexities to inspire a rich educational discussion. The researcher usually interviews a few principal "informants"—in our materials, the teacher and other involved participants—and, if possible, reviews the central episodes with them in order to get a textured picture of reality before distilling all the data for students to read and contemplate the night before the discussion. (Our minicases are so concentrated they can be read in class and discussed immediately.) In addition to the case, the researcher writes Suggested Study Questions and a parallel set of Discussion Questions for the discussion leader to indicate a path through the brambles and make reasonably certain that most of the participants will have considered similar issues before the discussion.

A note: our cases portray normal people—under stress, but still in reasonably familiar situations. Some of the events we depict are dramatic; some involve unpleasant "blowups." Still, the principles of abnormal psychology, however intriguing, are more or less irrelevant to what we are trying to accomplish with these materials. Most of our case characters face crises that reveal their vulnerability, but merely suggesting psychotherapy for them or their students begs the question. It is most fruitful to examine the dynamics that produce the irritation in their situations with an eye to finding ways to help within the normal parameters of most academic institutions. What might these teachers have foreseen or forestalled? Given similar early warning signs, what might you do?

The process of a case method discussion is less specialized and technical than many people assume. Its focus upon the elucidation of a central document recalls the classic *explication de texte* (or close reading) of literary studies. Its analytical component should be familiar to art critics, musicologists, physicians, historians, sociologists, students of politics—in short, anyone whose discipline involves reading or observing, analyzing, and presenting one's insights to a group for criticism and refinement.

Cases attempt to digest reality, with all of its deceptions, contradictions, discrepancies of perception, and general resistance to orderly analysis. Their irreducible core of ambiguity is one reason they are usually fun to discuss. In fact, fun, with its concomitant energy, is a major advantage of the case method. Controversy is another. Study Questions are always open-ended, and frequently involve judgments. They are not meant to entrap or breed hostility, but rather to help participants clarify their own and each other's unspoken assumptions because, as one woman put it, "People don't know what they think until they see what they say." Case discussions that include controversy can jostle participants into statements of principle that sometimes surprise them. One strength of the case method is that it encourages participants to defend their positions—which may result in jettisoning them. But effective teaching and learning have few worse enemies than complacency. If a focused, well-moderated discussion lures biases into the light for examination and assessment, the case method will have served a useful purpose.

What the case method absolutely will *not* do is offer a code of rules or techniques. Its suppleness precludes such rigidity. Each case is a slice of someone's life. The lessons it suggests will vary for each reader. To put it differently, each case is a kaleidoscope: what you see in it depends on how you shake it.

We present our teaching materials in the form of cases partly to generate empathy, both for the teachers and the students we describe. Empathy can supply leaven and spice to the discussion process. It is also the trait most students miss in their worst teachers. We do not confuse this quality with pity or softheartedness. On the contrary, empathizing with a student's true predicament (insofar as one human being can truly appreciate another's situation) might conceivably suggest a strict course of action. We suggest that teachers make the attempt to understand their students' points of view in order to assess their goals, strengths, and weaknesses as fairly as possible. To do less is to risk alienation, even hostility.

4. For Whom Do We Intend These Materials?

Anyone who teaches by means of a method other than straight "transfer of knowledge" (where a flypaper memory is the student's best friend) may benefit from working with our teaching cases, either in a full-length seminar or briefer workshop. We will *not* help teachers choose textbooks or primary readings, write watertight exam questions, ferret out plagiarism, or develop podium charisma. But we do claim to be able to stimulate insight into the complex of small skills that constitutes effective discussion leading. Time and again, such insight has stimulated practical improvement. Our materials invite attention to the discussion process as it occurs in the classroom. We take up basic questions such as how to choose an opening speaker, how to deal with belligerent, recalcitrant, retiring, or bored students, how to establish and maintain rapport with a group. These challenges face all teachers, regardless of their years in the classroom. Whether this is your first or fortieth year as a teacher, you will probably meet several groups of expectant strangers in the next year, attempt to involve them in your chosen subject, guide them from ignorance to sophistication, and, ultimately, evaluate them. Over the year, students' culture changes; teachers' personalities and attitudes alter as well. Experienced instructors may find that sure-fire material of a few years ago blows up or, perhaps worse, fizzles when they use it this year. We offer these materials to help newcomers conquer their insecurities, and old hands, their boredom. Each new class is an adventure and an opportunity. Growth is always possible.

5. What Might Participation in a Case-based Teaching Seminar Be Like?

Be warned: preparing to discuss teaching is not the same as preparing to teach. A group discussion is not a performance. First, of course, you read the case. Then you try to feel your way into it, from the major case character's point of view, and from as many other vantage points as you can discern. How might this teacher's students have felt in the case situations? How might a dean have viewed the whole sequence of events? What advice would you have given at different points in the case if you had been a good friend of one of the characters? For the purposes of preparing to discuss a case, it is probably more valuable to stockpile questions than answers. Heartfelt perplexity can kindle valuable insights.

The discussion itself usually begins with the leader asking one or two opening speakers to mark some terrain for further exploration by presenting overviews that raise central issues for the rest of the participants. Opening speakers steer and influence the discussion, and it is typical for them to play active roles in the whole session. After the initial presentations, the discussion leader may probe for greater depth or breadth, call for opposing views, or even slide into role-playing, but the overall goal of the first section of the discussion will probably be to cover the events of the (A) case. The (A) case usually ends with the main character facing some decision. The leader will probably ask the group for suggestions or predictions, and then if the case is so organized, distribute the (B) case, which details what did happen. As a rule, after evaluations of these events, the group turns to considerations of principle. After assessing the appropriateness of the main character's actions, the group applies whatever rules of general significance it has extracted from the case to its own concerns. Some of our cases continue with further segments—perhaps giving the case character's reflections upon the events or the researcher's analysis. These may be distributed for private reading or looked over in class and discussed.

Many participants experience a sort of double consciousness as they "play student" and watch someone else do what they have done for years: teach. Often they click in and out of single-minded participation, sometimes feeling playful and childlike, and at other times detached and superior to the proceedings. This is natural; sometimes, participants even interrupt the flow of discussion to challenge the leader's handling of some particular sequence, and a new line of inquiry emerges, to the benefit of all.

As we have noted, the character trait that participants most frequently find lacking in the case instructors they evaluate is empathy for students. There are few surer ways to develop such empathy than by actually filling their shoes. Most experienced teachers find it both frustrating and exhilarating to join a discussion group someone else is leading. On one hand, they relish the freedom from the responsibility of leadership; on the other, they find it painful to reexperience the powerlessness of the student's situation. Waving one's hand fruitlessly while the discussion leader ignores you can be infuriating, but even fury has its potential lessons. Appreciate the exaggerated impact of the discussion leader's movements in class; feel and evaluate the effects of tone of voice, volume, and speed of speech. Mentally compare these to your own. What, if anything, would you like to change?

6. Articles of Faith

Certain assumptions about the enterprise of teaching color all of our work. We take for granted that our participants wish to teach effectively, even as we acknowledge the other professional and personal demands, tensions, and pressures in every teacher's life. For us, the measure of good teaching is good learning. Even though we realize that there are no absolute scales to assess students' progress, most teachers and students can feel whether classes are "working" or not. We all know teachers who help, teachers who are ineffectual, and teachers who are downright obstructive. The key to helping is recognizing the enormous power of the classroom process. The teacher's task is to aid the students as they conquer the material, not demonstrate his or her own brilliance. Since the classroom is the prime arena for accomplishing this task, the means for improving one's teaching lie in attention to classroom practice. Teaching style has enormous impact. Fortunately, style can be adjusted without undue self-consciousness if one concentrates on small changes, one at a time. One can, for example, overcome a distracting habit of scratching an ear or speaking only to the left side of the classroom. One can learn to make eye contact, speak more clearly, move more smoothly. These seemingly small changes can make enormous differences in the emotional climate of the classroom. We believe that hostile or nervous students will not do as well as students who feel that the teacher genuinely hopes they will learn.

We further believe that the teacher's most powerful tools are the interrelated skills of posing questions, listening carefully, and responding to students' comments. All questions contain emotional components. Tone of voice and phrasing can turn an innocent request for information into a "third degree." There are hostile questions, supportive questions, condescending questions, sarcastic questions, questions of simple fact, questions that invite analysis, questions that elicit role-playing (and emotional involvement), questions that emphasize intellectual evaluation (and consequently cool the proceedings). The list of categories of questions is potentially infinite, as are the ways one can pose them. The same is true of responses. We believe that the most useful of these deflect the energy of the students' thoughts back to the group, rather than ending with a simple "yes" or "no" from the leader. One of our most abiding articles of faith is that no one has an exclusive patent on truth in discussion teaching.

It is also our belief that almost every basic principle of good teaching can be *operationalized*—put into practice—by word or gesture. One must take practical steps to put principles to use. How, for example, can you demonstrate a feeling of respect to a class? There are many ways. You might make it a point to use students' names and encourage them to use each other's. Nothing is more discouraging than the belief that teacher neither notices nor cares who one is. You can make a conscious attempt to look interested when students speak, making it physically apparent that you accord their comments serious—or at least good-humored—attention. Your posture and expression can show that you are actually listening. To encourage a group to cooperate, you might try to sidestep questions that refer issues only to the teacher by asking a student to address the question to a fellow student several seats away. These small techniques, and many more like them, can radically alter the whole tone of a class, making the difference between cooperation and apathy. To help sustain a smooth pace and further encourage the group to work together, you might call on two or three students at once and ask them to collaborate on some particularly elusive point of discussion for the rest of the class. How do you encourage a shy student? You might ask a serious question, but offer the student a chance to prepare an answer while the rest of the class discusses something else

for, say, five minutes. This combines respect for the student's ability to handle a useful issue with a soothing offer of time to compose the nerves.

These are the sorts of perennial teaching issues our materials address—basic, besetting, often deceptively simple matters, but all accessible to improvement, and central, we believe, to success. Our bias is toward formulating practical plans to achieve theoretical goals. We recognize that good teaching is an art that touches the heart as well as the brain, and we consider it, furthermore, a teachable art. Our method—cooperating with a group of colleagues to analyze other teachers' challenges, evolve recommendations, and deduce principles—can both create alertness to opportunities and deepen one's own appreciation of the power of the teaching process. We propose to help participants study teaching as a live thing. Unlike William Wordsworth's scientists, we will not *murder* teaching to *dissect* it.

Teachers Also Must Learn

CHARLES I. GRAGG

Reprinted with permission from Charles I. Gragg, "Teachers Also Must Learn," *Harvard Educational Review*, vol. 10, 1940, pp. 30–47.

The Queen seemed to guess her thoughts, for she cried, "Faster! Don't try to talk!"

Not that Alice had any idea of doing *that*. She felt as if she would never be able to talk again, she was getting so much out of breath; and still the Queen cried "Faster! Faster!" and dragged her along. "Are we nearly there?" Alice managed to pant out at last.

"Now! Now!" cried the Queen. "Faster! Faster!" And they went so fast that at last they seemed to skim through the air, hardly touching the ground with their feet, till suddenly just as Alice was getting quite exhausted, they stopped, and she found herself sitting on the ground breathless and giddy.

Alice looked around her in great surprise. "Why, I do believe we've been under this tree the whole time! Everything's just as it was!"

In any sensible discussion of teaching, emphasis of course must be upon learning rather than upon teaching. Teaching has no excuse except as it results in learning. Yet everyone who has been a student knows that it is possible, after even the most strenuous classroom exertions, to find, like Alice, that "everything's just as it was." The teacher's art lies in his ability to help his students to reach new positions, or, to put the matter with the utmost triteness, in his ability to help his students to learn.

Teaching is a social art, necessarily involving a relationship between people; and the success of a teacher in the practice of his art depends upon his possessing that quality or attitude of mind which enables him to make the relationship between himself and his students a reciprocal one. Not all the teaching should be done by the teacher. Not all the learning should be done by the students.

No one can learn in any basic sense from another except by subjecting what that other has to offer to a process of creative thinking; that is, unless the learner is actively and imaginatively receptive, he will emerge from the teaching experience with nothing more than a catalogue of facts and other people's notions. Anyone, consequently, who is to teach another must see to it that his pupil listens to him in an attitude of creative receptivity. But the teacher will not succeed in leading his students to receive ideas with a lively and formative spirit unless he, himself, shows toward his students a comparable attitude of being willing to learn from them.

Ideally, the only mark distinguishing the teacher from the student will be the teacher's greater learning.

Professor Whitehead in one of his powerful and compact essays, "The Aims of Education," has pointed out that those who seek to train the young must "beware of 'inert ideas'—that is to say, ideas that are merely received into the mind without being utilized, or tested, or thrown into fresh combinations."[1] In discussing the need for "self-education," or active participation by the learner in the process of learning, A. Lawrence Lowell wrote: "'Self-education' is based on the principle that, beyond the mechanical elements, no one can be really educated against his will, or without his own active effort."[2]

The passive reception of ideas or facts constitutes no education at all. In short, the learner must share actively in the task of learning; he must create for himself the ideas that the teacher seeks to communicate to him. The word "create" is used advisedly. The process is not one of absorption or of fitting pieces of knowledge into a pattern. The process of learning is truly one of creation. No teacher can take a concept, however simple, and place it intact and usable in the mind of another. The art of communication is too imperfect. From what the teacher says or writes or does, the learner must create his own concept. It may approach that of the teacher, but, like all created things, it will be to some extent original. The student has created something and it is his. He has learned, moreover, something of the labors and the joys of such activity. There is no serious doubt in educational circles that this process is desirable. No intelligent person maintains that any amount of listening and remembering will produce an educated man. As Professor Whitehead remarks later in his essay, "A merely well-informed man is the most useless bore on God's earth." If it be accepted that he who is to learn must take an active part in his own education, then from the point of view of the art of teaching the question becomes one of what the teacher can do to encourage his students to make the necessary exertion.

The teacher not only must have a genuine ability and desire to communicate to others the thoughts and concepts which have become his through his own imaginative thinking; he must go farther. He must have a genuine desire and ability to be communicated to, for it is this desire and ability which above all else will encourage, almost force, the student to the exertion necessary to the creation of something which will be his own, to the cultivation of a quality of thinking which ever will stand him and the world in good stead.

Teaching is not only the art of thinking and speaking. It is also the art of listening and understanding. Nor by listening is meant just the act of keeping still. Keeping still is a technique; listening is an art. Most of us, though all too infrequently, have experienced the stimulation of talking with someone whom we have felt to be genuinely willing to listen to us, that is, to exert himself to receive what we were saying and to comprehend it to the full extent of his capacity for imaginative understanding. In the presence of such a person we are carried out of ourselves, our minds become more active, our thoughts more vibrant and original. We see relationships and meanings that before were not apparent to us. We may even end by seeing that our notion was in truth a poor and feeble one. But whatever the outcome, it is something alive and real, not only for us, but also for our friend. Creative intercommunication has taken place though our companion may not have said three words.

In another connection Professor Henderson has stressed the importance of the attitude of receptivity. Speaking of the medical profession, he says:

> The doctors have always found it necessary to take account of what patients tell them. . . . The physician listens, first, to what the patient wants to tell, secondly, for implications of what he doesn't want to tell, and thirdly, for implications of what he can't tell.[3]

Also, in the field of employer-employee relations, Professor Roethlisberger has pointed out the importance of the listening attitude: "The first rule is that the supervisor should listen patiently to what

1. A. N. Whitehead, *The Aim of Education and Other Essays* (New York: The Macmillan Company, 1929).
2. A. Lawrence Lowell, *Report of the President of Harvard College and Reports of Departments,* 1931–1932.

3. L. J. Henderson, "Introductory Lectures, Sociology 23" (in mimeographed form). [For private distribution only, unpublished paper October 1938, pp. 13–14. In L. J. Henderson Papers, Baker Library, Harvard Business School.]

his subordinate has to say before making any comment himself. . . ."[4]

Just as everyone has had the invigorating experience of talking with persons of receptive minds, so too we have all had the experience of trying to communicate a thought to someone unwilling to receive it. Such a person, if we are fortunate, may keep quiet while we speak, but he will not exert himself to understand what we are saying. It is not, of course, that we need approval. Approval and disapproval are beside the point. We are never discouraged in our thinking by having our ideas disapproved of or disagreed with by someone we know understands them. But how stultifying is either approval or disapproval when it comes from a person who does not know what we are talking about! Everything such a person says, no matter how weighty, is without pertinence. Naturally so, for we are not talking about the same things. How chilling and futile is such an exchange of words! Our ideas wilt; our imagination retreats. In such an atmosphere nothing can come to life. The criticisms, comments, and suggestions offered by our adversary, for such he insists upon being though we looked for a friend, may be splendid and profound. The trouble is that they have no applicability in the situation. In the presence of such an attitude, creative thought is stifled. Neither we nor our companion have gained anything. Our idea is no different from what it was at the beginning though it now seems less alive to us. Our companion has had the satisfaction of stating his own views, but presumably he has had this satisfaction before and will have it again. Nothing creative has happened in either mind.

Expounders and debaters may thrive in an atmosphere of nonreceptivity. Blind opposition, flat denials, and the introduction of irrelevancies may spur them on. But, they are not thinking; their object is not to communicate with others, but to convince them. There are places in which such activity is valuable, though far fewer than is commonly thought. Certainly the classroom is not one of them. Persons of unreceptive minds are sorry sights in halls of learning. There, as in the marts of trade, "no sale is ever made by winning an argument."

Now, if we, who should be somewhat used to the ways of productive thinking, can feel our crea-

4. F. J. Roethlisberger, "Understanding: A Prerequisite of Leadership," address before Professor Cabot's Business Executives' Group, Boston, February 9, 1936.

tive faculties retreating in the presence of a mind which shows itself, to us at least, as opaque, how much greater is the effect of such an attitude likely to be upon the young? They know their ideas are untried and, though they may put up a bold front of confidence, they are easily discouraged. That they should be discouraged in their ideas may not matter, but that they should be discouraged from having ideas matters greatly. It is the teacher's task to establish a basis of communication between himself and his students which will lead them to the only type of mental activity through which they can learn, namely, the imaginative handling of ideas with the aim of creation.

I

It cannot be denied, and the writings of educators are filled with this plaint, that students in general resist "learning." At the same time they crave it. Neither of these tendencies is to be wondered at, for the acquiring of learning is as hard as it is happy. Every creator knows the torments and the joys of his art, and so does every "learner," for he too is a creator. Yet there is more behind the student's resistance to learning than the mere natural difficulty of the process. The unwillingness of students to work freely and wholeheartedly for what is their avowed objective, and for what is surely to their own self-interest, results perhaps from certain typical reactions of parents to their children's early efforts to acquire learning. The basic etiology of what in effect amounts to self-frustration by the student has a vital bearing upon the problem of teaching. It suggests both the attitudes which the helpful teacher must avoid and those which he must cultivate.

The child originally has no resistance to the creative incorporation of ideas or experiences; quite the contrary. He is eager to master the world, to make all knowledge, experience, and achievement his own. Unfortunately, the attitude of his elders is customarily far from encouraging. The child's eagerness for creative learning tends to arouse in his elders one of four commonly observed reactions. These reactions may be described as: the direct-withholding-of-information reaction; the depreciation-of-the-learner reaction; the drowning-of-the-learner reaction; and the talking-beside-the-point reaction. The withholding-of-information reaction is immediately recognizable.

"Why are my roosters so bad to my hens? They bite them all the time."

"Sh! Never mind. Don't pay any attention to that. You're just imagining things. Run on and play."

"I have answered three questions, and that is enough," said his father. "Don't give yourself airs. Do you think I can listen all day to such stuff? Be off, or I'll kick you downstairs!"

Then there is the depreciation-of-the-learner reaction, which, of course, amounts also to an exaltation of the elder.

"That's all wrong. Here, let me show you. You'll never be a good ball player if you hold the bat like that."

"This way's O.K., Daddy. See how far I can knock them!"

"Now look here. Don't be so *stubborn*. Don't you *want* to learn? I know what I'm talking about. Now watch me and try to do it right."

"I guess I'll play something else."

"I don't know what you mean by *glory*," Alice said.

Humpty Dumpty smiled contemptuously. "Of course you don't—till I tell you. I meant *there's a nice knock-down argument for you!*"

"But *glory* doesn't mean *a nice knock-down argument*," Alice objected.

"When *I* use a word," Humpty Dumpty said in rather a scornful tone, "it means just what I choose it to mean—neither more nor less."

"The question is," said Alice, "whether you *can* make words mean so many different things."

"The question is," said Humpty Dumpty, "which is to be Master—that's all."

Alice was too much puzzled to say anything. . . .

The drowning-of-the-learner reaction is another means for glorifying the adult. The adult, or educationally speaking, the teacher, often is unable to refrain from demonstrating his superior learning in response to a question. For example, an innocent inquiry as to why a flower is red while the leaves of the plant are green may produce a prolonged lecture drawn from ophthalmology, chemistry, and cosmology in the large. The effect of this flood of information quite inevitably is to make the squirming inquirer more cautious in the future about providing a similar opening.

"Oh, it needn't come to that!" Alice hastily said, hoping to keep him from beginning.

"The piece I'm going to repeat," he went on without noticing her remark, "was written entirely for your amusement."

Alice felt that in that case she really *ought* to listen to it, so she sat down and said, "Thank you," rather sadly.

Closely related to the drowning-of-the-learner reaction is the talking-beside-the-point reaction. Seldom is the child, or anyone else for that matter, able to convey by a single question or statement what really is on his mind. Yet how seldom the unlucky little questioner has an opportunity to clarify his position before his elder launches forth on a dissertation based upon faulty assumptions as to what the child wishes to talk about.

"Daddy, I think I'll be a soldier when I grow up because when you're a soldier, you can kill lots of people."

Now it happens that what the child is trying to express is his horror and amazement at the fact that if one is a soldier, it is his duty to kill as many people as he can; and if he is *not* a soldier, but merely a smuggler, or a bank robber, or a mastermind as in *Dick Tracy*, and he kills just one person, all the police and the coast guard and the detectives go after him and never rest until they get him, whereupon they throw him in jail and are very mean to him. But how does Daddy answer? It would not be at all surprising to learn that he replied:

"I've a darned good notion to take those toy pistols away from you and not let you listen to *Dick Tracy* on the radio any more. It's horrible all this gangster stuff they feed the kids. Why don't you listen to some good programs that teach you something, or read a book? I bought you a whole set of . . . ."

"I'd rather not try, please!" said Alice. "I'm quite content to stay here—only I *am* so hot and thirsty!"

"I know what *you'd* like!" the Queen said good-naturedly, taking a little box out of her pocket. "Have a biscuit?"

Alice thought it would not be civil to say "No," though it wasn't at all what she wanted. So she took it, and ate it as well as she could; and it was *very* dry;

and she thought she had never been so nearly choked in all her life.

"While you're refreshing yourself," said the Queen, "I'll just take the measurements. Have another biscuit?"

"No, thank you," said Alice. "One's *quite* enough!"

"Thirst quenched, I hope?" said the Queen.

Alice did not know what to say to this, but luckily the Queen did not wait for an answer, but went on.

Very likely this constitutes only a partial explanation of the student's attitude toward formal education. Nevertheless, a continual bumping against attitudes of these types is bound in the ordinary course of events to have a paralyzing effect upon free thought, free expression, and free reception. It produces a state of wariness, a reluctance either to try to give out or to receive. The cumulative effect on the child of the stereotyped reaction of parents, themselves similarly conditioned no doubt, tends toward a conviction, perhaps wholly unconscious, that learning is a curious process made up of helpless frustration, passive reception, unthinking imitation, and acquiescence in the elder's apparent eagerness to talk only about what interests *him*.

II

The teacher, both of elementary and advanced subjects, therefore, faces as a basic problem the need for encouraging, even of re-establishing, in his students the faculty of approaching the task of learning in a spirit of creative receptivity and independent accomplishment. One of the means sometimes suggested for solving the problem of the mental passivity of students is to bring them into contact with stimulating personalities. It is indeed an excellent thing when an institution of learning has upon its faculty teachers who can fill the young with a sense of the beauty and blessing of learning and with a desire to belong to the company of the learned. All good teachers will have this stimulating influence. Unfortunately, a spectacular personality which creates interest in itself is sometimes confused with the personality which inspires interest, not alone or chiefly in itself, but rather in the creative incorporation of knowledge. An ability to inspire students with a desire to listen to you and to learn from you is part of the art of teaching. It is not the whole art.

Inspiration, or stimulation, is a fine starting point for learning, but it needs to be translated into cre-

ative thinking. Most of us who have passed our youth can look back upon moments of being "inspired." But all too frequently we shall be able to remember nothing of the episode beyond the sweetness and the thrill of being so inspired. Too often we merely basked in the sensation of inspiration and failed to make our own the body of that inspiration which the teacher possessed and which he was endeavoring to communicate to us. It is sheer pleasure to be inspired. It is hard work to learn. We cannot make ideas our own except through a laborious and painful process. Nor is this process less painful for him who occupies the teacher's chair than it is for those who sit on the student benches.

The imaginative reception of another's thoughts, often only partially created and certainly often poorly expressed, is a grueling task. It is by the performance of this task that the teacher both fulfills his true function and reaches the real reward of his calling—the continual enrichment of his mind. But this is a reward truly earned by the sweat of the brow. That is why many teachers, even those who at one time were making progress in the art of learning, cease their efforts after a bit and become teachers only in the halfway sense of seeking to tell other people something. They do not wish to receive anything from their students except their own notions as little damaged as possible by their journey from teacher to students and back again. These teachers run a sort of lending library of facts, figures, and ideas. They desert the difficult practice of creative interchange of thought and so, while they may fill their students' heads with interesting and valuable ideas and facts, they nevertheless deprive those students, so far as lies in their power, of the precious opportunity to learn how to learn. The teacher who has given up the art of learning from his students should also give up the practice of teaching.

Some may think that if the teacher really wishes to enrich his own mind, he can find better ways of doing it than by listening to his students. He had best engage in original research and conversations with other learned men. There are several things to be said about this view. In the first place enrichment of the teacher's mind is not now under consideration except as such enrichment may be of help to his students. The idea that a man rich in knowledge is necessarily a valuable teacher is mostly poppycock. With the right attitude and little knowledge, a teacher still may be the gateway to great learning for his students. With much knowledge and the wrong attitude, a teacher, so far as his students' mental life is concerned, can be of no more value than a book, perhaps less. President Conant, speaking of the great interest in education in England in the seventeenth century, has said:

It was not so much the knowledge they acquired as the spirit they encountered which drew the young men. . . .

. . . If I understand the college tradition correctly, therefore, the liberal-arts colleges today should not worry too much about whether to require a knowledge of this or that but should rather direct their energies primarily to providing a Faculty which ensures the continuation of the university spirit. What, after all, determines whether a given course is part of a liberal education or is merely pre-vocational training? Clearly the outlook of the teacher.[5]

In the second place, a man cannot be enriched by contact with other men, no matter how learned, or by research, unless he has the capacity of imaginative receptivity. And this is not something which can be turned on or off at will. It is unlikely that a man who is not receptive where his students are concerned will be receptive in other directions. He may keep quiet longer when his learned associates are speaking than he does when his students speak, but it is doubtful if he will be listening any more in one case than in the other.

In the third place, the good old principle of teaching by example still applies. Most educators agree that students should be encouraged, not to a passive acceptance of ideas with a view to bringing them forth when a pat occasion arises, but rather to an active, imaginative receptivity of knowledge. How better then can the teacher indicate what is meant by this concept than by demonstrating it over and over again to his students by his own attitude?

And finally, it is by no means certain that for teachers original research or conversation with learned men is a more fruitful source for the enrichment of thought than is communication with students. An attitude of genuine receptivity to another's thoughts presupposes respect for that other; if respect is lacking, listening will be no more than

perfunctory. It is impossible for creative interchanges to take place between people who do not respect each other. This barrier is perhaps another reason why teachers sometimes fail to keep their minds open to their students so that the necessary incentive to communication will be present. Many teachers are filled with pride and pleasure when one of their students makes a contribution to their thinking. But all too often the teacher has a patronizing attitude toward his students. Sometimes this attitude amounts to an almost brutal depreciation, leading the teacher to endeavor to trip and embarrass the students. This does not of course refer to that good-natured tripping which uncovers sloth or brings to a halt a rambling medley of rationalization which the unfortunate perpetrator is probably relieved not to be able to get away with. Sometimes the teacher's patronizing attitude takes the form of the beautiful compassion expressed by Professor Palmer in his inspiring essay, "The Ideal Teacher,"[6] when he says:

In short, I was deficient in vicariousness—in swiftly putting myself in the weak one's place and bearing his burden. . . . Ours it should be to see that every beginning, middle, and end of what we say is helpfully shaped for readiest access to those less intelligent and interested than we.

A patronizing attitude must inevitably interfere with that desirable relationship between teacher and student upon which depends the effectiveness of the teacher as a stimulator of creative thinking. It is true, as Professor Palmer has said, that the teacher, for the time being, is in the stronger position. His then is the responsibility so to respect his students that they will feel free to think in his presence and to strive to communicate *their* thoughts, not his, to him. Nor is a mere pretense of respect of any avail. As a matter of fact, when no respect is felt, it is best that none be shown. Young people are no fools, and to add deception to disrespect is to make a bad matter worse.

Since no true intercommunication can exist in the absence of that mutual respect which is a requisite to an open mind, it is clear that, of all those who should not be teachers, the egoist ranks first. For the egoist cannot have a receptive mind; he is im-

5. James Bryant Conant, "The Role of the Privately Endowed College," an address at the celebration of the Fiftieth Anniversary of Bryn Mawr College on November 2, 1935, reported in *Harvard Alumni Bulletin*, November 8, 1935.

6. George H. Palmer, *The Ideal Teacher* (Boston: Houghton Mifflin Company, 1910).

pelled to hear only that which flatters him and must value ideas and persons according to how they minister to his egoistic needs. Unfortunately the profession of teaching is one that, while it attracts the noblest and most self-effacing personalities, also attracts egoists. Few other professions hold the promise of such rich rewards for the self-centered. In this high calling the egoist has the opportunity to display himself and his learning to large numbers of young people who by the rules of the game are bound at least to show him the signs of respect and to seek to please him. He usually can have the satisfaction of seeing in print whatever he may choose to write, particularly if he is employed by one of the great universities. Moreover, since accomplishment is peculiarly difficult to judge in the field of teaching, the egoist has an excellent chance of impressing his colleagues. He talks dramatically and firmly. He charges about. This combination is likely to be impressive. As Dean Wallace B. Donham has pointed out in another connection, "action may be esteemed evidence of accomplishment."

How difficult it is to know whether the teacher is fulfilling his high mission of creative intercommunication with his students! "What sort of conditions will produce the type of faculty which will run a successful university? The danger is that it is quite easy to produce a faculty entirely unfit—a faculty of very efficient pedants and dullards. The general public will detect the difference only after the university has stunted the promise of youth for scores of years."[7] Probably no one represents such a danger to the vital life of an educational institution as the egoist. He cannot teach others for he has shut his mind to being taught. Moreover, to whatever extent his influence reaches, he will perpetuate his own mediocrity for he is bound to sympathize with those who are of inferior abilities.

The notion that in order to teach, that is, in order to produce learning in someone else, the teacher must have an attitude of imaginative receptivity to the thinking of his students has a bearing upon the much debated question as to whether the same man can be both a good teacher and a good research man. Professor Philip Cabot has said: "It is a mistake to assume that the researcher and the teacher are always, or even commonly, united in the same person. The qualities needed for success in these two fields are different and are rarely found in the same man."[8] Inasmuch as Professor Cabot usually is right, he may be right in this. However, he is probably using "researcher" in a somewhat narrower sense than it is used by other authorities. It may be, too, that Professor Cabot is thinking of research men as they so often are and not as they sometimes are and always should be. President Conant describes research as "the advancement of learning . . . for I should like to include under one title not only the increase in our positive knowledge, the advances made in all science, but also the study and interpretation of those cultural values which come to us from the past."[9] If Professor Cabot is content to accept this interpretation of research, it will be evident that he, himself, is an excellent researcher and, thereby, a case in point against his own assertion.

Whether it is possible *in general* for men on our university faculties to be productive research workers and sound teachers is a controversial matter. Nevertheless, the same attitude of mind which characterizes the good teacher is also necessary for sound research: namely, an attitude of lively, imaginative receptivity. It is likely that one reason so much of our research, particularly our social and economic research, has been a failure is that it has been carried on by men who lack such receptivity. Professor Henderson has pointed out that: "In certain respects the observation, study, and interpretation of what men say is the characteristic feature of the social sciences."[10] In the pure sciences, the importance of being receptive to the creative thinking of others is at least not so apparent though the need is nevertheless there.

A laboratory is provided for the teacher by his classroom, his student interviews, and the papers of his students. In this laboratory he will find clues pointing to new hypotheses; will be able to test these hypotheses in order to modify, discard, or accept them. Professor Melvin T. Copeland, equally distinguished for his teaching and for his research work, recently offered a case in point. He had held the view that students entering a certain course

7. A. N. Whitehead, "Universities and Their Function," *Atlantic Monthly*, May 1928.

8. "Our Times and Your Future," commencement address, Juniata College, June 1, 1936.
9. James Bryant Conant, "The Mission of American Universities," an address before the Cincinnati Chamber of Commerce Forum, reported in *Harvard Alumni Bulletin*, February 26, 1938.
10. L. J. Henderson, "Introductory Lectures, Sociology 23," p. 19.

understood the meaning of the commonly used business concept of "general management" as something different from "departmental management." Various things which students said to him in the course of individual conferences, called for another purpose, suggested to him, however, that this concept might in fact mean very different things to different students, and that for some it might lack any meaning. Having in this way obtained a number of clues pointing in the same general direction, Professor Copeland undertook to retest his former hypothesis. Lack of alertness to the significance of seemingly irrelevant remarks made during the interviews would have prevented this particular strengthening of the understanding between teacher and students.

There is another implication of the theory of receptivity that should be mentioned. We hear much discussion of the proper age of retirement for teachers. If a teacher is good, he should be begged not to retire until he becomes too feeble to make intelligent motions. If a teacher has a truly receptive mind, he is bound to grow better and better until he totters to his grave. He can never be outmoded, for he is in incessant communication with the thought of the day; he cannot become stale, for he never has allowed his faculty for creative thinking to be dulled by lack of use.

> "The crinkled smile on the Dean's kind face is
>   Gone with a myriad smiles we miss;
> So please, dear God, don't fill the places
>   Quite yet of Kitty and Copey and Bliss."[11]

11. Lawrence McKinney, 1912, cited in the Tercentenary Graduates' issue of *The Lampoon*. [Reprinted with permission.] Reprinted in *Notes on the Harvard Tercentenary* (Cambridge:

The attitude of mind of the good teacher forms the bridge between two accepted principles of teaching. The first of these principles is that the teacher needs to have an imaginative and creative mind as well as a store of knowledge. It is deadening to a developing intelligence to come in contact with a mind loaded down with information to which it can give no life for lack of imagination and enthusiasm. While this principle unfortunately is often lost sight of in practice, in theory it cannot be questioned. The second accepted principle of teaching is that the student must recreate imaginatively the ideas and facts communicated to him by the teacher if those ideas and facts are to mean anything to him, if he is to be truly educated.

Given a teacher with a vivid creative intelligence, how can he lead his students to undertake for their own parts the creative interpretation of knowledge? The answer lies in part at least in the ability of the teacher to listen to his students, not with a view to appraising them, correcting their mistakes, and filling in the gaps in their knowledge, but rather in the constant and true expectation of learning something. A properly conducted class, however, is not one in which the teacher sits supinely wide eyed, beaming respect and approval, while his students in crescendoes of oratory pour forth their views as to what is what. Learning is hard, and there is much to be learned. There is no time for mawkish sentiment and backslapping. The teacher is the strong man, the center from which flows a fresh and vivifying stream of knowledge imaginatively conceived.

Harvard University Press, 1936), p. 24. (References are to George Lyman Kittredge, 1882, Charles Townsend Copeland, 1882, and Bliss Perry, Litt. D. (Hon.) 1925.)

READING

Why Teach?

MARYELLEN GLEASON

Not so long ago at one of those obligatory social functions, I was superficially engaged in conversation with a rather wearisome creature who inquired as to my profession. "I'm a teacher." Taking a sip of the warm, red punch, he smiled and asked me, "Why?" Confused, I echoed the question: "Why?" "Yes, why do you teach?" I stammered. The first reasons that came to mind were not right. For money. People who teach for money are a minority—poor, blinded souls who have yet to make the acquaintance of a banker, doctor, or mortician. For glory. The few who still teach for the glory tend to be young and idealistic—poor, blinded souls who have yet to read the fine print on promotion and tenure. For the opportunity to do research. Maybe; but unless you have a bevy of graduate assistants, objective tests, and no office hours, even the most elementary cost-benefit analysis reveals this to be a losing proposition. My inquisitor was out of punch, and I was out of time. I had to say something. "I teach for the students."

We parted—he for more punch, I to collect my thoughts. What kind of an answer had I given? Do I teach for the students? I felt myself wanting to smile. I caught myself trying to imagine the sophisticated, tweedy intellectuals among my colleagues admitting to such an unabashedly human reason. But before worrying about them I needed to answer the question for myself. Names and facts—some together, some separate—all flashed through my memory. Suddenly the movie stopped, and I remembered Scott.

I met Scott early in my teaching career one unfortunate semester when the two sections of my beginning speech course had been scheduled to meet at the same time. That meant I had sixty students instead of thirty. I was in no mood to sign overloads. Scott was patient, polite, and insistent. He had to have this course. He was going to be a doctor. "I have to communicate important messages. I want to learn how to do it right." The deep-set, brown eyes never wavered. Mine dropped; he had a point. Later, I chided myself for being a pushover. When would I learn a student could feign interest in any course if it fell into the right time slot?

My first mistake with Scott was the assumption his interest was feigned. It turned out to be all too genuine. This error was compounded by a second. I assumed I knew enough about communication to satisfy the intellectual curiosity of my students.

Scott's academic appetite was voracious. The course had barely begun and he was asking questions I couldn't answer, raising issues I'd never considered, and reading books I didn't know. Even my best-reasoned, most eloquent response did not settle an issue. It only stimulated more questions.

I was frightened—not just by the questions. It was his answers—to everything. One day on the way to class I wondered out loud why the yellow crocuses always bloomed first. Oh, that was easy, he assured me. It was a matter of dominant genes. The yellow plants had them, which meant they were the hardiest and therefore bloomed first. "Oh." I couldn't really think of anything else to say. I had only been trying to make conversation.

I couldn't help feeling a bit relieved when the semester ended. I didn't know anything else to teach Scott. The experience was humbling, and yet there was exhilaration as well. I was forced to admit here was a student more dedicated and determined about learning than I had ever been. Here too was a student brighter than I. The revelations startled me, but once the admissions were made I was ready to learn something far more significant: Students can teach us if we let them.

The pictures in my mind moved again. This time when they stopped I saw Ron—an average student thoroughly convinced of his ordinariness. Yes, he could play baseball, but that was just about it. "I'm not much of a student," he told me, and that pretty well summed up his less-than-adequate writing skills, his 2.1 GPA, and his general disinterest in anything academic. At the end of his sophomore year, Ron had yet to confront an intellectual idea that mattered.

Ron had also yet to confront a teacher who thought he mattered. I treated him like someone special. It wasn't hard. He was and is a unique human being without duplicate. It seemed like such a simple solution. Ron responded very much like my Swedish ivy when I finally got around to giving it some fertilizer. He started to grow. Almost before I knew what happened both Ron and my ivy were discovering places they had never been before. Ron found out that the nonverbal communication I lectured about in class he actually used when he played baseball. My ivy discovered the window latch around which it proceeded to grow. In both cases the very obvious changes attracted attention and the two continued to flourish.

From Ron I learned teachers have power—power that can affect and change students. It would be nice if the power was inherently creative. It is not. But then the power is not inherently destructive, either. Rather, the potential for teachers to influence students simply exists. Unfortunately, most teachers neglect to use this influence to accomplish any effect.

Ron was gone. I sighed as I remembered Richie—a black, ghetto kid raised in Watts who used to tell me he did not know ground could be green until he moved to Oregon. Later I wondered if it was a joke.

Richie lived with ignorance. His vocabulary permitted only the most rudimentary and repetitious descriptions of what happened. During one of many study sessions I was struggling, without apparent success, to explain inflation. I permitted a momentary diversion while I tried to brainstorm a better approach. Richie chatted amicably about the bank downtown where he had opened a savings account to keep his tuition for next semester. He was impressed by the size and security of the safe. "Well," he concluded, "That's the way it should be. I don't want nobody running off with my money." "Richie, your money is not in that safe." Feeling the tension, I began cautiously, "Banks are in business to make money. They do that by borrowing money. They've spent yours. You'll get somebody else's when you take yours out." The face was angry., "They can't do that! It's my money. How come they didn't tell me? Bastards!" "They thought you knew, Richie." My answer didn't touch his anger.

Richie astonished me. I had never seen the lonely islands of ignorance that still exist in our advanced, civilized society. Most of my time is spent at the higher levels of learning. My students are interested in actualizing; they want to realize their full potential. Richie was a tangible reminder that not all knowledge is luxury. Some is essential. Deprivation of these basic life facts relegates one to the peripheries of existence.

I wanted to move on. I remembered Eileen—what the professionals called a "nontraditional learner." Eileen was thirty, married, and a mother who wanted a college degree. For some reason she felt inferior—felt as if she had never accomplished much that mattered, at least to her. Get a college diploma and she would have tangible proof of an accomplishment that mattered. It was a noble challenge. Eileen had not been near a classroom since high school. She and her husband were struggling financially with a huge dairy farm, which meant there was no money for college. She financed the venture with a part-time secretarial job. Her arrival in class marked no small accomplishment, but for Eileen that was only the first step. She didn't anticipate the second step would be easier, and it was not.

As the date for the first exam approached, the tension rose noticeably. There were office calls and embarrassed questions asked quietly. "I don't know how to study the texts." "I don't understand things I've written in my notes." The very brown eyes twinkled, but the face was serious. "I tell the cows about what I read in the text. Some of them seem as slow as me."

On the day of the test the anguish was visible. I hoped for the best—so much appeared to be at

stake. The best turned out to be a C minus—a shaky two points from a D. Eileen was in my office when I returned from class. She quietly closed the door and sat down. There was stubborn determination as we painstakingly went through the test, question by question. Neither of us mentioned the tears that accidentally spilled on the last page.

By sheer gut determination Eileen made it in my class and many others. From that remarkably strong woman I learned there are values in education I have too long taken for granted.

I suppressed the urge to remember more. It was time to return. I took a sip from my still-full punch glass and smiled. I could live with the answer—even if it did open to public scrutiny my humanity. I owe students a great deal. The debt ought to be acknowledged.

In the educational journals, the definition of good teaching seems always to elude those who chase to capture and pin it to the dissecting table. This is not surprising. There are many kinds of good teaching situations at many different levels. Attempts to reduce it to a formula are doomed to failure. There will always be teachers who will break all the rules and yet be profoundly successful. In other words, it is the good teacher, not teaching in the abstract, that counts.

This is not to say that the art of teaching cannot be studied or its skills conveyed. It is to say that good teaching can never be successfully dealt with in a mechanical way. "Objective criteria" and "scientific evaluations" are attractive slogans to some in the world of education who are uneasy with anything that is not measurable. But such approaches to so complex and personal a thing as good teaching will always fall short. What is important is the *recognition* of it.

And here, I think, we should reject emphatically the proposition that "hearsay" is somehow not admissible or legitimate in judging teaching. How, really, do we know that Jinks Harbison was a great teacher? Because of the spoken testimony of hundreds of students and colleagues. I do not doubt that similarly the evidence on which tonight's awards are based is partly hearsay: diligently sought, carefully sifted and examined, and yet— hearsay. Apart from their scholarly writing, much of what we know of the teaching genius of other great teachers—Joseph Henry lecturing on electrical magnetism at Princeton, Mark Hopkins on the legendary log, Louis Agassiz in his zoological laboratory at Harvard, or Socrates in the marketplace—is based on hearsay.

Is this not perhaps another way of saying that the successful teacher is known by the mark he leaves on his students? If so, it is *not* the mark of indoctrination. (Someone recently described the indoctrinal sort of teaching as pouring from a big pitcher into many little pitchers, then *via* the final examination back into the big pitcher, so that all you have left is a lot of dirty little pitchers—and I am not referring to visual aids.) No, the kind of teaching which is significant at the college or university level—the kind involved in these Harbison Awards—is not indoctrination.

When Louis Agassiz was asked his greatest achievement, he replied that he had taught men to observe. Socrates taught men to question. Each

In Defense of Teaching

ROBERT F. GOHEEN

*This is an excerpt from a speech given by **Robert F. Goheen**, former president of Princeton University, at a presentation of the Harbison Awards in February 1966.*

Reprinted by permission from *Princeton Alumni Weekly*, February 22, 1966, pages 11 and 12.

great teacher has his own way. Yet, I suspect that more often than not two particular attributes will be found in the successful teacher. One is an ability to awaken and stimulate delight in the use of the mind. The second is attention to the effort to do so, together with a belief in its value to the student in *his* own right. Certainly those teachers I have admired most in Princeton (and Jinks Harbison was one) seem to have engendered in their students a pleasure, a joy, a raised awareness, in intellectual activity. Perhaps their students were not always the keenest of observers, or the most skillful interlocutors—but they had discovered the pleasure in discovering where they lead, the lift in the journey that carries beyond the misty flats of one's own experience.

I do not mean that this always comes easily either to student or to teacher. Undertaking to deal seriously with ideas is often a messy, difficult job for the young (even under the best tutelage); and undertaking to deal seriously with ideas is always a demanding, often a lonely, necessity of the teacher (even with the best of students). But vital connections do occur. Somehow the maturity of the teacher gets translated to the students so that they go beyond their years. This was one of the qualities of Jinks Harbison: his *maturity* was manifest, and he conveyed it in everything he wrote and said.

There is another role that the good teacher plays. He is interpreter in the house of learning. Now, the word *interpret* has several connotations: to explain—to translate—to construe. All involve the making of a connection. This is what the teacher does. He puts the student *in connection* with the problem at hand, and leads him to seek and press an engagement with it.

Finally, in the great teacher, no matter how unobtrusively, there will be found strength of conviction. Faulkner in his Nobel Prize speech said of the writer: he must "leave no room in his workshop for anything but old verities and truths. . . . Until he does so . . . he writes not of the heart but of the glands." We might say the same of the teacher. In his role of interpreter, his own heart and convictions will come through—subtly and quietly, perhaps, but they will come through.

We hear much these days about the bleakness of the impersonal university, the neglect of teaching, and the pressures for research and publication. There is ground for concern, as well as much exaggeration, in these charges. It is the more heart-

ening, therefore, that the Danforth Foundation has taken leadership in recognizing the crucial role of teaching—i.e., the presence and work of good teachers—in higher education. And it is most fitting that the Harbison Awards of the the Danforth Foundation should give emphasis to the teacher's concern with the personal dimension in education and the relevance of religious faith to the problems of our age.

Let me mention briefly just three of the many reasons why better teaching must be nourished and sustained on our campuses. One is obvious enough: the rapidly growing number of college and university students. A report of the United States Office of Education of December 27th [1966] indicates that this year's enrollments rose twelve per cent over last year's level to a total of nearly six million—more than double that of a decade ago. The new freshman crop is eighteen percent larger than that of 1964. Every state and territory showed an increase. Place alongside this the fact that the number of college and university teachers being produced (with or without doctorates) is falling far behind these burgeoning figures. The inference is clear. There are going to be proportionately fewer competent teachers to the number of students to be taught. Accordingly, the role of those teachers who can by leadership and contagion encourage and assist others is ever more crucial.

A second compelling argument for doing everything we can to strengthen and enrich the teaching on our campuses grows out of the exploding diversity of knowledge. The house of intellect, once so relatively tidy, has swollen and burst into fragments. As the late Professor Charles Osgood observed, anyone who tries to act as if this hadn't happened is like the man who gave up reading the encyclopedia because he couldn't follow the story!

Not only in the sciences and social sciences but also in the humanities, marked changes are discernible in the materials being studied and the approach to these materials. But on the whole the movement is, I think, a healthy one toward fundamental analysis and basic principles, away from mere memory work and dependence upon fixed segments of subject matter; but it does call for more talented teachers.

Rote learning never was much good. Today it is worth even less. The citizen of tomorrow must master the ways of analysis, must search deeply, if he is to cope with the uncertainties and changes of the decades ahead. The kind of education that will equip him to do so cannot be offered by second- and third-rate minds using second- and third-hand methods of instruction.

A third reason for stressing the importance of teaching in higher education today is the emphasis and glamor now so widely and strongly attached to research. Please do not mistake me. The quest for new knowledge is vital in the university, and the liberal arts college too. On campuses all over the country the stepped-up range and tempo of research have strengthened and enlivened instruction far more widely than they have deadened or disabled it. In the college or university, research and teaching are two poles of the same magnet; neither has much force without the other. That is what the ideal of the teacher-scholar is all about. But at a time when there are not enough good teachers to go around, and when the supply is falling still farther behind the demand, it is of national importance that such good teachers as we have not be lured or cudgeled away from teaching.

I am concerned here particularly with the drift toward sharply reduced teaching loads in many universities. It seems to me to have gone dangerously far. There is, to be sure, good reason for reducing the teaching duties of men and women with unusual capacities for research, or great gifts as lecturers or writers. It enables such people to bring their talents to bear in the best way. And as I have suggested in the image of the magnet, *all* college or university-level faculty members should have the time for search and inquiry, for scholarship, in their chosen fields of study. What I am dubious about is that by-product of today's intense competition for faculty wherein part of the lure is a weekly teaching assignment of no more than a few hours—and sometimes none at all. Whether they mean to or not, institutions which go in heavily for this kind of enticement are making the avoidance of teaching a reward and a mark of status in a way which cannot but be harmful to higher education.

Please understand that I am making no defense of the overly heavy teaching load, which is still too often the rule in some types of institutions. It, too,

is at odds with good teaching and brings low returns in students' learning. But in many of the leading institutions today the pendulum is toward the other extreme. So much so, I suspect the day may not be far off when legislators or trustees will be inquiring into the provision of substantial salaries for college and university faculty members on ridiculously low teaching schedules where there is not the exceptional promise or achievement to justify it. Some embarrassing questions may be asked.

Let this not be taken as a wail of despair. I believe that the link between good scholarship and good teaching is strong and will remain so. I also believe that the common sense of America's academic folk will prevail so that good teaching will have its proper place of honor among them. Meanwhile, it falls to all of us to help to keep the balance and preserve the dignity of the teacher-scholar as teacher, not solely as scholar. This cannot be the concern of deans and presidents only, but must be that of departments and individual faculty members as well. It is precisely there that the battle for effective teaching will be fought and won.

The nation cannot afford to have its best minds apart and aloof from the students thronging our college and university halls. There must be a meaningful connection between them. Woodrow Wilson once said:

> America will be great among the nations only in proportion as she finds an adequate voice. . . . Her wealth will not interpret her, or her physical power, or the breadth of her uncounted acres, or anything she has builded; but only such revealing speech as will hold the ear and command the heed of other nations and of her own people. Our thinkers must assist her to know herself.

In this same sense, America needs more than ever the men and women at all levels of education—school, college, and university—who will be interpreters to the coming generations, and leave their mark on them: the mark of maturity, of the use of the mind, of thoughtful conviction.

READING

Ana Roje

STEVE McFADDEN

This article is reproduced here as it first appeared in December 1977 in Boston Today.

Reprinted with permission of the author.

Copyright © 1977 by Steve McFadden.

There is never much fanfare when she arrives in Boston each September to begin her classes, but the news of her coming spreads quickly through the ballet community: Madame Ana Roje is here and ready to teach. Soon a select group of students will be arranged along a *barre*, waiting while she concentrates and prepares herself emotionally.

And then she begins, starting slowly. Always the start is slow, and the pace that follows is controlled by the condition of the dancers rather than the mood of the teacher.

Pacing is one of Madame Roje's secrets. It is pacing, personality, knowledge, experience, intuition, and love that combine to make her one of the outstanding ballet teachers in the world. Former Prima Ballerina of the Yugoslav State Ballet, ex-Ballet Mistress of the Ballet Russe de Monte Carlo and De Basil Companies, and protégé of the great Nicholas Legat, she is a uniquely learned and talented builder of dancers.

Madame teaches beauty of line, expressiveness of movement, softness of *port de bras*, passion, control, and understanding of the Russian style of classical ballet. Fluidity, continuity, and unity are her indelible trademarks. When dancers have sampled the wisdom and love that abound in her class, they must return. They know she is the source of a very special knowledge, and they want to move in front of her analytical eyes, to listen to her.

She, too, is a listener. Nicholas Legat, the chief architect of the Kirov Ballet, affectionately called her his "little rabbit," because she was "one big ear" while a student in his school in London. From 1933 until Legat's death in 1937, she was his first and only assistant.

Legat embodied the heritage of the great ballet masters of the world. He was born into a family of renowned dancers and was the most outstanding pupil of Christian Johannsen. By the start of the twentieth century Johannsen was, next to Marius Petipa, the most important figure in the development of Russian Ballet. When he retired he chose Legat to take his place as master of the Classe de Perfection of the Maryinsky Company (now the Leningrad Kirov) school. Some of the most respected artists in the world of dance attended his classes, including Nijinsky, Pavlova, Fokine, and Karsavina.

It was as a teacher that Legat achieved fulfillment. It was he who studied the Italian dancers and

74

gained an understanding of how they made their spectacular way of dancing. Then Legat taught Mathilde Kschessinska and Vera Trefilova to do the famous 32 *fouettes* in the third act of Swan Lake. During his career he had an immeasurable influence on hundreds of dancers, and in 1922 when he established his own school in London he attracted the world's premier dancers as pupils: Massine, Danilova, Dolin, Markova, Fonteyn, Shearer, and Ana Roje.

Ana Roje, who came to Legat late in his life, was especially selected and groomed to be his successor, and to be responsible for the preservation of his system. Legat could not have chosen anyone better suited to the task. She is a rare talent: born to dance with fire and strength, born to teach with patience and an astute understanding of how the body and mind work best.

Legat asked Ana Roje what she wanted out of life. Was it fame, fortune, flowers, or knowledge? With knowledge, he told her, she could have all the rest. At the time, she was widely recognized as a great dancer and was being solicited with offers from around the world. They wanted her to make movies, they wanted her to be in ads, they wanted her to dance. She stayed at Legat's side and listened, a decision she has never regretted. They would sit up until sunrise discussing the finest points of the art. They spent three days just talking about *battement tendu*. A single position of the arm could take hours of discussion.

His wisdom mingled with her passion for the dance. She became a connoisseur of people, of their similarities and differences. She learned to be analytical, to develop insights into personalities and physical abilities, and then to translate her insights into a way of reaching and teaching individuals to perform.

Madame Roje says it best herself: "I bring not only my knowledge, but my soul and my love to my work. I instinctively know how to pass my knowledge, to whom, and in what measure . . . I might scold you. I might bite you. I might kiss you. My passion becomes manifest, and I desire that I want you to do it. It doesn't matter which way I get you to go, sweet or drastic, I run the scale of emotions, but I must find a road for my students."

In her search for the most effective way to reach individual dancers, Madame Roje leads her class down a different road every day. To a casual observer there is no particular order to the ideas and techniques of her lessons. She never repeats any of her classes. Each is unique, created just for that moment and that group of pupils. When class is over, all combinations belong to the past.

But, there is a deep logic behind her operating procedure, and it is based on the wisdom Legat passed down to her: human beings are always changing; nature is constantly changing and man must adapt; variety in the class develops physical and intellectual capacity; and classes must not be stale since they are expected to give the student fresh strength, and to keep him or her eager for the next lesson.

The logic is effective in its application, and it is effective in terms of the results it produces. Many of the greatest artists of the dance world have benefited from her classes. Massine, Danilova, Markova, and Toumanova all studied under her when she was Ballet Mistress at the Ballet Russe de Monte Carlo.

She deals with each student in turn and has the capacity to instruct in such a way that all her students can perceive the logic and draw knowledge from her remarks.

"Your remarks must be to the individual," she says. "General remarks are too simple. My job is to make the dancers do it, and individual attention is the best way."

Yet, at times, when class is very crowded, she will employ general remarks. But she does it in a way that makes it seem intensely personal. From the back of the class, where the students cannot see her, she will call out "I am watching you"—and then if everyone does not strain all the harder—"You are not listening. Try harder; I am watching YOU." And of course, everyone in the class is sure that she is referring specifically to them. A native of Split, Yugoslavia, Ana Roje became the first soloist in the Split National Ballet at the age of 14, never having had a lesson, never having seen a ballerina. She was born to dance; her feet were formed in such a way that when she went *on pointe* all toes touched the stage. She could balance on them all, and she had an inherent talent for graceful motion. But she had an inextinguishable desire to refine her God-given abilities. She joined the Zagreb Ballet Company and later the Belgrade Ballet Company. Everywhere she danced she was praised by the critics, but she was never satisfied with what she was able to learn.

So, she went to London in 1933 to get a "little

polish" from Legat. He told her to forget everything she knew and start from the beginning. It was difficult for her to swallow her pride, but after a few of Legat's classes she began to understand ballet in a way she had never imagined. Ana Roje's experience as a student and assistant of Legat's made a profound difference in her life. She became dedicated to following and furthering the generations-old knowledge he passed to her.

Like Legat, Madame Roje wants all her dancers to strive for perfection, but she wants them all to do it with a personal style. "Individuality is important. This is dance, not the army. Individuality is the greatest virtue," she tells the class. "You must be unique. You must develop and exploit the portion of your uniqueness that is beautiful. On stage many are dancing; to be noticed you must maintain your individuality."

To encourage individuality from the outset, the first and most important thing she tells her students is "know your instrument perfectly. Everybody has some problems, but sometimes they can be exploited to advantage." Beyond this, she tells her students to be curious, to be always asking questions of her and to seek what is better.

Madame Roje is disappointed by what she sees in some ballet teachers around the world who use the Pavlov dog approach. "They think if they do the same things over and over, and reward and punish, they will achieve excellence. Dancers taught this way can rarely do anything right. The student should know exactly what is being done, why and how.

"My technique is valid," she says. "If a student is smart, she will realize where I am heading with each small part of the lesson. It all fits together. It is all so logical."

In a Class

Most noticeable is her voice, soft and cultured, but capable of coaxing greatness out of those who think they can only be good. Madame is in constant movement: lifting legs, putting arms into proper position, demonstrating the correct way to execute a *glissade* or *changement de pieds*.

The cadence is kept with castanets, the only instrument she knows how to play. The castanets are an integral part of the class because they keep the pace that guides the students in their development; their clacking contrasts sharply with her voice, and at each snap the dancers change position. Her eyes

are everywhere, constantly searching the dancers' bodies, analyzing each move.

Madame comes to a dancer's body and places her hands on the limb that has been giving trouble. "The leg," she says, "does not end at the thigh. It continues to the hip. To dance with the leg you must use the hip. It is natural." In the air or on the ground, her advanced pupils have beautiful body control and lyrical grace. Every move of the body is based on the same principle, the one Legat discovered while studying the motion of great dancers from all over the world: control in the hips.

Hip control is one of the techniques employed only in Russian style ballet, and it is one of the keys to the widely recognized superiority of Russian dancers.

Madame moves to the foot of a student, and then to the neck of another who is too tense. "Fill the lungs with air," she says soothingly. "Breathe deeply, then *plié* and exhale." The student relaxes.

She exaggerates breathing to emphasize it. She tells the members of the class they will turn blue if they do not breathe while working, and after each series of exercises there is a brief respite for a deep breath of air.

But the lessons are not always so placid. She can drive them hard, demanding that they do more. If necessary, Madame will force her students to do their exercises properly with a little physical persuasion. She may clutch a fistful of hair and pull up forcefully to encourage a student to "get tall," or she may strike from the rear: "Every time you stick out your 'rappapo,' I'm going to pinch it." And she is true to her word.

"Suffer," she entreats with enthusiasm. "You can all suffer. Show me how beautiful you are. Suffer pretty. It has to hurt you. Anybody can kick the leg, so what? Kicking the leg elegantly—that's it!" She tells her students not to avoid the pain in their arms and legs because someday the limbs will take them away like birds. "Think of every move up as a future jump."

The castanets click, and the dancers change position.

In Madame Roje's class, according to the Legat system, movement dictates the rhythms. If the rhythm is not right, dancers will have to battle their own bodies for control. Every gesture, as soon as it is created, carries its own special rhythm, without which that movement would not have any sense.

All these principles are based on sound knowledge of how the body works best. She has spent countless hours learning anatomy, visiting hospitals, and talking with doctors. Although injuries are common in ballet, none of Madame Roje's students have ever been injured in class or while performing under her guidance, "not even a little finger."

"Unfortunately," she says, "some dancers and choreographers do not take enough time to study so they can cope with physical reality, or see the limits and possibilities of individual dancers. They rush into a company and go overboard. That is the tragedy of ballet.

"Now who is the best? Those that come from somewhere else. But America can have the best," Madame asserts. She is sure of it. She has committed herself to helping it become reality.

During the summer months she works at her beautiful home and International School of Ballet in Primosten, Yugoslavia. There, with her husband and former dancing partner Oskar Hamos, they train a select group of dancers from Europe and America. But for nine months of the year she teaches in Boston. Several trips to America in the early 1960s convinced her that there was an opportunity for Russian style ballet to flourish in America, and she realized that American youth are good material for ballet.

Presently [1977] her classes are at the Ana Roje Studio of Russian Style Ballet, 667 Boylston St., opposite the Boston Public Library.

Beginning and continuing without local advertising, she has attracted a large and devoted group of pupils. They are her "children," and she loves them.

Some of the students are selected for training as teachers, so the traditions and knowledge of the Legat system will continue. But in the course of the last year Madame Roje has decided the time has come to more firmly establish Russian style ballet in America. So, with a group of supporters from the Boston area, she has formed the American Society of Russian Style Ballet (P.O. Box 219, Astor Station, Boston, Mass. 02123).

The purpose of the Society is to preserve and communicate the knowledge and performing methods of the great masters of the Russian ballet, and to further advance the art of classical dance in America. Toward that end the group co-sponsored a seminar and lecture-demonstration for teachers with M.I.T. in October. The Society plans future lecture-demonstrations, and also offers consultations and certification for dancers and dance instructors. Madame Roje and the Society's Board of Directors plan the activities, and have drafted a "syllabus" for certified instructors to employ in teaching Russian-style ballet.

Encouragement has come from around the world, and many of the most famous and respected figures in the dance world have agreed to serve as "Honorary Representatives" of the Society: Leonide Massine, Anton Dolin, Andre Eglevsky, Igor Youskevitch, Alicia Markova, Irina Baronova and Patricia Bowman.

What Her Students Say

"She has a wonderful common sense about the body," according to Stephanie Moy, a soloist with the Boston Ballet Company and a student of Madame Roje's for many years. Stephanie has been with the Boston Ballet for four years as a professional and is a rising star. When her busy rehearsal and performance schedule allow, she still takes classes from Madame.

"One of the major reasons Madame is a great teacher," Stephanie says, "is that she studied with a teacher who was a link in a long line of great tradition. The knowledge has been handed down from generation to generation, and each generation has added something to it. Also, she has a great knack of emotionally connecting to people. She cares intensely about her students, in the studio and out; she has a magnetic personality.

"Dance is a very hazardous profession, because the demands are so great. Madame makes a point never to hurt anyone physically," Stephanie says. "Dance is a very painful thing, but Madame is capable of making a distinction between good pain and bad pain. That is why none of her students have ever been injured."

Maggie Letvin, a celebrity in the Boston area through her physical fitness show on public television (Maggie and the Beautiful Machine), has recently become a student of Madame Roje's. She herself is a knowledgeable trainer of bodies, but she has recognized a level of understanding in Madame that she would like to attain.

For years, Maggie says, she led classes through exercises, knowing what the effect would be but never knowing why. Madame Roje has been able to explain why to her, because her philosophy toward the dance and the body is that understanding is as important as performance. "It's her experience and pacing that make her a superior teacher," according to Maggie. "It's almost uncanny the natural way that Madame paces her students through their exercises. And her personality is so strong that you are compelled to strive for perfection in her class."

My Own Experience

On the assumption that you cannot fully appreciate a teacher without having been a student, I enrolled in Madame Roje's class. At age 28 my physical abilities would give a choreographer nightmares. Corrupted by rich foods, cancerous from cigarettes, and atrophied from inaction, it seemed hopeless at the outset. I was bad material, and there was not enough time for any real progress, just three weeks.

But Madame Roje had many notable successes with me in that short span of time. She did it in little ways. She pulled my arm out straight. She told me to relax my neck. She told me she admired my courage, such as it is, although not my ability. And she made me suffer. "Suffer," she demanded, "you are not suffering enough." So, she would come to the leg I was struggling to lift and ensure that I suffered. I loved it.

I lumbered along at the *barre*, straining and sweating, and discovering how weak my body had become. After class I hobbled home to soak in the tub and reflect on my seemingly irrational attraction to her torture.

When Madame Roje enters the studio an infusion of energy infects all the students. She is a commanding figure, dressed in black tights, black slippers and a black skirt. Her brown eyes are piercing, and she walks to the center of the floor with a master's confidence.

She is steady, has an easily recognizable cadence to her commands, and has a sure touch evenly applied. Variously placid, passionate, exuberant, and stern, her personality pulls attention; and her spirit feeds back an enriched mixture of enthusiasm and love for the dance. Her mind contributes intellectual fodder that the students must assimilate and transfer to controlled yet graceful action.

Madame says: "Squeeze out more power than you think you have." And I squeeze and suffer.

I was not capable of grace. It was difficult enough just to follow along and mimic the moves of the other students, but Madame would not stand for mimicry. She compelled me to totally involve my mind in the control of the body. In time, I came to have a true sense of the beauty and depth of expression the human body is capable of when it is conditioned, disciplined, and directed by a creative intelligence. In no way was I capable of properly executing an arabesque, a glissade, or an *entrechat*. I could not conceive of my legs ever developing the quickness necessary for *battement frappé*. But, I could feel, I could taste, I could understand how they were done. If my body were capable of keeping up with my imagination, I could be a dancer.

In small ways that were difficult to perceive at first, my ballet training began to spill over into the rest of my life. It made me more alert, willing and able to work harder; it added a note of pride to my posture, and there was a pleasing precision to my stride.

I became hungry for physical grace, and I came to realize that Madame Roje's ballet class was the only source for satisfying this appetite.

The attention I received as a student in her class inspired me on a personal, rather than professional, level. She told me, "I firmly believe that each of us is here to do something, to create something, to be something the best we can. I try every day in my own way." She made me want to try harder.

She makes her dancers want to try harder. And since she is the contemporary link in a long line of ballet knowledge, she can feed her dancers with a nearly inexhaustible supply of wisdom.

Madame Roje's life has had one focus, to master the physical realities of the human body, and then to direct the body to express the most beautiful thoughts and feelings of the mind and spirit.

She has succeeded, realizing that perfection is unattainable, but the only valid goal, for the dancer. And with the newly founded American Society of Russian Style Ballet, her knowledge and experience will be made available to many more people.

Professor Shaler's Recollections

Agassiz's laboratory was then in a rather small two-storied building, looking much like a square dwelling-house, which stood where the College Gymnasium now stands. . . . Agassiz had recently moved into it from a shed on the marsh near Brighton bridge, the original tenants, the engineers, having come to riches in the shape of the brick structure now known as the Lawrence Building. In this primitive establishment Agassiz's laboratory, as distinguished from the storerooms where the collections were crammed, occupied one room about thirty feet long and fifteen feet wide—what is now the west room on the lower floor of the edifice. In this place, already packed, I had assigned to me a small pine table with a rusty tin pan upon it. . . .

When I sat me down before my tin pan, Agassiz brought me a small fish, placing it before me with the rather stern requirement that I should study it, but should on no account talk to any one concerning it, nor read anything relating to fishes, until I had his permission so to do. To my inquiry, "What shall I do?" he said in effect: "Find out what you can without damaging the specimen; when I think that you have done the work I will question you." In the course of an hour I thought I had compassed that fish; it was rather an unsavory object, giving forth the stench of old alcohol, then loathsome to me, though in time I came to like it. Many of the scales were loosened so that they fell off. It appeared to me to be a case for a summary report, which I was anxious to make and get on to the next state of the business. But Agassiz, though always within call, concerned himself no further with me that day, nor the next, nor for a week. At first, this neglect was distressing; but I saw that it was a game, for he was, as I discerned rather than saw, covertly watching me. So I set my wits to work upon the thing, and in the course of a hundred hours or so thought I had done much—a hundred times as much as seemed possible at the start. I got interested in finding out how the scales went in series, their shape, the form and placement of the teeth, etc. Finally, I felt full of the subject, and probably expressed it in my bearing; as for words about it then, there were none from my master except his cheery "Good morning." At length, on the seventh day, came the question, "Well?" and my disgorge of learning to him as he sat on the edge of my table,

READING

Louis Agassiz as a Teacher

LANE COOPER

Reprinted by permission of the present publisher, Cornell University Press, from Lane Cooper, ed. *Louis Agassiz as a Teacher* (Comstock Publishing Co., 1945).

puffing his cigar. At the end of the hour's telling, he swung off and away, saying: "That is not right." Here I began to think that, after all, perhaps the rules for scanning Latin verse were not the worst infliction in the world. Moreover, it was clear that he was playing a game with me to find if I were capable of doing hard, continuous work without the support of a teacher, and this stimulated me to labor. I went at the task anew, discarded my first notes, and in another week of ten-hours-a-day labor I had results which astonished myself and satisfied him. Still there was no trace of praise in words or manner. He signified that it would do by placing before me about a half a peck of bones, telling me to see what I could make of them, with no further directions to guide me. I soon found that they were the skeletons of half a dozen fishes of different species; the jaws told me so much at a first inspection. The task evidently was to fit the separate bones together in their proper order. Two months or more went to this task with no other help than an occasional looking over my grouping with the stereotyped remark: "That is not right." Finally, the task was done, and I was again set upon alcoholic specimens—this time a remarkable lot of specimens representing, perhaps, twenty species of the side-swimmers or Pleuronectidae.

I shall never forget the sense of power in dealing with things which I felt in beginning the more extended work on a group of animals. I had learned the art of comparing objects, which is the basis of the naturalist's work. At this stage I was allowed to read, and to discuss my work with others about me. I did both eagerly, and acquired a considerable knowledge of the literature of ichthyology, becoming especially interested in the system of classification, then most imperfect. I tried to follow Agassiz's scheme of division in the order of ctenoids and ganoids, with the result that I found one of my species of side-swimmers had cycloid scales on one side and ctenoid on the other. This not only shocked my sense of the value of classification in a way that permitted of no full recovery of my original respect for the process, but for a time shook my confidence in my master's knowledge. At the same time I had a malicious pleasure in exhibiting my "find" to him, expecting to repay in part the humiliation which he had evidently tried to inflict on my conceit. To my question as to how the nondescript should be classified he said: "My boy, there are now two of us who know that."

This incident of the fish made an end of my novitiate. After that, with a suddenness of transition which puzzled me, Agassiz became very communicative; we passed indeed into the relation of friends of like age and purpose, and he actually consulted me as to what I should like to take up as a field of study. Finding that I wished to devote myself to geology, he set me to work on the Brachiopoda as the best group of fossils to serve as data in determining the Palaeozoic horizons. So far as his rather limited knowledge of the matter went, he guided me in the field about Cambridge, in my reading, and to acquaintances of his who were concerned with earth structures. I came thus to know Charles T. Jackson, Jules Marcou, and, later, the brothers Rogers, Henry and James. At the same time I kept up the study of zoology, undertaking to make myself acquainted with living organic forms as a basis for knowledge of fossils.

Professor Scudder's Recollections

It was more than fifteen years ago [from 1874] that I entered the laboratory of Professor Agassiz, and told him I had enrolled my name in the Scientific School as a student of natural history. He asked me a few questions about my object in coming, my antecedents generally, the mode in which I afterwards proposed to use the knowledge I might acquire, and, finally, whether I wished to study any special branch. To the latter I replied that, while I wished to be well grounded in all departments of zoology, I purposed to devote myself specially to insects.

"When do you wish to begin?" he asked.

"Now," I replied.

This seemed to please him, and with an energetic "Very well!" he reached from a shelf a huge jar of specimen in yellow alcohol.

"Take this fish," said he, "and look at it; we call it a haemulon; by and by I will ask what you have seen."

With that he left me, but in a moment returned with explicit instructions as to the care of the object entrusted to me.

"No man is fit to be a naturalist," said he, "who does not know how to take care of specimens."

I was to keep the fish before me in a tin tray, and occasionally moisten the surface with alcohol from the jar, always taking care to replace the stopper tightly. Those were not the days of ground-glass stoppers and elegantly shaped exhibition jars; all the old students will recall the huge neckless glass bottles with their leaky, wax-besmeared corks, half eaten by insects, and begrimed with cellar dust. Entomology was a cleaner science than ichthyology, but the example of the Professor, who had unhesitatingly plunged to the bottom of the jar to produce the fish, was infectious; and though this alcohol had "a very ancient and fishlike smell" I really dared not show any aversion within these sacred precincts, and treated the alcohol as though it were pure water. Still I was conscious of a passing feeling of disappointment, for gazing at a fish did not commend itself to an ardent entomologist. My friends at home, too, were annoyed, when they discovered that no amount of eau-de-Cologne would drown the perfume which haunted me like a shadow.

In ten minutes I had seen all that could be seen in that fish, and started in search of the Professor—who had, however, left the Museum; and when I returned, after lingering over some of the odd animals stored in the upper apartment, my specimen was dry all over. I dashed the fluid over the fish as if to resuscitate the beast from a fainting-fit, and looked with anxiety for a return of the normal sloppy appearance. This little excitement over, nothing was to be done but to return to a steadfast gaze at my mute companion. Half an hour passed—an hour—another hour; the fish began to look loathsome. I turned it over and around; looked it in the face—ghastly; from behind, beneath, above, sideways, at a three-quarters' view—just as ghastly. I was in despair; at an early hour I concluded that lunch was necessary; so, with infinite relief, the fish was carefully replaced in the jar, and for an hour I was free.

On my return, I learned that Professor Agassiz had been at the Museum, but had gone, and would not return for several hours. My fellow-students were too busy to be disturbed by continued conversation. Slowly I drew forth that hideous fish, and with a feeling of desperation again looked at it. I might not use a magnifying-glass; instruments of all kinds were interdicted. My two hands, my two eyes, and the fish: it seemed a most limited field. I pushed my finger down its throat to feel how sharp the teeth were. I began to count the scales in the different rows, until I was convinced that that was nonsense. At last a happy thought struck me—I would draw the fish; and now with surprise I began to discover new features in the creature. Just then the Professor returned.

"That is right," said he; "a pencil is one of the best of eyes. I am glad to notice, too, that you keep your specimen wet, and your bottle corked."

With these encouraging words, he added:

"Well, what is it like?"

He listened attentively to my brief rehearsal of the structure of parts whose names were still unknown to me: the fringed gill-arches and movable operculum; the pores of the head, fleshy lips and lidless eyes; the lateral line, the spinous fins and forked tail, the compressed and arched body. When I had finished, he waited as if expecting more, and then, with an air of disappointment:

"You have not looked very carefully; why," he continued more earnestly, "you haven't even seen one of the most conspicuous features of the animal, which is as plainly before your eyes as the fish itself; look again, look again!" and he left me to my misery.

I was piqued; I was mortified. Still more of that wretched fish! But now I set myself to my task with a will, and discovered one new thing after another, until I saw how just the Professor's criticism had been. The afternoon passed quickly; and when, toward its close, the Professor inquired:

"Do you see it yet?"

"No," I replied, "I am certain I do not, but I see how little I saw before."

"That is next best," said he, earnestly, "but I won't hear you now; put away your fish and go home; perhaps you will be ready with a better answer in the morning. I will examine you before you look at the fish."

This was disconcerting. Not only must I think of my fish all night, studying, without the object before me, what this unknown but most visible feature might be; but also, without reviewing my new discoveries, I must give an exact account of them the next day. I had a bad memory; so I walked home by Charles River in a distracted state, with my two perplexities.

The cordial greeting from the Professor the next morning was reassuring; here was a man who seemed to be quite as anxious as I that I should see for myself what he saw.

"Do you perhaps mean," I asked, "that the fish has symmetrical sides with paired organs?"

His thoroughly pleased "Of course! Of course!" repaid the wakeful hours of the previous night. After he had discoursed most happily and enthusiastically—as he always did—upon the importance of this point, I ventured to ask what I should do next.

"Oh, look at your fish!" he said, and left me again to my own devices. In a little more than an hour he returned, and heard my new catalogue.

"That is good, that is good!" he repeated, "but that is not all, go on"; and so for three long days he placed that fish before my eyes, forbidding me to look at anything else, or to use any artificial aid. "Look, look, look," was his repeated injunction.

This was the best entomological lesson I ever had—a lesson whose influence has extended to the details of every subsequent study; a legacy the Professor has left to me, as he has left it to many others, of inestimable value, which we could not buy, with which we cannot part.

A year afterward, some of us were amusing ourselves with chalking outlandish beasts on the Museum blackboard. We drew prancing starfishes; frogs in mortal combat; hydra-headed worms; stately crawfishes, standing on their tails, bearing aloft umbrellas; and grotesque fishes with gaping mouths and staring eyes. The Professor came in shortly after, and was as amused as any at our experiments. He looked at the fishes.

"Haemulons, every one of them," he said; "Mr. — drew them."

True; and to this day, if I attempt a fish, I can draw nothing but haemulons.

The fourth day, a second fish of the same group was placed beside the first, and I was bidden to point out the resemblances and differences between the two; another and another followed, until the entire family lay before me, and a whole legion of jars covered the table and surrounding shelves; the odor had become a pleasant perfume; and even now, the sight of an old, six-inch, worm-eaten cork brings fragrant memories.

The whole group of haemulons was thus brought in review; and, whether engaged upon the dissection of the internal organs, the preparation and examination of the bony framework, or the description of the various parts, Agassiz's training in the method of observing facts and their orderly arrangement was ever accompanied by the urgent exhortation not to be content with them.

"Facts are stupid things," he would say, "until brought into connection with some general law."

At the end of eight months, it was almost with reluctance that I left these friends and turned to insects; but what I had gained by this outside experience has been of greater value than years of later investigation in my favorite groups.

As the sun's rays pass through a prism and diffuse into a radiance of separate colors, so too the teaching profession generates teachers with varying views. Here are three hues from that spectrum. From Dr. Haim G. Ginott, noted child psychologist, comes this view:

> I have come to a frightening conclusion. I am the decisive element in the classroom. It is my personal approach that creates the climate. It is my daily mood that makes the weather. As a teacher I possess tremendous power to make a child's life miserable or joyous. I can be a tool of humor, hurt or heal. In all situations it is my response that decides whether a crisis will be escalated or de-escalated, and a child humanized or de-humanized.
>
> Many teaching problems will be solved in the next decade. There will be new learning environments and new means of instruction. One function, however, will always remain with the teacher: to create the emotional climate for learning. No machine, sophisticated as it may be, can do this job.[1]

From Sophie Freud, granddaughter of Sigmund Freud and professor of Social Work at Simmons College, comes another view:

> Teachers are in an exposed position, scrutinized and judged daily by hundreds of students. There are days when I grow weary of performing, entertaining, and filling up others' emptiness. There are days when I tire of offering stimulation, encouragement, and comfort, and of being the target of my students' unresolved parental loves and hates. But curiously, as the years go by, those days grow fewer, perhaps because along with being more open, I have also become more detached. I used to get angry at students who did not meet my standards, and positively disliked and scorned them. With greater wisdom I have become less narcissistically engaged, both in my praise and criticism. I had to relearn the same lesson that motherhood taught me. Students, like children, must learn and achieve for themselves, not for their teachers. I must take care that my love and concern for my students, like motherly love and concern, does not become a prison. Sarton (1961) made this dilemma the subject of one of her early novels; it is one familiar to women teachers. The teacher role im-

READING

Teaching and Teachers: Three Views

HAIM G. GINOTT

SOPHIE FREUD

NEIL POSTMAN

1. Haim G. Ginnott, *Teacher and Child* (New York: Macmillan Co., 1972). Reprinted by permission.

plies distance, authority, evaluation, and objectivity, as well as warmth and nurturance.[2]

From Neil Postman, author and professor of English education at New York University, comes still another view:

> In spite of our attempts to make teaching into a science, in spite of our attempts to invent teacher-proof materials, and even in spite of our attempt to create 'relevant new curricula,' one simple fact makes all of this ambition quite unnecessary. It is as follows: when a student perceives a teacher to be an authentic, warm and curious person, the student learns. When the student does not perceive the teacher as such a person the student does not learn. There is almost no way to get around this fact, although technological people such as ourselves try very hard to.

We believe in experts and expertise, and we tend not to trust any activity that does not involve a complex technique. And yet, increasing the complexity of the act of teaching has not really made much difference, for there is always that simple fact that teaching is the art of being human and of communicating that humanness to others. Why is this so difficult for us to accept? Why do we trust our machines, our equations and our formulas more than we trust our humanity? Why do we think that a curriculum can do something that a person cannot? Our failure to place affection and empathy at the center of the education process says something very grave about us, and I do not think it will be of much value for us to persevere unless we can learn to love our technology less and ourselves more.[3]

2. Sophie Freud, "The Passion and Challenge of Teaching" in *Harvard Educational Review* 50, no. 1 (1980):10. Copyright © by the President and Fellows of Harvard College.

3. Excerpted from an article that first appeared in *Sensorsheet*, a publication of the Earth Science Educational Program in Boulder, Colorado, and later appeared in *Media Ecology Review*, published at the NYU School of Education. Reprinted by permission of the *Wall Street Journal* © Dow Jones and Company, Inc., 1972. All rights reserved.

PART II

**Seminar Program for
Liberal Arts Instructors:
Cases and Readings**

Section 1. Early Class Sessions: Establishing the Instructor-Student Learning Contract; Gaining Students' Respect; Adapting to a New Environment; Cultivating Rapport

Professor Benjamin Cheever stared disbelievingly at the Marine colonel whose public challenge had just interrupted a teaching workshop Ben was leading for the faculty of a military institute. Nothing in his twenty years of teaching—eight using the case method—had prepared Ben for a remark like this. He scanned the group for reactions as the colonel's words echoed in his ears: "...I am offended. Don't you think an apology is in order?"

Background

It was Friday morning. Ben Cheever, an economist and senior faculty member of Fairchild Graduate School of Organization and Management, had sensed from the outset of this case discussion that there would be difficulties getting the workshop moving in the right direction. Along with two colleagues, Ben had traveled from New England to Washington, D.C., to demonstrate case method teaching in a two-day workshop for the faculty of the Senior Commanding Officers' Executive Institute. Ben had come with only moderate expectations, but his instincts told him that this was, in fact, shaping up as a particularly lackluster discussion. The group, which included, in his recollection, "about 85% colonels and lieutenant colonels and some majors, as well as civilian faculty members of equivalent civil service rank," seemed wary, tentative, and unsure of how to proceed. This was particularly disheartening to Ben because his case—the first of the workshop—had been preceded by a rather long and thorough introduction, beginning with a friendly welcome from the commanding general of the institute, an old friend of Ben's.

According to Ben, the general had given the faculty "a warm and humorous speech in which he mentioned my military experience and the fact that he had once worked for me. He told them that he considered case method teaching something they ought to know a bit about and that we were the best." This introduction seemed auspicious to Ben, and it was followed by "about 30 minutes of detailed description of the case method by a colleague of mine who not only knows the method extremely well but also has a military background. He gave the group an encouraging overview, and used many military metaphors and references."

Nonetheless, Ben knew his efforts to make this workshop succeed had two strikes against them. First, the faculty at the institute was unlikely to

The Offended Colonel (A)

Dr. Abby J. Hansen, research associate, wrote this case for the Developing Discussion Leadership Skills and Teaching by the Case Method seminars. Data were furnished by the involved participants. All names and some peripheral facts have been disguised.

include many dedicated teachers. Most of the staff were military officers who had attended the institute's programs, as Ben put it, "to get their tickets punched," and fulfill a requirement for promotion. Having done well in the programs, these participants had received invitations to remain and teach for a few years. Second, the teaching staff usually had Fridays free, but today many instructors in the large, half-filled auditorium had been volunteered by their supervisors to attend this workshop.

Inwardly, Ben acknowledged that in some sense he, too, had come mainly to "get his ticket punched." His major reason for traveling to the institute had been to test some cases he had just written under a government contract which stipulated that the new materials be taught in a variety of official environments. Nevertheless, he hoped to find in this group at least some potential enthusiasm for exploring the possibilities of the case method. Ben truly enjoyed teaching and welcomed the challenge to make this workshop a success under these less-than-promised circumstances.

As usual, Ben had adopted a breezy, informal approach during the session. In contrast to the military audience—some in uniform, others in rather conservative civilian clothing—he wore no tie. Ben also joked often, hoping to create a relaxed atmosphere in which lively participation could arise spontaneously. He had asked the institute's faculty to prepare for the class and then join him, first for a regular class discussion, and then to analyze their own performance, his teaching techniques, and the case itself, considered as a teaching vehicle.

The case dealt with a civilian appointee heading a government agency responsible for military research. Faced with information leaks and unresponsiveness in the agency, the case protagonist, Claude La Fleur, resorts to declaring a moratorium on all research. After sketching the situation and briefly reviewing a few details of setting, Ben addressed a general question to the group: "Well, what's bothering Claude La Fleur? Can someone start us off?" The members of the faculty looked around, each seeming curious to see who would volunteer, but not personally interested in doing so. Once the dis-

cussion did get started, the speakers in this group avoided disagreement with their colleagues, much to Ben's annoyance—thus causing an early consensus that Ben feared would close off many possible areas of analysis. Worse, however, was Ben's discomfort at realizing that the ascendant point of view happened to be one he considered off the mark. He began to feel the necessity of getting the group to produce some opposition to this stifling premature conclusion. To accomplish this, he chose to play devil's advocate. In the character of a hostile opponent, Ben responded to one participant's formulation of the majority view with a good-natured "Bullshit!"

The ploy succeeded because, after a laugh, a few proponents of minority views did then raise their hands to speak, but Ben felt it was still hard work to keep the discussion open. By 11:45 he was, like the rest of the participants, looking forward to lunch. The group had moved from the case discussion to the analysis of the morning's proceedings.

All participants had remained seated to speak, but when Ben called on one uniformed Marine Corps colonel at the very back of the room, the man leaned forward and stood up, glaring.

"Dr. Cheever," he said in a strained voice, "I'm wondering about something. Do you always use profanity when you teach? Or is it that you just feel you have to talk down to us servicemen?"

Ben felt everyone's gaze. As an Army veteran and former civilian employee at the Pentagon, as well as the son of a career military officer, he was taken aback by the colonel's statement. His surprise was clearly evident on his face.

"Why no," he said quickly, "I'm not talking down to anybody. This is the way I usually conduct my classes."

"Well, I just want you to know, Dr. Cheever, that I am offended. Besides"—the colonel gestured to the only woman, seated a few rows ahead of him—"there are ladies present. Don't you think an apology is in order, Professor?"

Ben looked at the woman, at the rest of the group, and back at the colonel. The room was silent. Ben wondered, "How do I respond to that?"

When a malfunctioning heating system sent the classroom temperature up near 90°, Ellen Collins, a first-year assistant professor of Finance at Fleming Graduate School of Business and Public Management in Toronto, encountered an unexpected interruption. Although she always made it a rule to wear a jacket while teaching, the heat had become so stifling that she unobtrusively shed her blazer and draped it over a chair before turning back to the chalkboard. No sooner was Ellen's back turned than, from the rear of the large amphitheater-shaped classroom where sixty students sat, there came a long, loud wolf-whistle.

* * *

The Instructor

Before accepting her tenure track post with the Finance teaching staff at Fleming, Ellen, a recent Ph.D. in Economics from the University of Chicago, had already done two years of postdoctoral research in International Banking at the school. She was married, thirty years old, 5'4" tall, and slim, with collar-length brown hair, blue eyes, and a soft speaking voice. "Many of my male colleagues try to be tough," Ellen told the researcher, "and a few are really rough. But I don't admire that style and it wouldn't work for me anyway. I'm not tall; I can't physically dominate a large room; and nobody has ever called my voice 'booming.' I would never 'wipe the floor' with students, as they call it here—grill them so they look stupid in public—but there are teachers who do it regularly."

The School

Fleming Graduate School of Business and Public Management in Toronto enjoyed an admirable reputation for producing successful leaders who assumed influential positions all over the world. Advancement in this faculty was highly prized, as was its well-known master's degree, awarded after a two-year program to 430 students each year—about 25% of them women. The faculty ratio was similar.

At Fleming, the 500 first-year students were divided into units of 80 to 100 students called "learning groups" (LGs). Each LG met daily at 8:30 A.M. in a particular classroom permanently assigned to its use, and took three hour-and-a-half-long case discussion classes in a row with just one break for lunch. The first-year curriculum included nine

CASE

The Day the Heat Went On (A)

*Research Associate **Dr. Abby Hansen** wrote this case for the Developing Discussion Leadership Skills and the Teaching by the Case Method seminars. Data were furnished by the involved participants. All names and some peripheral facts have been disguised.*

different courses, most of them taught by the case method. Class participation usually counted heavily in course grades. Teachers "floated" from classroom to classroom to lead discussions with the LGs. Spending so much time together, and facing the pressure of the heavy workload, the LGs usually developed strong internal bonds. Most instructors described the LGs as self-protective.

The Situation

In her first year at Fleming, Ellen taught Finance to two LGs—III and VI. LG III had another woman teacher, but aside from Ellen, LG VI had only male instructors. These, according to her, constituted a mixed bag of personality types whose net effect was to create tension in the members of the group. Ellen mentioned various teachers whom LG VI thought "distant but cooperative"; some they thought "too strict" or "too lax"; one they thought "brilliant"; and one they thought "a tyrant." The "tyrant," Charlie Brennan, was their instructor in Organizational Psychology (OP). A notable practitioner of the tough style of teaching, Charlie started class on the dot of the hour, held students' presentations to a prescribed number of minutes, and had once made a lasting impression on the women of LG VI by calling a special meeting for them during which he said that because the professional world of bureaucracy had high standards for female decorum, he, too, would tolerate "no messy purses, no ungainly leg-crossing, no sloppy attire" in his class. According to Ellen, several women in the group described this meeting to her and mentioned how insulted Charlie's message had made them feel.

To make matters worse for Ellen, she usually taught LG VI immediately after Charlie's OP class with them. On these occasions Ellen found the group "so wound up that I had to do something to get them to relax before they could get their minds on the Finance class." To this end, Ellen made it a ritual to give them a few opening minutes for nervous joking. When one fellow began to use these openings for mildly flirtatious humor directed at Ellen, she tried to deflect it with good-humored shrugs. Once he opened the prediscussion joke session by saying, "Now, Ellen, smile if you have a secret crush on me!" Ellen was taken aback, but when she heard the LG laughing she good-naturedly smiled, too. "Aha! I knew it!", the student crowed, but he was laughing and Ellen read the incident as harmless and proceeded with the Fi-

nance discussion. Nonetheless, she considered his sexual undertones inappropriate and was very relieved when the jokes did not escalate any further in the direction of bad taste.

Although Ellen's relations with LG VI were generally satisfactory, she recalled having noticed right away that "the women in the group seemed demoralized. All the student association officers in this LG were male, and the women behaved particularly quietly in class, more so than in my other group, LG III. When one of the women spoke, the males tended to look bored or fidgety, as if Finance was so complex a subject that no female could possibly have anything worthwhile to say about it. I think Charlie Brennan was responsible for this intimidating atmosphere."

Ellen mentioned a further obstacle to her success with LG VI: a peculiarity of the scheduling at Fleming decreed that Finance should start in the spring semester—much later than most other courses—so that the students could accumulate technical background in economics and accounting and learn how to study by the case method before tackling its complexities. For Ellen, however, the late start also meant that she "inherited a section that had already set its social norms in the complete absence of women instructors." Nonetheless, Ellen hoped that LG VI would accept her simply as someone who could lead them through discussions of the Finance cases.

When she agreed to teach at Fleming, Ellen knew that its institutional culture could be very rough on women. Although women were significantly represented in the union faculty, only five women were tenured out of a senior faculty of 100 members. No one found Charlie Brennan's condescending attitude toward his female students particularly unusual. The master's-degree students at the school had a reputation for playing pranks, and those they sprang on women teachers often had sexual overtones. For example, when one woman teacher discovered that some fellows in her LG had hired a belly dancer to interrupt her class, she managed to intercept the woman and bar her from the classroom. But this lack of taste was quite common in all sorts of joking at Fleming.

Ellen mentioned to the researcher that, after her course with LG VI was over and she spoke less formally to some of the women of the group, they mentioned having been deeply offended by many things in their first year at Fleming—not only Char-

Section 1. Early Class Sessions: Establishing the Instructor-Student Learning Contract; Gaining Students' Respect; Adapting to a New Environment; Cultivating Rapport

CASE
The Day the Heat Went On (A)

lie Brennan's speech, but the general level of obscenity in the LG's humor and the tacit assumption of so many male students that women students couldn't possibly say anything useful about public administration. Ellen also mentioned that LG VI had included "three extraordinarily bright women—but oddly enough these three seemed to be having just as hard a time, for different reasons, as the less-gifted, more intimidated ones." Ellen described these three as "outstanding and outspoken," but she noticed that when any one of them began to speak, the rest of the group, male and female alike, put on expressions of bored tolerance, and "sarcastic chuckles" could be heard in the room as if to say "there goes old Sue, being so damned brilliant again—ho hum." Ellen felt "sorry to see these three—all of whom later won high honors, by the way—being almost systematically ostracized by their peers. All in all, I think their experience here was pretty negative, despite the honors. That just underlines the fact that women—all women—have a very tough time at Fleming."

Given this strained atmosphere and her late entry into the academic program of LG VI, Ellen worked hard to prepare herself to make a good impression on the group. "It sounds trivial," she smiled, "but women must worry about wardrobe in these public situations. If you look too frilly, you come across as an *airhead*; but if you look too severe, you're a *schoolmarm*. There's another aspect to dress here, too. Most of the male teachers begin class by removing their jackets and rolling up their shirtsleeves. Women can't do that because shedding an article of clothing in front of sixty students in an amphitheater might seem perilously close to some sort of striptease. I can't imagine any image less likely to bolster authority!"

*   *   *

The day the heat went on was a day in early April of her first year teaching at Fleming, during the third week of the Finance course. Ellen had worn a typically conservative outfit: dark skirt, high-necked white blouse, woolen tweed blazer. Unfortunately, by afternoon, the weather had turned unexpectedly warm. At 1:00 P.M. when she entered their classroom, Ellen noticed her LG VI students were all casually dressed; several were in running shorts. It was instantly apparent to Ellen that somehow the heat in their classroom had been turned on by mistake. Ellen got about fifteeen minutes into the discussion before beginning to feel extremely uncomfortable. She was putting a student's key points on the board when "the temperature felt as if it had gotten up near 90°. The students were all slumping. I was trying to listen to the speaker, but I, too, was beginning to succumb to the incredibly cloying atmosphere. That room was always stuffy. Now it was dizzyingly hot." As the student continued, Ellen stepped back from the board, shrugged out of her blazer as unobtrusively as possible, and turned to drape it over the chair that stood behind the instructor's desk near the blackboard. Then she turned to walk back to the board. As soon as her back was turned, the wolf-whistle rang out from the top row, where, Ellen knew, "a bunch of drinking buddies sat together." For a split second, anger crashed over Ellen. What nerve! How childish! What an insult! She clutched the chalk tightly and wondered what response to make.

CASE

One Teacher's Nightmare (A)

Jeff Freeman, a Columbia Ph.D. in Modern European History, had taught for six years as a graduate student before coming to Southwestern University on tenure track. He considered himself tough but fair in the classroom and was moderately alarmed to learn that his first course, "European Constitutional History"—a required unit in the undergraduate liberal arts program—had a reputation for furnishing an easy B. The other six instructors in the course were an easygoing lot, and all had the authority to set policies independently. Jeff decided to steer his own course and be rigorous. To his pleasant surprise, his students seemed to react well to his teaching policies. They came prepared for the discussions he always held after his standard half-hour lectures.

But not Bob Crane. He attended only sporadically, never spoke in class, wrote a farce of a research paper, and neglected even to show up for the required class debate, which most students considered the high point of the course. When Bob's final exam proved no better than the rest of his work, Jeff had little trouble giving him a D.

A week later, in mid-November, Bob stormed into Jeff's office—his first appearance since the beginning of the semester, despite Jeff's frequent requests that they meet for a progress review.

"You can't do this to me, Mr. Freeman," Bob exploded. "I *deserve* a better grade than this."

"I don't see why," Jeff said. "You consistently fell at the bottom of the grading curve. I could have flunked you outright, but I thought you deserved some credit for at least submitting some written work." He proceeded to outline in detail Bob's many errors and failings in the course.

Bob changed tack. "Look, Mr. Freeman," he said. "You're making a mistake here. I absolutely have to have a C."

There seemed to be some threat behind this; Bob's dictatorial tone made Jeff furious. "Then you should have worked harder," he said coldly. "Now please stop wasting your time and mine. I think you should leave right now."

Bob left. A half hour later Jeff's telephone rang. "This is Matt Crane. Bob's my kid brother," said a loud voice. "We're not going to stand for this crap. What the hell kind of credentials do you have, to teach at a place like this anyway? We're going straight to the dean and get you fired!"

Jeff hung up, shaking with fury. Then the phone rang again. "That was immature, I know," Matt's

Dr. Abby J. Hansen, research associate, wrote this case for the Developing Discussion Leadership Skills and the Teaching by the Case Method seminars. Data were furnished by the involved participants. All names and some peripheral facts have been disguised.

Section 1. Early Class Sessions: Establishing the Instructor-Student Learning Contract; Gaining Students' Respect; Adapting to a New Environment; Cultivating Rapport

CASE
One Teacher's Nightmare (A)

voice said. "I apologize. But it's like this: we're both on the football team, see? Bob's our star quarterback, and there are only two games left in the season. He's already on academic probation. If you don't give him a C, he'll be tossed off the team and out of our fraternity. This is really important!" Jeff was incensed. Football. Important? He had thought the issue was Constitutional History! "Your brother earned his D," he said. "Frankly, I doubt he even did the reading for the course. I don't see any reason to change the grade."

Matt's voice turned suddenly suave: "Well, look, Mr. Freeman. If he didn't do anything in your course, why can't you just give him a No Credit? That wouldn't pull down his average, and he could stay on the team. You don't know what that would mean to all of us. Can't you have a little compassion?"

Jeff hesitated. He was beginning to wonder how violently his standards clashed with the culture to which he had so recently come. He recalled an early academic meeting where a trustee had said, "We want a university our football team can be proud of!" Jeff had thought the statement funny at the time, but now he was inclined to wonder how important football really was at Southwestern.

It had not escaped Jeff's analytical mind that many Southwestern alumni who gave gigantic donations to the school based their allegiance on loyalty, not to the history department, but to the football team. Football was an obsession to many members of the Southwestern community. Was it possible, he wondered, that he had severely misjudged the whole value structure of the school? Had he placed expectations on Bob Crane that the situation did not, in fact, justify? In short, was there some sort of merit in Matt's argument?

Jeff clenched the receiver in his hand, muttered, "I'll see. Goodbye," and hung up. Then he sat alone in his office and stewed about this confrontation. What, he wondered, should he do? Submit to emotional extortion, or give the bastard the D he so richly deserved?

READING

Bike Riding and the Art of Learning

ROBERT G. KRAFT

From *Change* 10, no. 6 (1978). Reprinted with permission
of the Helen Dwight Reid Educational Foundation, 4000
Albermarle St., N.W., Washington, D.C. 20016
Owner of Copyright © 1978 Reid Foundation.

"If you reach 10 percent of your students, you're a good teacher." In 13 years as a college English teacher, I've heard that too often. Can you imagine your mechanic saying, "If I fix 10 percent of the cars in my shop, I'm a good mechanic"? Or your doctor: "If I heal 10 percent of my patients, I'm a good doctor"? That's a 90 percent kill rate.

For many of my teaching years, I had a 90 percent kill rate. I'd been talking my students to death. It was 1971 when it hit me. I was lecturing to my American literature class about Henry James. After class a student came to me and said, "Something you said I didn't get down right. Would you repeat it for me please? I'm student teaching in the fall and I want to give this stuff to my high school Lit class." I was stunned. This young man wanted to present my words and ideas to his students. He felt no need to stir my lecture into his own understanding. He felt no need to consider what high schoolers would respond to. He would just lecture them my lecture. Where had he gotten such ideas?

Obviously, from me. From all his teachers.

That student confirmed my suspicions about myself and most of my university teachers. We are teaching badly. Horribly, in fact. For me that day in 1971 started an anxious search. There had to be a better way. Since then I've come to some firm answers about these old questions. What is learning? When and how do people learn?

When and how did I learn? I sometimes ride a bike to school. When I think back to how I learned to ride, I remember a heavy green-and-white girl's bike from Sears. I was seven, the youngest in my family, and too small to reach the pedals on my brother's bike. My dad's store, with candy, cookies, and all that, was three blocks away. I went there several times a day, and I was tired of walking. Besides, smaller kids than I could ride two-wheelers.

I straddled the bike and came down hard on the top pedal. I tipped over. I got back on and tipped again. The bike pinned me under and I scraped a thigh on the sidewalk. But I had to learn, so I kept at it. In a week I could ride pretty well. Today I can also read, write, ski, and even fix the clothes dryer in my home. I learned them all the same way.

There is something so simple, so universal in this learning pattern. I needed to know or do something, so I went after it. It was hard and hurt sometimes, but it worked. But when I think about what

Section 1. Early Class Sessions: Establishing the Instructor-Student Learning Contract; Gaining Students' Respect; Adapting to a New Environment; Cultivating Rapport

READING
Bike Riding and the Art of Learning KRAFT

I learned in classrooms, that bike-riding pattern seldom happened. Often I sat passive, waiting for class to be over. Sometimes I got interested in something and read up on it. Twice I read an abridged *Moby Dick*. I did well on tests and everyone thought I was a good student. I remember some of the things I read in school too. Did you know King James I of England, remembered for the King James Bible, was fascinated by witches and liked to hunt them down? I don't know why I remember that. But mostly I learned how to succeed in school. This is a familiar story. A string of books have come out in the last two decades about our time-killing, dreary schools. But these told me little about college teaching. I had to provide the conditions for learning that made it possible for me to learn to ride a bike.

I started the search with a book of collected essays by reputedly great teachers. I don't remember the title now because the book made little impression on me. These were people students admired, and they came across as warm, witty, and altogether likable. Most were pleased and surprised at having been chosen. But baffled. They had no helpful advice to offer me except—this is one line I remember—"Wear a different tie to school each day."

I had a memorable teacher at the University of Minnesota in 1962. Her name was Emeline. She taught Victorian literature. She had a glass eye that fixed on your hairline when she talked to you. Emeline liked my paper on Robert Browning's play *A Blot on the Escutcheon,* and I loved her for liking it. The class smiled and applauded after her brilliant closing lecture. I was awash in admiration.

If I were to ask Emeline today what her teaching secrets are, she too would be baffled. She might say, "Prepare, be yourself, and be civil." As her student, I had a different view; she liked my paper and I liked her. But that was different from good teaching. My infatuation, her glass eye, even her bright and witty lectures were like my brown, leathery school bag. Nice, but only what's inside matters. How much Browning, Tennyson, and Arthur Hugh Clough (rhymes with "rough," I recall) are part of me today? What is still part of me measures Emeline's effectiveness, and only that.

Emeline, I'm sure, thought little about what her Victorian gentlemen would be to me 15 years later. She knew what these gentlemen had to say and what it meant. There was nothing in her literary Ph.D. studies that told her what would make Dante Gabriel Rossetti live in the hearts of her students. There was certainly nothing in mine. She learned teaching from watching her teachers. And their advice was, "Wear a different tie each day." I was back where I started.

But I pushed the question. How much Victorian literature do I recall? It seemed a fair test. I hadn't taught or read Victorian literature since Emeline's class. My specialty was modern American fiction, and I was barely able to keep up with that. So I asked, "Kraft, what do you know about Victorian literature?"

First, I remember everyone's names. (Roll this name off your tongue: Algernon Charles Swinburne.) I remember some Browning poems because I liked them. "Soliloquy in a Spanish Cloister" I can even recite. It's about monks, you see, and I went to a college that was part of a monastery. I knew about monks. Once I was even going to be one.

But most of all I remember that Browning play I wrote about; it was the paper Emeline liked so well. That play was full of phony love conflict and, above all, grand speeches. I said it was a bad play and Emeline agreed.

That paper set me thinking about other papers I wrote. I remembered one about Edgar Allen Poe's poem "Eureka," which describes how the universe came to be. It was the big bang theory long before scientists hit on the same idea. My teacher thought that was a fine essay. Another, about an early Hawthorne story, went over so well my teacher thought it should be published. I remembered my weaker papers too, but not so well.

I thought then about my other teachers and whether I liked or disliked them. There were good lecturers among them, but I had to admit I couldn't remember anything they'd said. I only remembered a crack a favorite English teacher once pitched at me when I protested the chaos of the class. He said, "Kraft, is your mind so small you have to keep it neat?" And that's what all those lectures came to. What I have left from all those college classes are the papers I wrote.

I have with me now what I did in school, and little of what I was told. That was a first principle I could use as a teacher. Ah, my carefully prepared lectures, useless.

But I was still in trouble. Papers were what we did outside class. Continue the papers, yes, but what do we do in class if not lecture? Discuss? Okay, but three fourths of my students won't discuss. I hadn't been a great discusser myself. I rarely had the confidence to speak in those formal and frightening classes.

One thing I had learned in my Ph.D. studies was how to research, how to track down answers, even if they were other people's. So when I was asked to teach a course called Teaching College English for graduate students, I decided to make that a forum for my search. Developmental psychologists seemed a splendid source of ideas. Psychology pursued answers objectively, using the scientific method. That appealed to me. I wanted the authority of science behind my conclusions. Carl Rogers, a humanistic psychologist, scotched my notions about objectivity and the scientific method. "Experience," he wrote, "is, for me, the highest authority." For Rogers, tests and measurements—science—that supposedly proved something never measured the important changes in people. He trusted only his "inner, nonintellectual sensing," which told him about his success and failure as a therapist and teacher. That made sense to me. I always knew without tests how my students were doing. Every teacher who watches and listens carefully knows. If I could never prove what good teaching was, my sensing would give me good directions. I would test the conclusions of psychologists against my experience.

Rogers's experience told him what mine told me: "I have come to feel that the only learning which significantly influences behavior is self-discovered, self-appropriated learning. Such learning, . . . assimilated in experience, cannot be directly communicated to another." My experience exactly. Since then I've been asking people these questions: "Think about what you know today. Did you learn it from being told? Or did you learn it from experience?" The answers always amount to, "Well, my dad told me lots of things. But I didn't really learn them until I lived a while and found out Dad was right." My dad and my teachers didn't teach me. They guided me and confirmed (or denied) what I learned from living.

A sabbatical gave me a chance to hunt further. There were lots of others I could look to. I had heard their names all my life. John Dewey, Jean Piaget, Jerome Bruner. If these people confirmed my experience, I would be satisfied.

Though Dewey had gone out of favor, what I read of his always struck me hard. So I went to his original great work, *Democracy and Education*, published in 1916. Dewey spoke confidently, dogmatically in fact, out of his experience. It was a posture I envied. He looked into the same gap I saw between learning and what so often goes on in schools.

"There is a strong temptation," Dewey wrote, "to assume that presenting subject matter in its perfected form provides a royal road to learning. What is more natural than to suppose that the immature can be saved time and energy, and be protected from needless error, by commencing where competent inquirers have left off?" That, to Dewey, was the worst, yet most frequent error. "No matter how true what is learned to those who found it out and in whose experience it functioned, there is nothing which makes it knowledge to the pupils. It might as well be something about Mars."

I needed no more reassurance but began to find it everywhere. Jean Piaget demands that students "undertake authentic work instead of accepting predigested knowledge from outside." Jerome Bruner points to the reasons students go along with their endless lecturers and fake it. "Telling children and then testing them on what they've been told inevitably has the effect of producing bench-bound learners whose motivation for learning is likely to be extrinsic to the task at hand—pleasing the teacher, getting into college, artificially maintaining self-esteem." Most universities continue down Dewey's royal road. That's why my teachers were so little help to me.

Faculty go on doing what they've always done—and blame the students when it fails. Piaget suggests that teachers should do some animal training, "since when that training fails, the trainer is bound to accept that it's his own fault, whereas in education failures are always attributed to the pupil."

Remember the bicycle? Tipping, scraping the thigh? How do we get some of that tipping, scraping, and riding experience into the classroom? Not by just sitting. In the journal *College English*, Vern Wagner of Wayne State University explained why students don't learn to read and write in English classes. "In the classroom no reading and little writing take place . . . we only talk about reading and writing." Carl Rogers put it simply: "Significant learning is acquired through doing."

Yet silence and passivity drift like fog through the classrooms and hallways of colleges. What students learn is to keep their mouths shut and let professors

Section 1. Early Class Sessions: Establishing the Instructor-Student Learning Contract; Gaining Students' Respect; Adapting to a New Environment; Cultivating Rapport

READING
Bike Riding and the Art of Learning KRAFT

do their thing. A couple of my professors dimly understood that. As a graduate student I once asked a favorite professor at the University of Washington when I should take my final exams. "Look," he said, "get out of here as soon as possible. You won't learn anything until you do." Now that I'm the professor, preparing the classes and writing articles, I'm learning almost as fast as I learned to speak English. And that was before I started school.

Dewey understood that too back in 1916. "Only in education, never in the life of farmer, physician, laboratory experimenter, does knowledge mean primarily a store of information aloof from doing." Piaget echoes: "A truth is never truly assimilated except insofar as it has first been reconstituted or rediscovered by some activity," which "may begin with physical motions" but grows to "the most completely interiorized operations." In discovery, Bruner says, the student learns how to learn more quickly and easily in the future, feels the excitement of learning and rushes to the next learning, remembers without memorizing.

But no real discovery and no learning take place unless the student is genuinely absorbed. He must feel a need to do and to know, and it cannot be for what Bruner calls extrinsic reasons, like passing courses, getting grades and degrees, or pleasing someone else. If such are his only purposes, then how to get high grades, degrees, and approval will be all he will permanently learn. A colleague told me of a student who supposedly learned all about punctuation and sentence structure in remedial English class. Next term, in a more advanced class, the student could no longer punctuate or structure sentences. When asked what had happened, he explained, "But I thought that stuff was for the bonehead class."

Piaget calls interest "that decisive factor." No permanent learning happens without it. The learning must touch the student, engage him in his concerns. So how can I get students interested in literature for its own qualities and use? What concern of students can the grammar teacher tap? Carl Rogers focused on this knotty problem for me: "A person learns significantly only those things which he perceives as being involved in the maintenance or enhancement of his own self." Since most of us want to talk and write to people, even grammar maintains and enhances.

Psychologist Abraham Maslow set up a beautiful scheme that explains what we are all after—his "hierarchy of human needs," a list of everything people need to stay alive, prosper, and be happy. Basic needs must be fulfilled before people turn to higher considerations. Here, oversimplified some, is Maslow's hierarchy:

1. Physiological needs: food, clothing, shelter, self-preservation, sex. A continually hungry person will seek to feed himself. Other needs are pushed to the background.
2. Safety needs: Once physically comfortable, a person will try to protect himself from physical harm. Thus government, laws, etc.
3. Love needs: Once fed and safe, a person seeks love and belonging.
4. Esteem needs: Once fed, safe, and loved, a person needs to respect himself and be respected by others.
5. Self-actualization needs: Once the earlier needs are taken care of, a person seeks to know, to understand, to appreciate. And he seeks to realize his potential.

According to Maslow, fulfilling these needs is what interests us. And it takes a lifetime. Schools, especially colleges, deal mostly with self-actualization. But we know hungry children will not learn to read and write. And the unloved and self-hating cannot lose themselves in literature. A college professor brings his subject to students who are at different stages of need. Younger students are feverishly interested in jobs and sex, love and self-esteem. Adults often make better students, because they've had more time to satisfy first needs.

A teacher can't find jobs or lovers for his students. But he can support their job hunting and treat them lovingly. He can respect them. He can treat his subject and arrange his class activity so that many needs are occasionally filled. He can boost self-esteem by starting his students on activities they can perform and then pointing to their successes. He can encourage them to experiment without threat. He can encourage cooperation, which earns them the respect and friendship of peers. No teacher can choose to ignore the range of student motivations that is part of what Piaget calls the laws of mental development. Ignoring the laws dooms a teacher to only partial, sporadic success and much failure. Honoring the laws won't guarantee success. Teaching is like that.

Not all motivation is personal; the group counts

for a great deal, too. There are critics who argue that learning together isn't necessary and that perhaps classes should be done away with. Aside from the impracticality of the suggestion, there are strong reasons for keeping classes. Though we learn much by ourselves, we all like to have other learners around. I did all the reading and writing for this essay alone, but it was stimulating to talk to others about it. I never would have learned to ski if I had gone to the mountain alone.

"The traditional school," says Piaget, "hardly offers scope for more than one type of social relationship: the action of the teacher upon the pupil. . . . The new methods of education, on the other hand, have allotted an essential place to the social life that develops among students. As early as the first experiments of Dewey . . . the students were free to work with one another, to collaborate in intellectual research as much as in the establishing of a moral discipline; this teamwork and self-government have become essential ingredients of active school practice."

As long as the individuals aren't lost in the bunch, bunching learners in classes may be the best part of the traditional school—but only if the groups have a chance to know each other and work together and the teacher can attend to individual needs too.

In the last year, I've been incorporating these principles into my English classes:

• I've cut the lectures. My talk can guide and support. It can awaken and enlighten. It cannot teach. When I talk I try to keep it under twelve minutes and never let it go longer than twenty. Psychologists say people stop listening after that. I don't try to cover everything anymore. When I did I always found I was the only one for whom it was covered. When I have something to say to students that could be especially useful, I write it. In that form they can use it in their activities, much as I have drawn on Dewey, Piaget, and others.

• I arrange for my students to do things, in and out of class. Since I'm an English teacher, I require that they read and write constantly. I don't judge all their writing because if I do they resort to pleasing me rather than trying to discover for themselves.

• I start students working on questions that touch their current interests. I can't motivate by appealing to future needs and concerns. People resist prophets. When my students read *Wuthering Heights*, I ask them why Kathy would fall in love with someone like Heathcliff. This leads them to examining character. The more advanced the students, the more naturally they lead themselves to literary history, mythic criticism, and other sophisticated literary matters. I found such matters fascinating (sometimes) as a graduate student, but not earlier.

• Students like to work together for support and friendship, so I ask small groups to write about questions like the one above and to read and talk to one another about findings and questions. Often they bring those questions to me and seem genuinely interested in my answers. Out of these inquiries they write finished papers, which are graded.

Planning and organizing all this has been demanding. It was easier to lecture, because I love to talk. But students say they like these workshop classes, and now I am convinced their learning will last.

Sylvia Nevins, associate professor of history at Farwestern College of the Liberal Arts, was living in New York for a year to research a new book. She had never taught night school before, but when an offer came from Downtown University Extension School to teach a course called "The American Family, An Historical Overview," she accepted, delighted with the extra income. The course met once a week from 8 to 10 P.M. She dedicated part of the time to students' "family history" reports, part to lectures, and part to discussions in which she encouraged them to participate as much as possible. The material, as indicated in the course description, included issues like sex, birth control, abortion, and other matters central to the family. She had taught the course before and assumed that, like her, the students found these matters worthy of serious intellectual consideration. Sylvia had, however, never taught such a heterogeneous group: young people pursuing B.A. degrees at night while working days, and retirees—some quite elderly— taking courses for intellectual stimulation.

Sylvia tried to strike a note of informality as she began the course. She invited students to participate—even to interrupt her lectures, if they had questions or comments. Then she embarked on her typical pattern: an hour's lecture, then a break, then a class discussion. The first three meetings went well. On the fourth evening, however, Sylvia encountered a surprise. She had spent the first half of the class lecturing on the practical implications of Victorian notions of "true womanhood" and "manliness," using one historian's concept of the "The Politics of Impregnation" as a central theme. She wrote the term on the board, with bibliography, and referred to it throughout her lecture. As the discussion began, one older man, who generally kept silent, raised his hand. "Yes?" Sylvia said, expectantly. "Professor Nevins," he said, in a strained voice. "I really do have to tell you I find that term very offensive!" He was glaring. Sylvia thought: Ouch! What he really means is that he finds *me* offensive for discussing impregnation in class!

Sylvia was shocked and a bit insulted. Given the subject matter of the course, what had he expected: no references to sexuality? Was he objecting to the term *impregnation* or to the fact that she, a woman, referred to sex in public? She wanted to deflect his comment somehow. But how? Ask the whole group if they were offended? Apologize and be done with it? Thank him for his forthrightness?

Sylvia stood there, perplexed.

CASE

A Night School Episode (A)

Dr. Abby Hansen, *research associate, wrote this case from material submitted by **Dr. Elaine Tyler May** for the Developing Discussion Leadership Skills and the Teaching by the Case Method seminars. Data were furnished by the involved participants. All names and some peripheral facts have been disguised.*

Assistant Professor Graham and Ms. Macomber (A)

This case was written by a member of the 1977 Developing Discussion Leadership Skills Seminar under the supervision of **C. Roland Christensen**. While the case is based on data supplied by participants involved, all names and some peripheral facts have been disguised.

Professor Charles Graham glanced at the clock on his left. The hands on the wall were not encouraging. One hour and ten minutes into the class—only ten minutes to go—and the discussion had gone nowhere. Charles reluctantly concluded he would have to exercise the basic dictatorial prerogative of any instructor: he would have to tell the class how wrong they were.

Charles was starting out his second year of teaching and, as he told his New Dominion faculty colleagues, he had developed a sincere commitment to the case discussion teaching methods and philosophy. Charles was in his second week of teaching Quantitative Analysis and Operations Management (QAOM). He wanted to give that class every chance, but he had not foreseen that 80 intelligent persons might, individually and jointly, entirely miss the main point of the case. Charles disapproved of the practice of giving a pat "answer" to a case at the end of class; on the other hand, he could not conscientiously allow 80 apprentice managers to leave class thinking that the last hour passed for an adequate case analysis. Charles drew a slow breath; one more comment, he thought, and then they are in for it.

The hand Charles recognized was in the back row: it belonged to one of the women students, Janet Macomber. Janet was one of the younger students in the section, a graduate of the California Institute of Technology with an excellent academic record but with limited work experience. She looked nervous and started speaking softly and hesitantly. "Louder, please!" came from somewhere on the other side of the room.

Janet stopped, and started again in a stronger voice. "I'm sorry, but according to my analysis, the class's recommendations simply do not answer the company's problem—which is how to move work-in-process through the plant the best way possible."

"And just what is your analysis, Ms. Macomber?" Professor Graham asked.

"Well"—there was a note of apology in her voice—"when I was doing the case last night, I multiplied Exhibit 1 times Exhibit 2."

Charles did not want to appear amazed that someone had apparently cracked the case after all. He only wanted the class—each and every one of the other 79—to realize the import of Janet Macomber's words. He interrupted: "Let me understand, Ms. Macomber. You actually took Exhibit 1"—he held up the case opened to the exhibits—"and

Section 2. Leading the Class: Direction vs. Control; Classroom Dialogue; Maintenence and Revisions of Contract; Retaining Authority

C A S E
Assistant Professor Graham and Ms. Macomber (A)

multiplied every number in Exhibit 1 times a number in Exhibit 2?"

"Times the corresponding number. Yes, sir."

"And how long did that take you?" (Snickers came from the side of the room.)

Janet Macomber appeared to be taken aback at such a personal question. "Not too long," she answered, adding, as if to justify her computational binge, "I used a calculator."

"And what exactly did you have, after you multiplied every number in Exhibit 1 times a corresponding number in Exhibit 2?"

"I had a matrix of the dollar-volume flow between departments." Janet stopped. She was obviously uncomfortable and ready to relinquish the floor. But Charles was determined to expose her reasoning, bit by bit.

"And what did you find . . . from this matrix?"

"I found that the flows were not all the same [pause]. Some departments had a much greater flow of work-in-process between them than others."

"And what did you conclude based on this observation?"

"I concluded that . . . if I were laying out the plant . . . I would put the departments with the most flow between them next to each other, lining them up, and I would put the other departments on the sides, or in other buildings, if I had to."

"Well, well." Charles looked around. The clock on the wall showed that the class was already two minutes overtime. There would be no chance to take further comments from the class, and anyway it might be more salutary for each individual to mull singly over Janet Macomber's analysis. So as not to end the class abruptly, Charles made a few extempore remarks about how this case was related to previous cases and to the course plan. He carefully refrained from passing judgment on Janet's analysis or on the preceding case discussion. Let 'em figure it out themselves, he thought, now they have something to think about. All in all, Charles was quite pleased with the way the class had turned out.

As he was leaving the room, Charles noted a group clustered around Janet Macomber's top row seat. There really is such a thing as section dynamics, he reflected. "When one of the class reasons through a case, everyone learns. This case method really works. What a break I had to start out my career teaching with cases; it sure is a lot more fun than lecturing."

*Dr. Abby J. Hansen, research associate, wrote this case
for the Developing Discussion Leadership Skills and the
Teaching by the Case Method seminars. Data were furnished by the involved participants. All names and some
peripheral facts have been disguised.*

CASE

The Case of the Dethroned Section Leader (A)

Several years ago, when I was a second-year teaching fellow in English Literature," Beatrice Benedict recalled, "I had a painful experience in a discussion class when my authority was directly—and publicly—questioned. I felt quite insulted at the time, and I still wonder how well I handled the situation."

The Instructor

In the fall of 1973 Bea Benedict was a fourth-year graduate student in Renaissance English Literature at Fairchild University, a large and famous institution in Arden, Connecticut. A tall, 26-year-old with dark hair reaching nearly to her waist, Bea had recently begun jogging two miles a day. Like many other graduate students, she dressed almost invariably in jeans, pullovers, and track shoes. After graduating with honors from Fairchild herself in 1966, Bea had spent four years in Chicago and Denver working in journalism and publishing. Although her assignments increased in challenge, she was always an "assistant" of some sort, and she felt that her salary had not advanced satisfactorily. Bea reported:

> There was just one woman editor at the last publishing house where I worked. She answered to the title "Doctor" on the job, and that's partly why I decided to go back to school and get a doctorate in English. The rest of the reason was probably that, after four years in the "real world," I was pretty sick of editing and writing trivia. I felt ready for a good, nourishing drink of great literature.

Early in the year in which this incident occurred, Bea had become a resident adviser (RA) in Falstaff House, one of Fairchild's coeducational dwelling units. She counseled English majors and advised graduating seniors seeking fellowships and other academic awards.

The Course

English 200, "Shakespeare," was a highly popular survey course taught to about 400 students in a large lecture room in Warwick Hall. Professor Owen Glendower, a celebrated scholar and raconteur, gave two formal lectures each week. The third meeting was a discussion section, led by one of the fourteen graduate teaching fellows (TFs) who, like Bea, had received their teaching assignments as a

Section 2. Leading the Class: Direction vs. Control; Classroom Dialogue; Maintenence and Revisions of Contract; Retaining Authority

C A S E
The Case of the Dethroned Section Leader (A)

precondition of their fellowship stipends. The TFs led discussions, made writing assignments, and were totally responsible for their students' grades. Professor Glendower's principal course assistant made up the section assignments under instructions to place 15 students in each group; scheduling problems, however, produced sections inevitably numbering from 8 to 20 students.

Bea had two sections. One—a group of 18—met in a classroom in Warwick on Thursday afternoons. Bea did more lecturing than discussing with this group because 14 of them were freshmen, unfamiliar with literary analysis. Her other class met after dinner the same evening in Falstaff House because, like the half-dozen other section leaders in English 200 who were also RAs, Bea had requested that at least one of her groups be made up of Falstaff residents. This was a much livelier group than Bea's other section.

[Because Bea considered Professor Glendower's lectures entertaining but superficial, she took a few hours each week from her own dissertation research (on Elizabethan political thought) to read literary criticism on the plays and cull excerpts to present to her sections.]

The Setting

Founded in 1778, Fairchild University included seven professional schools as well as a large, coeducational undergraduate division that enjoyed widespread praise for embodying the ideal of community (i.e., academic) fellowship. After their first year, all undergraduates lived in residential units like Falstaff House, each unit holding about three hundred and fifty students and twenty-five RAs like Bea. RAs ranged from graduate students through senior professors and occasional visiting celebrities—musicians, writers, scientists, and scholars.

Falstaff House, a red brick neo-Tudor compound on the west bank of the Avon River, included a large private dining hall, conference rooms, living suites, common rooms (lounges resembling living rooms), squash courts, a small gym, and a central courtyard where anything from political rallies to frisbee games could occur in good weather.

The Section

Bea's Falstaff House section included five men and three women; all lived in the House. Out of that group, Bea recalled four students especially:

Jack Kesselman was a sophomore from Lake Forest, Illinois. He was a political activist, particularly interested in organizing protests against the university's investments in South African companies. A folk singer and songwriter, Jack had a reputation for cleverness. He would often sit in the House courtyard playing his guitar and singing original ballads about people we all knew. He was also something of an operator: once he told me he had arranged to receive credit toward his degree for private guitar lessons he was taking from an upperclassman in the House.

Elke Gunnarson was a tall, blond woman from Kansas City, a senior in Political Science, and a star of the women's tennis team. She usually dressed either in tennis whites or her varsity sweatshirt when she came to the discussion section. Elke participated in the House Council, organized a formal dance, and served as hostess at sherry hours.

Elke's boyfriend, Cliff Farmer, was also in the group. Cliff was a hockey player born and raised in Rockport, Maine. His major was American History, and he planned to go to law school. I considered him steady—not overly brilliant, but a very reliable and pleasant sort of fellow.

Skip Townsend, a junior from Palo Alto, California, also participated in our group's discussions. He was an odd sort of guy, who wrote "beachcomber" under "Professional Plans, if Any" on the Student Information card I handed out. I recall him as ironic, fairly quiet, but with a sharp sense of humor.

Bea added:

By the way, the Student Information cards were my own idea. Glendower gave us almost no guidance in setting up our discussion groups. I had just started distributing the cards because the previous year I learned a week after the final exam that one of my students has spent the past three summers at the Stratford Shakespeare Festival. She'd understudied their Juliet one year. And I never even asked her to read in class.

Bea's section met just off the Falstaff courtyard in a small room furnished with an enormous rectangular oak conference table and straight-backed wooden chairs. Bea sat in the chair nearest the chalkboard, and the students arranged themselves in two rows along the sides of the table.

The Incident

[In the following section, Bea recalls in her own
words the circumstances leading up to the incident.]

It was the fourth session in the semester, and I
thought this group was doing quite well. The informality of meeting in the House after dinner
seemed pleasant for all of us. I used to bring my
coffee mug to class, and the students brought
pieces of cake from the dining hall. My usual
opening was to pass out photocopied excerpts
from published criticism about the play in question. The students then scanned the handout
while I stood at the board to write some key terms
for the evening's discussion or perhaps the title of
a particularly important book from the recommended readings list. Then I'd sit down and run
through a few administrative details—paper deadlines or in-class report assignments—and then
present a brief summary of some points from
Glendower's lectures. After this opening, I'd call
on the student whose turn it was to give a report—an analysis of an assigned passage—to kick
off our class discussion. I had asked the students
in the first two meetings to choose a date on
which they'd like to report, and I tried to accommodate their choices in my assignments. I had
stated at our first meeting that students should expect to give two reports during the semester. They
were to prepare them thoroughly, but not to read
criticism for their analyses. I wanted to hear their
own original ideas so I could form impressions of
their critical abilities that would help me grade
them.

That evening we were discussing Shakespeare's
Richard II. As usual, I sat in the chair nearest the
chalkboard. It was a warm night, and through the
open window of our conference room, the frisbee
players' shouts of "nice catch," and "whoa, boy,
look out for the bushes!" were almost louder than
our own voices. I toyed with the idea of asking
the students in the courtyard to be quiet, but I
knew that it would shortly be too dark to play
frisbee, and they would soon give up their game.
Skip sat halfway down the table from me. Jack sat
on my right. Elke and Cliff sat together just beyond him. (The other students in the section—Patricia Haley, Bob Connors, Charles Schwartz, and
Lisa Evans—were all present, but I confess I have
nothing in particular to say about them. In fact, I

hardly remember them. I had to look up their
names in my old gradebook.)

It was Jack Kesselman's turn to begin that night.
I sat down, put on my reading glasses, and
turned the pages of my text to the passage I had
assigned him. Then I said something like: "Well,
Jack, my syllabus has your name here under October 18. Could you tell us what you make of Richard's speech in the second scene of Act III where
we see and hear him grappling with the idea that
he may actually lose his throne? You remember,
as I've mentioned, of course, that the third act in
Shakespeare is pivotal. It's exactly in the middle of
the five-act structure, and it usually gives the audience the turnaround, the reversal of the world
we meet in the first act. I'm very interested, in
particular, to hear what you think of Richard's
rather pathetic lines 'Not all the water in the
rough rude sea/Can wash the balm off from an
anointed king'—especially here in the play, when
his enemies surround him and he is about to be
deposed?" Then, I think, I smiled, took off my
reading glasses, and turned to Jack. "Okay, you've
got the floor."

Jack slouched in his seat, looking away from
me, and riffled the pages of his text. Then he said,
"Bea, I'm not sure what I make of Richard's lines.
There's something else on my mind."

That took me by surprise. After all, he knew he
was being graded on his presentation. So I tried to
be encouraging.

I said: "You must have taken some time to think
about the passage. Why don't you just give us
your reactions. Do you think Richard has any idea
that he might lose his power despite his words?"

Jack still hadn't turned to meet my gaze. "Um,
I'd like to make a statement," he said.

"Go ahead," was my reply.

Jack said: "I think something's wrong here. In
this section. Bea, you talk too much. I timed your
introduction. Fifteen minutes. Of our time. And
you were just summarizing a lot of stuff we've already heard. It was pretty boring."

I remember I must have been blushing. I felt attacked. I think I sat there staring at Jack—at the
side of his head, that is. My first instinct was self-
defense.

I said, "I don't think you're being fair. I spent a
lot of time preparing for this discussion. I've been
studying this material intensively for four years
now, and I really want to convey some of what

Section 2. Leading the Class: Direction vs. Control;
Classroom Dialogue; Maintenence and Revisions of
Contract; Retaining Authority

CASE
The Case of the Dethroned Section Leader (A)

I've learned to you. Glendower hired me for a
purpose, you know. Don't you think I've got anything to teach you?"

Now Jack had turned to face me. I remember
thinking when I saw him full face how little I had
ever liked him. Now I could hardly stand to look
at him. Elke and Cliff had been exchanging
glances. Elke now telegraphed me a look of embarrassment. Cliff looked unnerved too. Skip was
leaning back on the rear legs of his chair. He was
grinning. I could imagine him thinking this whole
thing a fine joke.

Jack was talking again: "I think we should vote.
As far as I'm concerned, Bea, all your talking only
stifles us. Even if we're full of hot air, we ought to
hear each other's ideas and sort of feel our way
along with this material."

By this time I was really furious with Jack, but I
would have felt tyrannical if I'd refused to let the
section vote. Also, the situation had begun to appeal to my sense of adventure. I was wondering
how a leaderless discussion might turn out.

I stood at the board and faced the group, wondering what to do.

READING

The Professor-Student Barrier to Growth

MARCIA YUDKIN

From the *New York Times*, January 4, 1981, Educational Review. Reprinted by permission.

She sat down in the chair I indicated, unwound her scarf, and unbuttoned her jacket. "I don't know if you remember me," she began. "Of course I remember you!" I was astounded. Linda Harrison had been one of 15 students in a discussion section that had met weekly, just the previous semester—my first as a philosophy professor at Smith College. How could she suppose I wouldn't remember her?

When I thought about it later, my astonishment was tempered by the reflection that when I was an undergraduate I imagined myself part of a fog of names, faces and personalities to my professors, a fog that might clear when I spoke up in class or besieged them during office hours, but would quickly and inexorably descend again. After all, they had so very many other students and such other important things to think about. But later that week I heard my colleagues reminisce about students who had graduated five years previously. So it wasn't true!

That was the first of several startling comparisons I made between the views from the students' and the professors' sides of the desk. Another occurred after having brooded about what seemed to me an epidemic of absences from class. It had to mean that they thought me boring or incompetent. I confessed to a senior in my other class my anxiety over the number of students who skipped my intro course. "Hmmm," she said, "does it meet early in the morning? Or right after lunch? Or in the evening?" My worry dissipated.

I remembered that there were lots of reasons for skipping class, like all-nighters, personal crises, extracurricular commitments and general lethargy—reasons that had nothing to do with me, the professor.

It took another odd experience to make me recall that as a student I would not have believed that a professor could take my absence personally. A student in my intro course interspersed her written responses to assigned "thought questions" with remarks about the class, including one to the effect that she was able to observe me during class while remaining unobserved herself, so that while she knew a lot about me, I knew nothing about her.

"Not true," I wrote in the margin. "your face is a giveaway." Facial expressions, even in a class of 45, registered vividly. I would pick out resentment, interest, confusion, and happy struggling with new ideas. I would notice who was and wasn't there. I

Section 2. Leading the Class: Direction vs. Control; Classroom Dialogue; Maintenence and Revisions of Contract; Retaining Authority

READING
The Professor-Student Barrier to Growth YUDKIN

realized that when I was a student, I believed I was invisible, protected by a sort of one-way screen. That was mistaken too.

When I began teaching, I had a definite conception of my role in the classroom: I would provoke students to take responsibility for our progress through the course by being active participants in discussion. The goal of studying philosophy, I thought, was for them to incorporate the material, issues and questions into their lives. I would keep lectures to a minimum and encourage lively verbal exchanges in class and individual thinking on paper. I warned students at the outset that if they wanted to memorize without getting involved, they should go elsewhere. In my classroom they would be making discoveries. Unexpectedly, I made discoveries there, too.

One day, when everything was going right and there was an exhilarating interchange about whether Descartes' attempt to use reason to prove the existence of God made sense, a student turned toward me and asked, "What do *you* think?" All the other heads turned toward me, and there was silence while I balanced on the horns of a dilemma: if my opinion, as the professor's, carried more weight, I shouldn't give it. But if I held back my view I would be doing what I wanted none of the students to do. I took a deep breath and acted as if I were one of them. *I told.* Forty pencils moved, and the discussion ground to a halt. Anyone looking in would have seen me sitting in the circle, but really I was on the other side of the desk, standing in full academic regalia.

As much as I tried to subvert the traditional role of professor as authority figure, it refused to disappear. It would lurk like a ghost and materialize when I thought I had exorcised it. At evaluation time, I would get some evidence that my strategy worked: "Best course I've had at Smith. We were made to think for ourselves instead of having answers handed to us that we had to regurgitate." But I also got advice like this: "Less discussion by ignorant students and more lectures by the knowledgeable prof."

Why did she think I was knowledgeable? It was an assumption I might have made in her position too, that the Ph.D. after my name in the catalogue meant that I knew something.

I thought my age and appearance would aid me in transcending the traditional image of a professor. At 28 I still look about 20 and dress as I did when a student. Sometimes it does help, but when students cease to think of me as an authority figure, there is another role waiting in the wings: that of a pal. When that comes into play, if I announce firm deadlines for papers I am assumed not to mean it, or if I fail to give an A to someone with whom I have had good rapport, I am reproached: "How could you do this to me?" I have violated our compact as chums.

The upshot is after two and a half years of teaching I see the roles as obstacles I am not capable of removing alone. I can shove the desk into the corner of the room, but then I may be trampled upon by students unaccustomed to its absence. In any case, the struggle to move it away must begin again with each new group of students. The roles of professor and student prevent me, when a whole discussion section clams up, from finding out what is wrong. I also believe the roles prevent many students from developing a questioning habit of mind and self-reliance that would be theirs for life. As a philosopher, I am inclined to pose my concern as a question: wouldn't it be better for everyone if the views from the two sides of the desk were not so different, if the roles of professor and student were broken down?

Section 3. Responsibilities of Leadership: Protecting Students

CASE

Henry Jasper (A)

It was 8 A.M. on a cold and sunless winter day when Carol Cutler opened her statistics class. After a short summary of the major points covered by Professor Wilbar that week in lecture, she presented a simple problem.

"Can anyone get started on solving this?" Carol asked. No one volunteered. "Well, Henry, why don't you give it a try?"

Henry Jasper was sitting at the front of the class and at first just stared at Ms. Cutler, who was standing at the chalkboard. Then, suddenly, he replied in a loud, agitated, violent way: "Look, I'm sick of you women teachers always picking on me. I'm not going to take it anymore. That's just it, you're trying to castrate me and it's been that way since I was in elementary school. Well, you're not going to get away with it now. Professor Wilbar is going to hear what you're trying to do to me. You'll be sorry!"

Jasper was now standing by her desk. Carol looked at him, then at the class, then back to him. In the ensuing silence Carol frantically thought to herself, What's going on? What do I do?

Background

Located in a beautiful rural setting, Northern University was one of eight Ivy League Schools. The school's admission policy thus was selective. Northern's 12,000 undergraduates and 3,000 graduate students had the fortunate opportunity to choose between several specialized schools and departments, many of which were acknowledged to be the leading institutions in the field. This philosophy of excellence in very specialized areas permitted broad financial support for most graduate students and provided tuition, fees, and a small stipend to cover basic living expenses. Two part-time employment methods were extensively used for this purpose: research assistantships to aid professors engaged in critical work, and teaching assistantships for the large, required lecture courses. Northern's ratio of male to female undergraduates was about 3 to 1, and this ratio was even higher on the graduate levels.

The Statistics Course

In the section that follows, Carol Cutler describes in her own words the statistics course.

Statistics 210 is the introductory statistics course required of all sophomores in Human Ecology and

Tamara Gilman wrote this case under the supervision of *C. Roland Christensen* from data supplied by involved participants for the Developing Discussion Leadership Skills Seminar. All names and some peripheral facts have been disguised.

Industrial Relations, as well as in hotel management. There are about 300 captive students each semester, which provide five teaching assistants with half-time work. We teach three two-hour "labs" a week, each with about 24 students at a time. Since many of the students sleep or read the college newspaper during the three weekly 9 A.M. lectures by Professor Wilbar, we try to summarize the major points made that week and then hand out a problem set that requires use of the new techniques in order to solve the problems. We don't require attendance in the labs, but attendance is usually pretty high, since this is the only time students can practice doing problems similar to those on the exams. And because we only have a midterm and a final on which to base the course grade, most people show up on schedule.

The labs are held in one of two rooms called the machine rooms because they contain SCM calculating machines for student use in working out the numerical answers to problem sets. The SCMs are antiquated, compared to the new electronic calculators; they're incredibly noisy and so big they look like supermarket check-out machines; and they often jam up so that they either incorrectly calculate or don't work at all. Each machine is on a separate grey metal office-sized desk and they are lined up in four rows of six each. Given the drab decor, the lack of any windows, and the noise level when every machine is working, it can be pretty bleak in there.

The purpose of the T.A., as I see it, is to help the students learn how to do the problems and understand why they're doing them in a particular way or using a particular technique. The concepts aren't simple for people who don't have a strong background in math, and for most of them this will be their last quantitative course.

I begin my lab by listing the major issues Professor Wilbar has discussed at a theoretical level, and then I spend 15 or 20 minutes on how these can be used in a practical way to solve problems. Simple, somewhat humorous illustrations that somehow relate to the particular character and interest of the class work seem to work best. For example, in the lab I might use a hypothetical distribution of quarts of beer drunk by the various houses on campus that are predominantly male— since two out of three students in my class are male.

I also give the class the opportunity to work the problem out, or at least make a stab at it, by asking, "Can anyone suggest any way to go about solving this problem?" If no one raises his or her hand, I go ahead and work it out myself, explaining while I do it.

After going over the example, I hand out the worksheet and spend the rest of the period answering questions and helping students do the problems. The instructor's desk is at the head of one row of desks, and I usually just sit there for the next 15 minutes or so drinking a cup of coffee, but after that I wander around the lab so that people can stop me and show me their problem if they need help. Especially at the beginning of the semester I try to be enthusiastic and supportive, because I know so many are overly anxious about the math.

When they've completed the problems, the students hand in the finished sheets to me. If there is time left in the period, I check the answers, and if there are any mistakes we discuss them. However, most students take nearly the full time to do the work and I can't check them all at once, so I do that outside of the lab and then hand them back the next week. Often the individual discussions in lab are as much about the mistakes of the prior week as they are about the problems of the current week. The problem sets aren't "graded," but if there are errors I mark them, indicating what mistakes were made so that the student will understand what should have been done.

Besides discussing the problems in lab, I schedule six hours a week for conference time, so that the students can drop by for a private discussion if they want to. Well, it's almost private; although other students aren't around, my two officemates are often there. Most of my students come by infrequently and then only to discuss particularly troublesome problems or concepts. For instance, if a student makes the same error on the problems for two or three weeks in a row, I'll just put a note on the latest paper saying "Why don't you stop by my office and we'll try to clear this up once and for all."

However, there are two other types of students and both stop by almost every week. The first group really understands what's going on and just wants to "fine tune" that knowledge so that they will get an *A*. All of these students have aspirations for doing graduate work, often in law, and often at the top universities. They don't want a "dumb" statistics grade to jeopardize their chances.

The students in the second group are usually doing just adequate work and have little mathematical experience. I think that they're frightened by the very idea of a stat course and in some ways have a mental block against it, not lack of real ability. I try to encourage them to stop worrying by listening to them, patiently going over the problems—sometimes several times in a row in different ways—and by explaining really elementary operations, like how to take square roots. I can really sympathize with these people because I'm not in Math or Stat, and I know how anxious I'd feel if I was required to take a quantitative course which I thought was over my head.

However my officemate, Barry Gerber, a master's candidate in Stat, thinks I'm not tough enough. I remember one day I was listening to a young woman, after she had just gotten her midterm back: "I just don't understand it. I worked so hard for this exam and now I've done so poorly. I studied a lot for this. It's really upsetting, getting a grade like this after all that work."

"I know how you feel, Ginny," I said. "But I don't think that you did all that badly, and I'm sure if we work together for the next several weeks, you'll be able to do much better on the final. It is hard when you're not used to math. . . ."

At that point in my "sympathy" speech, Barry, who was sitting at his desk at the back of the office, literally flew over his desk and stood in front of us, berating the student for lying to me and trying to take advantage of me when she obviously hadn't done any work in the course at all. The student left in a hurry, as bewildered as I was! Then Barry, who had taught the course before, told me that after seeing me deal with students during conference hours, he was convinced I was "taking too much crap from them. You let them push you around with their sob stories." He kept telling me to "get tough with them!" I'm still not convinced that I should do that, but even if I was, I'm not sure at all how I would go about it. Being tough just isn't my style.

The Instructor's Background

[According to the case researcher, Ms. Cutler had just turned 22 and was in her first year of a master's program in industrial relations. She had graduated from a midwestern university with a major in economics. The following is Carol's own description of the events leading up to her role as instructor.]

I wasn't at all sure at the beginning of my senior year what I wanted to do after graduation—work or go to graduate school. My mother wanted me to work and thought that being a stewardess would be great, since I "wouldn't have to think so much" and I'd "meet a lot of nice men." She was worried because I wasn't dating anyone seriously, and she used to tell me that I'd be better off in a less "egghead" field, because men didn't like smart women! Since my sophomore year she had been sending newspaper clippings of the engagements and weddings of my high school girl friends, and I guess she thought I hadn't gotten the message. Besides, I didn't have the money for school, and she thought it was crazy to go into debt for something that I'd never have to use.

Well, I decided to apply anyhow. Although my average was only a $B-$, it was an $A-$ in economics and I was really interested in labor economics. I also applied for financial aid, but I really didn't hold out any hope. I was ecstatic when I learned that not only was I accepted, but that I would receive financial aid. Northern said that I'd be informed later in the summer which professor I'd be working for. When I told my family, the only positive comment my mother made was, "At least there's more men than women there."

I left in June for a summer exchange program job in a bank in Amsterdam. One day at work I received a letter from my mother which included a letter from Northern. It stated that I would be a teaching assistant for Professor Wilbar in the introductory Statistics 210 course. Was that a shock! I had been hoping for a research assistantship because I had never taught before and don't really like to be in the spotlight. Besides, I'd only had one course in statistics myself, and I only got a C in that. At first I considered forgetting the whole thing. I really didn't think I was up to it. Then some people I was working with convinced me to calm down and suggested that I get a few stat books to review. Luckily, English texts are used frequently in Holland and I found two on statistics, which I went over with the help of several Heinekens!

Carol Cutler

[According to Ms. Cutler's officemate, Barry Gerber, Cutler's arrival at the statistics department was something of a surprise. The following is Barry's own description of Carol Cutler.]

I walked into Professor Wilbar's office right before registration day and saw a mob of students. I thought I could help out so I started asking people if I could help them, answer any questions about the course, things like that. A small girl with long, brown hair was standing near me and I turned to her. She looked just like the rest of the kids—rather young and dressed casually. Was I surprised to discover that she was the new T.A. and my officemate! When Professor Wilbar's secretary heard her name, she was just as surprised and apologized for having her wait in line with the students. I guess Carol had been waiting there for some time. We finally got all the procedures taken care of—the books, assignments, things like that—and I showed her to our office.

We talked a little and then she left to see some professors about her own courses. She was very friendly and open, not at all formal, and with a kind of bouncy personality. She seemed nervous about teaching, though. I think this was partly because she wasn't getting an M.A. or Ph.D. in Stat like the rest of us and didn't feel all that comfortable with it, and partly because she hadn't taught before. Since we had all taught 210 last year, Carol got us all together one day before her first lab day and grilled us about how we ran a lab and what we did. She even asked us if she should wear a skirt or pants! I don't think we were very much help to her on that. The rest of us are all guys and had never thought about it. I remember seeing her after that first lab and she was pretty upset. I guess the guys in the class gave her a pretty rough time.

The First Lab

[According to Ms. Cutler, that first lab had been designed to enable students to develop a "hands on" familiarity with the calculators through a demonstration of how they worked and through a brief, purely mechanical problem set. The following is Carol's own description of that first lab session and the events that followed.]

Mine was scheduled for Tuesday at 2:30 P.M. Professor Wilbar was supposed to show me how to run the calculators the day before, but he didn't get around to it until noon of the same day. It wasn't difficult, but there were certain common mistakes he told me to watch out for. I just hoped I could remember all of them.

About 2:30 I finally conquered my doubts and walked into the machine room. Actually, I was a little late on purpose so I wouldn't have to stand up in the front of the class waiting for them. The first thing that I noticed was that there were no women in the lab. The second was the size of the guys. They were huge! I found out later that this was the "jock" section, made up of football and hockey players.

After introducing myself and talking a little about the purpose of the labs, I showed them how the SCMs worked and handed out the worksheet. I thought to myself, Well, at least you survived the first day. Was I mistaken!

Suddenly everything seemed to be going wrong. First, there was a rash of machine breakdowns. One right after another had keys that stuck, a carriage that wouldn't move, multiplied instead of added on command, or wouldn't respond at all. Then there were voices shouting throughout the room, "Hey, Teach, my machine won't work!"—accompanied by not very muffled snickers. On top of this, some guys decided to use a more direct approach and complained—rather, glared down at me—from a distance too close for comfort.

I didn't know what to do with the machines. Professor Wilbar hadn't said anything about mechanical problems. But by accident, while trying to fix one of them, I discovered that the plug was pulled out. Checking several others that wouldn't work at all revealed that they too had been disconnected. I finally realized that, at least in part, a concerted effort was being made to upset me.

I knew then that I had lost control and was in real trouble, but I hadn't the foggiest notion of what to do to regain any semblance of order. I had a terrible headache by this time and could hardly think with all these giants breathing down my neck. I guess I decided that the best thing that could happen would be for them to leave. Smiling and cajoling, I reminded them that if they quit horsing around, they'd finish and could leave early.

111

Appealing to their best self-interest didn't seem
to help much, though, until someone actually finished and left. That seemed to be the catalyst and
the turning point. Order, relatively speaking, then
prevailed and the guys focused more on the problems than on hassling me. But what a terrible 45
minutes it was! When the lab was over I immediately asked Professor Wilbar for a transfer to another section. I swapped with Barry and got primarily from Human Ecology a section that
happened to be mostly female.

After my trial by fire, I gradually began to feel
more comfortable in the classroom and the challenge became making sure I understood the statistical concepts and how to solve the problems. This
was more difficult than I had anticipated.

Professor Wilbar wrote the text, and it was different from the one I used and the ones I reviewed over the summer. Sometimes I just didn't
understand the answers on the "key" to the problem sets, and sitting in on the lectures didn't help.
I couldn't afford to lose the T.A. and by this time I
had a commitment to my students, so I felt I
couldn't let the department know how much trouble I was having. Usually one of my housemates
helped me work the problems out; she was a
Ph.D. in urban planning and had had a lot of stat
work.

But one night, before my first lab of the week,
neither of us could get the right answer and
match the "key." I couldn't wait until the next day
to get the solution because the lab was at 8 A.M. I
didn't know what to do. I couldn't go into the lab
not knowing how to do the problem, yet I didn't
have any way to find out how to do it. As it got
later and later I got more and more desperate. Ellie, my housemate, finally went to bed and I was
really all alone and didn't know where to turn.
Finally, at 1 A.M., I decided to call one of the other
T.A.s. I picked Barry because he seemed the most
approachable. Well, I woke both him and his
roommates up, but he explained it to me and I
finally could go to sleep.

The next morning at 10 A.M., just as the lab was
breaking up, Barry came into the machine room. I
thanked him again for his help. He looked at me
and said, "I want brownies!"

He had a whole batch of them on his desk the
first thing the next morning. I guess I had to swallow my pride and take a risk, but at least I started
getting the help I needed.

Henry Jasper

[The following is Carol Cutler's own description
of Henry Jasper.]

Henry Jasper was a sophomore in the Industrial
Relations School, with a quiet, serious manner not
usually found in the typical extroverted industrial
relations student. About 5'6" tall, he had dark
brown hair cut short and combed to the side,
wore glasses, and always had on a neat shirt and
a pair of slacks that contrasted sharply with the T-
shirt-and-jeans uniform the other three men in his
lab—as well as most of the male population at
Northern—wore.

He was one of the first to arrive in the machine
room on lab mornings and always sat in the first
desk of the row immediately in front of mine.
While many of the students drank coffee and
joked with each other while trying to wake up
waiting for the lab to start, Henry always took out
his stat book and reviewed the reading assignment for the week. During the lab time when students were working on the problems and comparing answers, Henry would just turn to me to
check the solution and ask any questions, because
our desks were so close. I don't think he knew
many other people in the lab because they were
mostly from Human Ecology, not Industrial Relations. He usually took the whole period to complete the problem set, and sometimes would stay
over to the next lab (10 A.M. to noon) if there were
calculators not being used.

Henry was extremely conscientious about doing
his problem sets right and came up to the office to
go over details all the time. For example, I remember one of his first office visits at the beginning of
the semester. He came in, put his books down
carefully, and took out a notebook with a list of
points he wanted to discuss. "I know you went
over this in class, Miss Cutler, but I want to make
sure I understand the difference between the
mean, the median, and the mode. The mean is
the average, the median is the 50th percentile, and
the mode is the most frequent value. Is that
right?"

"That's right, Henry. Do you understand the
formulas for calculating them?" I asked.

"I think so," he replied, "but I want to make
sure. Can we work through these problems at the
end of Chapter 2? I've already done them and

would like to check them against the correct answers."

"Of course," I said and reached for the text. Halfway through the second problem I saw that he had made a simple arithmetic error and I pointed it out. "But that's not really anything to worry about, Henry. You didn't have a calculator when you were doing these and anyone can make a mistake, dividing with such large numbers. Besides, you used the right formula, put the right numbers in it, and understand why you were doing it that way. I think you really know what's important."

Dejectedly he answered, "I don't know, Miss Cutler. I did these extra problems and thought I had worked them through very carefully. I took a lot of time with them. I thought I had the answers exactly right. I just don't seem to have much of a knack for math."

"When was the last time you took a math course?" I asked.

"High school algebra, four years ago when I was a sophomore," he responded. "I didn't do too well in it and stopped taking any more math after that. I tried to get out of Stat 210, but the registrar's office told me that I need it to graduate in IR, and there's no way I can avoid it. Do you think I'll do OK? If I work hard?"

Trying to be encouraging, I said, "I can't see why not, although it's just the beginning of the course. You understand everything so far and seem to be willing to work hard, even do extra work, and that's a good sign. But remember, if you ever want to go over the problems or need to discuss anything you just don't quite understand in the course, feel free to come up. If you can't make it during conference hours, we can always schedule another time that's convenient for both of us. And don't worry about those math errors—you'll get more and more used to the numbers as the time goes by."

As the semester went by, Henry came up to the office about every week. It became apparent that he understood basically what the course was about, but he had to work hard for that understanding.

Just a week ago, when we were in the section on confidence intervals, he told me during an office visit: "I think I've finally got down what a standard deviation is, but it keeps getting mixed up in my head, especially when I try to do prob-

lems. Now, it's the measure of how certain you are that a sample value is the true value, right?"

"Well, standard deviation is the measure of the variability of individual observations from the mean," I said. "And it can be used in hypothesis testing to see if a sample mean comes from a population with a certain hypothetical mean. And we use the confidence intervals, which are based on the standard deviation, to do the testing and give us a certain probability. You know, Henry, you keep telling me that you don't understand this, but it sounds like you do. You must, to answer your own questions the way you did."

"It may sound like it, but if I do understand it why can't I do the problems better? Why do I keep making the same mistakes?" he asked plaintively. He pulled the last two labs out of his notebook and said, "I know the final only has problems on it—not the definitions that I can memorize—and I just keep getting the labs wrong. Look at these! They have more red ink on them than pencil!"

"But you don't get the labs 'wrong,'" I insisted. "You make arithmetic mistakes, but everyone does that. Even when you attack a problem incorrectly, you always go back to it and make sure that you understand what you should have done. And that is the important thing—whether or not you do it perfectly right the first time isn't important. It's whether or not you understand it ultimately that counts."

He pushed his glasses back up and paused before he started putting his labs away. Then as he was picking up his books and coat, he said: "I'm getting tired of working so hard and not getting anywhere on this. It's frustrating. Completely frustrating! I know you're willing to help, but still, it doesn't get any easier and I put so much time into it that my other courses are suffering. I just can't afford that. Do you think I'm going to make it? Is it worth all this effort? What do you think?"

"I don't know for sure, Henry," I gently hedged. "But I do know that you can do the problems similar to those on the exams when you relax and think them through without getting all tensed up. The numbers on the exams are easier to work with—they're smaller and divide evenly—because we don't want students to get all hung up on that when we're trying to see if they know the concepts. And we don't mark down for stupid math errors that result from trying to work too fast, so you don't need to worry about that. And I know you've been working hard. If you're on the borderline of a grade, that can only help. Besides, you're one of the few people that goes regularly to the lectures, reads the assignments, and attends lab as well! I'm sure you'll do fine!"

*   *   *

Carol's Dilemma

Henry Jasper remained standing in front of Carol's desk as she thought to herself, "What's going on?"

Paula Wilson, a 30-year-old Ph.D. in English literature, had taught for four years as a graduate-student teaching assistant before accepting her first full-time job at the downtown campus of a large state university on the East Coast. Students at this university commuted to classes; many also held part-time jobs. Consequently there was very little student camaraderie. Many described the place as alienated or fragmented. The students were not noted for scholarly excellence, although Paula found many of them extremely talented and able. By and large, they were enthusiastic and, despite their other commitments, came to classes prepared. Paula's department included 40 full-time staff. The university's cumbersome administration occupied parts of several downtown buildings, some of which also housed classrooms. It wasn't an easy place to get to know.

Paula herself was slim, with blue eyes and long, dark hair. Many of her women colleagues taught in blue jeans, but Paula favored skirts or dresses and frequently wore silver jewelry. Her manner was cordial and her humor often based on wordplay. Successful in her own studies, she had chosen her academic career out of dedication to her subject. Helping students see the power and fascination of literature meant a great deal to her. In an era of scarce jobs, she felt fortunate to have found a teaching position near the university where her husband was finishing his Ph.D. dissertation, also in English literature. (Paula's marriage, which later ended in divorce, was already creating anxiety for her, and she looked to her professional life all the more to balance the growing unease at home.)

Paula Encounters Her First Challenge

The first stumbling block she encountered in her job was her department chairperson's phone call three weeks before the opening of the fall semester to inform Paula that the teaching assignments had been changed. One section she had expected to teach turned out to have insufficient enrollment, and the chairperson's suggestion was that she could pull together an advanced elective seminar instead of the English Novel course that she had already prepared. Could she do it? Paula gulped and said, "Of course!"

Paula took out her doctoral research, which included comparative studies of nature poems and satires, to cull material for a seminar to meet for three hour-long sessions each week of the semester.

CASE

The Handicapped Heckler (A)

Dr. Abby Hansen, research associate, wrote this case in collaboration with Professor C. Roland Christensen for the Developing Discussion Leadership Skills Seminar. While the case is based on data supplied by participants involved, all names and some peripheral facts have been disguised.

For herself, she made lists of critical readings to review before each class. But she expected the students to study only the primary literary texts and prepare to discuss them. Discussion would comprise the core of the learning experience in this course. She planned to lecture as little as possible, and only when historical data or critical interpretations were both important and obscure. Otherwise, she felt her task was to help her students talk—preferably to each other—so that they could learn to state, challenge, and refine their reactions to the literature. Paula managed to construct a coherent syllabus for this seminar, but never quite overcame a feeling of annoyance at the haste with which she had been forced to undertake the project.

When Paula got her room assignment for the course, she found the meeting place was grim—an old-fashioned room with fluorescent lighting, some twenty-odd assorted chairs, and a big oak desk pushed against a blackboard. It was located on the ground floor of a converted apartment building on a busy downtown street where traffic noise was a constant irritant.

A Greater Encounter Confronts Paula

The room was depressing, but not (Paula was soon to learn) the greatest challenge of this seminar. That challenge presented itself on the first day of classes. Paula always arrived early to teach, but a student in a wheelchair had preceded her. He sat in the middle of the room, staring out at the traffic. Paula walked around to greet him. He was a lanky, handsome young man of about 20, with broad, athletic shoulders—but his long legs appeared wasted in baggy blue jeans, and Paula found the unscuffed running shoes on his motionless feet particularly poignant. She felt a sharp stab of pity, even as she smiled at him. "Hello," she said brightly, "I'm Paula Wilson, and you are . . .?" He gave a spasmodic twitch, and answered in a strained voice, "Frank Edgerton." Paula wondered whether his paralysis had impaired his speaking ability. Would this student have extra difficulty in a discussion class? Frank resumed his study of the passing traffic, avoiding Paula's gaze and further conversation as she pulled chairs into a rough circle for the eight students in the seminar. As other students entered, no one sat beside Frank's wheelchair until there were only two empty seats left—one on each side of Frank. He greeted no one, nor did anyone greet him.

When the group was assembled, Paula introduced herself formally, described the subject matter and some class objectives, and gave a 15-minute minilecture on some critical issues and historical points that the students would find useful for their discussion. (This was a typical format but she often varied it.) Then she finished her minilecture, posed a general question about the time of the opening of a short passage she had distributed in class, and asked for a volunteer to begin the discussion. One brave soul complied. Another responded to his point, and then a third student spoke. As Paula recalled, the third student was saying, "I think the words *dark* and *shadow* in the first line of a nature poem warn us that there's going to be something sad."

"Sad?" Paula promoted encouragingly. "Like what?"

Suddenly Frank burst in: "Christ, how obvious! Why bother to make such a boring point?" The class fell silent.

Paula assumed that Frank's disability must be affecting his emotional state, and her pity squelched the urge to rebuke such rudeness. Instead of confronting him, she merely restated her original question to the previous student. Fortunately, the class seemed to have interpreted Frank's outburst more or less as Paula had. They, too, ignored it. But there was tension in the room as the discussion continued.

Paula recalled that during the next few sessions "Frank continued his disruptions. I would ask a question, somebody would answer, and he would burst out with an insult. The other students always became very quiet when he did this. He was terribly rude, but nobody challenged him."

Paula continued: "I noticed that he interacted little with the other students. He was always there first, and he stared out the window until class began. No one seemed to avoid him, but no one approached him either." After a week or two of this behavior Paula asked a few colleagues about Frank. No one knew him—not surprising in this environment. She decided to live with the situation a little longer.

One day, about four weeks into the term, Paula began an introductory minilecture: "Once again we see the presence of pastoral elegy in a satire. I wonder how this mixture works in stanzas one to five—"

"Oh, come *on*, we've talked that point to death!"

Frank's peevish snarl caught Paula by surprise. She took a deep breath and shifted ground swiftly to make another point before asking a student for a comment. The whole class seemed even more nervous than usual this time, and Paula found it difficult to prod them into making contributions.

On frequent occasions, Paula had held office hours; this university, however, was simply not the sort of place where students spent much time in casual conversation with their professors. For one thing, most of the students were under time constraints after class, and for another, the culture of the place was simply too alienated. Paula often mentioned office hours in class and urged the students to come. She singled Frank out with special cordiality a few times, pretending that he had made a point so interesting she wished he would come to discuss it further. She wanted to speak to him privately—possibly even to mention his disruptive behavior in some nonconfrontational way. But, although a few students came to office hours, Frank was never among them. Oddly enough, no one complained to her about his behavior. Paula did not ask any students about their reactions to Frank's behavior because she made it a policy never to discuss students with their colleagues—behind their backs, as it were.

During the next few class meetings, Frank's behavior deteriorated further. Someone would speak, he would interrupt, then dead silence would fall until Paula could scrape together a question interesting enough to shove the group into some forward momentum—always subject to the threat of another torpedo from Frank. When this situation had continued for six weeks, Paula realized that she was beginning to dread the class and was arriving in a state of nervousness. This was extremely unusual because Paula generally enjoyed teaching.

The time had come to do something. Paula had tried to live with the situation, but now she was fed up with Frank's bad manners, which appeared to be upsetting his classmates. She felt compelled to intervene. But how?

Section 4. Operations: Day-to-Day Classroom Practice; Implications of Teachers' Actions; Importance of Detail; Moral Issues

The French Lesson (A)

Bert Peters, an assistant professor of French at prestigious Bower College in rural Illinois, had four years of full-time college teaching experience. Today he was leading the twenty students in his 10 A.M. section of Intermediate French Grammar and Composition through an exercise in the subjunctive. They were three weeks into the fall semester and this group had already impressed Bert as outstandingly bright and enthusiastic, even for the generally high-caliber students at Bower.

As usual, Bert was trying to breathe life into the intrinsic boredom of pattern drills. He moved energetically around the classroom—whose movable desk-chairs he always had his students form into a U-shape—and tossed ridiculous sentences at them for translation from English to French.

Bert paused in front of Franny Ellis. "Franny," he said, "if this chalk were a piece of Camembert, I would eat it." He accompanied the sentence with a pantomime of gluttony directed at the chalk. Franny laughed and translated the sentence smoothly. Bert nodded and smiled and moved two chairs farther along the U. He pointed the chalk at Jack Sothern and said, "Jack, here's one for you: 'If I hadn't stolen that Citroen, I wouldn't be sitting in this ugly prison now!'" There was some laughter, but Jack didn't even smile. He grimaced, stared at the ceiling and, after a pause, produced a garbled string of French words. Bert had noticed from the first that Jack seemed nervous and translated more slowly than the others, but this was his worst performance to date. Instead of saying anything critical, however, Bert simply moved a few desks farther along the U and presented the same sentence to another student, who translated it perfectly. Bert nodded and continued the exercise, making up ever more outrageous sentences with similar grammatical structures.

Except for Jack, the students handled their assignments well, laughing and groaning at Bert's jokes with gratifying frequency. But Jack muffed every sentence Bert addressed to him. Finally, Bert stood at Jack's desk and lowered his voice and said, "If you didn't have a chance to study the lesson last night, Jack, tell me and I won't call on you."

Jack didn't answer. He just blushed and stared at his hands. This surprised Bert, who had expected something like a thank you; but instead of pursuing the subject further, he simply resumed the class exercise, trying not to look back at Jack. Soon he noticed that Jack had left the room. The other stu-

Dr. Abby Hansen, research associate, wrote this case for the Developing Discussion Leadership Skills and the Teaching by the Case Method seminars. Data were furnished by the involved participants. All names and some peripheral facts have been disguised.

Section 4. Operations: Day-to-Day Classroom Practice;
Implications of Teachers' Actions; Importance of Detail;
Moral Issues

CASE
The French Lesson (A)

dents noticed, too. About ten minutes later, Jack returned, a bit red-faced, and took his seat. The other students' awareness of his discomfort dampened the formerly jolly mood of the class. Bert's efforts to rekindle the humor became more and more self-conscious.

After class, Bert positioned himself near the door. He wanted to catch Jack and get the matter cleared up as soon as possible. But Jack slid by Bert when his back was turned.

He won't even talk to me, Bert thought. Uh oh, this kid is really ticked off!

Bert considered it essential to accord his students respect in the classroom because he knew that eroding their self-confidence could only destroy rapport and worsen their chances for conquering the complexities of good spoken and written French. He prided himself on putting students at their ease, but here was Jack Sothern acting as if Bert had attacked him! Dammit, Bert thought, he's got me all wrong. What's going on—is Jack an oversensitive baby, or am I just a lead-headed boor?

CASE

I Felt as if My World Had Just Collapsed! (A)

Dr. Abby Hansen and *Joy Renjilian-Burgy* prepared *this case in collaboration with* **Professor C. Roland Christensen** *for the Developing Discussion Leadership Skills Seminar. Although based on data supplied by participants involved, all names and some peripheral facts have been disguised.*

Racism!" Susan Roper gestured as if to push the word away. "This incident occurred a year ago, but I still shake when I recall it. If there's anything I have spent my life battling, it's racial prejudice. And the thought of its having cropped up in my classroom sickens me."

Sue was a 38-year-old lecturer in Spanish at Greenwood College for Women in Lancaster, Connecticut. An outgoing woman with long, dark hair and a ready smile, she was beloved by students and colleagues alike and had won several national teaching awards. She and her husband, Jed Henry (a composer-in-residence and professor of music theory at nearby Lancaster Community College), lived with their two young daughters in a rambling house near the Greenwood campus.

Sue's office was cluttered with Spanish books, posters, shawls, sombreros, toys, and other audio-visual aids as well as piles of photocopied materials for her classes, and stacks of notes for a literary project. It was usually populated by numerous students, fellow teachers, and friends. Speaking with the researcher in private, Sue tapped a pencil nervously on the stack of homework papers atop her desk.

"I never thought such a thing could happen in my classroom," she said. "I consciously model values as well as teach language and literature. It's my conviction that teachers shouldn't shy away from moral issues in class, so I don't hesitate to reveal myself. I refer to the kids and Jed, and I talk about the importance of families and the need for acceptance in society. I always assumed that my openness would automatically make something so vile, so pernicious as racism impossible in my classroom. Was I wrong! When this incident happened, I felt as if my world had just collapsed!"

The School

Greenwood College for Women had a pleasant, landscaped campus near enough to Yale University to permit cross-registration and regular travel on a shuttle bus. Founded in 1887, the college enjoyed an outstanding academic reputation. Though predominantly white and middle class, it had made significant efforts to recruit minority students. When this incident occurred in 1981, although 74 of Greenwood's 800 students were officially classified as minorities, most people still thought of the college as homogeneous—"a typical New England women's school."

Section 4. Operations: Day-to-Day Classroom Practice;
Implications of Teachers' Actions; Importance of Detail;
Moral Issues

C A S E
I Felt as if My World Had Just Collapsed! (A)

The Instructor

Sue and her husband Jed were both active in several civil rights organizations. They had worked with the Lancaster Upward Bound Program, and Sue was treasurer of the Mayor's Human Rights Commission, secretary of the Greenwood Community Action Commission, and a founder of CREATE (Citizens for Racial Equality in American Teaching and Education)—a national group promoting unbiased educational materials in elementary schools. Sue had completed all but her dissertation for a Yale Ph.D. She brought over fifteen years of teaching experience to the lectureship at Greenwood, which she had accepted in 1978. Over the years she had taught in Ivy League, state, and single-sex colleges as well as public and private secondary schools. Travel in Spain and Central and South America, in addition to numerous encounters with American black students and colleagues, had sharpened her sensitivity to prejudice and strengthened her commitment to social justice. She was a highly respected teacher at Greenwood, particularly well known for innovative reading lists, creative lesson plans, and effective classroom techniques.

The Course

Spanish 257, "Advance Conversation," met on Mondays, Wednesdays, and Fridays for an hour. The course required demonstrated proficiency in spoken Spanish, coupled with the ability to read and write sophisticated prose constructions. Many students took the course in the third or fourth year. According to Sue, "The composition of this group, like many of mine, was about 30% black—five students in a class of fifteen. Of all foreign languages, Spanish seems to attract the most minority students at Greenwood. Also, many black students tend to take my classes." Sue devised many assignments to get the students to speak Spanish, both in class and outside. One of her favorites was the so-called "minidrama," in which each student wrote a two-character dialogue and then worked with another student to memorize and perform one of their scripts for the whole class. Pairing the students for this exercise gave Sue the opportunity to encourage strangers to work together. The class met in a conventional classroom with movable desk-chairs. Sue urged her students to arrange their chairs in informal groupings and to vary their seating arrangements in order to sit beside different people.

The Students

Despite Greenwood's reputation for homogeneity, conservatism, and a certain affluence, over 35% of the students were receiving some sort of scholarship aid and working part time. There were also many foreign students, as well as feminists, nonconformists, and eccentrics in their ranks. In her class, Sue recalled no particularly unusual young women, however. "This group was very much like most I've had at Greenwood," she reported. "There was the same racial composition, too. Of the black students, there were some from professional families and others from the working class. Of the nonblacks, there were no obvious problems. I recall them as pleasant, competent, and basically cooperative."

The Incident

[In the following section, Sue recalls in her own words the events leading up to the incident.]

It was a Friday in the third week in October. Classes had been in session for over a month. We had gotten about forty minutes into the hour and were finishing a discussion of the reading assignment from the previous day. I had begun to prepare the students for their next task—the minidrama—for which they had already written their scripts and brought them to class. I intended, as usual, to use the exercise to strengthen language acquisition skills and to develop public presence. It's also important to get people to talk to each other in a conversation course. I try to break up cliques in order to help people expand their horizons and maybe even form new friendships. At the very least, they can experience new and different conversational styles.

For one team, I paired Carrie Draper—a rather quiet, white girl from Ohio, a sophomore interested in European Art History—with Sarah Hawley, a black girl from Washington, D.C., who had declared her major as Economics. Sarah was a junior. Both girls had shown strong language skills. I picked them as a team simply because I hadn't previously seen them speaking together.

"Carrie," I began—all this was in Spanish, of course—"would you please sit beside Sarah so you two can read each other's dramas and choose which you'll memorize to perform for the rest of the class next Monday? Please remember to include simple props in your planning and preparation." I was giving my standard speech—I always mention props, for example—so I don't think I looked very intently at Carrie as I stood before the class. Then I went right on and turned to Sarah, saying, "Sarah, would you please take out your minidrama and get ready to work with Carrie?" It was only then that I realized that Carrie hadn't budged. Instead of getting up to go sit beside Sarah, as students usually do, she had simply turned her face directly to me. She avoided Sarah's gaze and said, "I'm sorry, I'm not going to work with Sarah. I mean, I can't work with Sarah. We're . . . we're not in the same dormitory." (In Spanish, "No voy a trabajar con Sarah.")

In all my years of teaching, never before had a student refused to work with another in class. This was a stunning slap in the face to Sarah and a shock to me. I was so horrified I felt positively sick. I stiffened and flushed. Some students had obviously heard Carrie, because I noticed that they looked stricken and embarrassed. No one dared look at Sarah. My body felt hot, and my hands felt icy as they somehow rose before me in a robot-like gesture that was very uncharacteristic for me. I don't think I focused clearly on the class's reaction, because I was so utterly taken aback. But I vividly remember feeling them watch me to see what I'd do.

A friend of mine was made an assistant professor. This fellow—we'll call him Lee—was *very* bright, very nice, sympathetic, also an athlete, a devoted husband, and new father. He was very excited about the undergraduate course he would offer in the fall. The topic was quite interesting. It was a history-of-ideas course of the highest academic integrity and he was writing a book on the subject at the same time.

Well, Lee prepared and prepared and prepared for the course. We talked a good deal with him about what material he wanted to cover and how to acquire it. I must say that he got me very interested in the topic. The semester passed, and Lee—very much worn out from preparation and grading—got through the course. (His mode was to lecture.)

At the end of the year Lee was distinguished in the student newspaper as the most boring professor on campus—a fact which was picked up and reprinted in the wider press.

I suspect his lectures were brilliant, that he was "superstudent," and that he had geared his lectures to the intellectual level of the Society of Fellows with all its Nobel Prize scholars.

As I went over in my mind what went wrong despite all Lee's good intentions and preparation, I began to come up with this idea that he'd overlooked all sorts of basic questions about what he wanted to do and was doing in the course, and that asking them might relieve the catatonic anxiety he now has about teaching. Let's review those questions.

1. *Do all students start equal?*
   Level of Learning. Where do I want to end? Amount of material in the syllabus? If not equal, strengths and weakness of students? How to get this information: class cards?
2. *How am I asking them to learn?*
   Mode of Learning. Programmatic, exploratory, group effort, lecture, attack? Level of uncertainty? Variety of modes? Silent signals, self-referring, teacher-referring?
3. *What's going on in class?*
   Room dynamics; interpersonal dynamics? Are the talkers representative of rest of class?

READING

Seven Questions for Testing My Teaching

LAURA L. NASH

Abstracted from a speech, "Questions You Forgot to Ask; Roles and Responsibilities of Teaching," delivered at Harvard-Danforth Learning Center Workshop, February 19, 1982, by Assistant Professor **Laura L. Nash,** *Harvard University Graduate School of Business Administration.*

Did they get it? Can I help them next time with a summary?

4. *What's going on outside of class?*

Chem. 20 midterm, football weekend, recruiting week?

5. *How does my mode of evaluation affect learning?*

When does it occur; feedback expected?
Where does it occur, how often, what forms?

6. *Who do I want to be?*

Personal Role. Expert, best friend, senior professor, popularity queen, remote, developer, mentor?

How do these roles affect learning? Do students see me in same role as I see myself?
What is an inappropriate role?

7. *What do I owe myself?*

Complete graduate work? Research?
Family?
How to get perspective on what I am doing, teaching included; is this enjoyable?

PART III

Seminar Program for Instructors in Professional Schools: Cases and Readings

Section 1. Introduction

"Several years ago, when I was a second-year teaching fellow in English Literature," Beatrice Benedict recalled, "I had a painful experience in a discussion class when my authority was directly—and publicly—questioned. I felt quite insulted at the time, and I still wonder how well I handled the situation."

The Instructor

In the fall of 1973 Bea Benedict was a fourth-year graduate student in Renaissance English Literature at Fairchild University, a large and famous institution in Arden, Connecticut. A tall, 26-year-old with dark hair reaching nearly to her waist, Bea had recently begun jogging two miles a day. Like many other graduate students, she dressed almost invariably in jeans, pullovers, and track shoes. After graduating with honors from Fairchild herself in 1966, Bea had spent four years in Chicago and Denver working in journalism and publishing. Although her assignments increased in challenge, she was always an "assistant" of some sort, and she felt that her salary had not advanced satisfactorily. Bea reported:

> There was just one woman editor at the last publishing house where I worked. She answered to the title "Doctor" on the job, and that's partly why I decided to go back to school and get a doctorate in English. The rest of the reason was probably that, after four years in the "real world," I was pretty sick of editing and writing trivia. I felt ready for a good, nourishing drink of great literature.

Early in the year in which this incident occurred, Bea had become a resident adviser (RA) in Falstaff House, one of Fairchild's coeducational dwelling units. She counseled English majors and advised graduating seniors seeking fellowships and other academic awards.

The Course

English 200, "Shakespeare," was a highly popular survey course taught to about 400 students in a large lecture room in Warwick Hall. Professor Owen Glendower, a celebrated scholar and raconteur, gave two formal lectures each week. The third meeting was a discussion section, led by one of the fourteen graduate teaching fellows (TFs) who, like Bea, had received their teaching assignments as a

The Case of the Dethroned Section Leader (A)

Dr. Abby J. Hansen, research associate, wrote this case for the Developing Discussion Leadership Skills and the Teaching by the Case Method seminars. Data were furnished by the involved participants. All names and some peripheral facts have been disguised.

precondition of their fellowship stipends. The TFs
led discussions, made writing assignments, and
were totally responsible for their students' grades.
Professor Glendower's principal course assistant
made up the section assignments under instructions
to place 15 students in each group; scheduling problems, however, produced sections inevitably numbering from 8 to 20 students.

Bea had two sections. One—a group of 18—met
in a classroom in Warwick on Thursday afternoons.
Bea did more lecturing than discussing with this
group because 14 of them were freshmen, unfamiliar with literary analysis. Her other class met after
dinner the same evening in Falstaff House because,
like the half-dozen other section leaders in English
200 who were also RAs, Bea had requested that at
least one of her groups be made up of Falstaff residents. This was a much livelier group than Bea's
other section.

[Because Bea considered Professor Glendower's
lectures entertaining but superficial, she took a few
hours each week from her own dissertation research
(on Elizabethan political thought) to read literary
criticism on the plays and cull excerpts to present
to her sections.]

The Setting

Founded in 1778, Fairchild University included
seven professional schools as well as a large, coeducational undergraduate division that enjoyed
widespread praise for embodying the ideal of community (i.e., academic) fellowship. After their first
year, all undergraduates lived in residential units
like Falstaff House, each unit holding about three
hundred and fifty students and twenty-five RAs like
Bea. RAs ranged from graduate students through
senior professors and occasional visiting celebrities—musicians, writers, scientists, and scholars.

Falstaff House, a red brick neo-Tudor compound
on the west bank of the Avon River, included a
large private dining hall, conference rooms, living
suites, common rooms (lounges resembling living
rooms), squash courts, a small gym, and a central
courtyard where anything from political rallies to
frisbee games could occur in good weather.

The Section

Bea's Falstaff House section included five men
and three women; all lived in the House. Out of
that group, Bea recalled four students especially:

Jack Kesselman was a sophomore from Lake Forest,
Illinois. He was a political activist, particularly interested in organizing protests against the university's
investments in South African companies. A folk
singer and songwriter, Jack had a reputation for cleverness. He would often sit in the House courtyard
playing his guitar and singing original ballads about
people we all knew. He was also something of an
operator: once he told me he had arranged to receive
credit toward his degree for private guitar lessons he
was taking from an upperclassman in the House.

Elke Gunnarson was a tall, blond woman from
Kansas City, a senior in Political Science, and a star of
the women's tennis team. She usually dressed either
in tennis whites or her varsity sweatshirt when she
came to the discussion section. Elke participated in
the House Council, organized a formal dance, and
served as hostess at sherry hours.

Elke's boyfriend, Cliff Farmer, was also in the
group. Cliff was a hockey player born and raised in
Rockport, Maine. His major was American History,
and he planned to go to law school. I considered him
steady—not overly brilliant, but a very reliable and
pleasant sort of fellow.

Skip Townsend, a junior from Palo Alto, California,
also participated in our group's discussions. He was
an odd sort of guy, who wrote "beachcomber" under
"Professional Plans, if Any" on the Student Information card I handed out. I recall him as ironic, fairly
quiet, but with a sharp sense of humor.

Bea added:

By the way, the Student Information cards were my
own idea. Glendower gave us almost no guidance in
setting up our discussion groups. I had just started
distributing the cards because the previous year I
learned a week after the final exam that one of my
students has spent the past three summers at the
Stratford Shakespeare Festival. She'd understudied
their Juliet one year. And I never even asked her to
read in class.

Bea's section met just off the Falstaff courtyard in
a small room furnished with an enormous rectangular oak conference table and straight-backed
wooden chairs. Bea sat in the chair nearest the
chalkboard, and the students arranged themselves
in two rows along the sides of the table.

The Incident

[In the following section, Bea recalls in her own words the circumstances leading up to the incident.]

It was the fourth session in the semester, and I thought this group was doing quite well. The informality of meeting in the House after dinner seemed pleasant for all of us. I used to bring my coffee mug to class, and the students brought pieces of cake from the dining hall. My usual opening was to pass out photocopied excerpts from published criticism about the play in question. The students then scanned the handout while I stood at the board to write some key terms for the evening's discussion or perhaps the title of a particularly important book from the recommended readings list. Then I'd sit down and run through a few administrative details—paper deadlines or in-class report assignments—and then present a brief summary of some points from Glendower's lectures. After this opening, I'd call on the student whose turn it was to give a report—an analysis of an assigned passage—to kick off our class discussion. I had asked the students in the first two meetings to choose a date on which they'd like to report, and I tried to accommodate their choices in my assignments. I had stated at our first meeting that students should expect to give two reports during the semester. They were to prepare them thoroughly, but not to read criticism for their analyses. I wanted to hear their own original ideas so I could form impressions of their critical abilities that would help me grade them.

That evening we were discussing Shakespeare's *Richard II.* As usual, I sat in the chair nearest the chalkboard. It was a warm night, and through the open window of our conference room, the frisbee players' shouts of "nice catch," and "whoa, boy, look out for the bushes!" were almost louder than our own voices. I toyed with the idea of asking the students in the courtyard to be quiet, but I knew that it would shortly be too dark to play frisbee, and they would soon give up their game. Skip sat halfway down the table from me. Jack sat on my right. Elke and Cliff sat together just beyond him. (The other students in the section—Patricia Haley, Bob Connors, Charles Schwartz, and Lisa Evans—were all present, but I confess I have nothing in particular to say about them. In fact, I

hardly remember them. I had to look up their names in my old gradebook.)

It was Jack Kesselman's turn to begin that night. I sat down, put on my reading glasses, and turned the pages of my text to the passage I had assigned him. Then I said something like: "Well, Jack, my syllabus has your name here under October 18. Could you tell us what you make of Richard's speech in the second scene of Act III where we see and hear him grappling with the idea that he may actually lose his throne? You remember, as I've mentioned, of course, that the third act in Shakespeare is pivotal. It's exactly in the middle of the five-act structure, and it usually gives the audience the turnaround, the reversal of the world we meet in the first act. I'm very interested, in particular, to hear what you think of Richard's rather pathetic lines 'Not all the water in the rough rude sea/Can wash the balm off from an anointed king'—especially here in the play, when his enemies surround him and he is about to be deposed?" Then, I think, I smiled, took off my reading glasses, and turned to Jack. "Okay, you've got the floor."

Jack slouched in his seat, looking away from me, and riffled the pages of his text. Then he said, "Bea, I'm not sure what I make of Richard's lines. There's something else on my mind."

That took me by surprise. After all, he knew he was being graded on his presentation. So I tried to be encouraging.

I said: "You must have taken some time to think about the passage. Why don't you just give us your reactions. Do you think Richard has any idea that he might lose his power despite his words?"

Jack still hadn't turned to meet my gaze. "Um, I'd like to make a statement," he said.

"Go ahead," was my reply.

Jack said: "I think something's wrong here. In this section. Bea, you talk too much. I timed your introduction. Fifteen minutes. Of our time. And you were just summarizing a lot of stuff we've already heard. It was pretty boring."

I remember I must have been blushing. I felt attacked. I think I sat there staring at Jack—at the side of his head, that is. My first instinct was self-defense.

I said, "I don't think you're being fair. I spent a lot of time preparing for this discussion. I've been studying this material intensively for four years now, and I really want to convey some of what

129

I've learned to you. Glendower hired me for a purpose, you know. Don't you think I've got anything to teach you?"

Now Jack had turned to face me. I remember thinking when I saw him full face how little I had ever liked him. Now I could hardly stand to look at him. Elke and Cliff had been exchanging glances. Elke now telegraphed me a look of embarrassment. Cliff looked unnerved too. Skip was leaning back on the rear legs of his chair. He was grinning. I could imagine him thinking this whole thing a fine joke.

Jack was talking again: "I think we should vote. As far as I'm concerned, Bea, all your talking only stifles us. Even if we're full of hot air, we ought to hear each other's ideas and sort of feel our way along with this material."

By this time I was really furious with Jack, but I would have felt tyrannical if I'd refused to let the section vote. Also, the situation had begun to appeal to my sense of adventure. I was wondering how a leaderless discussion might turn out.

I stood at the board and faced the group, wondering what to do.

Professor Benjamin Cheever stared disbelievingly at the Marine colonel whose public challenge had just interrupted a teaching workshop Ben was leading for the faculty of a military institute. Nothing in his twenty years of teaching—eight using the case method—had prepared Ben for a remark like this. He scanned the group for reactions as the colonel's words echoed in his ears: "...I am offended. Don't you think an apology is in order?"

Background

It was Friday morning. Ben Cheever, an economist and senior faculty member of Fairchild Graduate School of Organization and Management, had sensed from the outset of this case discussion that there would be difficulties getting the workshop moving in the right direction. Along with two colleagues, Ben had traveled from New England to Washington, D.C., to demonstrate case method teaching in a two-day workshop for the faculty of the Senior Commanding Officers' Executive Institute. Ben had come with only moderate expectations, but his instincts told him that this was, in fact, shaping up as a particularly lackluster discussion. The group, which included, in his recollection, "about 85% colonels and lieutenant colonels and some majors, as well as civilian faculty members of equivalent civil service rank," seemed wary, tentative, and unsure of how to proceed. This was particularly disheartening to Ben because his case—the first of the workshop—had been preceded by a rather long and thorough introduction, beginning with a friendly welcome from the commanding general of the institute, an old friend of Ben's.

According to Ben, the general had given the faculty "a warm and humorous speech in which he mentioned my military experience and the fact that he had once worked for me. He told them that he considered case method teaching something they ought to know a bit about and that we were the best." This introduction seemed auspicious to Ben, and it was followed by "about 30 minutes of detailed description of the case method by a colleague of mine who not only knows the method extremely well but also has a military background. He gave the group an encouraging overview, and used many military metaphors and references."

Nonetheless, Ben knew his efforts to make this workshop succeed had two strikes against them. First, the faculty at the institute was unlikely to

CASE

The Offended Colonel (A)

Dr. Abby J. Hansen, *research associate, wrote this case for the Developing Discussion Leadership Skills and Teaching by the Case Method seminars. Data were furnished by the involved participants. All names and some peripheral facts have been disguised.*

131

include many dedicated teachers. Most of the staff were military officers who had attended the institute's programs, as Ben put it, "to get their tickets punched," and fulfill a requirement for promotion. Having done well in the programs, these participants had received invitations to remain and teach for a few years. Second, the teaching staff usually had Fridays free, but today many instructors in the large, half-filled auditorium had been volunteered by their supervisors to attend this workshop.

Inwardly, Ben acknowledged that in some sense he, too, had come mainly to "get his ticket punched." His major reason for traveling to the institute had been to test some cases he had just written under a government contract which stipulated that the new materials be taught in a variety of official environments. Nevertheless, he hoped to find in this group at least some potential enthusiasm for exploring the possibilities of the case method. Ben truly enjoyed teaching and welcomed the challenge to make this workshop a success under these less-than-promised circumstances.

As usual, Ben had adopted a breezy, informal approach during the session. In contrast to the military audience—some in uniform, others in rather conservative civilian clothing—he wore no tie. Ben also joked often, hoping to create a relaxed atmosphere in which lively participation could arise spontaneously. He had asked the institute's faculty to prepare for the class and then join him, first for a regular class discussion, and then to analyze their own performance, his teaching techniques, and the case itself, considered as a teaching vehicle.

The case dealt with a civilian appointee heading a government agency responsible for military research. Faced with information leaks and unresponsiveness in the agency, the case protagonist, Claude La Fleur, resorts to declaring a moratorium on all research. After sketching the situation and briefly reviewing a few details of setting, Ben addressed a general question to the group: "Well, what's bothering Claude La Fleur? Can someone start us off?" The members of the faculty looked around, each seeming curious to see who would volunteer, but not personally interested in doing so. Once the dis-

cussion did get started, the speakers in this group avoided disagreement with their colleagues, much to Ben's annoyance—thus causing an early consensus that Ben feared would close off many possible areas of analysis. Worse, however, was Ben's discomfort at realizing that the ascendant point of view happened to be one he considered off the mark. He began to feel the necessity of getting the group to produce some opposition to this stifling premature conclusion. To accomplish this, he chose to play devil's advocate. In the character of a hostile opponent, Ben responded to one participant's formulation of the majority view with a good-natured "Bullshit!"

The ploy succeeded because, after a laugh, a few proponents of minority views did then raise their hands to speak, but Ben felt it was still hard work to keep the discussion open. By 11:45 he was, like the rest of the participants, looking forward to lunch. The group had moved from the case discussion to the analysis of the morning's proceedings.

All participants had remained seated to speak, but when Ben called on one uniformed Marine Corps colonel at the very back of the room, the man leaned forward and stood up, glaring.

"Dr. Cheever," he said in a strained voice, "I'm wondering about something. Do you always use profanity when you teach? Or is it that you just feel you have to talk down to us servicemen?"

Ben felt everyone's gaze. As an Army veteran and former civilian employee at the Pentagon, as well as the son of a career military officer, he was taken aback by the colonel's statement. His surprise was clearly evident on his face.

"Why no," he said quickly, "I'm not talking down to anybody. This is the way I usually conduct my classes."

"Well, I just want you to know, Dr. Cheever, that I am offended. Besides"—the colonel gestured to the only woman, seated a few rows ahead of him—"there are ladies present. Don't you think an apology is in order, Professor?"

Ben looked at the woman, at the rest of the group, and back at the colonel. The room was silent. Ben wondered, "How do I respond to that?"

This note describes the educational environment at a two-year graduate business school.

The School

Many of the cases used in the Harvard Business School teaching seminar take place at a fictitious two-year graduate school of business management called, for example, "Metropolitan," "Bay" "Farwestern" and "New Dominion." The school includes 800 first-year students in the Master's program in business administration, with the entire student population (including participants in short-term advanced courses in professional management) numbering some 2,000. The school prepares men and women to enter both public and private organizations as managers. Most of the students are college graduates, median age between 26 and 27, with some managerial experience. The administration divides the first-year class into ten "sections" of 80 students each—about 25% of whom are women (a percentage that increased from approximately 8% in the early seventies). Another 10% will be foreign students.

During the first year all students follow a uniform prescribed program. Courses in the first-year program are scheduled in free-form fashion so that they relate to and build upon one another rather than being fitted into a rigid quarter or semester system. The effect of this scheduling arrangement is to begin some courses in September and others at various times during the school year. Course lengths also vary; some run for a few months, stop, and then begin again later in the program.

In the second year, students' course programs reflect personal choice. Students often specialize in a functional area—e.g., marketing, finance, or production—or choose a broader orientation, e.g., concentrating in Control (accounting and statistics), Organizational Behavior, or Business Policy (problem solving from the point of view of a firm's general manager).

The mission of the school is to prepare students for general management positions—in other words, to give them the ability to lead specialists in such fields as accounting, production, and marketing toward the accomplishment of the goals of the larger organization. To this end, qualitative, rather than purely quantitative, approaches to management prevail.

READING

Background Information on a Graduate School of Business Administration

Dr. Abby J. Hansen prepared this note for the Developing Leadership Skills and Teaching by the Case Method seminars.

133

The Section

In many of the teaching cases set in schools of management, the class group is called a section. This implies that it is one of the ten subgroups of the first-year MBA class, numbering approximately 80-plus students. Each section meets daily in the same amphitheater-shaped classroom at 8:30 A.M. for its first hour-and-a-half-long class. The second and third discussion classes continue, with a break for lunch, until 2:30 P.M. Instructors float from classroom to classroom, leading discussions in rooms that the sections grow to regard with a certain proprietary feeling.

Each section elects an educational representative and a social representative. The ed rep's mission is to coordinate the section's reactions to the educational process and, when appropriate, represent its point of view to teachers and administration (and, conversely, theirs to the section). The social rep coordinates informal gatherings and parties, which are numerous, and—in reaction to the pressure of an extremely heavy workload and the frequently tense atmosphere in the school—sometimes very "lively." As the academic year progresses, the section's social organization strengthens, as evidenced by the frequent development of in-class skits which parody study materials or the instructor's teaching style.

For better or worse, the evolution of a strong group dynamic is produced and fostered by the section system, which endeavors to give students a foretaste of the sort of teamwork that management often requires. Learning to function cooperatively in a highly organized and competitive setting is part of the whole enterprise of the first year.

The Faculty

Many of the first-year required courses are taught by a junior faculty group with limited case-discussion teaching experience. Each year a number of these junior instructors or assistant professors are newcomers to the faculty of that graduate business school, often finishing their discipline-based dissertations at other schools while undergoing their first teaching experience in a professional school of business administration. Other instructors are products of that graduate business school's own doctoral program. About a third of the overall teaching group hold associate- or full-professor rank.

The Case Method

Cases used in MBA programs generally present descriptions of real, but sometimes disguised, business situations from the point of view of an actual participant. Cases may run to 30 or more pages plus several exhibits including, for example, charts, balance sheets, profit-and-loss statements, diagrams of factories, and other such technical data. Students receive study questions that help guide them through analysis of the situation. The last study question generally calls for recommendations to the viewpoint character.

Researchers prepare cases from field data and interviews. It is the students' job to sift the wheat from the chaff, make diagnoses, present recommendations, and defend them in open discussion.

Case discussions often begin with the instructor calling on a student "cold" (without previous warning) to ask for a coherent analysis of the major issues inherent in the welter of historical detail in the case. Following the student's presentation, the rest of the section members enter the discussion after being recognized by the instructor. In many courses, class participation accounts for as much as 50% of the students' final grades. Ideally, the discussion allows the participants to practice both analytical and rhetorical skills: they think, speak, react, persuade, and judge.

In the course of the subsequent discussion, the instructor often writes significant points on the chalkboards at the front of the amphitheater. The goal of the method is to engage the students' interest, and thus stimulate them to participate and learn from each other in order to produce from their varied and often contradictory approaches to the administrative problems some set of graspable alternatives for action. The process by which this all happens in the classroom is the instructional heart of the method.

Grading

There is a premium on class participation, since a substantial part of the general manager's daily world is verbal. Grades given are Excellent, Satisfactory, Low Pass, and Unsatisfactory. Students who receive eight units of any combination of Low Pass or Unsat or three units of Unsat, regardless of any other grading, are screened out—asked to leave the school (although some petition, successfully, to be allowed to return and complete their degrees).

Faculty protocol insists that an instructor restrict Excellent grades to 15% or 20% of the class and to give a minimum of 10% to 15% Low Passes and Unsatisfactory grades. The latter grade designation is rarely used.

I wish to present some very brief remarks in the hope that if they bring forth any reaction from you, I may get some new light on my own ideas.

I find it a very troubling thing to think . . . about my own experiences and try to extract from those experiences the meaning that seems genuinely inherent in them. At first such thinking is very satisfying, because it seems to discover sense and pattern in a whole host of discrete events. But then it very often becomes dismaying, because I realize how ridiculous these thoughts, which have much value to me, would seem to most people. My impression is that if I try to find the meaning of my own experience it leads me, nearly always, in directions regarded as absurd.

So in the next three or four minutes, I will try to digest some of the meanings which have come to me from my classroom experience and the experience I have had in individual and group therapy. They are in no way intended as conclusions for someone else, or a guide to what others should do or be. They are the very tentative meanings, as of April 1952, which my experience has had for me, and some of the bothersome questions which their absurdity raises. I will put each idea or meaning in a separate lettered paragraph, not because they are in any particular logical order, but because each meaning is separately important to me.

a. I may as well start with this one in view of the purposes of this conference. My experience has been that I cannot teach another person how to teach. To attempt it is for me, in the long run, futile.

b. It seems to me that anything that can be taught to another is relatively inconsequential, and has little or no significant influence on behavior. That sounds so ridiculous I can't help but question it at the same time that I present it.

c. I realize increasingly that I am only interested in learnings which significantly influence behavior. Quite possibly this is simply a personal idiosyncrasy.

d. I have come to feel that the only learning which significantly influences behavior is self-discovered, self-appropriated learning.

e. Such self-discovered learning, truth that has been personally appropriated and assimilated in experience, cannot be directly communicated to another. As soon as an individual tries to com-

READING

Personal Thoughts on Teaching and Learning

CARL R. ROGERS

*This was a speech given by noted psychologist **Carl R. Rogers**, and taken from Carl R. Rogers,* On Becoming a Person *(Boston: Houghton Mifflin Co., 1961), pp. 275–78. Reprinted with permission of publisher.*

municate such experience directly, often with a quite natural enthusiasm, it becomes teaching, and its results are inconsequential. It was some relief recently to discover that Soren Kierkegaard, the Danish philosopher, had found this too, in his own experience, and stated it very clearly a century ago. It made it seem less absurd.

f. As a consequence of the above, I realize that I have lost interest in being a teacher.

g. When I try to teach, as I do sometimes, I am appalled by the results, which seem a little more than inconsequential, because sometimes the teaching appears to succeed. When this happens I find that the results are damaging. It seems to cause the individual to distrust his own experience, and to stifle significant learning. Hence I have come to feel that the outcomes of teaching are either unimportant or hurtful.

h. When I look back at the results of my past teaching, the real results seem the same—either damage was done, or nothing significant occurred. This is frankly troubling.

i. As a consequence, I realize that I am only interested in being a learner, preferably learning things that matter, that have some significant influence on my own behavior.

j. I find it very rewarding to learn in groups, in relationship with one person as in therapy, or by myself.

k. I find that one of the best but most difficult ways for me to learn is to drop my own defensiveness, at least temporarily, and to try to understand the way in which [the other person's] experience seems and feels to the other person.

l. I find that another way of learning for me is to state my own uncertainties, to try to clarify my puzzlements, and thus get closer to the meaning that my experience actually seems to have.

m. This whole train of experiencing, and the meanings that I have thus far discovered in it, seem to have launched me on a process which is both fascinating and at times a little frightening. It seems to mean letting my experience carry me on, in a direction which appears to be forward, toward goals that I can dimly define, as I try to understand at least the current meaning of that experience. The sensation is that of floating with a complex stream of experience, with the fascinating possibility of trying to comprehend its everchanging complexity.

I am almost afraid I may seem to have gotten away from any discussion of learning, as well as teaching. Let me again introduce a practical note by saying that by themselves these interpretations of my own experience may sound queer and aberrant, but not particularly shocking. It is when I realize the implications that I shudder a bit at the distance I have come from the commonsense world that everyone knows is right. I can best illustrate that by saying that if the experiences of others had been the same as mine, and if they had discovered similar meanings in it, many consequences would be implied.

a. Such experience would imply that we would do away with teaching. People would get together if they wished to learn.

b. We would do away with examinations. They measure only the inconsequential type of learning.

c. The implication would be that we would do away with grades and credits for the same reason.

d. We would do away with degrees as a measure of competence partly for the same reason. Another reason is that a degree marks an end or a conclusion of something, and a learner is only interested in the continuing process of learning.

e. It would imply doing away with the exposition of conclusions, for we would realize that no one learns significantly from conclusions.

I think I had better stop there. I do not want to become too fantastic. I want to know primarily whether anything in my inward thinking, as I have tried to describe it, speaks to anything in your experience of the classroom as you have lived it, and if so, what the meanings are that exist for you in your experience.

Until a few decades ago, it was generally agreed that the most important part of the legacy from one generation to another consisted in a kind of wisdom: In what does the good life consist? What is worthy of one's commitment? What is more important than self-gratification? What is good or honorable or true? The second part of that legacy consisted of knowledge and skill: teaching a younger generation how to make a living, how to master a profession, how to become a productive citizen. But through it all, education was seen as a moral endeavor, not because it sought to indoctrinate but because it was a sharing of things that people held to be important. Faculty had authority not only because they were experts in their disciplines, but because they had common commitments and took seriously the important questions and the responsibility of their answers before a younger generation.

All of us are aware that the collegiate tradition in this country grew out of such an understanding of education. In the colleges that were founded in the eighteenth and nineteenth centuries, there was an ethos, an atmosphere of expectation, embodied in ceremonies and traditions as well as in courses, in which all of these things were fused together and passed on. Education was the institutionalization of what we as a people deemed to be important. And through that process, that institutionalization, we sought to prepare oncoming generations for their role and responsibility in society.

The wisdom that underlay such preparation, as we all know, was a distillate of the Bible and of the classical tradition, and it included a strong dose of literature. Through those courses and subjects one encountered life vicariously. Reality was served up not in piecemeal fashion but in and through the larger conflicts and tensions, aspirations and dichotomies, hypocrisies and hopes of the people portrayed in that literature. Virtue had a role—not in a preening self-regarding sense but as the embodiment of certain qualities of life and of their importance for the body politic—qualities such as fidelity, good will, patience, discipline, restraint, promise-keeping. This was a legacy that took precedence over self.

There are some thoughtful testimonies in our time to the power of that kind of education. Many of us were products of it. Theodore White has written movingly in his *In Search of History* of his first encounter, as a young Harvard student out of a Boston

READING

The Education of the Heart

JAMES T. LANEY

*This essay by **James T. Laney**, president of Emory University, originated as an address to the directors of the Harvard Alumni Association, and was published in* Harvard Magazine, *September–October 1985.*

ghetto, with John K. Fairbank. He tells how this gangling North Dakotan—who taught Chinese, of all unlikely subjects—drew him to himself and taught him how to live in the mannered atmosphere of Cambridge. But beyond that, White says that he remembers Fairbank for having sculpted and polished a rough stone into something that was worthwhile. And he was talking about himself. We've all known the impact of that kind of teaching. One doesn't need to be sentimental to acknowledge the role of that wisdom and of that kind of teaching and of that kind of education.

But times have changed. For at least three decades, that received wisdom has been under attack. We have lost the confidence to share those dimensions of life, to express those opinions, to give vent to our deepest longings in behalf of others as our own mentors once did.

That wisdom has been under attack because, for one thing, its focus was too exclusive, too parochial. It was too WASPish. It contributed to a disenfranchisement of too many in a full life. And its conventional morality too easily accommodated injustice and hypocrisy. That wisdom has also wilted under the harsh analysis of Marx and Freud, which sees goodness as a cover for imperialism or a mask for self-aggrandizement, placing all virtue and wisdom under suspicion. Within the academic community that wisdom has become embattled because it seems too amateurish, and there is no charge more intimidating for us in the academic world than to be told that we are amateurs. The received wisdom seems too didactic, too preachy. Expertise has now become the necessity.

The result is that authority has retreated to that which is more certain, known and demonstrable. A more comprehensive and holistic view of life has given way to specialization. The shared outlook which that wisdom represented has fragmented. In many of our faculties across the country there has been such a focus upon research and teaching that the interaction with students has become limited to the classroom. Today few colleges have shared public events beyond commencement. I'm not talking just about chapel, but about any kind of assembly where the community gathers.

In many academic disciplines there has been a retreat from the attempt to relate values and wisdom to what is being taught. Not long ago, Bernard Williams, the noted British philosopher, observed that philosophers have been trying all this century to get rid of the dreadful idea that philosophy ought to be edifying. Philosophers are not the only ones to appreciate the force of that statement. Others have written of the shift in the humanities from the life portrayed to emphasis upon methodology.

Obviously in all of this something is missing. Surely we can recall that the events at Berkeley in the sixties not only introduced us to the notions of free speech, but also taught us that students feel deprived when teachers only teach or, even more tellingly, only do research. The brightest of students want to get inside their professors' minds, not to be indoctrinated but to learn why they think the way they do and how they have arrived at their conclusions. If this seems strange, look at what law students and medical students and other professional students remember most vividly from their education: their clerkships with judges and the moments over coffee, or the grand rounds when the doctor begins to tell anecdotes that reveal something of his or her humanity. It is precisely in those moments that values and wisdom are shared.

Not too long ago a magazine commissioned a writer to go back to his college and write an article about undergraduate life. He observed that the only two things he could find that all undergraduates shared were a sense of having to survive and a desire for self-gratification. He is not alone in this observation. Education no longer seems to be the institutionalization of what we think is important to society. Instead, what we are emphasizing today, largely by default, is careerism. We seem to be turning out people who are bent upon exploiting careers for their own ends rather than upon service through their professions for the sake of society.

And that is exactly what we are bound to do if we do not educate the heart. Without virtue, without the education of the heart, expertise and ambition easily become demonic. How can society survive if education does not attend to those qualities which it requires for its very perpetuation? Witness the decline of the sense of service in the field of medicine or law or nursing or even the ministry. To be sure no one, with the possible exception of the Moral Majority, questions the inadequacy of the old, received wisdom. But more and more people are acknowledging now the need for a new wisdom, a wisdom that is compatible with contemporary knowledge and our new pluralism and that grows out of an appreciation of our common heritage. There is a growing realization that we can no longer operate under the popular conceit that the mere aggregation of individual pursuits and successes will somehow redound to the best interests of our commonweal.

To speak of virtue in education does not necessarily entail being ideological or doctrinaire. Nor does it imply being moralistic. But in our concern to avoid these excesses and intrusions we have tended to evacuate the field of value and meaning altogether. And in our understandable honoring of the freedom of others we have allowed our students to conclude that we don't much care.

So it seems to me that we need to permit ourselves to teach more comprehensively, more personally. We need to encourage our institutions to be hospitable to a broader range of discussions concerning purpose and meaning. We in the universities are not only guardians of the pursuit of knowledge but stewards of the tradition in which that knowledge is applied for the good of society—indeed the world. This stewardship cannot be left to chance or to self-appointed moral monitors who would impose their judgments upon us from outside. The problem is ours. I am persuaded that all of us in higher education share these concerns, however much addressing them may complicate our personal careers and our institutional goals.

Section 2. The Early Class Sessions: Establishing the Instructor-Student Learning Contract

CASE

Henry Jasper (A)

It was 8 A.M. on a cold and sunless winter day when Carol Cutler opened her statistics class. After a short summary of the major points covered by Professor Wilbar that week in lecture, she presented a simple problem.

"Can anyone get started on solving this?" Carol asked. No one volunteered. "Well, Henry, why don't you give it a try?"

Henry Jasper was sitting at the front of the class and at first just stared at Ms. Cutler, who was standing at the chalkboard. Then, suddenly, he replied in a loud, agitated, violent way: "Look, I'm sick of you women teachers always picking on me. I'm not going to take it anymore. That's just it, you're trying to castrate me and it's been that way since I was in elementary school. Well, you're not going to get away with it now. Professor Wilbar is going to hear what you're trying to do to me. You'll be sorry!"

Jasper was now standing by her desk. Carol looked at him, then at the class, then back to him. In the ensuing silence Carol frantically thought to herself, What's going on? What do I do?

Background

Located in a beautiful rural setting, Northern University was one of eight Ivy League Schools. The school's admission policy thus was selective. Northern's 12,000 undergraduates and 3,000 graduate students had the fortunate opportunity to choose between several specialized schools and departments, many of which were acknowledged to be the leading institutions in the field. This philosophy of excellence in very specialized areas permitted broad financial support for most graduate students and provided tuition, fees, and a small stipend to cover basic living expenses. Two part-time employment methods were extensively used for this purpose: research assistantships to aid professors engaged in critical work, and teaching assistantships for the large, required lecture courses. Northern's ratio of male to female undergraduates was about 3 to 1, and this ratio was even higher on the graduate levels.

The Statistics Course

In the section that follows, Carol Cutler describes in her own words the statistics course.

Statistics 210 is the introductory statistics course required of all sophomores in Human Ecology and

Tamara Gilman wrote this case under the supervision of *C. Roland Christensen* from data supplied by involved participants for the Developing Discussion Leadership Skills Seminar. All names and some peripheral facts have been disguised.

Industrial Relations, as well as in Hotel Management. There are about 300 captive students each semester, which provide five teaching assistants with half-time work. We teach three two-hour "labs" a week, each with about 24 students at a time. Since many of the students sleep or read the college newspaper during the three weekly 9 A.M. lectures by Professor Wilbar, we try to summarize the major points made that week and then hand out a problem set that requires use of the new techniques in order to solve the problems. We don't require attendance in the labs, but attendance is usually pretty high, since this is the only time students can practice doing problems similar to those on the exams. And because we only have a midterm and a final on which to base the course grade, most people show up on schedule.

The labs are held in one of two rooms called the machine rooms because they contain SCM calculating machines for student use in working out the numerical answers to problem sets. The SCMs are antiquated, compared to the new electronic calculators; they're incredibly noisy and so big they look like supermarket check-out machines; and they often jam up so that they either incorrectly calculate or don't work at all. Each machine is on a separate grey metal office-sized desk and they are lined up in four rows of six each. Given the drab decor, the lack of any windows, and the noise level when every machine is working, it can be pretty bleak in there.

The purpose of the T.A., as I see it, is to help the students learn how to do the problems and understand why they're doing them in a particular way or using a particular technique. The concepts aren't simple for people who don't have a strong background in math, and for most of them this will be their last quantitative course.

I begin my lab by listing the major issues Professor Wilbar has discussed at a theoretical level, and then I spend 15 or 20 minutes on how these can be used in a practical way to solve problems. Simple, somewhat humorous illustrations that somehow relate to the particular character and interest of the class work seem to work best. For example, in the lab I might use a hypothetical distribution of quarts of beer drunk by the various houses on campus that are predominantly male—since two out of three students in my class are male.

I also give the class the opportunity to work the problem out, or at least make a stab at it, by asking, "Can anyone suggest any way to go about solving this problem?" If no one raises his or her hand, I go ahead and work it out myself, explaining while I do it.

After going over the example, I hand out the worksheet and spend the rest of the period answering questions and helping students do the problems. The instructor's desk is at the head of one row of desks, and I usually just sit there for the next 15 minutes or so drinking a cup of coffee, but after that I wander around the lab so that people can stop me and show me their problem if they need help. Especially at the beginning of the semester I try to be enthusiastic and supportive, because I know so many are overly anxious about the math.

When they've completed the problems, the students hand in the finished sheets to me. If there is time left in the period, I check the answers, and if there are any mistakes we discuss them. However, most students take nearly the full time to do the work and I can't check them all at once, so I do that outside of the lab and then hand them back the next week. Often the individual discussions in lab are as much about the mistakes of the prior week as they are about the problems of the current week. The problem sets aren't "graded," but if there are errors I mark them, indicating what mistakes were made so that the student will understand what should have been done.

Besides discussing the problems in lab, I schedule six hours a week for conference time, so that the students can drop by for a private discussion if they want to. Well, it's almost private; although other students aren't around, my two officemates are often there. Most of my students come by infrequently and then only to discuss particularly troublesome problems or concepts. For instance, if a student makes the same error on the problems for two or three weeks in a row, I'll just put a note on the latest paper saying "Why don't you stop by my office and we'll try to clear this up once and for all."

However, there are two other types of students and both stop by almost every week. The first group really understands what's going on and just wants to "fine tune" that knowledge so that they will get an A. All of these students have aspirations for doing graduate work, often in law, and often at the top universities. They don't want a "dumb" statistics grade to jeopardize their chances.

The students in the second group are usually doing just adequate work and have little mathematical experience. I think that they're frightened by the very idea of a stat course and in some ways have a mental block against it, not lack of real ability. I try to encourage them to stop worrying by listening to them, patiently going over the problems—sometimes several times in a row in different ways—and by explaining really elementary operations, like how to take square roots. I can really sympathize with these people because I'm not in Math or Stat, and I know how anxious I'd feel if I was required to take a quantitative course which I thought was over my head.

However my officemate, Barry Gerber, a master's candidate in Stat, thinks I'm not tough enough. I remember one day I was listening to a young woman, after she had just gotten her midterm back: "I just don't understand it. I worked so hard for this exam and now I've done so poorly. I studied a lot for this. It's really upsetting, getting a grade like this after all that work."

"I know how you feel, Ginny," I said. "But I don't think that you did all that badly, and I'm sure if we work together for the next several weeks, you'll be able to do much better on the final. It is hard when you're not used to math. . . ."

At that point in my "sympathy" speech, Barry, who was sitting at his desk at the back of the office, literally flew over his desk and stood in front of us, berating the student for lying to me and trying to take advantage of me when she obviously hadn't done any work in the course at all. The student left in a hurry, as bewildered as I was! Then Barry, who had taught the course before, told me that after seeing me deal with students during conference hours, he was convinced I was "taking too much crap from them. You let them push you around with their sob stories." He kept telling me to "get tough with them!" I'm still not convinced that I should do that, but even if I was, I'm not sure at all how I would go about it. Being tough just isn't my style.

The Instructor's Background

[According to the case researcher, Ms. Cutler had just turned 22 and was in her first year of a master's program in industrial relations. She had graduated from a midwestern university with a major in economics. The following is Carol's own description of the events leading up to her role as instructor.]

I wasn't at all sure at the beginning of my senior year what I wanted to do after graduation—work or go to graduate school. My mother wanted me to work and thought that being a stewardess would be great, since I "wouldn't have to think so much" and I'd "meet a lot of nice men." She was worried because I wasn't dating anyone seriously, and she used to tell me that I'd be better off in a less "egghead" field, because men didn't like smart women! Since my sophomore year she had been sending newspaper clippings of the engagements and weddings of my high school girl friends, and I guess she thought I hadn't gotten the message. Besides, I didn't have the money for school, and she thought it was crazy to go into debt for something that I'd never have to use.

Well, I decided to apply anyhow. Although my average was only a $B-$, it was an $A-$ in economics and I was really interested in labor economics. I also applied for financial aid, but I really didn't hold out any hope. I was ecstatic when I learned that not only was I accepted, but that I would receive financial aid. Northern said that I'd be informed later in the summer which professor I'd be working for. When I told my family, the only positive comment my mother made was, "At least there's more men than women there."

I left in June for a summer exchange program job in a bank in Amsterdam. One day at work I received a letter from my mother which included a letter from Northern. It stated that I would be a teaching assistant for Professor Wilbar in the introductory Statistics 210 course. Was that a shock! I had been hoping for a research assistantship because I had never taught before and don't really like to be in the spotlight. Besides, I'd only had one course in statistics myself, and I only got a C in that. At first I considered forgetting the whole thing. I really didn't think I was up to it. Then some people I was working with convinced me to calm down and suggested that I get a few stat books to review. Luckily, English texts are used frequently in Holland and I found two on statistics, which I went over with the help of several Heinekens!

Carol Cutler

[According to Ms. Cutler's officemate Barry Gerber, Cutler's arrival at the statistics department was something of a surprise. The following is Barry's own description of Carol Cutler.]

I walked into Professor Wilbar's office right before registration day and saw a mob of students. I thought I could help out so I started asking people if I could help them, answer any questions about the course, things like that. A small girl with long, brown hair was standing near me and I turned to her. She looked just like the rest of the kids—rather young and dressed casually. Was I surprised to discover that she was the new T.A. and my officemate! When Professor Wilbar's secretary heard her name, she was just as surprised and apologized for having her wait in line with the students. I guess Carol had been waiting there for some time. We finally got all the procedures taken care of—the books, assignments, things like that—and I showed her to our office.

We talked a little and then she left to see some professors about her own courses. She was very friendly and open, not at all formal, and with a kind of bouncy personality. She seemed nervous about teaching, though. I think this was partly because she wasn't getting an M.A. or Ph.D. in Stat like the rest of us and didn't feel all that comfortable with it, and partly because she hadn't taught before. Since we had all taught 210 last year, Carol got us all together one day before her first lab day and grilled us about how we ran a lab and what we did. She even asked us if she should wear a skirt or pants! I don't think we were very much help to her on that. The rest of us are all guys and had never thought about it. I remember seeing her after that first lab and she was pretty upset. I guess the guys in the class gave her a pretty rough time.

The First Lab

[According to Ms. Cutler, that first lab had been designed to enable students to develop a "hands on" familiarity with the calculators through a demonstration of how they worked and through a brief, purely mechanical problem set. The following is Carol's own description of that first lab session and the events that followed.]

Mine was scheduled for Tuesday at 2:30 P.M. Professor Wilbar was supposed to show me how to run the calculators the day before, but he didn't get around to it until noon of the same day. It wasn't difficult, but there were certain common mistakes he told me to watch out for. I just hoped I could remember all of them.

About 2:30 I finally conquered my doubts and walked into the machine room. Actually, I was a little late on purpose so I wouldn't have to stand up in the front of the class waiting for them. The first thing that I noticed was that there were no women in the lab. The second was the size of the guys. They were huge! I found out later that this was the "jock" section, made up of football and hockey players.

After introducing myself and talking a little about the purpose of the labs, I showed them how the SCMs worked and handed out the worksheet. I thought to myself, Well, at least you survived the first day. Was I mistaken!

Suddenly everything seemed to be going wrong. First, there was a rash of machine breakdowns. One right after another had keys that stuck, a carriage that wouldn't move, multiplied instead of added on command, or wouldn't respond at all. Then there were voices shouting throughout the room, "Hey, Teach, my machine won't work!"—accompanied by not very muffled snickers. On top of this, some guys decided to use a more direct approach and complained—rather, glared down at me—from a distance too close for comfort.

I didn't know what to do with the machines. Professor Wilbar hadn't said anything about mechanical problems. But by accident, while trying to fix one of them, I discovered that the plug was pulled out. Checking several others that wouldn't work at all revealed that they too had been disconnected. I finally realized that, at least in part, a concerted effort was being made to upset me.

I knew then that I had lost control and was in real trouble, but I hadn't the foggiest notion of what to do to regain any semblance of order. I had a terrible headache by this time and could hardly think with all these giants breathing down my neck. I guess I decided that the best thing that could happen would be for them to leave. Smiling and cajoling, I reminded them that if they quit horsing around, they'd finish and could leave early.

143

Appealing to their best self-interest didn't seem to help much, though, until someone actually finished and left. That seemed to be the catalyst and the turning point. Order, relatively speaking, then prevailed and the guys focused more on the problems than on hassling me. But what a terrible 45 minutes it was! When the lab was over I immediately asked Professor Wilbar for a transfer to another section. I swapped with Barry and got primarily from Human Ecology a section that happened to be mostly female.

After my trial by fire, I gradually began to feel more comfortable in the classroom and the challenge became making sure I understood the statistical concepts and how to solve the problems. This was more difficult than I had anticipated.

Professor Wilbar wrote the text, and it was different from the one I used and the ones I reviewed over the summer. Sometimes I just didn't understand the answers on the "key" to the problem sets, and sitting in on the lectures didn't help. I couldn't afford to lose the T.A. and by this time I had a commitment to my students, so I felt I couldn't let the department know how much trouble I was having. Usually one of my housemates helped me work the problems out; she was a Ph.D. in urban planning and had had a lot of stat work.

But one night, before my first lab of the week, neither of us could get the right answer and match the "key." I couldn't wait until the next day to get the solution because the lab was at 8 A.M. I didn't know what to do. I couldn't go into the lab not knowing how to do the problem, yet I didn't have any way to find out how to do it. As it got later and later I got more and more desperate. Ellie, my housemate, finally went to bed and I was really all alone and didn't know where to turn. Finally, at 1 A.M., I decided to call one of the other T.A.s. I picked Barry because he seemed the most approachable. Well, I woke both him and his roommates up, but he explained it to me and I finally could go to sleep.

The next morning at 10 A.M., just as the lab was breaking up, Barry came into the machine room. I thanked him again for his help. He looked at me and said, "I want brownies!"

He had a whole batch of them on his desk the first thing the next morning. I guess I had to swallow my pride and take a risk, but at least I started getting the help I needed.

Henry Jasper

[The following is Carol Cutler's own description of Henry Jasper.]

Henry Jasper was a sophomore in the Industrial Relations School, with a quiet, serious manner not usually found in the typical extroverted industrial relations student. About 5'6" tall, he had dark brown hair cut short and combed to the side, wore glasses, and always had on a neat shirt and a pair of slacks that contrasted sharply with the T-shirt-and-jeans uniform the other three men in his lab—as well as most of the male population at Northern—wore.

He was one of the first to arrive in the machine room on lab mornings and always sat in the first desk of the row immediately in front of mine. While many of the students drank coffee and joked with each other while trying to wake up waiting for the lab to start, Henry always took out his stat book and reviewed the reading assignment for the week. During the lab time when students were working on the problems and comparing answers, Henry would just turn to me to check the solution and ask any questions, because our desks were so close. I don't think he knew many other people in the lab because they were mostly from Human Ecology, not Industrial Relations. He usually took the whole period to complete the problem set, and sometimes would stay over to the next lab (10 A.M. to noon) if there were calculators not being used.

Henry was extremely conscientious about doing his problem sets right and came up to the office to go over details all the time. For example, I remember one of his first office visits at the beginning of the semester. He came in, put his books down carefully, and took out a notebook with a list of points he wanted to discuss. "I know you went over this in class, Miss Cutler, but I want to make sure I understand the difference between the mean, the median, and the mode. The mean is the average, the median is the 50th percentile, and the mode is the most frequent value. Is that right?"

"That's right, Henry. Do you understand the formulas for calculating them?" I asked.

"I think so," he replied, "but I want to make sure. Can we work through these problems at the end of Chapter 2? I've already done them and would like to check them against the correct answers."

"Of course," I said and reached for the text. Halfway through the second problem I saw that he had made a simple arithmetic error and I pointed it out. "But that's not really anything to worry about, Henry. You didn't have a calculator when you were doing these and anyone can make a mistake, dividing with such large numbers. Besides, you used the right formula, put the right numbers in it, and understand why you were doing it that way. I think you really know what's important."

Dejectedly he answered, "I don't know, Miss Cutler. I did these extra problems and thought I had worked them through very carefully. I took a lot of time with them. I thought I had the answers exactly right. I just don't seem to have much of a knack for math."

"When was the last time you took a math course?" I asked.

"High school algebra, four years ago when I was a sophomore," he responded. "I didn't do too well in it and stopped taking any more math after that. I tried to get out of Stat 210, but the registrar's office told me that I need it to graduate in IR, and there's no way I can avoid it. Do you think I'll do OK? If I work hard?"

Trying to be encouraging, I said, "I can't see why not, although it's just the beginning of the course. You understand everything so far and seem to be willing to work hard, even do extra work, and that's a good sign. But remember, if you ever want to go over the problems or need to discuss anything you just don't quite understand in the course, feel free to come up. If you can't make it during conference hours, we can always schedule another time that's convenient for both of us. And don't worry about those math errors— you'll get more and more used to the numbers as the time goes by."

As the semester went by, Henry came up to the office about every week. It became apparent that he understood basically what the course was about, but he had to work hard for that understanding.

Just a week ago, when we were in the section on confidence intervals, he told me during an office visit: "I think I've finally got down what a standard deviation is, but it keeps getting mixed up in my head, especially when I try to do prob-

lems. Now, it's the measure of how certain you are that a sample value is the true value, right?"

"Well, standard deviation is the measure of the variability of individual observations from the mean," I said. "And it can be used in hypothesis testing to see if a sample mean comes from a population with a certain hypothetical mean. And we use the confidence intervals, which are based on the standard deviation, to do the testing and give us a certain probability. You know, Henry, you keep telling me that you don't understand this, but it sounds like you do. You must, to answer your own questions the way you did."

"It may sound like it, but if I do understand it why can't I do the problems better? Why do I keep making the same mistakes?" he asked plaintively. He pulled the last two labs out of his notebook and said, "I know the final only has problems on it—not the definitions that I can memorize—and I just keep getting the labs wrong. Look at these! They have more red ink on them than pencil!"

"But you don't get the labs 'wrong,'" I insisted. "You make arithmetic mistakes, but everyone does that. Even when you attack a problem incorrectly, you always go back to it and make sure that you understand what you should have done. And that is the important thing—whether or not you do it perfectly right the first time isn't important. It's whether or not you understand it ultimately that counts."

He pushed his glasses back up and paused before he started putting his labs away. Then as he was picking up his books and coat, he said: "I'm getting tired of working so hard and not getting anywhere on this. It's frustrating. Completely frustrating! I know you're willing to help, but still, it doesn't get any easier and I put so much time into it that my other courses are suffering. I just can't afford that. Do you think I'm going to make it? Is it worth all this effort? What do you think?"

"I don't know for sure, Henry," I gently hedged. "But I do know that you can do the problems similar to those on the exams when you relax and think them through without getting all tensed up. The numbers on the exams are easier to work with—they're smaller and divide evenly—because we don't want students to get all hung up on that when we're trying to see if they know the concepts. And we don't mark down for stupid math errors that result from trying to work too fast, so you don't need to worry about that. And I know you've been working hard. If you're on the borderline of a grade, that can only help. Besides, you're one of the few people that goes regularly to the lectures, reads the assignments, and attends lab as well! I'm sure you'll do fine!"

*   *   *

Carol's Dilemma

Henry Jasper remained standing in front of Carol's desk as she thought to herself, "What's going on?"

CASE

Ernie Budding (A)

B ay Area Graduate School of Management (called Bay by its students) was a large, well-reputed business school that conducted most instruction by the case method, dividing its first-year class of MBAs into approximately 10 sections of 80 students each. Each section was assigned an amphitheater-shaped classroom in which the students assembled daily at 8:30 for the first of three hour-and-twenty-minute classes. The instructors taught their courses by moving among the sections' classrooms.

Included in the required first-year curriculum at Bay were Organizational Psychology and Management, Business Economics, Comparative Political Economy, Business English, Marketing, and Manufacturing Management.

That year, many instructors agreed that Section I, of all the first-year groups, seemed to be the brightest, hardest working, and liveliest. Assistant Professor Ernie Budding, new to Bay that year, taught the course Manufacturing Management (MM) to Section I. He found teaching by the case method to be exciting, and he especially enjoyed teaching Section I. Despite the technical nature of much of the MM material, Ernie was quickly impressed with Section I's desire to learn and its high level of preparation and participation. By second semester, however, he began to notice sluggishness in class participation and a widening gap between his continued commitment to preparation and theirs.

This case details Ernie's perceptions of the section's deteriorating behavior through the year and his various attempts to improve the situation.

The Instructor

Ernie Budding came to Bay with a brand new Ph.D. in economics from Carnegie Tech. Teaching MM, a required first-year course, to Section I was his primary assignment. Ernie commented to the case researcher: "I established rapport with Section I very early in the first semester, and heard about their excellent reputation from other instructors. I was glad that we got along so well."

Ernie was 28 and unmarried when he began teaching MM. He looked like one of the MBA students, except that he always wore a tie when teaching; the students usually dressed more casually. He was enthusiastic, extremely energetic, and active—always moving around the classroom when he taught. Asked his favorite sports, he replied, "You name it. Swimming, running, tennis, skiing, rock-

*Dr. Abby J. Hansen wrote this case in collaboration with
C. Roland Christensen for the Developing Discussion
Leadership Skills Seminar. While the case is based on data
supplied by participants involved, all names and some peripheral facts have been disguised.*

climbing. But I dislike competitive sports, probably because I'm so competitive by nature. I prefer to compete against myself." He described his family as "a whole bunch of high achievers," both in academics and the business world.

Ernie told the researcher that he chose Carnegie Tech for graduate work after he graduated from Berkeley because, as he put it, "I'm not instinctively quantitative, so I wanted the rigor that their program offered." He smiled and added:

> I'm not a masochist; I needed a rigorous program because, with my interest in organizations and their behavior, I would be labeled suspect if I didn't have quantitative skills. But I'm never willing to quantify things like human motivations. I created havoc at Carnegie Tech by always asking, "What's that number good for? What does it do?" It's a very theoretically oriented place, but I wrote my thesis on a rather practical subject. It's coming out this fall as a book, by the way.

When asked to describe his basic approach to teaching, Ernie replied:

> I have a concern for rigor. Of course, in and of itself rigor probably isn't a virtue, but deep down I feel dissatisfied about data that come to me with loose ends. Generally, I look for order and logic in the presentation of material. That doesn't necessarily require mathematics. T. S. Kuhn's *The Structure of Scientific Revolutions*, for example, is the most rigorous piece of analysis I've ever seen, and it isn't at all quantitative. Rigor is a matter of reasoning, accounting for everything in a problem.

Ernie attributed his decision to become a teacher to two major considerations: independence and potential influence. He said:

> I like doing what I want to do. I'd never be comfortable in a hierarchy because I wouldn't be any good at taking directions when I didn't think the directions made any sense. In the classroom, I can run it my way. Also, I consider teaching to be a way to bring human beings across. Manufacturing, for example, has a bearing on a variety of human issues. In one case, when we talked about the 20 years it took some guy to start a factory and the consequent personal toll that the start-up took, I was able to raise the issue of the corporation's responsibility to this

man. Moral issues often get ignored in business environments.

A Profile of Section I

[Ernie's overall evaluation of the section was glowing. The following is his own description.]

In general, they were a wonderful section, very highly motivated. If I warned them about a tough case and said, "You'd better plan on putting in five hours," they'd do more. Their preparation exceeded my recommendations. The section was balanced intellectually, but a few students stood out. Tom Selig and Barbara Reinhardt, for example, were so bright and articulate that the section perceived them as leaders almost immediately. Others stood out because of substantive preparation in their backgrounds: the engineers Jack Mannix, Mandy Farmer, Jeannette Bell, and Bill Sims, for example. Socially, Al Carpenter and Eric Schuyler were leaders. Arlene Allen, the educational representative, handled the students' complaints, so she had the closest communication with the faculty.

Section I performed extremely well as a group. The administration requires 15% to 20% Excellents and 10% to 15% Low Passes for the grading curve. I gave 19.8% Excellents with no trouble, but agonized over the 10.2% LPs because a few of these were marginal. They could have been considered higher.

The Course

[Ernie considered it significant that MM was the only course in the first-year curriculum with an interrupted schedule. Here is Ernie's own description of the course.]

We met for three months at the beginning of the term (September to November); then, except for one class meeting, we took a long break until late February, when we resumed a normal schedule. It's also worth noting that the material wasn't everyone's cup of tea. Most students come to Bay to specialize in finance or marketing, but MM is required. It was clear to me that many of the students, even the most brilliant, were uncomfortable with the material, for it teaches a way of thinking that was foreign to most of them. Inventory policy, aggregate planning, scheduling—few were familiar with these concepts. As a result, I was

extremely directive, sharpening their focus and
clarifying the details in every case.

Oddly enough, despite my own very theoretical
background and complete lack of experience in
manufacturing—I've never worked in a factory, for
example—I found the material fascinating. In micro-
economics you make the assumption that firms have
inputs a and b. Then you apply a production function—a mathematical relationship—and get results y
and z. Whatever actually happens between inputs
and results occurs in a black box. For me, MM
opened that box and showed what a production process really is. I certainly enjoyed teaching the course,
and the feedback I got, in conferences and at some
parties with the students, was excellent. In fact, some
of them told me they considered me their best
teacher.

First Semester ("When Things Went Well")

[In the following section, Ernie describes in his
own words a typical early class.]

By the sixth case, the one on Sullivan Watch
Company, I had memorized all the students'
names and backgrounds. We were getting along
well. I started by calling on one of my strongest
students, Harris Pauley, who is very, very smart.

"Harris," I said, "tell me about the company."

"Well, they make watches."

"What kind of watches?"

"Well, digital watches."

I was at the left-hand board, which I used for
facts about the company. I wrote down "digital
watches," and asked, "What's special about that?"

"They use a certain kind of manufacturing
process."

"Certain kind? What kind? What's it like to be
on that line? How many people stand there
working?"

"In total, you mean?"

"If that's what you want to tell me."

"Well, there are two or three at each station on
the line, and. . . ."

"Two or three? Wait, let me write that on the
board, too. Say, Jeannette, I notice you had your
hand up a second ago. Did you have something to
add?"

"Yes, a calculation. The exact time the watch
took to go through the line."

"Great. What was that number?"

"The watch comes down the line in 20 minutes—"

"Wait. What does that tell us?"

"It means the whole assembly process takes 20
minutes."

I was getting at the difference between labor
time—the actual work on the watch—and
throughput time—the time the watch spent on the
line, some of it just sitting. We were moving in
the direction of talking about minimum possible
labor time, in which there would be no idle time
at all. There were lots of figures in this case, and
we'd develop each part of the discussion for about
15 minutes. While I was at the board, I'd continually call on people, since I was able to remember
whose hands had been up and didn't like to lose
time while my back was turned and I was writing.
I'd ask questions like, "What's throughput time?"
"What's labor time?" "Describe the assembly process." "How are low-priced watches different from
high-priced watches?"

I'd use the middle board for analysis, the left-
hand one for basic facts about the company and
market, and the right-hand board for recommendations. By now, we would have gotten to new
ground where students didn't know quite what
was coming next. It was a question of comparing
two different manufacturing processes. They'd
never done this before. At this point, I'd be going
back to Harris fairly regularly, but other hands
were going up continually and I went on questioning students quite closely.

Ernie's Choice of Teaching Style

[In the following section, Ernie explains his selection of a directive approach by citing the highly
technical material in the early MM cases.]

The first semester focused on the nitty-gritty
concepts like the nature of production methods,
which can range from "job shops" to "continuous"
processes. The early cases demanded simple algebra, but many students felt uncomfortable even
with this, so I'd always ask, "Where did that calculation come from? How did you get that particular number?" My purpose was to have students
clarify their answers for the whole class.

In the first eight to ten cases we discussed
basics—materials, inventory, work force management, and capacity planning. I tried to get the

students to realize that an understanding of production systems was important in a number of everyday contexts. A restaurant, for example, is a production process. I wanted them to see the relevance of the material to their lives.

Especially in the case of calculations, I wanted the section to understand each case as well as I did. I went slowly and asked, "Does everybody have that?" I guess it's possible that people nodded simply to avoid the embarrassment of admitting they didn't understand, but I was doing my best to get the explanations clearly laid out. I also wanted to give all the students a chance to participate because they're graded 50% on participation. I kept comments short, partly because I thought it less painful for them, if they were dead wrong, to embarrass themselves with a brief, rather than a long, comment.

I didn't take volunteers to start the cases, although once things were under way people volunteered freely and were recognized. I asked students to start the case "cold," without forewarning, because this opening allowed me to decide who had the best chance of making a good showing. I spent a great deal of time figuring out whom to call on, matching background with material. If the case involved the steel industry, I'd call on a guy who'd worked in a steel mill. I didn't mind at all the possibility that he might know much more than I did about steel. In fact, I'd have been upset if he didn't.

In the early cases I called on people with public speaking experience because I knew they'd be less nervous than the others. I'd start with general questions about the setting. After the student had started, I made it clear that this was his or her case to continue by frequent contributions throughout the rest of the discussion. I would usually cross-question the student closely to expose any faulty reasoning, so as not to confuse the class. Each lead speaker got about 10 or 15 minutes to dissect the case, aided by very specific questions from me, and then got the opportunity for additional comments later in class. I expected all students to prepare all cases, so I didn't think it necessary to warn them when they were going to be called on.

Going through the "blocks," as I call it, was another aspect of my teaching style. I generally organized my class notes in analytical blocks, and reviewed these notes right up until class. I'd bring

the notes into class with me and toss them on the desk before beginning the case. I tried to get the class to go through those analytical blocks in order, because that was the most coherent sequence for the case. Although I didn't refer to my notes during the class, the blocks did govern my organization of the discussion. Actually, I only brought my notes into the classroom because, if a student were to come up after class and ask for a calculation I'd forgotten, I wanted to be able to furnish it right there on the spot. But some students later told me, "Wow, you're the only teacher who comes in and doesn't even refer to his notes. We're impressed!" That made me feel uncomfortable: it seemed as if I'd brought in the notes just to show that I didn't need to refer to them.

As for the "directive style," I guess that encompasses several things, including cold calls, cross-questioning, and going through the blocks in order. Frankly, as a new instructor, uncomfortable with new material, I found it easier to channel the discussion in areas I had prepared. I didn't feel competent enough to recognize a promising line of discussion in an area I hadn't prepared, let alone to ask relevant questions on the subject. Second, at the beginning anyway, the students gave me very positive feedback. They desired guidance, wanted to be led carefully through the technical intricacies of MM. Whatever its drawbacks, the directive style does make the reasoning process clear.

[Ernie's conclusion:]

I tried my best to prepare each case thoroughly. If the students did five hours' work, I did fifteen. It was my goal to learn the material thoroughly and help them understand things as well as I did.

Things Begin to Change

[Ernie continues his description as he recalls how things began to change.]

The first semester ended uneventfully. I taught the last class in my usual directive fashion and the section responded well, with high performance. My feedback at this point was gratifying, and I had high hopes for an equally good second semester. But I began to notice a slight difference in Section I's general attitude and performance when I met them briefly in January for a two-case module that was part of a Combined Business Exercise in which the whole first year participated. After that, we didn't meet until late February, when MM resumed a normal schedule.

[In the second semester, a few benchmarks of deterioration stood out to Ernie: the emergence of game playing in class; the section's raucous behavior during a power failure; and Ernie's subsequent speech to the class about maintaining standards. Ernie continues with his recollections.]

Several trends emerged in the second semester. MM's emphasis changed from quantitative analysis to strategic planning; the students had become more confident and less willing to be led; and the section had developed into a stronger social unit with different operating modes in class. It took me a while to notice the impact of these changes.

During MM's break in December and January, other courses continued as usual. We did meet once during this period, as part of the Combined Business Exercise. As it happened, some students told me that another instructor's cases had turned out to be a disaster. I noticed a certain leaden quality to my class as well, perhaps because of outside factors, but, on the other hand, perhaps because the section had changed style in the interim and I hadn't. Also, I co-taught this unit with Ted Kleber, whose subject is organizational psychology. Ted is practically my opposite number. He's completely nondirective. At some points, he simply removed himself from the students' line of vision and let them talk with each other. I was fascinated to see how well Section I performed under those conditions. Our unit was an unqualified success. Of course, Ted's material, unlike MM, lends itself to long, uninterrupted speeches by students. But watching him gave me a hint at some changes I might make in my own style.

When MM resumed its normal schedule, Section I's students had changed in several respects. They had evolved several new modes of behavior, both to amuse themselves and to offer help to some slower members of the group. The "learning curve game" illustrates the former, and "triage," the latter.

Buzzwords started to come up in the technology unit, the first unit of the second term. For example, one day a student said, "The most important consideration in this case is the product life cycle."

"What does product life cycle mean?" I asked.

He just hemmed and hawed. Buzzwords like that—"learning curve," "sequential decision making," and "flexibility"—seemed to have a magical appeal. As soon as the students learned them, they started to use them indiscriminately. "Learning curve," for example, has a precise meaning. With a doubling of cumulative output, costs per unit decline a certain percentage because the workers learn how to produce more efficiently. But the concept must be applied carefully if it is to have any usefulness as a management tool.

In one case, a student who had been having some problems in the course said, "The company should not go along with this process because they're going to be overcommitted." As he used it, with no explanation, "overcommitted" was just a buzzword. Later, when he came to see me privately, I said, "There were three ways you could have made that comment. An average way would have been to say they should not go ahead because of x, y, and z other processes they're already using. You could have named them. An excellent way would have been to say, 'Because it's a family-owned business, the scarce resource in this firm is management talent, and that's why the additional processes would be overcommitting their management.'" But simply saying "overcommitted" without further comment contributed little to the discussion.

It was about this time that some students came up and told me that the group actually had played a "learning curve game" one day to see how many buzzwords could be inserted into a class discussion. They had kept score. I was chagrined. I'd certainly noticed buzzwords coming up, but the idea of an organized game hadn't occurred to me. I still think I should have picked up on it.

Triage was a different sort of strategy they used. It took two forms. In one, the students decided for themselves which courses they could let slip and which they wanted to concentrate on. They knew that each of them could get three Low Passes without being screened out of the MBA program, so they worked hardest where the probability of doing well existed. That eliminated MM for many of them. Also, I learned from one student that the section had started to play triage as a group. The brighter students, who were in no danger of failing MM, had been asked to step back in class discussion to give the weaker stu-

dents more class participation time so they could
improve their grades. That meant the better ones
were putting themselves at a disadvantage.

A Disquieting Episode: The Power Failure

[Ernie recalls the power failure.]

In the second week in April, there was a power
failure in our building, and what happened afterwards showed me that the group's discipline and
self-control had deteriorated. Twenty minutes into
class the lights went out. I left the room to call
maintenance to make sure that someone was
aware of the problem. When I got back into the
classroom, I was amazed to see that the students
had unrolled a roll of toilet paper and draped
every single seat in the classroom with it. They
were stamping and clapping and yelling, "Tell us
a ghost story!"

Now, even when I'd been extremely demanding, I'd always been ready to share a joke with the
students. I'd only drawn the line at really bad
taste. I said, "But I don't know any ghost stories."

"Then tell us a story," they shouted.

I'd been dragging in anecdotes all along, and I
happened to have read a funny story, so I told it.
"Once," I said, "at a Berkeley final exam in a large
course, the proctor cleared the room and picked

up all the exam books. About a half-hour after
everyone had left, he noticed a student way in the
back, still writing. He went up to the student and
said, 'The exam's over. I can't accept your bluebook.' The student drew himself up tall and said,
'My dear fellow, do you know who I am?' 'No,'
said the proctor, very unimpressed. 'Good,' said
the student, and he jammed his bluebook into the
middle of the pile of others and ran out of the
room."

The class laughed, but we finally did get back to
order and finish the case that day. From that time
on, though, "Tell us a story" became a favorite demand of the class.

It wasn't too long after this that I began to
worry seriously about the way the class was slip-
ping. The buzzword situation was bad, games
seemed more important than cases, and we were
beginning to lose rigor entirely. I decided to do
something about the situation.

I knew that making a formal speech of
reprimand would damage my excellent rapport
with Section I. We had been getting along beautifully since the earliest classes of the first semester,
and I like to be liked as much as anybody does.
But the obvious drop in preparation and performance really upset me. I knew I had to do something. I agonized for a while about whether or not
to make a formal speech.

After serious deliberation, Ernie Budding decided to deliver a formal reprimand to Section I. He recalled the speech as follows:

In the past few weeks I've noticed that your comments have become peppered with buzzwords. I can't count the number of times I've heard phrases like "ride the learning curve," "product life cycle," "flexibility," "dominant design," or "sequential decision making." There's nothing inherently wrong with those phrases. They all represent important concepts and are valuable tools of analysis. The problem lies in how you are using them. Don't just tell me that a company should pursue a "flexible" manufacturing strategy; tell me what that *means*. These phrases are without content if you don't tie them down to the particulars of a case. All companies can "ride the learning curve" to achieve lower costs through higher cumulative output. So what? Tell me *why* that is important for a particular company. Tell me *how* those cost reductions will be achieved. Otherwise, you really haven't said anything.

I raise this issue now because I think it is a special problem for Bay MBAs, particularly when they first enter the work force. By the time you leave here you will have absorbed an enormous number of concepts and a wide variety of buzzwords. The tendency of Bay graduates to use these phrases loosely, often as a *substitute* for hard analysis, only worsens the school's reputation for "blue-skying." I'd like to put a stop to that right now.

Another thing. In recent weeks the leadoff speakers have done a very poor job starting off the discussion. A leadoff is your chance to lay out a case, to walk other students through your analysis, and to work through a business problem logically from beginning to end. It serves a valuable educational purpose. Rather than making a few minor points and then reserving your major contributions for later in the class—as recent leadoff speakers have done—you should be prepared to start off with an organized presentation of the issues, backed by solid analysis.

OK, that pretty much covers it. Any questions?

[Ernie continues with his recollection.]

You could have heard a pin drop. It felt like a scolding, and they seemed as chastened as first- or second-graders. It was very uncomfortable for a

CASE

Ernie Budding (B)

Dr. Abby J. Hansen wrote this case in collaboration with C. Roland Christensen for the Developing Discussion Leadership Skills Seminar. While the case is based on data supplied from participants involved, all names and some peripheral facts have been disguised.

Copyright © 1980 by the President and Fellows of Harvard College. HBS Case No. 9-381-039.

few minutes, but when I called on one of the best students in the class to start off the case, he did a superb job. I ended the class by complimenting the section on how well they'd done that day, hoping that we would have no further problems that semester. I had felt extremely uncomfortable lecturing a section of adults as if I were their parent—after all, I was younger than some of the students—but I also felt I had a responsibility to uphold standards, and that was more important.

Afterwards, I collared six to a dozen students and asked them their reactions. Some said, "It's about time somebody said something about buzzwords. We wanted to, but nobody would listen." Others said "It's unreasonable to 'cold call' and expect students to lay the whole case out." That surprised me. I thought I had addressed one problem: the decline in the quality of section performance. Instead, I got reactions to two issues: the use of buzzwords and my policy of "cold calls" which held a student responsible for the case he or she started.

I've always been very uncomfortable in the multifaceted role of the section person. The satisfactions you get from each of the roles are by no means complementary, and for a long time it seemed to me that successfully performing one role meant that the others were sacrificed.

In particular, it's very hard to establish satisfactory relationships with both the professor and the students. What you really want from the professor is patronage. You want him to help you get where he is now. You want him to like you and you want him to support you. On the other hand, what you want from the students is fear and respect. You want to cash in on all the agony you've gone through to master the material by making sure they suffer. You want them to be in awe of the searing brilliance of your intellect. You want to dominate them, exploit them, pure and simple.

Getting both the professor and the class to see you as you'd like them to is hard. You want to impress the professor with the clarity of your perception, which means you agree with him. But you need to distinguish yourself to the class, which means you don't. Professors in my experience get very nervous when you steal their students. But students get really snotty when they realize you're a lapdog.

So what do you do? The root of the problem is that the teaching fellow [TF] is no longer an undergraduate and not yet a professor. The answer is to remember that he once was an undergraduate and soon will be a professor. This is a subtle distinction. But the point is that the teaching fellow stands somewhere between the class and the professor. In the course of the semester the two of them are going to have to come together—and that means they're headed in the teaching fellow's direction.

A successful course is one in which students get out of it something like what the professor puts in. This doesn't happen often. The professors I've worked with spend hours, literally, on a single lecture. No student puts in that kind of time understanding it. And they come at the material with much less background. So it is clear that students never manage to pump all the depth out of the material.

For a professor, a good lecture is one in which the subtlest relationships are revealed with wit of the most refined, penetrating sort; where all the points of view are caressed and molded into a unity

READING

Hybrids Are Successful Adaptations

JEFFREY ZAX

This article is reproduced from a speech given by Dr. Jeffrey Zax at the Harvard-Danforth Center for Teaching and Learning. It was printed originally in the Harvard Crimson, *January 1981.*

Reprinted with permission of the author and of the publisher of the *Harvard Crimson.*

that hits with a little pop of clarity and he goes away feeling smug.

Students generally have notes on this kind of lecture which wander off the page or don't stay within the lines or go both ways on the same page. They look like zombies when they leave. And there's a reason for this. Professors, really, can't be any less abstruse. Most of them want or need to get a book out of their lecture notes, and that immediately means that the tone is going to be less than conversational. Those who don't are at least mildly interested in the abstract beauty of the whole thing, which means again that the tone will be anything but conversational.

In any event, it's common for a professor to spend lecture after lecture on nuances which resolve contractions which students never perceived as a problem in the first place. Students have three other courses, they have social lives (that's something teaching fellows find very hard to relate to), they are majoring in something else. The big difference is that all this is new to them, each lecture unfolds a new chapter, and they really don't know where it's all heading until it gets there.

Until then, they don't understand why what they're doing right now is important. They have trouble identifying the main thread. The professor knows the whole story already; he's been anticipating the punch line since the first lecture. The way he retraces his path is by no means the way you would go exploring it for the first time. The students and the professor are by necessity operating at completely different intellectual levels and neither has the freedom to move closer to the other.

That's where teaching fellows come in. Luckily, teaching fellows combine the worst characteristics of both student and professor. Teaching fellows think they like the nuances, but they're not sure they follow them. They like to worry about the subtle problems, but they'd like their degree and tenure first. They know the punch line, but they don't think it's funny (but they will). They can follow the flow, but they don't know how to contribute to it. This is their strength, and it is when they exercise it that they are most appreciated. There are imbalances in any course which only the teaching fellow is sufficiently detached to observe.

What, specifically, can the teaching fellow do? An example: Suppose the reading list in the undergraduate course is more demanding than in the graduate course. The professor thinks it's all very necessary,

and the teaching fellow knows that. The students are never going to read more than a quarter of it, and the teaching fellow knows that too. Now, the teaching fellow could keep quiet. Each student would guess at the 20 articles which will be most important, so that no two students will have read more than five articles in common. They'll all be petrified at the exam because they'll each be prepared to answer at best a third of each question and they'll do miserably. There will be no pattern to the ignorance and grading will be difficult. The professor will be horror-struck and his response will be to assign more readings. A situation like this can often be foreseen by the second week of the term.

The teaching fellow's strategy is obvious. He organizes a conspiracy. In sections he makes it clear that a quarter of the readings are absolutely critical, double and triple asterisks, and he talks about which these are. At first this may feel subversive, but it's really a completely positive step. He is giving nothing away to the students, since whatever he says, they are only going to read a quarter of the readings.

He certainly has not undermined the professor, since now at least the class will be homogeneous in its ignorance. And the thing works itself out so much more nicely. When the test comes the whole class is well prepared for two out of five questions. The answers to the other three will be uniformly gibberish. So the two questions will be the basis of the grading, which is fair. Furthermore, any professor will immediately notice that there is this collective myopia and reconsider the sections the class seems to have ignored and either cut or improve them.

There are many other opportunities to pull the same kind of maneuver. It's very popular, for instance, for professors (especially in survey courses) to deal with an issue by taking two lectures and presenting all sides of the debate, all the strengths and weaknesses, and the names associated with each position. In order to impress students with the solemnity of the whole thing, he speaks of the interchanges with the kind of reverential awe that makes you feel the discussion has taken place at a very stately pace since the Middle Ages.

And that's exactly what it sounds like to the students. The proof of this is that the instant they're asked a question, they ascribe opposing views to the same person, or they talk about the opinions and names they remember in such vague terms that they'll never positively associate one with the other. They hope you'll just impute the correct relationships and give them full credit. Here again, without hurting anyone you can make everyone happier by simply having an opinion.

The professor will probably have summed up the discussion by indicating what he believes to be the truth of the matter, the academic truth, which amounts to saying that the question requires more study. That is not the same as the undergraduate truth. In sections, the TF picks a likely opinion and states that while it has not been conclusively proven, for the purposes of the class it is correct. This may seem overassertive, but it's not. It gives the students a chance to bring focus into a subject that they would have ignored altogether otherwise. And when the professor sees on all the exams these cogent arguments all in favor of the same viewpoint, he is going to rethink his own presentation. He'll be surprised that his lectures were so conclusive; he didn't realize he felt so strongly, but next year he'll be more explicit. Again, everyone profits.

One last example. Even when everything about the course is right, it is easy for the motivation to be missing. It's easy for the professor to spend hours on material that doesn't suffer from ambiguity or multiple viewpoints, where the reading list is manageable and helpful, and where the students simply don't care. Unfortunately, there are occasions when, fundamentally, there's no reason why they should. But there are times when the professor just doesn't get around to addressing the relevance directly. Such comments just don't fit into the flow of what he's trying to do. Anyhow, relevance for him means something he can write an article on. Relevance for the students means something they can talk about at parties. There may be no relation.

Sections on current events are an obvious ploy, but students do not demand anything that bald. I once had a very successful section in which I discussed a research idea that the professor and I had developed in casual conversation earlier that day. Anything which breathes life into the litany of constructs and generalizations is going to be well-appreciated, whether it sheds light on the process of real life—or just academic life. The students will follow the lectures with renewed enthusiasm, and the professor will be very grateful for a class that stops sleeping.

I think the lesson to be learned from these examples is that the most precious thing the teaching fellow possesses is his independence. That's a commodity which is easy to forgo. If he finds himself spending all his section time working problem sets step-for-step, he's become another button on the students' calculators. If he finds himself being asked to spend sections re-delivering the professor's last lecture, he has become a phonograph.

His perspective is unique; it is all the more valuable the more acutely he feels within him the contradictions of being a teacher while simultaneously being a student.

Professors and students are often unsatisfied, but they have to talk to each other to resolve anything. A teaching fellow is both, so he only has to talk to himself—and there it's much easier to get an answer. Changes that would make the teaching fellow feel more comfortable with the course are changes which will make everyone feel more comfortable. In the end, making the course better is the only role for the teaching fellow.

Assistant Professor Graham and Ms. Macomber (A)

Professor Charles Graham glanced at the clock on his left. The hands on the wall were not encouraging. One hour and ten minutes into the class—only ten minutes to go—and the discussion had gone nowhere. Charles reluctantly concluded he would have to exercise the basic dictatorial prerogative of any instructor: he would have to tell the class how wrong they were.

Charles was starting out his second year of teaching and, as he told his New Dominion faculty colleagues, he had developed a sincere commitment to the case discussion teaching methods and philosophy. Charles was in his second week of teaching Quantitative Analysis and Operations Management (QAOM). He wanted to give that class every chance, but he had not foreseen that 80 intelligent persons might, individually and jointly, entirely miss the main point of the case. Charles disapproved of the practice of giving a pat "answer" to a case at the end of class; on the other hand, he could not conscientiously allow 80 apprentice managers to leave class thinking that the last hour passed for an adequate case analysis. Charles drew a slow breath; one more comment, he thought, and then they are in for it.

The hand Charles recognized was in the back row: it belonged to one of the women students, Janet Macomber. Janet was one of the younger students in the section, a graduate of the California Institute of Technology with an excellent academic record but with limited work experience. She looked nervous and started speaking softly and hesitantly. "Louder, please!" came from somewhere on the other side of the room.

Janet stopped, and started again in a stronger voice. "I'm sorry, but according to my analysis, the class's recommendations simply do not answer the company's problem—which is how to move work-in-process through the plant the best way possible."

"And just what is your analysis, Ms. Macomber?" Professor Graham asked.

"Well"—there was a note of apology in her voice—"when I was doing the case last night, I multiplied Exhibit 1 times Exhibit 2."

Charles did not want to appear amazed that someone had apparently cracked the case after all. He only wanted the class—each and every one of the other 79—to realize the import of Janet Macomber's words. He interrupted: "Let me understand, Ms. Macomber. You actually took Exhibit 1"—he held up the case opened to the exhibits—"and

This case was written by a member of the 1977 Developing Discussion Leadership Skills Seminar under the supervision of C. Roland Christensen. While the case is based on data supplied by participants involved, all names and some peripheral facts have been disguised.

multiplied every number in Exhibit 1 times a number in Exhibit 2?"

"Times the corresponding number. Yes, sir."

"And how long did that take you?" (Snickers came from the side of the room.)

Janet Macomber appeared to be taken aback at such a personal question. "Not too long," she answered, adding, as if to justify her computational binge, "I used a calculator."

"And what exactly did you have, after you multiplied every number in Exhibit 1 times a corresponding number in Exhibit 2?"

"I had a matrix of the dollar-volume flow between departments." Janet stopped. She was obviously uncomfortable and ready to relinquish the floor. But Charles was determined to expose her reasoning, bit by bit.

"And what did you find . . . from this matrix?"

"I found that the flows were not all the same [pause]. Some departments had a much greater flow of work-in-process between them than others."

"And what did you conclude based on this observation?"

"I concluded that . . . if I were laying out the plant . . . I would put the departments with the most flow between them next to each other, lining them up, and I would put the other departments on the sides, or in other buildings, if I had to."

"Well, well." Charles looked around. The clock on the wall showed that the class was already two minutes overtime. There would be no chance to take further comments from the class, and anyway it might be more salutary for each individual to mull singly over Janet Macomber's analysis. So as not to end the class abruptly, Charles made a few extempore remarks about how this case was related to previous cases and to the course plan. He carefully refrained from passing judgment on Janet's analysis or on the preceding case discussion. Let 'em figure it out themselves, he thought, now they have something to think about. All in all, Charles was quite pleased with the way the class had turned out.

As he was leaving the room, Charles noted a group clustered around Janet Macomber's top row seat. There really is such a thing as section dynamics, he reflected. "When one of the class reasons through a case, everyone learns. This case method really works. What a break I had to start out my career teaching with cases; it sure is a lot more fun than lecturing."

CASE

Bill Jones (A)

At 2:20 P.M. Bill Jones concluded his class and made his way out through the swinging doors of the classroom, heading for his office. As he walked through the noisy corridor, he reflected, "In my eight years of teaching I don't think I have ever had to handle a more potentially explosive situation than I did this afternoon. Did I do the right thing?"

Background on Bill Jones

Bill Jones, a young associate professor at Metropolitan Business School, had been at the school for six years as a member of the Production and Operations Management faculty. An Arkansas native, Bill had received his doctorate in economics from the University of Texas. Prior to that Bill had received his bachelor's degree from Tulane University, where he had been a member of Phi Beta Kappa as well as a second-string quarterback for the varsity football team.

Immediately after receiving his doctorate he had been hired by Metropolitan to teach a first-year MBA course in Production and Operations Management. Although Bill had never been exposed to the case method of teaching before, he had become quite successful as a classroom teacher, consistently receiving high ratings from students in course surveys.

Bill spent four years teaching the first-year MBA course and two years teaching a second-year course on the Management of Nonprofit Organizations, which he had designed himself. Bill had become very interested in case method teaching and brought a great deal of enthusiasm to each class. He had a booming voice, a very dramatic style of teaching which he complemented with a quick wit.

In the spring Bill was asked by the chairman of his department to teach a new second-year MBA course called Labor and Production Policy. The department chairman would teach one section and Bill the other. Bill was somewhat apprehensive about teaching a new course, especially since he felt he had a meager background in labor relations. However, he did look forward to the challenge of teaching a different course and the opportunity to learn more about a new field. Bill spent most of the summer writing cases and preparing materials for the course, which was to be taught in the fall semester.

The Labor and Production Policy Course

In October, as Bill Jones was about halfway through the semester, he set out to review course

*This case was written by a member of the Teaching by the Case Method Seminar under the supervision of **C. Roland Christensen**. While the case is based on data supplied by Bill Jones, all names and some peripheral facts have been disguised.*

progress. First, he noted, enrollment had been very high: Bill had about 90 students in his section. The case material had proved to be very exciting and evoked a great deal of student discussion. During most classes Bill was unable to call on all of the students who wanted to participate. Bill felt that part of the excitement in his class was due to the fact that students had such diverse opinions and experiences with respect to labor relations. This diversity often sparked open conflict that produced exciting discussion sessions.

One of the section students who, in Bill's judgment, represented a somewhat radical point of view about labor policy was Dave Young. Dave was 27 years old and a graduate of the University of Wisconsin. After receiving his bachelor's degree with honors in economics, Dave had spent one year working in California with Cesar Chavez, helping to organize the United Farm Workers Union. After that he worked for two years in the California State Department of Labor as an assistant to the secretary.

Earlier in the semester Bill had asked students to submit a proposal for a paper topic. At that time Dave had come to Bill to discuss his ideas on writing a paper on participative management. Bill was impressed with Dave's intellectual ability, but he felt that his emotional intensity and aggressive manner often prevented him from successfully persuading others to accept his point of view.

In the course of the semester Bill found that many students came to his office to talk about career counseling. One such student was Paige Palmer. Paige was a graduate of a well-known Eastern women's college and had come directly to Metropolitan after receiving her bachelor's in art history. Although she had done well academically in the first year, many of her class comments were viewed as naive by some of her more experienced colleagues. They believed she was bright but lacked a certain "savvy" in her analysis of a case situation.

Bill felt that it was important to continue to encourage Paige to participate in class even though some of her classmates might rush to criticize and attack her point of view. There were 12 women in Bill's class of 90 students. Traditionally the production area had been viewed as "male domain," but increasingly women students had shown an interest in taking electives in this area. Bill felt that it was important for the women students to participate as actively as the men and to have their views heard, and he encouraged them to do so.

Another student with whom Bill had talked outside of class was Fred Wilkens. Fred had attended private schools, was an only child, and both of his parents were very active in professional work. He was a Stanford graduate in engineering, and after receiving his master's degree at that school he worked for Hewlett-Packard for two years prior to coming to the business school. He was basically a shy person, slightly built and studious in appearance. Fred was the only black student in Bill's section. Bill was concerned that Fred had not participated at all during the semester, although Fred seemed to be always prepared for class and had an excellent background in manufacturing. He had asked to see Fred after the student handed in an excellent paper on production planning earlier in the semester.

Fred told Bill during their meeting that he was primarily interested in leaving the manufacturing area to follow a career in finance. He confided to Bill that he had taken the Labor and Production Policy course primarily as an "easy" course so that he could devote the major part of his effort to his finance courses, which he found more difficult. Bill told Fred that he understood his reasoning, but that he hoped Fred would make an effort in the future to share some of his insights and experience with the other members of the Labor and Production Policy course. After this meeting Bill had been pleased to see that Fred had started contributing to class discussions.

The General Motors Case

In mid-October a case on the General Motors Corporation was assigned, dealing with a plant manager's decision to experiment with "stall" or "team" building of automobiles to replace the traditional assembly line method of production. The case made the point that after labor difficulties had forced the closing of the Lordstown Vega plant, General Motors began in earnest to re-evaluate some of its traditional labor policies. The company had found that younger workers were far more discontented with traditional production jobs than older workers and in general were also less productive.

One suggested remedy was to replace the monotonous tasks of the assembly line with a team-building concept. With "team build," four workers would be responsible for the final assembly of the car and each worker would be expected to learn all of the jobs associated with this phase of the production process. General Motors' top management chose a Cleveland, Ohio, assembly plant to experiment with the team-build concept. The case described the labor force as being about 60 percent black, with almost all of the black workers under 40 years of age. The remaining older workers were mostly white.

The plant manager in the case had chosen four workers out of a pool of volunteers for the team-build experiment. He was primarily interested in determining how long it would take the team to begin working together harmoniously and how many production hours would be required to assemble a car using this method. Based on the results of this experiment, he would have to predict the total cost of assembly using the team-build method and then make a recommendation to top management on whether to expand the experiment, discontinue it, or convert the entire plant to team build.

During the first few months of the experiment the four workers involved in the project worked very hard to reduce the total amount of production time required for team-build assembly. The four workers, three black and one white, took a great deal of pride in their work and at one point asked the plant manager if they could put their pictures in the glove compartment of each car assembled, to inform the customer that they were personally responsible for the product.

While it was true that total production time kept decreasing as the workers discovered better methods or more efficient ways of doing things, still, the total cost for the assembly phase of the operations was considerably higher than for the traditional automated method. However, absenteeism had dropped drastically and quality had improved considerably.

The Class Discussion

Labor and Production Policy met at 1:00, right after lunch, and students began filing into Bill Jones's class about ten minutes early. Bill was at the front of the room laying out his notes for the afternoon session while he talked and joked with students as they came in. He anticipated a lively discussion, particularly between Dave Young and Jim Casey, who had been a General Motors' employee and was fairly conservative.

Early student comments were directed toward the problem of determining the actual cost of the team-build method compared with traditional methods. One student offered the theory that as more and more cars were built using the team-build method, a "learning curve" effect would take place and eventually one could project that the cost would be driven down close to the assembly-line cost. After that comment Jim Casey, who sat in the middle section of the amphitheater, raised his hand. Bill knew that Jim was well regarded by his classmates as a bright and articulate spokesman. Also, because of his four years' experience with General Motors, he would often include in his class comments interesting anecdotes or helpful insights. Bill called on Jim, who said, "I think it is important to bear in mind that four people on one team-build project is a very limited sample on which to base long-run cost projections. After all, these four people have been hand-picked for this project, and even though their production time has been dramatically decreasing they are probably 'rate busters' anyway, and their performance in no way indicates how the average worker would perform under this system."

Bill Jones thought that Jim had raised a good point for discussion and he scanned the room looking for the next person to call on. Sitting in the back row by the door, Dave Young had been raising his hand continually and trying to get into the discussion. Bill decided to wait and not call on Dave at that point. In the front row, at his right side, Fred Wilkens was sitting with his notes spread out, but Fred's hand was not raised. Sitting next to Fred was Paige Palmer, who raised her hand immediately after Jim had finished speaking. Bill decided to call on Paige. Her reply: "Well, I disagree with Jim; I don't think the workers could be 'rate busters' because three of them are black, and . . . "

At that moment Fred Wilkens shot back in his seat so that his chair seat banged loudly; his fingers tensely gripped the desk. A hush fell over the classroom. Most students looked down at their desks; others stared at Paige in disbelief. Paige did not finish her sentence; an icy silence prevailed in the room. Fred Wilkens put his head down for a moment. Then slowly he gathered his papers in a pile, ready to slide them into his attaché case, and half turned his chair seat as if to leave the classroom. Dave Young began to rock back and forth in his chair in an agitated manner.

Kurt Jacobs, 31, married, of German nationality with a student visa, had been a "quiet" member of the Business Policy's Section A for the first eight weeks of the course's 13-week term. Kurt, one of the older members of the section, was tall, thin, angular of face, and solemn of demeanor. In Metropolitan's amphitheater-type classroom, he sat in the front row, aisle seat. Although the seat next to his was assigned to another student, it was rarely occupied. The seat directly behind Kurt was one of the two seats in the 100-seat room not assigned to any section member; it was occasionally used by visitors.

Since the classroom contributions were important to the section's overall learning experience, all faculty members encouraged this activity. Individual student reinforcement was provided via the assignment of 50 percent of the course grade to classroom work. A section member could make "alternative arrangements" with his instructor (for example, the submission of a number of written reports) if there were medical or psychological extenuating circumstances preventing classroom contribution.

Professor Brett, as part of this effort, had become concerned about Kurt's silence during the early weeks of the course. His first step in dealing with the situation had been a personal, handwritten note attached to a course report that was being returned to Kurt at the end of the fourth week of the semester. In sum, the note complimented Kurt on his excellent report, reminded him of the importance of classroom contribution, noted that Kurt had not spoken yet in class, and suggested that perhaps professor and student should discuss the situation.

Kurt's response was immediate. He scheduled a 10:00 A.M. Monday appointment with Professor Brett. After Ms. Ash, Professor Brett's secretary, had noted his arrival, Kurt entered the office and asked if he might sit down. Coming quickly to the note attached to his report, he explained that he did come to each class with the case well prepared and that he did follow the classroom dialogue closely. Both of those observations seemed accurate to Professor Brett; he had often noticed handwritten pages of analysis at Kurt's classroom desk. Kurt continued:

> Professor, I do not feel comfortable talking in large groups. This case method teaching is so different from the Technical Institute in Germany and my

CASE

Kurt Jacobs

*This case was written by **C. Roland Christensen** for the Developing Discussion Leadership Skills Seminar. While the case is based on data supplied by participants involved, all names and some peripheral facts have been disguised.*

industrial experience involved only small-staff group work.

Professor, I don't like to talk either unless I have something *worthwhile* to say. Some members of your section just talk because it is required or they want to please you. Perhaps we need less talking and more thoughtful, constructive reflection. There is so much rubbish, just rubbish, in all classes here—yours too.

Professor, I *will talk* in class when I have worthwhile points to make which might help students in the section to learn. Not talking in class hurt my first year's grades; it may happen again during my second year, but that is all right with me. When my experience and background make it relevant, I will contribute! Then I will help the section to learn. They are very young!

Professor, my next class starts in a few minutes and I do not like to be late to class! Please excuse me.

Kurt then abruptly left Professor Brett's office.

During the next weeks, Kurt continued his established class routines. His desk top always seemed crowded with handwritten case analysis notes and calculations to which he referred. He checked these as points were made in classroom discussion. His only visible personal involvement came when questions arose involving the ethics and morality of corporate and personal decisions.

In the ensuing weeks, Professor Brett gained some additional information about Kurt Jacobs. Kurt, he noted, did not appear to participate in the social "chit-chat" of the section before or after class. His relationships with other section members were courteous and formal, being limited primarily to social conventions. Professor Brett on several occasions did see Kurt checking his notes after class with another section member, Bob Anderson. Anderson, 31, had been an engineering supervisor before attending Metropolitan. The Student Association representative for Section A mentioned that both men were active members of a university religious club that met on a regular basis, and both lived in the same married students' housing development.

The student representative also mentioned an incident that had occurred the previous year at a first-year section social event, one of the few attended by Kurt. It involved Millicent Wyeth, who was currently a member of Business Policy Section A. "Mil," described by the student representative as "liberated," had been engaged by Kurt in a discussion of the appropriate societal role of women. Cit-

ing biblical sources, he had sought to convince Millicent that the proper role for women was the "traditional" one. The student reported that Ms. Wyeth had responded in an extremely spirited way; her most restrained suggestion had been that Kurt ought to at least try to crawl into the Dark Ages.

The cases scheduled for the first class day of the ninth week were Heublein (A) and (B). The cases involved an analysis of Heublein's success in the vodka market, with key discussion questions focused on whether Heublein should move into new fields. Specifically, should it buy a beer company?

Class discussion for the first 50 minutes could, at best, be described as dull, Brett thought. The class did cover the basic areas of the case, but the students seemed to be going through a required exercise with little interest and zero excitement. Yawns increased, doodling became the order of the day, and two "back benchers" started to read the *Times*.

Approximately 30 minutes before the end of the class, Mike Healey, a recognized academic leader of the section, entered the discussion. Noting that he had experience in the industry, he summarized Heublein's strategy, noted major areas such as Scotch and bourbon into which the company might expand, gave a financial analysis which indicated the company's ability to finance these moves, and then presented a series of recommendations to senior management that directly followed his diagnosis. The presentation was impressive to the section, and Healey's demeanor and tone of voice indicated personal involvement and conviction.

Mike's contributions were followed by a series of useful questions and comments by other section members, which indicated at least modest case preparation and some interest in Heublein's strategic problems. The section seemed to agree that the company should expand its line of liquors and buy the beer company with which they were negotiating. The "back benchers" put down their newspapers and the section pace seemed to pick up a bit—though it still seemed to Professor Brett to be tedious.

As the pros and cons of Mike's recommendations were being debated, Tom Mooney, Mike's roommate and sidekick, broke into the discussion. Tom's section role had often been that of "the jester" although certainly not "the buffoon." On several occasions Tom's wit and perspicacity had turned routine discussions into sparkling, high-interest, productive class sessions. Professor Brett assumed

Tom was again trying to increase the fun and interest level of the section discussion.

"Mike is too darn conventional! This company really needs some jazz—some new thinking." With a hint of merriment in his voice, he proposed a series of recommendations. "Let's expand our present markets. Why not put vodka in square bottles for the over-50-year-olds," he said, looking at the professor. "And we can start working to lower the drinking age—get teenagers to drink beer—the demographics are super. Why—why not have beer-flavored baby foods? And then there is the women's market. Why not break down hard liquor television advertising restraints—if we can sponsor 'soaps' on the tube—look at the potential!"

Other section members joined what Professor Brett perceived to be "the game" with a series of nontraditional recommendations. One student suggested diversification in marijuana and another reinforced Tom's comment about the women's afternoon cocktail market by saying that liquor could change the entire concept of mother's milk.

"No! No! This is sickening." Kurt Jacobs was standing. He walked slowly into the open area of the classroom amphitheater, his face flushed, his arms close to his body, his fists clenched; he turned and faced the section.

No! No! What are you doing? Why are we spending our time discussing the debauchery of the young—the degradation of motherhood? Are there no limits? Is there nothing we will not do? Do you not know that your words break His injunction to love, to help those less fortunate, to honor your mothers?

Is this professional education? Is this education for leadership—to entice the young into self-abuse—to destroy family life? It is wrong. It is a sin!

What does this discussion tell us about ourselves? Are you proud of it? What do your comments tell us about this school? I am ashamed of this discussion. . . .

"Professor. . . ." Kurt turned and looked at Professor Brett, who was standing near the chalkboard. The remainder of the sentence did not follow.

To Professor Brett the room seemed frozen: no sound, no movement. His mind raced through Kurt's comments. It seemed as if the contribution had lasted for hours, instead of the reality of three or four minutes. He could at best remember the major points of Kurt's comments, none of the multitude of biblical references. Brett's eyes swept the room; his throat muscles seemed set in concrete. Kurt remained standing.

"Professor," he said again.

READING

Active Listening

CARL R. ROGERS

RICHARD E. FARSON

Reproduced by special permission from the University of
Chicago, Industrial Relations Center.

The Meaning of Active Listening

One basic responsibility of the supervisor or executive is the development, adjustment, and integration of individual employees. He tries to develop employee potential, delegate responsibility, and achieve cooperation. To do so, he must have, among other abilities, the ability to listen intelligently and carefully to those with whom he works.

There are, however, many kinds of listening skills. The lawyer, for example, when questioning a witness, listens for contradictions, irrelevancies, errors, and weaknesses. But this is not the kind of listening skill we are concerned with. The lawyer usually is not listening in order to help the witness adjust or cooperate or produce. On the other hand, we will be concerned with listening skills which *will help* employees gain a clearer understanding of their situations, take responsibility, and cooperate with each other.

Two Examples

The kind of listening we have in mind is called "active listening." It is called "active" because the listener has a very definite responsibility. He does not passively absorb the words which are spoken to him. He actively tries to grasp the facts and the feelings in what he hears, and he tries, by his listening, to help the speaker work out his own problems.

To get a fuller picture of what is meant by active listening, let us consider two different approaches to the same work problem.

Example No. 1

FOREMAN: Hey, Al, I don't get this production order. We can't handle this run today. What do they think we are?

SUPERVISOR: But that's the order. So get it out as soon as you can. We're under terrific pressure this week.

FOREMAN: Don't they know we're behind schedule already because of that press breakdown?

SUPERVISOR: Look, Kelly, I don't decide what goes on upstairs. I just have to see that the work gets out, and that's what I'm gonna do.

FOREMAN: The guys aren't gonna like this.

SUPERVISOR: That's something you'll have to work out with them, not me.

Example No. 2

FOREMAN: Hey, Ross, I don't get this production

order. We can't handle this run today. What do they think we are?

SUPERVISOR: Sounds like you're pretty sore about it, Kelly.

FOREMAN: I sure am. We were just about getting back to schedule after that press breakdown. Now this comes along.

SUPERVISOR: As if you didn't have enough work to do, huh?

FOREMAN: Yeah. I don't know how I'm gonna tell the guys about this.

SUPERVISOR: Hate to face 'em with it now, is that it?

FOREMAN: I really do. They're under a real strain today. Seems like everything we do around here is rush, rush.

SUPERVISOR: I guess you feel like it's unfair to load anything more on them.

FOREMAN: Well, yeah. I know there must be plenty of pressure on everybody up the line, but—well, if that's the way it is—guess I'd better get the word to 'em.

There are obviously many differences between these two examples. The main one, however, is that Ross, the supervisor in the second example, is using the active-listening approach. He is listening and responding in a way that makes it clear that he appreciates both the meaning and the feeling behind what Kelly is saying.

Active listening does not necessarily mean long sessions spent listening to grievances, personal or otherwise. It is simply a way of approaching those problems which arise out of the usual day-to-day events of any job.

To be effective, active listening must be firmly grounded in the basic attitudes of the user. We cannot employ it as a technique if our fundamental attitudes are in conflict with its basic concepts. If we try, our behavior will be empty and sterile, and our associates will be quick to recognize this. Until we can demonstrate a spirit which genuinely respects the potential worth of the individual, which considers his sights and trusts his capacity for self-direction, we cannot begin to be effective listeners.

What We Achieve by Listening

Active listening is an important way to bring about changes in people. Despite the popular notion that listening is a passive approach, clinical and research evidence clearly shows that sensitive lis-

tening is a most effective agent for individual personality change and group development. Listening brings about changes in people's attitudes toward themselves and others; it also brings about changes in their basic values and personal philosophy. People who have been listened to in this new and special way become more emotionally mature, more open to their experiences, less defensive, more democratic, and less authoritarian.

When people are listened to sensitively, they tend to listen to themselves with more care and to make clear exactly what they are feeling and thinking. Group members tend to listen more to each other, to become less argumentative, more ready to incorporate other points of view. Because listening reduces the threat of having one's ideas criticized, the person is better able to see them for what they are and is more likely to feel that his contributions are worthwhile.

Not the least important result of listening is the change that takes place within the listener himself. Besides providing more information than any other activity, listening builds deep, positive relationships and tends to alter constructively the attitudes of the listener. Listening is a growth experience.

These, then, are some of the worthwhile results we can expect from active listening. But how do we go about this kind of listening? How do we become active listeners?

How to Listen

Active listening aims to bring about changes in people. To achieve this end, it relies upon definite techniques—things to do and things to avoid doing. Before discussing these techniques, however, we should first understand why they are effective. To do so, we must understand how the individual personality develops.

The Growth of the Individual

Through all of our lives, from early childhood on, we have learned to think of ourselves in certain very definite ways. We have built up pictures of ourselves. Sometimes these self-pictures are pretty realistic, but at other times they are not. For example, an average, overweight lady may fancy herself a youthful, ravishing siren, or an awkward teenager regard himself as a star athlete.

All of us have experiences which fit the way we need to think about ourselves. These we accept. But it is much harder to accept experiences which don't fit. And sometimes, if it is very important for us to hang on to this self-picture, we don't accept or admit these experiences at all.

These self-pictures are not necessarily attractive. A man, for example, may regard himself as incompetent and worthless. He may feel that he is doing his job poorly in spite of favorable appraisals by the company. As long as he has these feelings about himself, he must deny any experiences which would seem not to fit this self-picture—in this case any that might indicate to him that he is competent. It is so necessary for him to maintain this self-picture that he is threatened by anything which would tend to change it. Thus, when the company raises his salary, it may seem to him only additional proof that he is a fraud. He must hold onto this self-picture, because, bad or good, it's the only thing he has by which he can identify himself.

This is why direct attempts to change this individual or change his self-picture are particularly threatening. He is forced to defend himself or to completely deny the experience. This denial of experience and defense of the self-picture tend to bring on rigidity of behavior and create difficulties in personal adjustment.

The active-listening approach, on the other hand, does not present a threat to the individual's self-picture. He does not have to defend it. He is able to explore it, see it for what it is, and make his own decision about how realistic it is. And he is then in a position to change.

If I want to help a man reduce his defensiveness and become more adaptive, I must try to remove the threat of myself as his potential changer. As long as the atmosphere is threatening, there can be no effective communication. So I must create a climate which is neither critical, evaluative, nor moralizing. It must be an atmosphere of equality and freedom, permissiveness and understanding, acceptance and warmth. It is in this climate and this climate only that the individual feels safe enough to incorporate new experiences and new values into his concept of himself. Let's see how active listening helps to create this climate.

What to Avoid

When we encounter a person with a problem our usual response is to try to change his way of looking at things—to get him to see his situation the way we see it or would like him to see it. We plead,

reason, scold, encourage, insult, prod—anything to bring about a change in the desired direction, that is, under these circumstances, we are usually responding to *our own* needs to see the world in certain ways. It is always difficult for us to tolerate and understand actions which are different from the ways in which *we* believe *we* should act. If, however, we can free ourselves from the need to influence and direct others in our own paths, we enable ourselves to listen with understanding and thereby employ the most potent available agent of change.

One problem the listener faces is that of responding to demands for decisions, judgments, and evaluations. He is constantly called upon to agree or disagree with someone or something. Yet, as he well knows, the question or challenge frequently is a masked expression of feelings or needs which the speaker is far more anxious to communicate than he is to have the surface questions answered. Because he cannot speak these feelings openly, the speaker must disguise them to himself and to others in an acceptable form. To illustrate, let us examine some typical [employee] questions and the types of [active listener] answers that might best elicit the feelings beneath them.

Q. Just whose responsibility is the toolroom?
A. Do you feel that someone is challenging your authority in there?
Q. Don't you think younger, able people should be promoted before senior but less-able ones?
A. It seems to you they should, I take it.
Q. What does the super expect us to do about those broken-down machines?
A. You're pretty disgusted with those machines, aren't you?
Q. Don't you think I've improved over the last review period?
A. Sounds as if you feel like you've really picked up over these last few months.

These responses recognize the questions but leave the way open for the employee to say what is really bothering him. They allow the listener to participate in the problem or situation without shouldering all responsibility for decision making or actions. This is a process of thinking *with* people instead of *for* or *about* them.

Passing judgment, whether critical or favorable, makes free expression difficult. Similarly, advice and information are almost always seen as efforts to change a person and thus serve as barriers to his self-expression and the development of a creative relationship. Moreover, advice is seldom taken, and information hardly ever utilized. The eager young trainee probably will not become patient just because he is advised that "the road to success in business is a long, difficult one, and you must be patient." And it is no more helpful for him to learn that "only one out of a hundred trainees reaches a top management position."

Interestingly, it is a difficult lesson to learn that positive *evaluations* are sometimes as blocking as negative ones. It is almost as destructive to the freedom of a relationship to tell a person that he is good or capable or right, as to tell him otherwise. To evaluate him positively may make it more difficult for him to tell of the faults that distress him or the ways in which he believes he is not competent.

Encouragement also may be seen as an attempt to motivate the speaker in certain directions or hold him off, rather than as support. "I'm sure everything will work out O.K." is not a helpful response to the person who is deeply discouraged about a problem.

In other words, most of the techniques and devices common to human relationships are found to be of little use in establishing the type of relationship we are seeking here.

What to Do

Just what does active listening entail, then? Basically, it requires that we get inside the speaker, that we grasp, *from his point of view,* just what it is he is communicating to us. More than that, we must convey to the speaker that we are seeing things from his point of view. To listen actively, then, means that there are several things we must do.

LISTEN FOR TOTAL MEANING. Any message a person tries to get across usually has two components: the *content* of the message and the *feeling* or attitude underlying this content. Both are important; both give the message *meaning.* It is this total meaning of the message that we try to understand. For example, a machinist comes to his foreman and says, "I've finished that lathe setup." This message has obvious content and perhaps calls upon the foreman for another work assignment. Suppose, on the other hand, that he says, "Well, I'm finally finished with that damned lathe setup." The content is the

same, but the total meaning of the message has changed—and changed in an important way for both the foreman and the worker. Here sensitive listening can facilitate the relationship. Suppose the foreman were to respond by simply giving another work assignment. Would the employee feel that he had gotten his total message across? Would he feel free to talk to his foreman? Will he feel better about his job, more anxious to do good work on the next assignment?

Now, on the other hand, suppose the foreman were to respond with, "Glad to have it over with, huh?" or "Had a pretty rough time of it?" or "Guess you don't feel like doing anything like that again," or anything else that tells the worker that he heard and understands. It doesn't necessarily mean that the next work assignment need be changed or that he must spend an hour listening to the worker complain about the setup problems he encountered. He may do a number of things differently in the light of the new information he has from the worker—but not necessarily. It's just that extra sensitivity on the part of the foreman which can transform an average working climate into a good one.

RESPOND TO FEELINGS. In some instances, the content is far less important than the feeling which underlies it. To catch the full flavor or meaning of the message, one must respond particularly to the feeling component. If, for instance, our machinist had said, "I'd like to melt this lathe down and make paper clips out of it," responding to content would be obviously absurd. But to respond to his disgust or anger in trying to work with his lathe recognizes the meaning of this message. There are various shadings of these components in the meaning of any message. Each time, the listener must try to remain sensitive to the total meaning the message has to the speaker. What is he trying to tell me? What does this mean to him? How does he see this situation?

NOTE ALL CUES. Not all communication is verbal. The speaker's words alone don't tell us everything he is communicating. And hence, truly sensitive listening requires that we become aware of several kinds of communication besides verbal. The way in which a speaker hesitates in his speech can tell us much about his feelings. So, too, can the inflection of his voice. He may stress certain points loudly

169

and clearly and may mumble others. We should also note such things as the person's facial expressions, body posture, hand movements, eye movements, and breathing. All of these help to convey his total message.

What We Communicate by Listening

The first reaction of most people when they consider listening as a possible method for dealing with human beings is that listening cannot be sufficient in itself. Because it is passive, they feel, listening does not communicate anything to the speaker. Actually, nothing could be farther from the truth.

By consistently listening to a speaker, you are conveying the idea that "I'm interested in you as a person, and I think that what you feel is important. I respect your thoughts, and even if I don't agree with them I know that they are valid for you. I feel sure that you have a contribution to make. I'm not trying to change you or evaluate you. I just want to understand you. I think you're worth listening to, and I want you to know that I'm the kind of a person you can talk to."

The subtle but most important aspect of this is that it is the *demonstration* of the message that works. While it is most difficult to convince someone that you respect him by *telling* him so, you are much more likely to get this message across by really *behaving* that way—by actually *having* and *demonstrating* respect for this person. Listening does this most effectively.

Like other behavior, listening behavior is contagious. This has implications for all communication problems, whether between two people or within a large organization. To ensure good communication between associates up and down the line, one must first take the responsibility for setting a pattern of listening. Just as one learns that anger is usually met with anger, argument with argument, and deception with deception, one can learn that listening can be met with listening. Every person who feels responsibility in a situation can set the tone of the interaction, and the important lesson in this is that any behavior exhibited by one person will eventually be responded to with similar behavior in the other person.

It is far more difficult to stimulate constructive behavior in another person but far more profitable. Listening is one of these constructive behaviors, but if one's attitude is to "wait out" the speaker rather than really listen to him, it will fail. The one who consistently listens with understanding, however, is the one who eventually is most likely to be listened to. If you really want to be heard and understood by another, you can develop him as a potential listener, ready for new ideas, provided you can first develop yourself in these ways and sincerely listen with understanding and respect.

Testing for Understanding

Because understanding another person is actually far more difficult than it at first seems, it is important to test constantly your ability to see the world in the way the speaker sees it. You can do this by reflecting in your own words what the speaker seems to mean by his words and actions. His response to this will tell you whether or not he feels understood. A good rule of thumb is to assume that you never really understand until you can communicate this understanding to the other's satisfaction.

Here is an experiment to test your skill in listening. The next time you become involved in a lively or controversial discussion with another person, stop for a moment and suggest that you adopt this ground rule for continued discussion: Before either participant in the discussion can make a point or express an opinion of his own, he must first restate aloud the previous point or position of the other person. This restatement must be in his own words (merely parroting the words of another does not prove that one has understood but only that he has heard the words). The restatement must be accurate enough to satisfy the speaker before the listener can be allowed to speak for himself.

This is something you can try in your own discussion group. Have someone express himself on some topic of emotional concern to the group. Then, before another member expresses his own feelings and thought, he must rephrase the *meaning* expressed by the previous speaker to that individual's satisfaction. Note the changes in the emotional climate and in the quality of the discussion when you try this.

Problems in Active Listening

Active listening is not an easy skill to acquire. It demands practice. Perhaps more important, it may require changes in our own basic attitudes. These changes come slowly and sometimes with considerable difficulty. Let us look at some of the major problems in active listening and what can be done to overcome them.

The Personal Risk

To be effective at all in active listening, one must have a sincere interest in the speaker. We all live in glass houses as far as our attitudes are concerned. They always show through. And if we are only making a pretense of interest in the speaker, he will quickly pick this up, either consciously or unconsciously. And once he does, he will no longer express himself freely.

Active listening carries a strong element of personal risk. If we manage to accomplish what we are describing here—to sense deeply the feeling of another person, to understand the meaning his experiences have for him, to see the world as he sees it—we risk being changed ourselves. For example, if we permit ourselves to listen our way into the psychological life of a labor leader or agitator—to get the meaning which life has for him—we risk coming to see the world as he sees it. It is threatening to give up, even momentarily, what we believe and start thinking in someone else's terms. It takes a great deal of inner security and courage to be able to risk one's self in understanding another.

For the supervisor, the courage to take another's point of view generally means that he must see *himself* through another's eyes—he must be able to see himself as others see him. To do this may sometimes be unpleasant, but it is far more *difficult* than unpleasant. We are so accustomed to viewing ourselves in certain ways—to seeing and hearing only what we want to see and hear—that it is extremely difficult for a person to free himself from his needs to see things these ways.

Developing an attitude of sincere interest in the speaker is thus no easy task. It can be developed only by being willing to risk seeing the world from the speaker's point of view. If we have a number of such experiences, however, they will shape an attitude which will allow us to be truly genuine in our interest in the speaker.

Hostile Expressions

The listener will often hear negative, hostile expressions directed at himself. Such expressions are always hard to listen to. No one likes to hear hostile words. And it is not easy to get to the point where

one is strong enough to permit these attacks without finding it necessary to defend oneself or retaliate.

Because we all fear that people will crumble under the attack of genuine negative feelings, we tend to perpetuate an attitude of pseudo peace. It is as if we cannot tolerate conflict at all for fear of the damage it could do to us, to the situation, to the others involved. But of course the real damage is done to all these by the denial and suppression of negative feelings.

Out-of-Place Expressions

There is also the problem of out-of-place expressions—expressions dealing with behavior which is not usually acceptable in our society. In the extreme forms that present themselves before psychotherapists, expressions of sexual perversity or homicidal fantasies are often found blocking to the listener because of their obvious threatening quality. At less extreme levels, we all find unnatural or inappropriate behavior difficult to handle. That is, anything from an off-color story told in mixed company to a man weeping is likely to produce a problem situation.

In any face-to-face situation, we will find instances of this type which will momentarily, if not permanently, block any communication. In business and industry, any expressions of weakness or incompetency will generally be regarded as unacceptable and therefore will block good two-way communication. For example, it is difficult to listen to a supervisor tell of his feelings of failure in being able to "take charge" of a situation in his department, because *all* administrators are supposed to be able to "take charge."

Accepting Positive Feelings

It is both interesting and perplexing to note that negative or hostile feelings or expressions are much easier to deal with in any face-to-face relationship than are truly and deeply positive feelings. This is especially true for the businessman, because the culture expects him to be independent, bold, clever, and aggressive and manifest no feelings of warmth, gentleness, and intimacy. He therefore comes to regard these feelings as soft and inappropriate. But no matter how they are regarded, they remain a human need. The denial of these feelings in himself and his associates does not get the executive out of

171

the problem of dealing with them. They simply become veiled and confused. If recognized, they would work for the total effort; unrecognized, they work against it.

Emotional Danger Signals

The listener's own emotions are sometimes a barrier to active listening. When emotions are at their height, which is when listening is most necessary, it is most difficult to set aside one's own concerns and be understanding. Our emotions are often our own worst enemies when we try to become listeners. The more involved and invested we are in a particular situation or problem, the less we are likely to be willing or able to listen to the feelings and attitudes of others. That is, the more we find it necessary to respond to our own needs, the less we are able to respond to the needs of another. Let us look at some of the main danger signals that warn us that our emotions may be interfering with our listening.

DEFENSIVENESS. The points about which one is most vocal and dogmatic, the points which one is most anxious to impose on others—these are always the points one is trying to talk oneself into believing. So one danger signal becomes apparent when you find yourself stressing a point or trying to convince another. It is at these times that you are likely to be less secure and consequently less able to listen.

RESENTMENT OF OPPOSITION. It is always easier to listen to an idea which is similar to one of your own than to an opposing view. Sometimes, in order to clear the air, it is helpful to pause for a moment when you feel your ideas and position being challenged, reflect on the situation, and express your concern to the speaker.

CLASH OF PERSONALITIES. Here again, our experience has consistently shown us that the genuine expression of feelings on the part of the listener will be more helpful in developing a sound relationship than the suppression of them. This is so whether the feelings be resentment, hostility, threat, or admiration. A basically honest relationship, whatever the nature of it, is the most productive of all. The other party becomes secure when he learns that the listener can express his feelings honestly and openly to him. We should keep this in mind when we begin to fear a clash of personalities in the listening rela-

tionship. Otherwise, fear of our own emotions will choke off full expression of feelings.

Listening to Ourselves

To listen to oneself is a prequisite for listening to others. And it is often an effective means of dealing with the problems we have outlined above. When we are most aroused, excited, and demanding, we are least able to understand our own feelings and attitudes. Yet, in dealing with the problems of others, it becomes most important to be sure of one's own position, values, and needs.

The ability to recognize and understand the meaning which a particular episode has for you, with all the feelings which it stimulates in you, and the ability to express this meaning when you find it getting in the way of active listening will clear the air and enable you once again to be free to listen. That is, if some person or situation touches off feelings within you which tend to block your attempts to listen with understanding, begin listening to yourself. It is much more helpful in developing effective relationships to avoid suppressing these feelings. Speak them out as clearly as you can, and try to enlist the other person as a listener to your feelings. A person's listening ability is limited by his ability to listen to himself.

Active Listening and Company Goals

"How can listening improve production?"

"We're in business, and it's a rugged, competitive affair. How are we going to find time to counsel our employees?"

"We have to concern ourselves with organizational problems first."

"We can't afford to spend all day listening when there's a job to be done."

"What's morale got to do with production?"

"Sometimes we have to sacrifice an individual for the good of the rest of the people in the company."

Those of us who are trying to advance the listening approach in industry hear these comments frequently. And because they are so honest and legitimate, they pose a real problem. Unfortunately, the answers are not so clear-cut as the questions.

Individual Importance

One answer is based on an assumption that is central to the listening approach. That assumption is: The kind of behavior which helps the individual will eventually be the best thing that could be done for the group. Or saying it another way: The things that are best for the individual are the best for the company. This is a conviction of ours, based on our experience in psychology and education. The research evidence from industry is only beginning to come in. We find that putting the group first, at the expense of the individual, besides being an uncomfortable individual experience, does *not* unify the group. In fact, it tends to make the group less a group. The members become anxious and suspicious.

We are not at all sure in just what ways the group does benefit from a concern demonstrated for an individual, but we have several strong leads. One is that the group feels more secure when an individual is being listened to and provided for with concern and sensitivity. And we assume that a secure group will ultimately be a better group. When each individual feels that he need not fear exposing himself to the group, he is likely to contribute more freely and spontaneously. When the leader of a group responds to the individual, puts the individual first, the other members of the group will follow suit, and the group will come to act as a unit in recognizing and responding to the needs of a particular member. This positive, constructive action seems to be a much more satisfying experience for a group than the experience of dispensing with a member.

Listening and Production

Whether listening or any other activity designed to better human relations in an industry actually raises production—whether morale has a definite relationship to production—is not known for sure. There are some who frankly hold that there is no relationship to be expected between morale and production—that production often depends upon the social misfit, the eccentric, or the isolate. And there are some who simply choose to work in a climate of cooperation and harmony, in a high-morale group, quite aside from the question of increased production.

A report from the Survey Research Center[1] at the University of Michigan on research conducted at the Prudential Life Insurance Company lists seven

1. "Productivity, Supervision, and Employee Morale." *Human Relations*, Series I, Report 1, Survey Research Center, University of Michigan, Ann Arbor, Michigan.

findings relating to production and morale. First-line supervisors in high-production work groups were found to differ from those in low-production work groups in that they

1. are under less close supervision from their own supervisors;
2. place less direct emphasis upon production as the goal;
3. encourage employee participation in the making of decisions;
4. are more employee-centered;
5. spend more of their time in supervision and less in straight production work;
6. have a greater feeling of confidence in their supervisory roles;
7. feel that they know where they stand with the company.

After mentioning that other dimensions of morale, such as identification with the company, intrinsic job satisfaction, and satisfaction with job status, were not found significantly related to productivity, the report goes on to suggest the following psychological interpretation:

People are more effectively motivated when they are given some degree of freedom in the way in which they do their work than when every action is prescribed in advance. They do better when some degree of decision making about their jobs is possible than when all decisions are made for them. They respond more adequately when they are treated as personalities than as cogs in a machine. In short, if the ego motivations of self-determination, of self-expression, of a sense of personal worth can be tapped, the individual can be more effectively energized. The use of external sanctions or pressuring for production may work to some degree, but not to the extent that the more internalized motives do. When the individual comes to identify himself with his job and with the work of his group, human resources are much more fully utilized in the production process.

The Survey Research Center has also conducted studies among workers in other industries. In discussing the results of these studies, Robert L. Kahn writes:

In the studies of clerical workers, railroad workers, and workers in heavy industry, the supervisors with the better production records gave a larger proportion of their time to supervisory functions, especially to the interpersonal aspects of their jobs. The supervisors of the lower-producing sections were more likely to spend their time in tasks which the men themselves were performing, or in the paperwork aspects of their jobs.[2]

Maximum Creativeness

There may never be enough research evidence to satisfy everyone on this question. But speaking from a business point of view, in terms of the problem of developing resources for production, the maximum creativeness and productive effort of the human beings in the organization are the richest untapped source of power still existing. The difference between the maximum productive capacity of people and that output which industry is now realizing is immense. We simply suggest that this maximum capacity might be closer to realization if we sought to release the motivation that already exists within people rather than try to stimulate them externally.

This releasing of the individual is made possible, first of all, by sensitive listening, with respect and understanding. Listening is a beginning toward making the individual feel himself worthy of making contributions, and this could result in a very dynamic and productive organization. Competitive business is never too rugged or too busy to take time to procure the most efficient technological advances or to develop rich raw material resources. But these in comparison to the resources that are already within the people in the plant are paltry. This is industry's major procurement problem.

G. L. Clements, president of Jewel Tea Co., Inc., in talking about the collaborative approach to management, says:

> We feel that this type of approach recognizes that there is a secret ballot going on at all times among the people in any business. They vote for or against their supervisors. A favorable vote for the supervisor shows up in the cooperation, teamwork, understanding, and production of the group. To win this secret ballot, each supervisor must share the problems of his group and work for them.[3]

The decision to spend time listening to his employees is a decision each supervisor or executive has to make for himself. Executives seldom have much to do with products or processes. They have to deal with people who must in turn deal with people who will deal with products or processes. The higher one goes up the line, the more one will be concerned with human relations problems, simply because people are all one has to work with. The minute we take a man from his bench and make him a foreman, he is removed from the basic production of goods and now must begin relating to individuals instead of nuts and bolts. People are different from things, and our foreman is called upon for a different line of skills completely. His new tasks call upon him to be a special kind of person. The development of himself as a listener is a first step in becoming this special person.

2. Robert L. Kahn, "The Human Factors Underlying Industrial Productivity," *Michigan Business Review*, November 1952.

3. G. L. Clements, "Time for 'Democracy in Action' at the Executive Level," address given before the AMA Personnel Conference, February 28, 1951.

I. Allegro Vivace: Learning to Teach

Mary Dare Hitchcock taught Human Growth and Development, 3 credits, to sophomore students in the teacher education program at my undergraduate university. I remember her very well; she was a southern lady who spoke in the soft, drawn-out vowel tones of eastern Geo-ja. Her distinguishing characteristic was that she always managed to look cool and unperturbed on those beastly hot and humid days that slip too early into the New York spring, while we lot, scraped from the New York sidewalks, were always sweating and grubby. Her presence alone made us feel less dignified. From the raised teacher's platform where she sat, distant from us in metre and in measure, she told us that children were different—physically, intellectually, emotionally, and socially different from each other. (If we could only remember P-I-E-S, that would surely help us to pass the final exam. We copied pies into our notebooks.) And because children are different in pies ways, our teaching methods should emphasize INDIVIDUALIZATION OF INSTRUCTION. She spoke the words in capital letters—it was the *only* sensible way to teach.

Individualization of instruction was a foreign idea to all of us who had spent twelve or so years in the nailed-down desks of the New York City Board of Education standard classroom issue. But in our willingness to please—and pass—we embraced it. It was *the* current motto of the faculty of education— the new panacea and holy grail of methodology. We learned that the amount of emphasis we gave to the slogan in writing essays and final exams directly correlated with higher grades. We mouthed the slogan, as we had the rule, "invert the divisor and multiply," in Grade 5. Naturally, in our understanding of and in our ability to apply theory, we were as ignorant of the how as we had been unable in Grade 5 to figure out which fraction was the divisor. Mary Dare wasn't much of a virtuoso on the how, either. As she sat on her platform, day after blah-blahing day, we sat, too, in straight rows of tablet armchairs, listening, taking notes, and collecting our 3 credits' worth of human growth and development.

READING

How I Taught Myself How to Teach

SELMA WASSERMANN

Selma Wassermann *is professor of Education at Simon Fraser University.*

Reproduced from *Teacher Education*, October 1980. Reprinted with permission.

175

In my teacher education program, we were required to collect 36 hours of credits in course work theoretically designed to teach us to become "good" teachers. With the exception of my practice teaching (which deserves a story of its own), the style and manner of the courses we took were the same: distinguished professors of education, lecturing to students, with an occasional counterpoint of question and answer. That is how we were taught to teach. Needless to say, what I learned best was how to listen, how to take notes, how to read quickly, and most important, how to take and pass exams with high marks.

I remember my first day of teaching as clearly as I would recall sinking with the Titanic. A small detail had been left out of my preparation: I had no teaching skills. I fumbled and bumbled and limped through five interminable hours of the school day, frequently wishing to die. Kenny Henderson didn't help either. He kept tagging along behind me telling me that his last year's teacher never did it *that* way. At the end of the day, I was very close to leaving that room, that school, that city, that world. Who the heck wanted to be a teacher, anyway? I could always earn my living making cabbage rolls—a profession in which I had at least some minimal competence.

In the years to come, I found to my astonishment and consternation that what I had endured during my first days of teaching was not unique. It is the same for very many of us entering the classroom for the first time—a universally shared trauma. The ordeal of those first 60 days are the beginning teacher's initiation rites into the profession, the time during which we face up to the bankruptcy of what little we know about teaching. It is the time during which we begin to teach ourselves how to survive in the classroom. Some of us teach ourselves to teach in the process. It's either that, or making cabbage rolls—in the kitchen, or in the classroom.

What is it, exactly, that is missing from our training programs? Why do beginning teachers feel disabled, rather than enabled, during those first, critical days of teaching? Imagine, for a moment, a scenario in which a student wished to learn to play the harpsichord. Imagine her attending university classes for four years, during which she engaged primarily in listening to her teachers play *their* harpsichords, and which culminated in a practicum experience of actual harpsichord playing lasting only five months. It would be silly to expect this student to perform as a competent professional. We are content that she has learned to play "The Happy Farmer." Her technical skills are understandably weak, and her artistry nonexistent. We would not dream of awarding her a certificate so that she might now teach others. Yet, this is the route by which students are expected to learn how to become classroom teachers. It is no wonder that so many graduate lacking both the technical skills and the artistry.

A pair of seemingly incompatible ideas are being presented in this paper—and as a closing note to this section, it may be of value to look at each, and their relationship to each other. Theme A, carrying the melody, takes the position that a teacher ought to leave his professional training program with at least a set of skills which will enable him to function with some degree of competence in the classroom. In the development of this very familiar theme, it is suggested that such an idea is subscribed to more in theory than in practice.

Theme B, in a somewhat discordant tone, suggests that the artistry found in excellent teaching comes about largely as a result of the process of self-teaching. There is no contradiction here. As the contrapuntal melody does not exist outside of the main theme, so can artistry not evolve in the absence of skill mastery. It is on both themes—how a training program may help a student to move from technical competence toward the evolving of personal artistry—that the following three movements play.

II. Andante Cantabile: What Is Teaching?

> I have come to feel that the only learning which significantly influences behavior is self-discovered, self-appropriated learning.[1]

It may well be that the most important process learnings of life are actually self-taught. How else do we learn about loving, about parenting, about artistry? Who taught Beethoven to compose the Eroica? Where did Einstein learn about the theory

1. Carl Rogers, *On Becoming a Person* (Boston: Houghton Mifflin Co., 1961), p. 276.

of relativity? (His Ph.D. thesis was rejected by his examining committee.) How did Michelangelo learn to sculpt David?

I want to go off, for a moment, to play a small cadenza on the act of teaching—a word which seems to be at the heart of this report. I believe that there is *teaching*, and there is *Teaching*. Almost any damn fool may think he knows all there is to know about teaching—and given half the chance, without benefit of consultant's fee, will gladly tell a teacher *exactly* what that teacher *ought* to be doing. A six-year-old shows his five-year-old brother how to tie his shoelace. He is teaching. Your mother explains why your rye bread did not rise. She is teaching. The tax consultant tells you what deductions are allowed on your tax form. She is teaching. In all of these acts, teaching is occurring and it doesn't take a lot of teacher training to do it. Almost anyone with knowledge and skill in a particular content area might teach that skill to another with relative ease. The common thread which runs through all of these "anyone can teach" examples is that teaching is telling—informing, explaining, demonstrating, showing how. This kind of teaching goes on much of the time and most of us interchange learner and teacher roles many times a day. Yet, in spite of what we can and do learn as a result of teaching by telling, I have come to call this "small 't' teaching."

> It seems to me that anything that can be taught to another is relatively inconsequential, and has little or no significant influence on behavior.[2]

But there is also Teaching—what I call "capital 'T' Teaching"—the Teacher as Artist. While content, knowledge and skills are also learned as part of the process of capital "T" Teaching, it goes much, much further than the mere act of informing, explaining and showing how. It is different in style, in the strategies employed and the attitudes conveyed. Its end result is that the learner is *enabled* by the process. The outcome of capital "T" Teaching is that the learner becomes more free to engage in a process of self-teaching. (To call it self-learning is redundant. There is no other kind of learning.) Capital "T" Teaching is liberating; the learner increases his autonomy, his self-initiative, his confidence in himself and consequently his ability to take risks. He therefore grows in his ability to teach himself.

(On the other hand, the end result of small "t" teaching is that the learner is informed. Frequently, the act of informing by itself results in the learner's decrease in autonomy. He learns dependence upon the teacher, since it is the teacher who sets himself up as the one who "knows.")

How does the capital "T" Teacher achieve these awe-inspiring goals? It is difficult to describe with precision, but if you've been lucky enough to have studied with such a Teacher, you will have shared some of these observations.

Goldhammer[3] has said, "It is the relationship that teaches, rather than the text." And that is the starting point—the quality of the relationship which the capital "T" Teacher is able to achieve with the learner, and what is communicated to the learner via that relationship.

In his teaching, the capital "T" Teacher communicates a genuine prizing and valuing of the student. He listens deeply—and this communicates that he is attentive, caring, interested in what the student has to say. The student does not have to be concerned about defending himself against ridicule, belittlement or rejection. There is a deep respect for the dignity of the learner—for his individuality, for his capacity, for his gifts, for his right to make choices—and there is also a sensitivity to the needs, problems and feelings of the student.

This Teacher reveals an openness to growing and learning; and the student comes to see that self-teaching is a continuous process for him. He has sufficient self-regard that he does not become defensive when his beliefs are under question. He communicates a joy—almost a passion—about his work, and it is clear that he loves what he is doing.[4] The student experiences this teacher not as an "all-knowing sage" but as a resource person who has faith and trust in the learner's ability. While in almost every sense the capital "T" Teacher is a model to the learner, the message communicated to the learner is that he is free to develop his own unique style.

There is, of course, more. The Artist Teacher has the skill which enables him to make accurate assessments of student performance and initiate teaching strategies which help the student grow in

2. Ibid., p. 176.

3. Robert Goldhammer, *Clinical Supervision* (New York: Holt, Rinehart and Winston, 1969).
4. Gerald Pine and Angelo Boy, *Learner Centered Teaching* (Denver: Love Publishing Co., 1977).

autonomy. All of this is done in a way which does not undermine the learner's confidence in himself, and does not diminish his self-esteem. A student's mistakes are seen as opportunities for understanding how the learner perceives the learning task, rather than as misdemeanors with penalties owing.

Recapitulation. In small "t" teaching, we can and do teach by informing, explaining and showing how. This can be done stylishly, or it can be done in a dull and boring manner. Either way, it is an act which requires a high degree of teacher control over learner behavior.

In capital "T" Teaching, the Teacher not only provides for the development of knowledge and skill, but he does this in such a way that *enables* the learner to move to higher positions on the continuum of personal autonomy.

While it is true that skill mastery will never guarantee the quantum leap to artistry, there can be no artistry without the skills and the development of personal autonomy.

III. Menuetto. Allegretto: Promoting Artistry in Teaching via the Harpsichord Theory of Teaching Education

What does it take to produce a Landowska? A Segovia? A Rostropovich? A Menuhin? A musician of incomparable artistry and skill, who will thrill you with his/her performance, as the capital "T" Teacher thrills you with his/her teaching?

In the beginning, there is the *Passion*—the all-consuming desire that makes it possible to give your life to the art. Without the passion, there cannot be the commitment to endless hours of *Practice*; without the practice, there can be no mastery of technique, no musical understanding, no development of style, of performance skill, musicianship. Finally, there is the intervention of the *Master Teacher*, who enables in a variety of ways. The Master Teacher enters into a relationship with the student that is consistently enabling. He provides practice tasks which will help you to advance your technical know-how. He knows just how to identify your specific performance difficulties and, what's more, introduce procedures which help to alleviate the

difficulty. Wrong notes are not matters for ridicule; they are important keys to understanding how the process of learning has been impeded. The sum of all the strategies used by the Master Teacher is that you become more and more enabled, more skilled, more confident. You are able to take more risks. And as you gain in skill and in personal autonomy, you increase your self-teaching capabilities.

There are some clear parallels for the training of Teachers. Because of these parallels, I have come to call this training model the Harpsichord Theory of Teacher Education. The theory attempts to do the following:

a. It attempts to show that current teacher education requires students to learn the wrong skills. (In effect, students engage in practicing the wrong tasks.)
b. It attempts to identify those practice tasks which are related to developing skill in classroom teaching.
c. It attempts to show that these skills can be taught effectively and in enabling ways.
d. It attempts to establish a relationship between skill mastery, personal autonomy and the process of self-teaching required of the Artist Teacher.

It has been said that there is nothing new under the sun, and I would like to admit straight away that the Harpsichord Theory is only a new name for what we already know and for what many of us deeply believe about teaching and learning. It rests primarily on the "theory of engaged time" which is in current vogue in some educational research circles. In laymen's terms, this means that the more time a person spends on a particular task, the more competent he is apt to become at that task. Not only is the idea not new, but it is at least as ancient as my old grandmother, who, while thoroughly unschooled, used to tell me that "practice makes perfect." Even John Dewey was known to have written, "We learn what we do."[5]

If we examine current practices in most teacher education programs, we can see pretty clearly what students are spending most of their time practicing. It is listening, note-taking, reading, exchanging ideas, writing and passing exams. It should, therefore, come as no surprise that this is what they learn

5. John Dewey, *The Child and the Curriculum* (Chicago: University of Chicago Press, 1906).

to do, and to do very well. These types of learning experiences are found in courses in theory, in courses in "foundations" and curiously enough, in courses in methodology. If an observer were to follow a randomly selected teacher-trainee around from class to class during the course of a university day, he would find that students are engaged more than 80% of the time in practicing listening, talking, and note-taking, while the professor is actively engaged in teaching (telling). If the theory of engaged time has any validity, it is little wonder that students emerge from these programs without the competence in the highly sophisticated and complex skills required of the Teacher.

Playing on the harpsichord metaphor a little more, we can also say with some confidence that if practice tasks are to be introduced into the existing course work structure, these tasks ought to have some relevance to those professional skills that are required of the classroom teacher. In other words, in order to perform more competently on the harpsichord, it is essential that the student engage in practicing scales and arpeggios, fingering, sight reading, phrasing. Seeing a film about Chopin and making a harpsichord out of papier-mâché are quite nice to do, but largely irrelevant to the development of technical keyboard know-how.

Teacher trainees may engage in reviewing children's books, making phonics games and learning about the difference between reliability and validity. But such practice tasks do little to increase skill in the teaching of reading, or in the development of classroom tests. Segovia once told an aspiring musician, "I never practice my scales more than five hours a day." And that was when the maestro was 75 years old. There is a vast difference between *learning about* teaching, and practicing the tasks of teaching.

There is little in the whole of the educational process that is actually enabling. Moreover, it is pretty clear that many students leave school at the end of Grade 12 as less autonomous learners than they were when they started. In what other institutions, after all, do we have so much emphasis on controlling and directing the behavior of others—with very little opportunity for exercising personal options? A Grade 3 class in Salmon Arm participates in "organized peeing"—an activity which may only occur at half-past ten in the morning.

Teacher trainees come into university programs needing very much to be more enabled—and this

process ought to be the primary outcome of what we do in our courses. It is not enough to help our students to practice the right tasks. It is vitally important that we teach them in enabling ways—so that they may embark in a direction of self-teaching. Without the enabling, their teaching may never be more than mechanical and deadly dull. It is through the enabling that the self-teaching required to become the Artist Teacher is made possible.

What follows now is the articulation of three categories of experiences which I believe to be essential in the education of self-teachers. These, of course, are not the *only* experiences in which teacher-trainees need to engage. However, I believe each of these to be not only vitally important to competent teaching—but *the* key practice tasks, providing the skills as well as the enabling, and without which the self-teaching required at the capital "T" level of performance cannot occur.

A. The Development of a Clear Set of Educational Beliefs from Which Teaching Practices May Flow

In almost every teacher education program, there is at least one course devoted to the "foundations" of education, dealing with the analysis and articulation of educational issues and ideas. The focus of such courses, however, is usually upon the examination of the ideas and beliefs of others; and/or the presentation of ideas by the teacher—hopefully to be examined, but in any event, embraced by the students. Exhortations to the students to "feel free to disagree" are quickly seen as phony. What the teacher really wants is for the students to accept his/her point of view and, what's more, to trade it in on the final exam for a good grade. The practice tasks in which the student engages are primarily those of listening, note-taking, reading, and group discussions.

Most of the current literature dealing with the preparation of teachers emphasizes the need for the student's development and articulation on his own beliefs, since it is the student's own beliefs about teaching and learning which will guide his/her actions in the institutional press of the classroom. If a student's beliefs are unclear, unformed, uncritically derivative, confused, the resulting teaching behavior is likely to be erratic, confused, inconsistent, chaotic.

Unfortunately, we cannot *give* students beliefs. Beliefs do not come about from reading or listening or group discussion. A belief one truly owns comes about as a result of having had an opportunity to reflect on that belief, over a period of time, having had many opportunities to turn it over in the mind, this way and that way, examining it from many angles, and finally, by testing it in the marketplace of life. All of this has to take place before a belief can be truly owned, and it is generally a long-term process.

A teacher helps a student to reflect upon his beliefs through the use of clarifying questions. Can you give me an example of what you mean?, What data support that point of view?, What might be some assumptions you are making? are the types of questions that allow the student to examine his belief from a variety of angles. Moreover, these clarifying questions are raised without verbal or nonverbal cues which in any way undermine the student's confidence in deciding the issue for himself. Clarifying a student's idea is not to be confused with manipulating the student around to the teacher's point of view. If the student is not permitted the freedom to choose for himself, the process of enabling is greatly impeded.[6]

In the absence of sufficient practice in reflecting upon and working through their own educational beliefs, students will most likely revert to using those classroom practices through which they themselves have been heavily programmed, perpetuating the small "t" teaching cycle.

How much practice does a teacher-trainee need in the task of reflecting on educational beliefs? If Segovia can be believed, certainly not more than five hours a day, for about 75 years. Like learning to play the harpsichord, the practice of a skill is a life-long activity. But more, much more, of this kind of practice experience needs to find its place in the teacher-education curriculum.

B. Practicing the Skills of Teaching

Toward the end of almost every teacher-education program is an experience called practice teaching. It *is* there—but, in most programs, there is too little of it, and it occurs only at the culmination of the program. Five months of limited harpsichord practice may help the budding artist to become proficient at "The Happy Farmer" stage of musical performance, but it is hardly a sufficient practice ex-

perience for the Goldberg Variations. Not only that; we do expect the student, in his practicum, to perform at the level of the Goldberg Variations, playing the correct notes, the correct fingering, the correct phrasing, with much attention to the crescendoes and decrescendoes, if you please.

There is very little opportunity in teacher education courses for the student to begin practicing at "The Happy Farmer" stage and proceed through increasingly difficult stages of performance. Our programs only create the illusion that this is happening, but in actual fact, few courses allow for the student to engage in those practice tasks that have direct relevance to classroom teaching skill. A glance into any methods course will reveal that it is the professor who is practicing the methods, while the student is primarily practicing the listening, the note-taking and the group discussions.

What is proposed then, is not only the addition of more practice teaching time in actual classrooms, but also the inclusion in methods courses of opportunities for students to engage in those professional practice tasks which will help them to acquire skill in a variety of teaching strategies.

For example, in a course dealing with the teaching of reading, instead of learning *about* the teaching of reading, students ought to be engaged in practicing tasks such as conducting reading conferences; making diagnoses of weaknesses in reading performance; using remedial intervention strategies; using a variety of different reading programs in practice sessions; providing instruction in word analysis skills; providing instruction in comprehension/thinking skills. What's more, students should be required to practice these tasks until the professor has seen a demonstration of the student's ability to perform the task competently.

In a course in evaluation, instead of learning *about* evaluation, students should be practicing at the professional tasks of providing informed, non-punitive feedback to pupils; developing good evaluative procedures; conducting parent-teacher conferences; writing thoughtful and accurate descriptions of pupil performance.

Where the practice tasks may be continually interfaced with actual classroom teaching performance, under the rigorous scrutiny of a videotape feedback system, the student's opportunities to strengthen his skills grow enormously. This is due to the added dimensions of practice, combined with actual performance and focused self-scrutiny, which

6. Louis E. Raths, et al., *Teaching for Thinking: Theory, Strategies and Activities for the Classroom* (New York: Teachers College Press, 1986).

require the student to undertake the self-teaching necessary for improved performance levels. Without the advantages of the practice task/classroom teaching interface, students may have to practice primarily in role-playing contexts, which, like dummy pianos, can also help to sharpen technique, facility and overall skill in quite adequate ways.

C. The Intervention of the Master Teacher

I have said in an earlier section that the critical dimension in Master Teaching is that of *enabling*. Students who have undertaken studies with a Master Teacher find themselves more enabled in a variety of ways—more skilled, more knowledgeable, more self-confident, and most certainly, more autonomous. The Master Teacher employs strategies which, in the end result, enable the student to move forward on the self-teaching continuum.

There are hundreds of statistical studies which attempt to zero in on what it is a teacher actually does in the classroom to bring about certain learning outcomes, and the results are, at best, ambiguous and inconsistent. Yet, if we have been lucky enough to have been a student in the class of a Master Teacher, we *know* it—and we come away from the experience deeply affected in profound and intense ways.

The Master Teacher functions in at least three domains. First of all, he functions as a *person*—and in doing so, he reveals much about himself via his very presence. What's more, the qualities which are being revealed about his person are the very qualities which we admire, value, prize and respect. To merely possess information about his subject is not sufficient. A Master Teacher who has acquired knowledge, but behaves in ways that are churlish, hostile, or morally repugnant does not earn our esteem. What he does, what he says, and who he is speaks loudly to us, and on that basis, we make our assessments of him. He is, of course, eminently knowledgeable in his field; he is open and nondogmatic about ideas; his behavior may be characterized as "thoughtful" in that his actions seem reasoned and reasonable. He is a person who is able to take risks, to take and defend an unpopular stand, to take initiatives. There is a consistency about him that is clearly observable—not only is there consistency about his beliefs, but between what he says and what he does. Some call this *congruence*—the quality of authenticity. He is no phony. The admired Master Teacher functions

much of the time as a "problem solver"—as one who is unafraid of the challenges of new problems and undertakes to solve them in imaginative and highly skillful ways. There are qualities of creativeness attached to his Teaching and to his thinking that are both refreshing and stimulating. Moreover, as a person, he is reliable and dependable with respect to his obligations to students, to colleagues and to his own scholarly activities.

Another domain in which we assess the Master Teacher is through his interactions with his students and the quality of the relationship that occurs as a direct consequence of those interactions. In the very first order of priority, there is communicated in this Teacher's interactions a deep and genuine prizing and caring about the learner. He reveals this through his ability to be undogmatic and nonjudgmental in the face of students' ideas, opinions, beliefs. He is considerate of the feelings of students and communicates genuine warmth and regard for them.

A second type of interactive skill has to do with this Teacher's ability to make astute observations of individual pupil performance, diagnose specific weaknesses and suggest plans of action that are truly helpful. Casals listened intently to the young cellist perform and said, "You are playing the trill with the third and fourth fingers. I think if you use the fourth and fifth fingers instead, you will get a better, fuller tone." An English teacher writes on a student's essay, "You seem to be having difficulty with your syntax. Please come to me for some help with it." In each of these instances, the student is not made to feel stupid as a consequence of his inability; evaluative judgments are not demeaning nor punitive. They are specifically diagnostic to the individual learner's difficulty. As a consequence of these specific diagnostic interventions, the learner is enabled to understand a little more about his performance and he is enabled to do the self-teaching required to move himself to the next level of mastery. The teacher who attempts to help a student learn by writing "tighten your style" on his paper, is not only nonspecific in pinpointing weakness, but also nonhelpful in directing remediative procedures. The consequence for the student is increased confusion and frustration.

I have heard students say about a Master Teacher, "He makes me think"—at first said grudgingly, and then with admiration. The teacher who, through his questions and responses, expands and extends

181

the thought processes of his students puts into operation a process of enabling which may serve the students throughout their lives.

There is a third domain in which the Master Teacher outperforms the rest and that is in the area of curriculum. In his classroom, whether at the music school, or in the kindergarten, or at the university, there is a quality about what is happening in the class that might be called "dynamic." The Master Teacher may achieve this through a combination of his own enthusiasm, his choices of curriculum materials, the content and purposefulness of the subject matter, and the way he organizes and orchestrates the learning experiences. His class is never boring or routine; it is alive and zestful and rich. The student comes away from it inspired, knowing more, being more interested, and feeling good—and all of these contribute richly to his movement along the self-teaching continuum.

In all of what the Master Teacher does, he is continually a model for us, to which we frequently aspire. Yet, we are free to develop in our own unique ways, our own talents and our own capabilities.

If you have had the good fortune of studying with such a Teacher, you will know the feeling of being liberated instead of being controlled, of being invited instead of being dismissed, of being enabled instead of being disabled. The Master Teacher thus plants the seeds by which the student, in turn, may grow to teach himself to become a Master Teacher.

IV. Allegro Molto: How I Taught Myself How To Teach

Marshall McLuhan told us: "The medium is the message."

Postman and Weingartner also told us: "The critical content is the process through which learning occurs."

Teachers teach not as they are taught *how* to teach, but as they themselves are taught.

It was perfectly natural then, that one day, early in my teaching career, in a blinding recognition scene, I should find myself teaching as a cloned version of Mary Dare Hitchcock. There were my students—sitting in their tablet armchairs. There

was I, elevated, not in wisdom, alas, but on the teacher's platform, telling them about pies, day after blah-blahing day. There is a lot of safety in doing things in the same old way. There are no risks, no personal involvement, no putting your tenure on the line, no making waves in your faculty boat which might rock that solid ship of state. But then, Beethoven did not write the Rasoumowsky Quartets by following mechanically in the footsteps of Haydn.

I guess all significant learning comes about as a consequence of the need for resolution of cognitive dissonance. One cannot endure for long a period of such disharmony as is encountered in a clash between a conflict of personal beliefs and discrepant personal behavior. Once you have identified such a conflict, something has to give if you are to restore homeostasis. It is as uncomfortable as hearing the last movement of a symphony, without the concluding tonic chord.

After that first awareness, some change must inevitably follow.

> I find that another way of learning for me is to state my own uncertainties, to try to clarify my own puzzlements, and then get closer to the meaning that my experience has for me.[7]

Alas, there is no magical transformation, no chemical potion that allows you to awaken in the morning as THE NEW YOU, no telephone booth scene in which you shed the garments of the ordinary teacher and leap out as Superteacher! There is, instead, after the initial insight, the beginning of a growth process which is as slow, and as painful, as teething.

Once your teaching performance has become unacceptable to you, you begin a self-teaching program to change, so that what you do in the classroom may be more congruent with your personal beliefs. First, there is the undertaking of "field trials"—the setting up of your classroom as a laboratory in which the testing of new ideas, the examination and interpretation of results, the learning to live with failure, the recreating, retesting, reshaping of methodology, materials, interactive strategies, may all occur. There is the continued seeking of additional information, the identification and selection of specific new teaching skills, of sharpening

7. Rogers, *On Becoming a Person*, p. 277.

old ones and discarding others which are no longer appropriate. There is the continuous and painful process of self-assessment, in which you learn to depend more and more upon your own internal evaluation system. In the process of self-teaching, the locus of evaluation rests heavily within the learner.

None of this is very easy. Most colleagues and friends don't seem to understand what all the fuss is about and why you can't be content with what you are doing. Some students, like Kenny Hender-son, find the difference in your classroom expectations extremely unsettling. ("Why can't you just *tell* us what to do?") Support systems fail all around you when you travel uncharted territory, and the open hostility can be very punishing.

What, then, have I taught myself about teaching? That I am discontent to follow in the footsteps of Mary Dare Hitchcock; that I must learn to do it better. I am deep in the process of teaching myself how, and there is only one thing left for me to learn. Everything.

Section 4. Leading the Discussion Process: The Critical Instructional Choice—Direction vs. Control

The Section Just Took Over: A Student's Reflections

C. Roland Christensen wrote this case from data supplied by a member of the Developing Discussion Leadership Skills Seminar. All names and some peripheral facts have been disguised.

I 'll never forget that class as long as I live! There was Associate Professor Kenneth Webster; we thought he was the case method instructor *par excellence*, the professor who was always in perfect control—simply nonplussed—just out of it! The section simply took the class discussion away from him. He was left up front, standing by the instructor's desk, just watching the parade go by. At that time it was just an interesting episode to talk about at the weekend beer party. But now, as I'm about to start out teaching myself, I keep thinking about the class; it poses so many tough questions for me.

Nobody ever came late to Professor Webster's 8:30 A.M. Marketing Policy class. Besides being a key first-semester MBA course, many of us were almost intimidated by the highly polished "performance" of the professor. He was able to needle students into corners, only to lead them out again when the time was ripe by getting someone to dredge up the three numbers in Exhibit 2 which "cracked the case." His sense of timing in a case discussion was flawless, although he was never seen glancing at the clock; the class myth attributed part of his mystique to his having eyes in the back of his head. Professor Webster was always "on top" of the discussion, leading us through the relevant and the obscure to the climax and his brilliant five-minute windup. His smooth performance was always given in one of Southeastern's few amphitheater classrooms with their left, right, and center subsections of seats.

I was in the classroom a bit early that day. Webster came in and, as usual, removed his coat and carefully arranged the mechanical chalkboard so that only his class discussion outline could be seen by the students as they came in. He then stood taking a last look at his carefully prepared notes, finally putting them in a neat stack at one side of the instructor's table. Once class started, at least in those early weeks of the course, I could never remember him using those notes; he must have memorized an outline of the case as he would have done it. He had told us in his introductory speech for the course that he worked to combine class discussion freedom with a logical, scientific, and disciplined approach to marketing problems and solutions.

The case for this particular day concerned the marketing of birth control pills in an underdeveloped country by a large, multinational drug company. The issues ranged from problems of pric-

Section 4. Leading the Discussion Process: The Critical Instructional Choice—Direction vs. Control

CASE
The Section Just Took Over: A Student's Reflections

ing, to distribution of the product to diverse market segments in terms of literacy, income levels, and physician contact. Side issues included overcoming possible parochial government resistance to the "invasion" of local markets by a foreign company, and the powerful resistance of the Catholic Church, the country's dominant religion, to the distribution of such a product. It was the first case we had involving this kind of complicated product-market situation.

The case began with a mediocre "kickoff" performance by the first student called on: many of the distinctions between marketing sophisticated products in underdeveloped versus highly industrialized nations were missed. Contributions were slow in coming, perhaps indicating less than adequate overall class preparation. Webster kept slugging away, I thought, with the objective of getting more meat on the bones of his visible board class outline before revealing the "fat" hidden on the board beneath. His disappointment, however, was clearly visible in his frequent gazing around the room during student comments, and in a lack of continuity between his questions and student comments.

Just about halfway through the session, Kay Woodward raised her hand—one of the only times she had done so during the semester. I didn't know her well, but I gathered she had not had business experience. But a member of one of the small "study groups" in the section told me not to mistake her quietness for an absence of feeling or a lack of depth of conviction on social issues. Was she right! She brought everyone up short!

"I think," Kay said, "we are avoiding the most important issues presented by this case, and that's discouraging to me if I am to believe that we are the leaders of tomorrow. This company's marketing plan should strike everyone's conscience as being highly unethical, even immoral. I read the case last night and thought I was studying a chapter out of *The Ugly American*. Here is this huge drug company, restricted in its own country from distributing the pill without careful medical supervision, pushing wholesale distribution of a hazardous drug to illiterates under the guise of doing them a favor. The only favor being done is to the stockholders of the company. Not only are the long-term effects of the drug acknowledged to be potentially dangerous, but the drug is also forbidden by the religious authority of the country. This is a gross example of the exploitation of women—endangering their health and encouraging them to defy their religious beliefs—all done in the pursuit of Almighty Profits."

Bob Kinney—I believe he had been in the investment business for a number of years—wheeled his seat around and without even looking at Professor Webster shot back as soon as Kay finished: "Well, that's not really the main issue here. That kind of problem is a personal one for you, and not what I'd really like to have to listen to in class. I didn't come here to learn what I'd missed in Sunday School. . . ."

Wow, did that create an explosion. Almost everyone got in the act. There were students on the left side arguing with students on the right side of the room, plus at least several dozen neighbor-to-neighbor private discussions going on at once. The arguments, as far as I can remember, were all over the place. The only "quiet" part of the room was the first few rows of the center section. Students there just seemed half bored and half irritated.

With about 20 minutes remaining, Harry Jones, an older member of the section and a former divinity school student, came into the act. From his seat toward the rear of the center section, he took over: "I disagree with Bob Kinney and I don't think his response to Kay was fair. We should discuss the ethics of this issue. You have to consider ethical issues in the real world, and that's what we're here for, to learn how to handle these problems within the organizations we will be working for. I think the drug companies have suffered from a moral lapse in many instances; I have a big question in my mind about the way they influence doctors with their armies of salesmen. My brother is a doctor and when he graduated from med school, he and all his classmates received boxfuls of drug samples and instruments from the drug and instrument manufacturers. I don't like the idea that my doctor is prescribing a drug to me because some guy is a good salesman—a better word for it might be 'pusher'. . . ."

The class pace slowed and Professor Webster, who had made several attempts to bring the class back to "normal" operating patterns, held up his hands and stepped forward. The room slowly became quiet. Focusing his eyes on the back wall of the classroom he said, "Kay's question is not appropriate to discuss in marketing class. You all have the opportunity to air your views privately with each other outside the class. Now, let us get back to how you would approach *the* problem of the case—how should the company distribute this product. Peter, what would you do?"

The discussion resumed on a subdued note. At the end of class, Professor Webster gave a summary of the marketing issues involved in the case and the problems they presented to the company. No further "social-ethical" questions were raised in his marketing course that semester.

One mid-October Friday afternoon Ed Sherman, assistant professor of Marketing at San Francisco Bay Area Graduate School of Management, asked a student, Charles Finch, to open a case discussion. Charles mumbled "I pass," which surprised and annoyed Ed because he had asked students to inform him discreetly before class when they couldn't prepare a case, in order to avoid general embarrassment. Nonetheless, Ed made sure to smile as he asked Charles to please come see him in his office. Then he called on someone else and the discussion began.

It seemed a minor incident; however, when Ed learned later that not only was Charles furious but many other members of the class were extremely upset, his anxiety began to tighten, notch by notch. "Over the weekend," he told the researcher, "I realized that I was actually in very big trouble with this group. We were miles apart, and not only because they thought I had embarrassed Charles, though I thought it was just the other way around. Rapport is everything in case method teaching, and we'd lost it. I felt I was on the precipice. As the ed rep later told me, at that point the section was mine to lose."

The School

San Francisco Bay Area Graduate School of Management, called "Bay" by its students, enjoyed a fine reputation in the business world. Like admission to its two-year MBA program, advancement in its faculty's ranks was highly prized. Bay divided its 800 first-year students into ten groups called sections, which met daily at 8:30 A.M. for three hour-and-a-half case discussions. Teachers "floated" from classroom to classroom.

Characteristically, the student called upon to open the discussion took at least 10 minutes to present analysis and recommendations for the case, which the section then used as the basis for a broader and deeper discussion. Class participation counted heavily in most course grades. Since first-year students carried nine courses, most of them technical and unfamiliar, the taxing workload created tight social units among the sections, initially for mutual psychological protection. In the third week of classes, each section elected representatives to provide liaison among them, their teachers, and the administration.

CASE

The Section Was Mine to Lose (A)

Dr. Abby J. Hansen, research associate, wrote this case for the Developing Discussion Leadership Skills and the Teaching by the Case Method seminars. Data were furnished by the involved participants. All names and some peripheral facts have been disguised.

The (B) case presents key events in Ed Sherman's dealings with Section VI from his perspective; the (C) case presents parallel comments from the point of view of the section's educational representative, Hayes Latham.

The Course

Marketing, a first semester course, was considered difficult. Many students found the initial several weeks of Marketing bewildering. As Ed Sherman pointed out, "The cases are broad-based and challenging; in the assignment summary book all students receive here, other course assignments have specific questions, like 'What level of inventory should Company X maintain?' In Marketing the only assignment is: 'Prepare to discuss the case.'"

I am something of an anomaly among Bay professors," Ed Sherman told the researcher, "because I had neither an MBA nor practical business experience when I was hired two years ago." Ed's background was, instead, strongly academic, including a doctorate in sociology from Berkeley. His only preparation to teach marketing had been original research in organizational cultures. He was a seasoned teacher, however, having taught during graduate school and in a one-year appointment at Pomona College. While at Pomona, Ed won and accepted a fellowship to do research on American business corporations at Bay. Supplementing his library work there with class visits and meetings with faculty, he began to find the school intriguing.

The Instructor: A Self-Description by Ed Sherman

"When Phil Meyer, the head of the marketing course, invited me to teach here," Ed recalled, "I was both exhilarated and intimidated. I turned down a more conventional job in sociology at Purdue to accept Bay's offer, but I knew that I'd have to work extremely hard to master the material and the case method of teaching. I'm not especially good at numbers, and my discipline-oriented background is the sort that many people here would call 'soft.' I had to learn to read a balance sheet and an income statement just as my students did." Nonetheless, Ed thought he had personal resources to draw on. "I'm very quick-witted," he said. "I was brought up on repartee, and I have a sense of humor and the ability to think on my feet—all useful qualities in case method teaching."

In his first year at Bay Ed concluded:

"I had blossomed. I knew my students, I was really getting by on my wits, and I thought everything was just wonderful. It was a high. Research became a burden. At Pomona, where I mostly lectured, I had consumed a great deal of antacid. But at Bay, in my first year, I heard nothing but compliments on all sides from my students. 'Edward, you're the best thing ever!' Of course, I knew not to believe the flattery, but nevertheless I did believe it. Unfortunately, when the year was over I learned that my students had given me an overall teaching rating of 3.5 out of a possible 5 [the top rating]. Not awful, but below the course mean. I had underperformed my colleagues! That really bothered me, especially because some students' comments showed that my humor made them fear I might direct it at

CASE

The Section Was Mine to Lose (B)

Dr. Abby J. Hansen, research associate, wrote this case for the Developing Discussion Leadership Skills and the Teaching by the Case Method seminars. Data were furnished by the involved participants. All names and some peripheral facts have been disguised.

them. I vowed that in my second year I would learn to lean less on their approval."

At this point it is relevant to mention that Ed was the only child of parents in their late sixties, and quite concerned about his father's chronic heart condition.

The rest of this case is related in Ed Sherman's own words, as he describes the situation and the events leading up to the incident.

The Section

For some reason, this was an oddball group. One time a student arrived 45 minutes into the 8:30 A.M. class, walked right in front of my desk, said, "Sorry, I overslept," and then just continued up the aisle to find a seat.

In our first two and a half weeks together, I had not been altogether pleased with Section VI, although I thought they liked me pretty well. Having taught the course the previous year, I now felt comfortable with the material—at least enough so that I knew I wouldn't worry too much. But somehow I felt Section VI lacked a certain *joie de vivre*. These people weren't sharp and defined in my mind. For instance, there were two women whose names I confused so consistently that I had to give up using their names at all. Once on campus I bumped into the two social reps of the group and they asked, "Don't you think our section lacks humor?" To ask a question like that is to answer it. This seemed to be a stick-in-the-mud section. Also, I had an odd sense of being closed in with them: The classroom was bare, institutional, and ugly, with faded curtains hanging over windowless cinderblock walls, and signs saying "Don't do this, don't do that." It was a *hard* room.

Context of the Incident

As I mentioned, I was determined not to repeat one mistake I'd made in my first year—getting too wrapped up in my students. You don't get ahead by stewing about students, so in my return bout, I had decided to be more independent. I was a bit seasoned. I'd already seen a whole year of section dynamics. I'd seen students bored and edgy; I'd seen them play games in class. This time I felt unfrightened of their ability to humiliate me. Perhaps my increased confidence had something to do with finding Section VI timid and self-protective.

Late arrivals became an issue between me and

this group. It annoyed me when people came in late and interrupted the flow of discussion, but I didn't like to stop class and make a big deal about it, so I simply wrote their names down.

Another issue that raised tension had to do with my calling on a certain student to speak. In our ninth case, two weeks before the incident that really derailed things, I asked Margaret Peters to open. She had not previously spoken, but when she moved forward from her usual seat way in the back, I interpreted this as a signal that she felt ready to participate. I was willing to risk letting a weak student open a case because I now felt confident of my own familiarity with the material and ability to get a good discussion started even after an uncertain start. Margaret was hesitant. I had anticipated that. But then she stumbled and said, "I can't talk, I'm too nervous." I wanted to help her continue, so I kept questioning her, with easier and easier questions, which she still couldn't handle. Finally, I said, "It's okay, you can wait." But she really couldn't speak. As it turned out, she left the program not too long thereafter. I realize now that my questions could have seemed like a third degree, but really I was trying to be helpful.

The Incident

The incident that bothered me so much happened on Friday, October 10, at 1:00 P.M. It was our fourteenth case—"Royal Foods Co." I called on Charles Finch, who was 30, married, and a former employee of the marketing department at Bendix. Charles had previously come to my office to ask how I thought he was doing, but since he had spoken neither very well nor very badly in class, I had little feeling for his participation. I said to myself, "Okay, give him a chance to start a case." Just before class, Charles sought me out to say he wanted to make an announcement. If a student wants to avoid a teacher, he usually slinks in a minute or two late and stays far away, so I assumed that Charles was prepared. He also had several piles of notes on his desk. I opened the class saying, "Charles has an announcement he'd like to make after class." Then I smiled at Charles and said, "Charles, I'd also like you to start the case today." Then I turned my back to write on the board, feeling perfectly confident that he was about to speak. When I turned around, he was shuffling papers. I thought he had several classes'

Section 4. Leading the Discussion Process: The Critical
Instructional Choice—Direction vs. Control

CASE
The Section Was Mine to Lose (B)

worth of notes there so I made a typical sort of joke: "Charles, it's the Royal Foods case." Charles started, hesitantly, to say something, then stopped and said, "I'm not prepared to open. Please call on someone else."

On reflection, I'm sorry about the way I replied, although at the time it seemed innocuous—even pleasant. I smiled and said, "Okay, but would you mind, if you get a chance, coming to see me in my office?" The fact was I was pretty annoyed. Charles should have warned me if he wasn't prepared. I was careful, though, to speak politely, even sweetly. As it turned out, though, I had underestimated the effect of my words and the general level of tension in that classroom.

The Aftermath

Later that afternoon, after I'd seen a few people from the section, Charles burst into my office and said, "Edward, I don't know what to say. I had a special assignment last night—a big essay for Industrial Psychology. Also, my car was towed. I just didn't have time to prepare the marketing case."

"Charles, you know there's no passing in my class," I answered. "You should have told me before the hour began if you weren't prepared." (I had explained this policy in the second or third class of the year.) I went on, "Working for someone else's course is no excuse for not doing your marketing assignment anyway."

"Look," he said, "if you don't believe my car was towed, I can show you the towing company's receipt."

"I believe you," I replied, "but it's irrelevant. You're either prepared or you're not, and if you're not, you should tell me before class. Let's forget the whole thing now, okay? You'll have the opportunity to show what you can do during the rest of the course."

I could tell that he was still angry when he left. As the afternoon wore on, several other students came to see me. We discussed what had happened. One—the General Affairs Committee rep—said, "You did what you had to do." That reinforced me then, but later I realized that he was something of a company man and a pretty tough character himself. His approval didn't represent the whole section's feelings. A bunch of others who came that afternoon also agreed I'd been fair to Charles. One woman, however, said, "Tell me

something, Edward. Have you got a good memory?"

"I guess so," I answered.

"Can't you remember the names of people who come in late without writing them down?"

As I reflected on her question, it now seems obvious to me that her particular phrasing was extremely hostile. She was trying to trap me into saying, "Yes, I've got a good memory" so she could pounce and say, "Then why do you write names down?" Even then I took her question as a real clue showing that her annoyance was just the tip of the iceberg. The section wasn't happy with me.

By late Friday afternoon I was disturbed with the section and very annoyed at their overreaction. That evening, I had dinner with a friend and complained to her that the students were bitching and moaning. She said, "Be tough." I also spoke with some other colleagues from school and they agreed. Over the weekend my parents drove down from Seattle, and I put the whole Charles Finch episode out of my mind. But on Sunday, Hayes Latham told me on the phone that the section had held one of their regular meetings Friday and a focus of the discussion had been discontent about me. The Charles incident had been a catalyst. My writing down people's names was bothering them a lot, and so was a certain lack of direction in my style of teaching—I wasn't giving summaries at that point. I thought a lot about the section's general confusion, and fear of the system at Bay was focusing on me. But Hayes made me realize that, whatever the real causes of our problems, I'd have to do something. I knew I'd have to display an officially understanding manner, but inside I was thinking, "Look, students, I've got problems too, you know!" Because of my position of authority I couldn't seem to retreat. It was like the Falkland Islands dispute. The section was angry; so was I. Who would back down? It's a rather unpleasant memory. As I recall, I spoke with Hayes several times by phone at this point.

On Monday, my mother phoned to say that the drive back to Seattle had been too much for my father. He was in the hospital. That tightened the vise for me. That personal worry formed the backdrop for the anxiety I began to feel about the whole situation with Section VI. I sought advice from a senior professor in another area who, I knew, wished me well. He was busy and apparently preoccupied because he told me two completely contradictory things without meaning to. "You shouldn't have written down names," he said first.

"But what should I do now?"

"Well, I hate to let problems fester," he answered. "Maybe you should take the bull by the horns. But on the other hand, going public with a problem is risky. You can't revoke words once you've said them."

Ed Sherman Voices His Reflections

Personally, I was worried about control. If you let up in October, will you pay for it in May? I think there's a ratchet effect in teaching. You can always make things less tense if you start hard, but you can't tighten up once you've released the tension. By then I was really sweating. "Jeepers," I thought, "What if *I'm* late to class one day?"

I asked Sue Cameron, a senior member of the Finance teaching staff, what she would do. She said, "You were right; the student shouldn't have passed, but you have to lessen the tension. Why not do something natural to your style—maybe open the next class with a joke to relieve tension?" I considered saying to Section VI, "I had a nightmare last night. I dreamed I came in late and you all wrote my name down."

We were in the middle of a two-part case. The second half was material I had never taught, so I knew that on Thursday morning at 8:30 I was not only going to face Section VI across a great chasm of alienation, teaching material I barely knew myself, but my larger task would be to get things back on track.

On that same Sunday, Hayes and I spoke on the phone. I had really learned that I hadn't understood the situation when we last met, on Friday afternoon. It was a full-blown crisis. As confident as I had felt in class when I simply let

Charles pass and went on to another student, that's how unconfident I now felt. I talked things through with Hayes, but made no decisions about what to do.

By Wednesday night—the night before my next class with Section VI—I was a wreck. Besides being worried about my father, I had also caught a cold, and I was too congested as well as too worried to sleep. In my state of general misery, I simply couldn't figure out a teaching plan for the next discussion. Late that night I gave up and phoned Ellen Banks, an instructor in the course with a Bay MBA. Ellen gave me a detailed teaching plan for the case; at 6:30 A.M. on Thursday, I found I couldn't speak, so I phoned another colleague and just barely made myself understood over the phone; I asked if he'd fill in for me if my voice didn't return in time for class. I was in agony. I had wanted my work to be enjoyable, despite its inherent tensions, but this was pure misery. Fear was gnawing at me. I was afraid of losing the section completely, of being humiliated in public, of acting nervous in class and looking absurd. I knew we were all overreacting, and that I had to end the tension between Section VI and me.

What on earth to do in the next class was a major decision. How should I go in there (assuming my throat cleared up and I could speak) and start? With a joke? An apology? A sermon on passing in class? I didn't want to humiliate Charles by dwelling on the incident, nor did I want to create any more negative tension. But I also didn't want things to go lax. Spring is famous at Bay for courses going to pieces: students skip classes and read their *Wall Street Journals* right under the teachers' noses. I certainly didn't want that to happen in my marketing class. I was a mess.

My work is my life. I damn well didn't relish the idea of doing it badly. "What," I asked myself, "am I going to do when I walk into that classroom?"

Hayes Latham, Ed Rep of Section VI, relates his own version of the section's prevailing situation to the researcher, told as follows in his own words.

The Instructor

Edward is a very sharp guy. Intimidation and our own early insecurity gave him power over our section in the first semester. He had an incredible grasp of the concepts in marketing. I think we came to respect his analytical capabilities, but when this incident occurred, we were still very defensive. In class Edward moved around a lot, more than most other teachers. He spoke fast, and demonstrated a fantastic memory—even citing people's remarks from discussions days before. He was very intense about teaching. I don't think anyone ever said to himself, "Edward is uptight; he is nervous." But just the same, he built an atmosphere of tension which the section caught from him. Particularly in the first year—when sections are susceptible—teachers' moods are contagious. Our class had a split opinion of Edward. Some thought him our best teacher; some thought him our worst. He called on people according to background, home town, or work experience—which showed that he knew a lot about us. That built a picture of his not leaving us anywhere to hide. Also, his preparation and interest in the subject overwhelmed people, while his high-energy style and fast patter made them nervous. As Ed Rep, I encouraged people to talk to him. In his office, Edward would yak and yak away happily—which offset some tension for those who did go to see him. It's fair to say also that some of the tension came from the material, which is difficult and often frustrating. You can drown in detail until principles emerge. Many people were uptight in the course, but in mid-October Edward hadn't perceived that yet.

In a typical class, Edward would come early, chat with people, fiddle with his many sheets of notes, and then open with jokes, housekeeping details, and such. Then, with no warning, he would make the first call. That made many people tense. It was consistent with his high-energy style. One student told me that his stomach knotted up so badly before Edward's class that he felt like going to the bathroom.

CASE

The Section Was Mine to Lose (C)

Dr. *Abby J. Hansen*, research associate, wrote this case for the *Developing Discussion Leadership Skills* and the *Teaching by the Case Method* seminars. Data were furnished by the involved participants. All names and some peripheral facts have been disguised.

The Section

I'd say that we were a bit more laid back than most. We were supportive, not insulting, and not hostile. About the second week of school, before we elected officers, one guy stood up after our last class and said, "Let's stop interrupting each other." We agreed to this and took to having frequent meetings on matters of classroom procedure, usually during morning break or right after our last class. Attendance was high at meetings because class attendance was high.

I don't think we had many really unusual people in the group, although I recall that in the second month one foreign student came in late and, instead of sneaking in at the back, walked right in front of Edward, collided with him, and said, "Oh, good morning." Edward answered, "Well, good morning," and the student just kept walking up to an empty seat. That was a rather strange incident. Other than that, I think we were a pretty normal group.

Context of the Incident

By mid-October, everybody in the first-year class was depressed. We were over our initial excitement about being at Bay, and beginning to fall into a rut as we struggled up a pretty steep learning curve, mastering hard concepts. We were taking Accounting, Business Economics, Accounting for Control, Manufacturing Management, Marketing, Industrial Psychology, Business Writing, and Introduction to Strategy—a staggering load. And there was no break in sight till Thanksgiving, when we'd be worrying about mid-terms instead of relaxing. We were saying to ourselves, "My God, just think—this pressure goes on for the next two years." We felt there was no day when we could afford to be unprepared—that we'd be doing three cases a night forever.

It was at that psychological point in the year that I was elected Ed Rep. A written survey I took of my section's reactions to our course showed a lot of negative response to Edward, but comments in conversation were even worse. It was a question of tension. Part of my aim in giving out the survey had been to get material to help get our relationship with Edward back in synch. I thought he could change, and that he probably didn't mean to project the image that was making us all nervous.

At this point, dissatisfaction with Edward was building. We were frustrated by the way he would dash down to the teacher's desk to write down absentees' and latecomers' names. Also, some people thought he had grilled Margaret Peters by asking her questions when she stumbled and asked to pass. It seemed like a third degree.

Another Anxiety-Producing Vignette

In our classroom the rear doors have little windows with shutters that open and close. Nobody ever fiddles with the shutters. They were left open. Latecomers used to peer through them to find seats. That was a kind of game, actually—to wait till the teacher's back was turned, spot an empty seat, and dash into it without being noticed. Edward, apparently, found it disturbing when people peeked in, so one day he walked all the way up the aisle—where most teachers never ventured because it was *our* territory—and he closed one of the shutters dramatically. A bunch of people thought that was symbolic. Edward showed us it was *his* sacred class!

The Incident

Charles was asked to open, and he wasn't prepared. He said, "I pass," and Edward said, "Why don't you stop by and see me after class?" Then Edward called on someone else.

Charles was sitting down front, on Edward's left. Edward called on someone up and to the right. You can just *feel* people reacting badly sometimes, and that's how it was then. It was as if Edward had said, "You have to stay after school today." I was sitting in the left-hand part of the middle section where I could see people's faces. They looked worried, sympathetic, and embarrassed for Charles. I imagine they were thinking, "My God, this could happen to me."

The Aftermath

Because it was an unhappy time of the year and Edward had been doing a number of little things that bothered people, negative reactions to him grew out of proportion. People got together and said, "God, do you believe how bad this Edward character is? He's our worst teacher; all the others are good. He actually blocked the window in the classroom; he takes attendance; he embarrassed Charles in class. What are we going to do about Edward?" Actually this was incredibly overstated.

Section 4. Leading the Discussion Process: The Critical
Instructional Choice—Direction vs. Control

CASE
The Section Was Mine to Lose (C)

Many of our other teachers *weren't* good, but people's emotional perceptions were running against Edward.

I went to see Edward right after the incident with Charles and, in order not to be too blunt, presented some of the class's dissatisfaction in the form of survey results. He was silent through my oration, and seemed not particularly comfortable. I felt very gingerly about it. I was impressed, though, that he picked up on what I was saying. He had been losing credibility with us and had to get it back. He was overly controlling—making us nervous. I knew he didn't want us to turn on him—that would be a personal insult, and Edward was image-conscious and interested in tenure.

Edward said he'd think about things—attendance taking, for example—and call me back. But at this point I felt I hadn't made much of an impression. In fact, I wished I'd been a bit more blunt.

After I spoke to Edward on the phone I started running around to the class informally, to tell people Edward was concerned and intended to change. I knew 10 or 12 very yikky-yakky types and they were reliable about spreading the word for me. I also met with Charles, who was really ticked off. He felt put upon and embarrassed and told me that he thought that he had implied very clearly to Edward before class that he wasn't prepared. Somehow, he thought he'd conveyed the message. Edward's "come see me in my office" and the conversation they had actually had there increased the annoyance. Charles, I should mention, had impressed some people in the section as, how shall I say it—a bit pedantic? He wore glasses and said, "etcetera" a lot. He had been one of the

two students who volunteered to do an extra essay for class discussion in Industrial Psychology, but that was an informal sort of thing. The other student had gotten hers in on time and typed, but Charles, for some reason, had problems writing his. Then at the last minute, he expected secretarial help with the typing and was annoyed not to get it. He was also annoyed because he had to xerox the essay himself and didn't get any extra recognition for it. That, having his car towed, and Edward's calling on him made him really mad.

It was Sunday night, I believe, when Edward called me back. He was really quite upset. I remember I was standing in my kitchen cooking a hamburger and by the time I was through with Edward the hamburger was completely burnt. At that point, Edward was even considering replacing our next class with a meeting to discuss how to improve our relationship. He hadn't yet decided what to do. Have a meeting? Explain his goals and procedures and say he hadn't meant to make a big deal out of the little irritating things he'd been doing? Perhaps have me tell the section about his concern and say he'd agreed to stop taking attendance and that he really wanted people to tell him if they weren't prepared and not to pass in class? He was trying to decide whether to confront the issue head on, chart a middle course by having me tell the class he was going to loosen up, or take a third option and just ignore the whole thing and go on.

In our phone conversation, Edward laid out the alternatives and told me honestly that he hadn't made up his mind.

READING

The Gifted Can't Weigh That Giraffe

SELMA WASSERMANN

Selma Wassermann, "The Gifted Can't Weigh That Giraffe," Educational Review, *New York Times*, November 15, 1981. Copyright © 1981 by The New York Times Company. Reprinted by permission.

The turbojet descends from 32,000 feet into the purple air and the rainy-wintry Vancouver morning left far behind is transformed magically into spring. On the freeway the cars wear yellow and blue license plates reading KING NI and M. BENZ and HOT TUBS and you know you are in Southern California.

The school is low and wide-flung and I am led into an attractive room—the "center" for working with gifted children. A group of nine volunteers, ages 10 to 12, are led in to participate in a demonstration of a "teaching for thinking" lesson with this teacher who has just dropped out of the skies. Around the periphery of the room is a large group of teachers who have come to observe teaching strategies that emphasize higher-order cognitive skills.

Perspectives

The pupils are reserved and there is some evidence of anxiety. My attempts to establish rapport are not very successful.

I offer them a piece of wisdom. "How do you suppose birds learn to fly?"

"What do you mean?" asks Chris.

"I don't understand what you want us to do," says Mark, his body shifting uncomfortably.

"We didn't study birds yet," says Ann, explaining the lack of response.

The children are clearly troubled.

I make several attempts, using a variety of different open-ended tasks that have no clear, definitive answers, to tap the creative thinking capabilities of these children, and I am dead-ended every time.

Again and again I encounter responses in which the pupils try to manipulate me into helping them "get the right answer." The more I avoid doing this, the more tense they seem. Their dependency, their rigidity, their intolerance for ambiguity, their inability to take cognitive risks and their anxiety are astonishing.

The pupils I see later that afternoon are representatives of a different group. Although the school has a more benign name for them, they are the low achievers.

"How could you weigh a giraffe?" I begin. They immediately rise to the challenge.

"You put em' on a bathroom scale," says Maria.

"Dummy, he ain't gonna fit," says Benedetto, smiling at his wisdom. "You gotta put two scales.

Section 4. Leading the Discussion Process: The Critical
Instructional Choice—Direction vs. Control

READING
The Gifted Can't Weigh That Giraffe SELMA WASSERMANN

Put his back feet on one and his front feet on the other."

More and more responses of equally refreshing ideas keep coming. Then Sam offers: "I'd get a big truck and fill it with food that giraffes like to eat. Then I'd weigh the truck. Then, I'd hide inside of it and call, 'Here, giraffe. Here, giraffe.' When he got inside, I'd slam the doors and weigh the truck again."

I am astonished at the difference in responses of both groups, and even more concerned about the "single, right answer" orientation of the pupils identified as gifted. I am flabbergasted at their limited personal autonomy and their difficulty with questions that do not call for single, correct answers. I want to find out more, so I ask for time to talk with small groups of children from both schools.

The children from the gifted classes tell me that they carry with them anxiety that is constant and pervasive. They worry about their school performance and grades.

Pressures from parents and teachers to perform at high levels is subtle, but excessive. The children are *always* on guard. They use their considerable talents to try to figure out what their significant adults demand of them, and their lives are tilted in the direction of performance up-to-expectations.

They are crippled by fears of making mistakes and their anxieties are manifest in a variety of stress-related physical symptoms. Because school tasks are largely of the "single, correct answer" type (e.g., "The sea is made of water"), these children have become gifted lesson learners—excelling at the lower-order cognitive tasks found in traditional text-book and workbook exercises.

Unfortunately, the transfer of these lower-level thinking skills to the higher-order tasks of problem solving, creating, and imagining does not occur magically. There is even evidence to suggest that such activities are counterproductive to higher-order functioning. And so we have a group of gifted children who are exceptionally good at the very narrow tasks of finding single, correct answers to the most mundane questions but who lack experience and therefore expertise in the more intellectually rigorous and more creative stuff.

But what about the low achievers? How is it they were able to outperform the gifted group? Though the in-school experiences are largely similar (lots and lots of textbook and workbook activities requiring single, correct answers), the out-of-school experiences of these children appear to be significantly different. Most of them are out on the streets involved in many activities that require high levels of creative problem-solving capabilities. They have become "street wise"—experienced and talented problem solvers; while the gifted and talented group attends music lessons and French lessons and does prodigious amounts of homework.

What does it add up to? Can this one event have any educational significance at all? Perhaps not. On the other hand, if you were to look at children's behavior and see excessive anxiety about school performance, considerable dependency, preoccupation with single, correct answers, and inability to think creatively in the face of new problems, then it might be fair to conclude that our teaching is decreasing their autonomy and is substantially disabling them as problem solvers.

Section 5. Leading the Discussion Process: Some Basic Operating Issues

Trevor Jones

This case was a collaborative effort of a member of the Developing Discussion Leadership Skills Seminar and C. Roland Christensen. While the case is based on data supplied by participants involved, all names and some peripheral facts have been disguised.

I n my book, you're one son of a bitch!" Bob Smith, heretofore our section's model of discipline, consideration, and moderation, was speaking. Bob's face was flushed, his eyes angry. He seemed to hurl his words at Professor Vinceberg. The class waited expectantly.

The Organizational Behavior Course

Organizational Behavior, or OB as it was called, was a required first-year course at New Dominion's Graduate School of Business. Dealing with the human problems of administration, OB was one of the shorter class modules in the two-year MBA program; it was allocated only 30 sessions instead of the usual 50 classes.

OB classes started up just after Christmas vacation. Therefore, OB professors, along with those teaching the Business and Government course, were faced with sections that had worked together for four months and had formed their own social organization and discussion norms.

OB cases usually included only a modest amount of quantitative data, if any. For many students, Professor Vinceberg believed, these "human" cases came as a welcome relief from "number-crunching" courses such as Finance and Operations Management. But he was also aware that some students thought OB was not a real, hard-core MBA course. Their attitude seemed to be that there was too much *feeling* and not enough *hard facts* for OB to be taken too seriously. He knew that some of his colleagues were having disciplinary problems with their sections.

Al Vinceberg: Background

Al Vinceberg's academic training had been in sociology. Before joining New Dominion's Graduate School of Business faculty, Al had done research in the business sphere. He found this type of research most stimulating and had continued those efforts during his five years on New Dominion's faculty. Many of Al's faculty associates concentrated on investigating psychological problems and group dynamics issues within organizations. Al, however, preferred to study overall organizational structures and was an expert on matrix organization problems.

Al indicated in conversations with colleagues that he had mixed feelings about his teaching assignments at New Dominion. He found case teaching to be a stimulating experience that fit well with his own vigorous approach to any task. He enjoyed the dialectic of class discussion and the clash of personalities so often accompanying it. He said, however, that he sometimes became impatient with the elementary nature of the first-year OB course and that he wished he could share with his students the intricacies of the sophisticated forms of organization with which he was researching and living in the real world.

Al's Teaching Style

Al's teaching style, as described by one of the informal leaders of the section, was "blunt, aggressive and demanding, but with a vein of good humor." This section member's description continues in his own words in the following paragraphs.

He evidently saw himself as embodying a gutsy, down-to-earth approach to people and to the organizational problems described in the cases he taught. In class he showed that he respected and liked those who tended to see the case situation the way he did. In return, many students admired and respected him for his "no nonsense" outlook, and his ratings on student polls were good.

Vinceberg was very tall, and with his long strides and his loud voice he easily dominated the classroom. During class he would pace restlessly in the front of the room, as well as up and down the aisles between the blocks of seats. He liked to rest one foot on the instructor's table as if it were a low stool, and he seemed to enjoy striking vigorous shirt-sleeve poses at the chalkboard.

Vinceberg had strong ideas about what his students should know. He would often interrupt class discussion to summarize and give lectures on points he felt to be important. Lots of my sectionmates welcomed this approach, especially those who found OB's "soft" psychological and sociological concepts difficult to grasp. In keeping with his tough-minded approach, Vinceberg felt it important to get across to the section the gritty realities of everyday, blue-collar work life. I think he may have come from that background himself. Anyway, he often commented on this subject and in one of our early course sessions, he read aloud extracts from Studs Terkel's book *Working*, including a lengthy piece full of oaths and profanity.

And, he clearly believed in the importance of classroom contributions for he announced at the beginning of the course that 70 percent of the course grade would rest on class performance and 30 percent on the final exams. In most of the other courses it was 50/50.

His teaching style was hard to describe—you really had to experience it to understand. Sometimes he tended to shape and guide the class discussion to the point where—well, you know how it works—you knew what he wanted you to say and you went right along. Other times he was confrontational. He put you in a position where your ego was involved, and you had to defend your position well. Also, I often felt that with his forceful manner he was "broadcasting with too loud a signal"; it drowned out much of the individual student responses. Yet, he could listen and understand.

He always tried to deal with us each as individuals. He referred to our backgrounds and interests. I got the feeling he liked us and liked our section. Yet we never felt close to him. I didn't ever feel like just going to his office for a chat, and I don't think others did either.

The Section

Like all New Dominion sections, students had been assigned carefully, so that each group had a balance of students of different ages, sexes, management interests and experiences, and geographical backgrounds. More than 10 percent of the students came from overseas, mostly from Europe and Latin America. The school considered this heterogeneity a valuable enricher of the learning experience.

As described by its educational representative,[1] the section was "a most interesting agglomeration. There was, naturally, plenty of rivalry among its members, but the general atmosphere was friendly and tolerant. We weren't a 'dog-eat-dog' section like many of the others. Individual differences were respected and even encouraged." The following paragraphs contain the ed rep's further description, in his own words, of the section and its members.

Surely there were no hard and fast lines dividing up the section. People just fell into the obvious social groupings: those from the same living halls, geographical areas, or business interests. There was quite a strong awareness that nobody

---

1. A student-selected member of the group, who, with colleagues from other sections, represents student interests on New Dominion faculty–student committees.

had a monopoly on the truth. Midwesterners were keen to hear what foreign students had to say about particular issues. Female students listened to the CPAs. All the students knew they would get a hearing from their associates.

As one would expect, the male, white, conservative group was large. Typical of these students was Bob Smith, a stocky, ex-Navy submarine officer and graduate of Kansas State, who was one of the "senior citizens" group. He knew what he wanted to do: to run his own business. And he wasn't afraid to state his mind. We sometimes jokingly called him "Mr. Middle America."

A more unusual student was Trevor Jones from Wales. Trevor was younger (25 years old), came from a working class background, had achieved a first-class honors degree in economics, and then spent two years in banking. Trevor seemed to get along with the rest of the section outside of class, though socially he preferred to mix primarily with those from the U.K. and the Commonwealth. The fascinating thing about Trevor was his academic conduct; he never spoke in class. This, of course, put him in a very disadvantageous position in terms of grades.

I talked with Trevor many times. In appearance and speech you certainly knew he wasn't Oxbridge. He had a burning desire to succeed at New Dominion. He felt that it would put a seal of approval on his career-to-date and free him for good from any social origin slurs.

The fact that he didn't talk in class was not, we believed, that he lacked ability or strongly held opinions. As he explained his position to his friends, he felt quite unable to put forward or defend his views in class because, in his opinion, the rough-and-tumble of case discussion was completely unreal and, therefore, irrelevant. It was confined within a set of artificial nonbusiness rules; a good student classroom "operating technique" was most of what was needed to ensure success. By participating, he said, one was agreeing to be judged according to this undignified and juvenile code of conduct, and therefore one would inevitably end up making a fool of himself. It also encouraged people to grab the maximum amount of "air time," run off at the mouth, and rarely listen to what other people were saying. Trevor said he always followed the case discussions attentively and said he learned a lot from them. I noted, however, that he was sometimes scathingly

critical of his fellow students and teachers when he felt they made themselves look ridiculous in class.

Naturally, it was necessary for Trevor to explain his point of view toward class participation to his instructors. At the beginning of each course, therefore, Trevor would see the new professor in his office and explain his situation. Invariably teachers never called on him in class and graded him solely on his written work. Trevor said he had been to see Professor Vinceberg and thought they had developed a good understanding. During their conversation they had discussed the attitudes of shop floor workers, and Trevor had mentioned some of the experiences of his father who worked in one of the Welsh plants of the declining British steel industry.

The Situation

The following is another section member's own description of the situation.

That was a class never to be forgotten; an experience that still gets talked about at our class get-togethers.

It was our sixth session; the beginning of our third week. The case concerned the use of various formal manager evaluation techniques to select personnel for dismissal during a period of company retrenchment. In addition, we had to grapple with the social and personality problems of carrying out such a drastic and unpleasant operation in a small, closely-knit southern community, where the company was the sole employer and where it had a long-standing reputation for taking a personal, even a paternal, interest in its employees.

That day Al Vinceberg, as usual, strode into class, stripped off his jacket, and rolled up his sleeves in the vigorous mode he had used since our first session. He quickly established order in the room; we had just finished our first class.

I was never sure whether or not Vinceberg used a formal, planned call-list; he would always just call on someone to start off. That day he immediately called on Trevor Jones to "lay out the case." A ripple of surprise ran around the section. I watched Trevor closely. Trevor looked up quizzically at Al who, by this time, had his back to him as he paced toward the other side of the room. Then Trevor glanced around, took a deep breath, and started. He spoke disjointedly for about five minutes without coming to grips with the main issues of the case. When he finished, Al turned to the rest of the class and said, "Well, you're his colleagues; what sort of job do you think he did?" He paused; the class looked puzzled. Vinceberg went on, "How would you evaluate Trevor? Has he done a good job or a bad job?"

"Hands up for those people who thought he did not do a good job," Al continued. About two-thirds of the class hesitantly raised their hands. "How many think Trevor did a good job?" The rest of the class put up their hands, a bit quicker this time. Al stopped his pacing, wheeled on Trevor Jones, who sat three-quarters of the way toward the back in the center section of seats. "Your colleagues don't think you've done an adequate job. You're fired!"

The silence was frightening. We waited! Trevor started slowly to gather his papers together. He appeared stunned and surely was humiliated. He glanced up, looked around the class, and then at Vinceberg again. Then he carefully and deliberately pressed his briefcase shut, stood up, struggled along the row of occupied seats, and exited by the rear door.

Vinceberg continued with the case, seemingly unconcerned. He called on another student for an opinion on the case issues. He paced up and down the front of the room as usual, listening to the student. The door at the back of the class remained closed. A few minutes passed by, and suddenly Al was taking the steps three at a time from the front of the room toward the door, and he disappeared into the corridor. The student who had been speaking stopped. The section just sat silent for the few minutes Al was outside the classroom. He returned alone and called on the student to continue his contribution. When that student finished he called on another. Nobody raised a hand to volunteer. The level of tension in the section was overpowering.

Suddenly Vinceberg stopped. "I don't think we can continue like this. We're all a bit on edge at what's happened. I'm going to break for a few minutes and get myself a cup of coffee. We'll start the class all over again at 10:15."

When Vinceberg left the room everyone seemed to burst into conversation at once. One of Trevor's close friends, a quiet New Zealander, got up and went out in search of Trevor.

Al soon returned with a cup of coffee and began the class again. The discussion was sluggish. The section refused to make any voluntary contributions, and it seemed to me that the tension was rising rapidly again. Al stopped pacing up and down. Surely he must have felt the hostility but struggled on for a few more minutes. Then he stopped.

"We still haven't gotten over our bad start to the class today. I think we should discuss what happened and get our thoughts out in the open. That way we can clear the air. I confess that I did not intend this to happen like this. I didn't think Trevor would react the way he did. I realize I may have blown it with all of you. I'm very keen that that should not happen. Until now I think we've had an excellent relationship. Please help me."

The words were barely out of his mouth when Bob Smith burst out, "I'll tell you what I think. As far as I'm concerned you're nothing but a son of a bitch for doing what you did. You know what Trevor is like. You know he doesn't talk in class. Calling on him like that was wrong. And what came after was worse—much worse. In my book you're one son of a bitch."

Vinceberg appeared stunned. Bob Smith had always been one of Vinceberg's "stars," one of the section who appreciated his teaching program a great deal.

The entire section seemed to me to radiate hostility toward Vinceberg. Here we had had such a fine section working atmosphere and good relationships with all our faculty. Now that had blown. What a mess!

CASE

The Handicapped Heckler (A)

Dr. Abby Hansen, *research associate, wrote this case in collaboration with* **Professor C. Roland Christensen** *for the Developing Discussion Leadership Skills Seminar. While the case is based on data supplied by participants involved, all names and some peripheral facts have been disguised.*

Paula Wilson, a 30-year-old Ph.D. in English literature, had taught for four years as a graduate-student teaching assistant before accepting her first full-time job at the downtown campus of a large state university on the East Coast. Students at this university commuted to classes; many also held part-time jobs. Consequently there was very little student camaraderie. Many described the place as alienated or fragmented. The students were not noted for scholarly excellence, although Paula found many of them extremely talented and able. By and large, they were enthusiastic and, despite their other commitments, came to classes prepared. Paula's department included 40 full-time staff. The university's cumbersome administration occupied parts of several downtown buildings, some of which also housed classrooms. It wasn't an easy place to get to know.

Paula herself was slim, with blue eyes and long, dark hair. Many of her women colleagues taught in blue jeans, but Paula favored skirts or dresses and frequently wore silver jewelry. Her manner was cordial and her humor often based on wordplay. Successful in her own studies, she had chosen her academic career out of dedication to her subject. Helping students see the power and fascination of literature meant a great deal to her. In an era of scarce jobs, she felt fortunate to have found a teaching position near the university where her husband was finishing his Ph.D. dissertation, also in English literature. (Paula's marriage, which later ended in divorce, was already creating anxiety for her, and she looked to her professional life all the more to balance the growing unease at home.)

Paula Encounters Her First Challenge

The first stumbling block she encountered in her job was her department chairperson's phone call three weeks before the opening of the fall semester to inform Paula that the teaching assignments had been changed. One section she had expected to teach turned out to have insufficient enrollment, and the chairperson's suggestion was that she could pull together an advanced elective seminar instead of the English Novel course that she had already prepared. Could she do it? Paula gulped and said, "Of course!"

Paula took out her doctoral research, which included comparative studies of nature poems and satires, to cull material for a seminar to meet for three hour-long sessions each week of the semester.

For herself, she made lists of critical readings to review before each class. But she expected the students to study only the primary literary texts and prepare to discuss them. Discussion would comprise the core of the learning experience in this course. She planned to lecture as little as possible, and only when historical data or critical interpretations were both important and obscure. Otherwise, she felt her task was to help her students talk—preferably to each other—so that they could learn to state, challenge, and refine their reactions to the literature. Paula managed to construct a coherent syllabus for this seminar, but never quite overcame a feeling of annoyance at the haste with which she had been forced to undertake the project.

When Paula got her room assignment for the course, she found the meeting place was grim—an old-fashioned room with fluorescent lighting, some twenty-odd assorted chairs, and a big oak desk pushed against a blackboard. It was located on the ground floor of a converted apartment building on a busy downtown street where traffic noise was a constant irritant.

A Greater Encounter Confronts Paula

The room was depressing, but not (Paula was soon to learn) the greatest challenge of this seminar. That challenge presented itself on the first day of classes. Paula always arrived early to teach, but a student in a wheelchair had preceded her. He sat in the middle of the room, staring out at the traffic. Paula walked around to greet him. He was a lanky, handsome young man of about 20, with broad, athletic shoulders—but his long legs appeared wasted in baggy blue jeans, and Paula found the unscuffed running shoes on his motionless feet particularly poignant. She felt a sharp stab of pity, even as she smiled at him. "Hello," she said brightly, "I'm Paula Wilson, and you are . . .?" He gave a spasmodic twitch, and answered in a strained voice, "Frank Edgerton." Paula wondered whether his paralysis had impaired his speaking ability. Would this student have extra difficulty in a discussion class? Frank resumed his study of the passing traffic, avoiding Paula's gaze and further conversation as she pulled chairs into a rough circle for the eight students in the seminar. As other students entered, no one sat beside Frank's wheelchair until there were only two empty seats left—one on each side of Frank. He greeted no one, nor did anyone greet him.

When the group was assembled, Paula introduced herself formally, described the subject matter and some class objectives, and gave a 15-minute minilecture on some critical issues and historical points that the students would find useful for their discussion. (This was a typical format but she often varied it.) Then she finished her minilecture, posed a general question about the time of the opening of a short passage she had distributed in class, and asked for a volunteer to begin the discussion. One brave soul complied. Another responded to his point, and then a third student spoke. As Paula recalled, the third student was saying, "I think the words *dark* and *shadow* in the first line of a nature poem warn us that there's going to be something sad."

"Sad?" Paula promoted encouragingly. "Like what?"

Suddenly Frank burst in: "Christ, how obvious! Why bother to make such a boring point?" The class fell silent.

Paula assumed that Frank's disability must be affecting his emotional state, and her pity squelched the urge to rebuke such rudeness. Instead of confronting him, she merely restated her original question to the previous student. Fortunately, the class seemed to have interpreted Frank's outburst more or less as Paula had. They, too, ignored it. But there was tension in the room as the discussion continued.

Paula recalled that during the next few sessions "Frank continued his disruptions. I would ask a question, somebody would answer, and he would burst out with an insult. The other students always became very quiet when he did this. He was terribly rude, but nobody challenged him."

Paula continued: "I noticed that he interacted little with the other students. He was always there first, and he stared out the window until class began. No one seemed to avoid him, but no one approached him either." After a week or two of this behavior Paula asked a few colleagues about Frank. No one knew him—not surprising in this environment. She decided to live with the situation a little longer.

One day, about four weeks into the term, Paula began an introductory minilecture: "Once again we see the presence of pastoral elegy in a satire. I wonder how this mixture works in stanzas one to five—"

"Oh, come *on*, we've talked that point to death!"

Frank's peevish snarl caught Paula by surprise. She took a deep breath and shifted ground swiftly to make another point before asking a student for a comment. The whole class seemed even more nervous than usual this time, and Paula found it difficult to prod them into making contributions.

On frequent occasions, Paula had held office hours; this university, however, was simply not the sort of place where students spent much time in casual conversation with their professors. For one thing, most of the students were under time constraints after class, and for another, the culture of the place was simply too alienated. Paula often mentioned office hours in class and urged the students to come. She singled Frank out with special cordiality a few times, pretending that he had made a point so interesting she wished he would come to discuss it further. She wanted to speak to him privately—possibly even to mention his disruptive behavior in some nonconfrontational way. But, although a few students came to office hours, Frank was never among them. Oddly enough, no one complained to her about his behavior. Paula did not ask any students about their reactions to Frank's behavior because she made it a policy never to discuss students with their colleagues—behind their backs, as it were.

During the next few class meetings, Frank's behavior deteriorated further. Someone would speak, he would interrupt, then dead silence would fall until Paula could scrape together a question interesting enough to shove the group into some forward momentum—always subject to the threat of another torpedo from Frank. When this situation had continued for six weeks, Paula realized that she was beginning to dread the class and was arriving in a state of nervousness. This was extremely unusual because Paula generally enjoyed teaching.

The time had come to do something. Paula had tried to live with the situation, but now she was fed up with Frank's bad manners, which appeared to be upsetting his classmates. She felt compelled to intervene. But how?

"A camel is a horse put together by a committee" is a saying frequently applied to group decision making. What is it that makes so many groups inefficient, slow, and frustrating, instead of effectively combining the insights and expertise of its members? To some extent the answer may be found in the formal group design. Perhaps the people chosen were not the ones who should have been included in such a group, or perhaps the group's goal was simply unattainable. More often, however, the difficulties encountered have less to do with content of task issues than with the *group process*, or how the group is going about achieving its formal task.

Each group member is a unique individual, bringing certain expectations, assumptions, and feelings to the group, not only about his or her own role but also about the roles of other members in the group. As a result of these expectations certain interrelationships develop. These patterns may become either beneficial or detrimental to the group's purpose. Spotting detrimental patterns is the first key to understanding and improving the functioning of any group; but often these patterns are hard to identify because you cannot read each person's mind. For instance, how do you know that everyone understands what the agenda is, or that person X understands it but is likely to deviate from it if possible, or whether person X has the leverage to change the agenda if he or she wants to? While you cannot see inside others' minds, you can develop a greater awareness of what is and what is not likely to happen in a group, and of what the group is or is not capable of doing at a given meeting by being attentive to what is happening among group members.

Being able to observe and understand a group's process is important for two reasons. First, it enables you to understand what is taking place covertly as well as overtly in the group's behavior. Second, it can provide you with insights into what you and others can do to make the group's interactions more productive.

Listed below are seven aspects of group behavior that can furnish valuable clues on how effectively a group functions. It is unlikely that all of these will be relevant to your concerns at a given point in time, or that you can attend to them all simultaneously. The more adept you are at observing and assessing them, however, the more likely it is that

READING

Note on Process Observation

JOHN J. GABARRO

ANNE HARLAN

John J. Gabarro and *Assistant Professor* **Anne Harlan**
*prepared this note. Portions of it were excerpted from an
earlier note by Assistant Professor* **Eric H. Nielsen** *on influencing groups.*

you will spot potential difficulties early and act on them to improve the group's effectiveness.

Participation

Participation—who participates, how often, when, and to what effect—is the easiest aspect of group process to observe. Typically, people who are higher in status, more knowledgeable, or simply more talkative by nature, tend to participate more actively. Those who are newer, lower in status, uninformed, or who are not inclined to express their feelings and ideas verbally, generally speak less frequently. Even in groups composed of people of equal status and competence, some people will speak more than others; this variation is to be expected and is not necessarily a sign of an ineffective group. When large disparities exist among the contributions of individual members, however, it is usually a clue that the process is not effective—particularly when individuals or coalitions dominate the group's discussion.

There are many reasons why unequal participation can reduce a group's effectiveness. Low participators often have good ideas to offer but are reluctant to do so, or they cannot contribute their ideas because they are squeezed out by high participators who dominate the meeting. This imbalance can be a potential problem when we consider that those ideas receiving the most attention inevitably become the ones that are most seriously considered when it is time to make a decision. Considerable research shows that the most frequently stated ideas tend to be adopted by the group, regardless of their quality. Maier calls this the *valence effect*[1] and it is one of the reasons why groups often make poor decisions. Thus, large imbalances in participation can result in potentially good ideas being underrepresented in the discussion, or perhaps not even expressed.

Another negative consequence of uneven participation, understood through common sense as well as research, is that low participators are likely to tune out, lose commitment to the task, or become frustrated and angry—especially if they have tried to get into the discussion but have been ignored or cut off by high participators. These negative attitudes result not only in poorer quality decisions but also in less commitment to implementing the group's decision.

Several factors contribute to uneven participation. One is that people who have the most at stake in a given issue (and may therefore be the least objective) are more motivated to participate than others who may have better ideas to offer. Another is that different people have different internal standards on which they judge whether or not an idea they have is worth offering to the group. Thus, people with higher internal standards may be less likely to contribute than those with lower internal standards, with negative consequences for the quality of the group's discussion.

A marked change in a person's participation during a meeting is also a clue that something important may be going on. If a person suddenly becomes silent or withdraws during part of a meeting, it could suggest a number of possibilities (depending on the person's nonverbal behavior). For example, it might simply mean that the person has temporarily withdrawn to mull over the comments of a prior speaker. It may also be that the person has tuned out, or it may be a sign of hostility or frustration. Whatever the case, it could be a sign that something is not right.

Some questions to consider in observing participation include the following:

1. Who are the high participators? Why? To what effect?
2. Who are the low participators? Why? To what effect?
3. Are there any shifts in participators, such as an active participator suddenly becoming silent? Do you see any reason for this in the group's interaction, such as a criticism from a higher-status person or a shift in topic? Is it a sign of withdrawal?
4. How are silent people treated? Is their silence taken by others to mean consent? Disagreement? Disinterest? Why do you think they are silent?
5. Who talks to whom? Who responds to whom? Do participation patterns reflect coalitions that are impeding or controlling the discussion? Are the interaction patterns consistently excluding certain people who need to be supported or brought into the discussion?
6. Who keeps the discussion going? How is this accomplished? Why does the group leader want the discussion to continue in such a vein?

---

1. Norman R. F. Maier, "Assets and Liabilities in Group Problem Solving: The Need for an Integrative Function," *Psychological Review*, vol. 74, no. 4 (July 1967), pp. 239–248.

INTERVENTIONS. There are a number of simple and unobtrusive process interventions that you can make, either as a group leader or group member, to bring about a better balance in participation. These interventions are particularly important if you think that potentially valuable minority views are not getting their share of time, that certain people have not had a chance to develop their ideas fully, or that some group members seem out of the discussion. One intervention is to try to *clarify* a point that someone had made earlier which seemed to fall through the cracks—going back to that person's point by saying something like "Tom, let me see if I understood what you said a moment ago." A related technique is simply to *reinforce* a prior point by asking the person to elaborate on it—"Sue, I was interested in what you were saying earlier; can you elaborate on it?" Similarly, a very direct technique for bringing out silent people is to simply *query* them—"Mary, you haven't said a word during this discussion; what are your ideas on it?" or to make a comment as direct as "We've heard a lot from the marketing people, but very little from production scheduling. What do you guys think about the problem?"

Influence

Influence and participation are not the same thing. Some people may speak very little, yet capture the attention of the whole group when they do speak. Others may talk frequently but go unheard. Influence, like participation, is often a function of status, experience, competence, and to some degree personality. It is normal for some people to have more influence on a group's process than others, and this fact is not necessarily a sign that a group is ineffective. However, when one individual or subgroup has so much influence on a discussion that others' ideas are rejected out of hand, it is usually a clue that the group's effectiveness will suffer and that the discussion will fail to probe alternatives. This imbalance is particularly dangerous when minority views are systematically squelched without adequate exploration.

An asymmetry in influence can have a number of negative consequences on a group's effectiveness. As we have already noted, it can result in the suppression of potentially valuable minority views, it can contribute to imbalanced participation, and it will inevitably result in hostility and lack of commitment by group members who feel that they have been left out. As with participation, considerable research on group behavior and alienation shows that the more influence people feel they have had on a group's discussion, the more committed they are likely to be to its decisions, regardless of whether their own point of view has been adopted by the group.

One way of checking relative influence is to watch the reactions of the other group members. Someone who has influence is not only likely to have others listening attentively but is also less likely to be interrupted or challenged by the others. He or she may also be physically seated at or near the head of the table or near the center of a subgroup.

Struggles for influence and leadership often characterize the early stages of a group's life, especially in temporary groups such as task forces, project teams, or committees. To some extent these struggles occur in most groups, although usually in a mild, covert fashion. Vying for leadership can become a problem, however, when it disrupts the group's ability to deal with the task at hand. The disruption occurs when being dominant is an important need for those who are vying for leadership. Under these circumstances, the competition gets played out in a sub-rosa fashion with one person disagreeing with the other because of his or her need to establish dominance, regardless of the relative merits of the other's arguments. The hidden agenda then becomes scoring points rather than working on the problem. Often two people engaged in such a power struggle are not even aware of their hidden motives and genuinely think that they are arguing about the problem at hand.

In assessing influence patterns within a group, you may find the following questions useful:

1. Which members are listened to when they speak? What ideas are they expressing?
2. Which members are ignored when they speak? Why? What are their ideas? Is the group losing valuable inputs simply because some are not being heard?
3. Are there any shifts in influence? Who shifts? Why?
4. Is there any rivalry within the group? Are there struggles among individuals or subgroups for leadership?
5. Who interrupts whom? Does this reflect relative power within the group?

6. Are minority views consistently ignored regardless of possible merit?

INTERVENTIONS. If you observe that the opinions of an individual or subgroup of people appear to be unduly influencing a group's progress, there are several brief interventions that can be made to open up the discussion. One strategy is simply to *support or reinforce* the views of minority members—"I think there is some merit to what Jane was saying earlier and I'd like to elaborate on it," or "I think that we're not giving enough thought to Jane and Sam's position and I think we should explore it further before dropping it." Another intervention is to actually *point out* that the opinions of certain people are dominating the discussion—"Mary, you've made your point quite forcefully and clearly, but I'd also like to hear the other side of the question before we go further." Similarly, another technique is to ask the group to *open up* the discussion—"So far we've spent a lot of time talking about Jane and Bill's proposal, but I'd like to hear some differing opinions," or "The managers seem to agree strongly on what needs to be done, but I'd like to hear more about what the customer representatives think are the problems."

Group Climate

Members bring with them many assumptions of how groups ought to function generally and how their particular group should function. Frequently, these expectations of assumptions will be quite different from one member to another. One person may feel that the way for a group to work effectively is to be strictly business—no socializing and with tight leader control over the group. Others may feel that the only way a group can work creatively is to give each person equal time for suggestions, get together informally, and use relatively loose leadership. After group members have tested each others' assumptions early on in the group, a climate or atmosphere becomes established that may or may not facilitate effective group functioning. Different group climates are effective in different situations; what is good for one situation is not necessarily good for another.

For example, if the problem to be solved is one that demands a creative, new solution and the collaboration of a number of different experts (such as on a task force problem), then a climate of openness in which everyone has an equal opportunity to par-

ticipate will be most effective. In other situations, however, a more competitive or structured group climate might encourage a higher quality solution, especially if expertise is not distributed equally among all group members. To gauge a group's climate you should observe:

1. Do people prefer to keep the discussion on a friendly, congenial basis? Do people prefer conflict and disagreement?
2. Do people seem involved and interested? Is the atmosphere one of work? Play? Competition? Avoidance?
3. Is there any attempt to suppress conflict or unpleasant feelings by avoiding tough issues?

For most task groups an unstructured, laissez-faire, or conflict-free climate is not effective: Important issues and conflicts are not explored. sufficiently, and the quality of the group's work is sacrificed for the maintenance of friendly and smooth relations. Conversely, a highly structured climate can impede effective problem solving because members do not allow each other enough freedom to explore alternatives or consider creative solutions. A highly competitive climate can also be dysfunctional; competition can get in the way of thoughtful deliberation and exchange, resulting in failure to build on other people's ideas.

INTERVENTIONS. Intervening to alter a group's climate is more difficult than the previous interventions described. It can be done, however, by reinforcing and supporting desirable behavior, as well as by raising the issue directly. Where a group is smoothing over and avoiding important problems, for example, a useful intervention would be, "We seem to have a lot of agreement, but I wonder if we have really tackled some of the tougher underlying issues." When a group seems to be tied up by its own structure, often a comment as simple as the following will suffice: "I think that maybe we're looking at the problem too narrowly, and it might be useful to discuss whether we should also consider X which isn't on the agenda but seems to have relevance to what we're talking about."

Membership

A major concern for group members is their degree of acceptance or inclusion in the group. Different patterns of interaction may develop in the group, providing clues to the degree and kind of membership:

1. Is there any subgrouping? Sometimes two or three members may consistently agree and support each other or consistently disagree and oppose one another.
2. Do some people seem to be outside the group? Do other members seem to be insiders? How are outsiders treated?
3. Do some members move physically in and out of the group—for example, lean forward or backward in their chairs, or move their chairs in and out? Under what conditions do they come in or move out?

The problem of in-groups and out-groups is closely related to the earlier discussion of influence within the group. The interventions described earlier are also useful for bringing in marginal members—for example, supporting, querying, and opening up the discussion.

Feelings

During any group discussion, feelings are frequently generated by interactions among members. These feelings, however, are seldom talked about. Observers may have to make guesses based on tone of voice, facial expressions, gestures, and other non-verbal cues.

1. What signs of feelings (anger, irritation, frustration, warmth, affection, excitement, boredom, defensiveness, competitiveness, etc.) do you observe in group members?
2. Are group members overly nice or polite to each other? Are only positive feelings expressed? Do members agree with each other too readily? What happens when members disagree?
3. Do you see norms operating about participation or the kinds of questions that are allowed (e.g., "If I talk, you must talk")? Do members feel free to probe each other about their feelings? Do questions tend to be restricted to intellectual topics or events outside of the group?

Most groups in business develop norms that only allow for the expression of positive feelings or feelings of disagreement, but not for anger. The problem with suppressing strong negative feelings is

that they usually resurface later. For example, a person who is angry about what someone said earlier in the meeting gets back at that person later in the discussion by disagreeing or by criticizing his or her idea regardless of the idea's merit. The person's hidden motive becomes getting even and he or she will do so by resisting ideas, being stubborn, or derailing the discussion. This retaliation is usually disguised in terms of substantive issues and often has an element of irrationality to it. It is often more effective to bring out the person's anger in the first place and deal with it then.

Task Functions

In order for any group to function adequately and make maximum progress on the task at hand, certain task functions must be carried out. First of all, there must be *initiation*—the problem or goals must be stated, time limits laid out, and some agenda agreed upon. This function most frequently falls to the leader, but may be taken on by other group members. Next, there must be both *opinion* and *information* seeking and giving on various issues related to the task. One of the major problems affecting group decisions and commitments is that groups tend to spend insufficient time on these phases. *Clarifying* and *elaborating* are vital not only for effective communication but also for creative solutions. *Summarizing* includes a review of ideas to be followed by *consensus testing*—making sure all the ideas are on the table and that the group is ready to enter into an evaluation of the various ideas produced. The most effective groups follow this order rather than the more common procedure of evaluating each idea or alternative as it is discussed. Different group members may take on these task functions, but each must be covered.

1. Are suggestions made as to the best way to proceed or tackle the problem?
2. Is there a summary of what has been covered? How effectively is this done? Who does it?
3. Is there any giving or asking for information, opinions, feelings, feedback, or searching for alternatives?
4. Is the group kept on target? Are topic jumping and going off on tangents prevented or discouraged?
5. Are all the ideas out before evaluation begins? What happens if someone begins to evaluate an idea as soon as it is produced?

Maintenance Functions

Groups cannot function effectively if cohesion is low or if relationships among group members become strained. In the life of any group, there will be periods of conflict, dissenting views, and misunderstandings. It is the purpose of maintenance functions to rebuild damaged relations and bring harmony back to the group. Without these processes occurring, group members can become alienated, resulting in the group's losing valuable resources.

Two maintenance activities that can serve to prevent these kinds of problems are *gate keeping*, which insures that members wanting to make a contribution are given the opportunity to do so; and *encouraging*, which helps create a climate of acceptance.

Compromising and *harmonizing* are two other activities that have limited usefulness in the actual task accomplishment, but they are sometimes useful in repairing strained relations.

When the level of conflict in a group is so high that effective communication is impaired, it is often useful for the group to suspend the task discussion and examine its own processes in order to define and attempt to solve the conflicts. The following questions will focus attention on a group's maintenance functions:

1. Are group members encouraged to enter into the discussion?
2. How well do members get their ideas across? Are some members preoccupied and not listening?

Are there any attempts by group members to help others clarify their ideas?
3. How are ideas rejected? How do members react when their ideas are rejected?
4. Are conflicts among group members ignored or dealt with in some way?

Process Observation and Feedback

This note has covered seven important aspects of group process that can influence a group's effectiveness. The interventions suggested are relatively simple and can be made naturally and unobtrusively during the normal progress of a meeting. The more people in a group skilled at making process observations, the greater the likelihood that the group will not bog down, waste valuable time, or make poor decisions. For this reason an increasing number of U.S. and foreign firms have developed norms that encourage open discussions of group process. In many companies, meetings are ended with a brief feedback session on the group's process, during which the meeting's effectiveness is critiqued by the group members.

It is not necessary, however, to be in such a firm or to use terms such as *process feedback* to contribute to a group's effectiveness. Most of the ideas presented in this note are based on common sense; practicing them does not require using the terms described here. The underlying ideas described here are more important than the specific labels, such as task and maintenance functions, applied to them.

The only privilege a student had that was worth
his claiming, was that of talking to the professor, and
the professor was bound to encourage it. His only
difficulty on that side was to get them to talk at all.
He had to devise schemes to find what they were
thinking about, and induce them to risk criticism
from their fellows.

THE EDUCATION OF HENRY ADAMS

The conspiracy of silence is breaking up: we
are learning to talk more openly about our
joys and fears as teachers, our achievements
and frustrations in the classroom. As I have listened
to my colleagues talk about their students and their
classrooms, the one fear and frustration mentioned
more than any other, as for Henry Adams, was in
leading a discussion. No matter how many articles
on technique we read, or workshops we attend, the
dreaded discussion continues to bother us more
than any other part of our daily teaching lives.
Freshman seminar and discussion-based core programs continue to develop. Pressures not only to
"do more discussion" but to do it well, reinforced
by student evaluations and faculty development
centers, do not go away. We are learning, alas, that
to walk into class and hold up one's copy of the
assigned text, asking, "How'd you like that?" does
not necessarily guarantee an enthusiastic, rewarding discussion.

We need, first of all, to acknowledge our fears in
facing discussion classes: the terror of silences, the
related challenges of the shy and dominant student,
the overly-long dialogue between ourself and one
combative student, the problems of digression and
transitions, student fear of criticism, and our own
fear of having to say "I don't know." Worst of all,
perhaps, is the embarrassment of realizing, usually
in retrospect, that "about half way through the period I lapsed, *again,* into lecture." I suspect that our
fears about discussion (and our lapses) have a great
deal to do with the issue of who controls the classroom. Although psychologically rooted, the control
issue is best dealt with as a nitty-gritty practical
question of how to plan and how to begin.

My first assumption is that an effective discussion, like most anything, depends upon good planning. The content goals for any given class period
usually suggest employing different teaching strategies. We would like to be able to select from among
many discussion possibilities with confidence. The
purpose of this article is to expand the range of our

READING

The Dreaded Discussion:
Ten Ways to Start

PETER FREDERICK

From *Improving College and University Teaching* 29, no. 3
(1980): pp. 109–114. Reprinted with permission of the
Helen Dwight Reid Educational Foundation. Published by
Heldref Publications, 4000 Albemarle Street, N.W., Washington, D.C. 20016. Copyright © 1980 Heldref Publications.

options by describing very precisely several different ways of starting a discussion. Like Henry Adams, we "devise schemes" to find out what our students are thinking.

My particular schemes are guided by the following assumptions and principles about discussions:

- because we have much to learn from each other, all must be encouraged to participate
- it is important to devise ways in which each student has something to say, especially early in the class period
- students should be expected to do some (often highly structured) thinking about a text or issue before the discussion class begins
- students should know and feel comfortable with each other and with the teacher. As Carl Rogers and others keep reminding us, learning is aided perhaps most of all by the equality of personal relationships
- those relationships are enhanced by a climate of trust, support, acceptance, and respect: even "wrong" answers are legitimate
- a student's self-image is always affected by his or her participation in discussions: feedback, therefore, is crucial for self-esteem
- the primary goal in any discussion is to enhance the understanding of some common topic or "text" (in the broadest sense)
- different kinds of texts, purposes, and faculty teaching styles suggest using different kinds of discussion schemes.

My hope and expectation is that other teachers will adapt these suggestions and devise schemes for their own texts, purposes, and teaching styles.

(1) GOALS AND VALUES TESTING: The students are asked to pair off and decide together what they think is the primary value of the particular text for the day, and how their consideration of it meshes with course goals. "Why are we reading this?" "Why now?" After five minutes or so, invite reactions. It is not necessary to hear from each pair, but hearing from a few provides a public reality test for the teacher's course goals ("Is this text serving the purpose I had hoped it would?"), as well as providing a mutual basis for further probing into the text. An alternative initial question for the pairs is to ask for a list of relationships (comparisons and contrasts) between this text and another, usually the

most recent one. Make the instructions explicit: "Identify three themes common to both texts," "Suggest the two most obvious differences between the two texts," "Which did you like best and why?" [and] "Make a list of as many comparisons (or contrasts) as you can in ten minutes." In this case, in order to benefit from the richness of diversity, as well as to confirm similar insights, it is probably best to check in with each pair.

(2) CONCRETE IMAGES: It is obvious, of course, that discussions go better when specific references are made. Yet I think we often need help remembering the content of our text. A few minutes at the beginning can guarantee that the sophisticated analysis we seek will be based on specific facts. Go around the table and ask each student to state one concrete image/scene/event/moment from the text that stands out. No analysis is necessary—just recollections and brief description. As each student reports, the collective images are listed on the board, thus providing a visual record of selected content from the text as a backdrop to the following discussion. Usually the recall of concrete scenes prompts further recollections, and a flood of images flows from the students. A follow-up question is to invite the class to study the items on the board, and ask: "What themes seem to emerge from these items?" "What connects these images?" "Is there a pattern to our recollected events?" "What is missing?" This is, obviously, an inductive approach to the text. Facts precede analysis. But also, everyone gets to say something early in class and every contribution gets written down to aid our collective memory and work.

(3) GENERATING QUESTIONS: We have our own important questions to ask about a text. And we should ask them. But students also have their questions and they can learn to formulate better ones. Being able to ask the right questions about a particular text may be the first way of coming to terms with it. There are many ways of generating questions:

a. Ask students ahead of time (Wednesday for Friday's class) to prepare one or two questions about their reading. One can vary the assignment by specifying different kinds of questions: open-ended, factual, clarifying, connective and relational, involving value conflicts, etc.

212

b. As students walk into the classroom ask them to write down (probably anonymously early in the term) one or two discussable questions about the text. "What questions/issues/problems do you want this group to explore in the next hour about this reading?" Hand all questions to one student (a shy one, perhaps) who, at random, selects questions for class attention. Do not expect to get through all of them, but the discussion of two or three questions usually will deal with or touch on almost every other one. Students, like all of us, ask questions they really want to answer themselves, and they will make sure their point is made somehow.

c. Same as *b*, except the teacher (or a student) takes a minute or two to categorize the questions and deals with them more systematically.

d. Ask each student to write down one or two questions (either ahead of time or at the start of class), but in this case the student owns his/her question and is in charge of leading the discussion until he/she feels there has been a satisfactory exploration of the issues. Start anywhere and go around the table. This obviously works best in smaller groups with longer periods than 50 minutes.

e. Divide the class into pairs or small groups and charge each group to decide upon *one* salient question to put to the rest of the class.

(4) FINDING ILLUSTRATIVE QUOTATIONS: We do not often enough go to the text and read passages out loud together. Students, we are told, do not know how to read any more. If so, they need to practice and to see modeled good old-fashioned *explication de texte*. Ask each student, either ahead of time or at the start of class, to find one or two quotations from the assigned text that he/she found particularly significant. There are many ways in which the instructions may be put: "Find one quotation you especially like and one you especially disliked." Or, "Find a quotation which you think best illustrates the major thesis of the piece." Or, "Select a quote you found difficult to understand." Or, "Find a quotation which suggests, to you, the key symbol of the larger text." After a few minutes of browsing (perhaps in small groups of three to four), the students will be ready to turn to specific passages, read out loud, and discuss. Be sure to pause long enough for everyone to find the right spot in their books: "Starting with the middle para-graph on page sixty-one—are you all with us?" Lively and illuminating discussion is guaranteed because not all students will find the same quotations to illustrate various instructions, nor, probably, will they all interpret the same passages the same way. It is during this exercise that I have had the most new insights into texts I had read many times previously. And there may be no more exciting (or modeling) experience than for students to witness their teacher discovering a new insight and going through the process of refining a previously held interpretation. "Great class today! I taught Doc Frederick something he didn't know."

(5) BREAKING INTO SMALLER GROUPS: No matter the size of a class, sixty or six or one hundred and sixty, it can always be broken down into smaller groups of four, five, eight, fifteen, or whatever. The purpose, quite simply, is to enable more people to say something and to generate more ideas about a text or topic. Also, groups lend themselves usually to a lively, competitive spirit, whether asked to or not. We are interested not only in the few people we are grouped with but also in "what they're doing over there." Furthermore, reticent students often feel more confident in expressing themselves in a larger group after they have practiced the point with a safer, smaller audience. There are three crucial things to consider in helping small groups to work well. First, the instructions should be utterly clear, simple, and task-oriented. Examples: "Decide together which of the brothers is the major character in the novel." "Which person in the *Iliad* best represents the qualities of a Greek hero? Which person, the same or different, best represents a hero by your standards?" "Why did the experiment fail? What would you suggest changing?" "Identify the three main themes of this text." "What is Picasso's painting saying?" "Identify three positive and three negative qualities of King David's character." "What do you think is the crucial turning point in Malcolm's life?" "If you were the company treasurer (lawyer), what decision would you make?" "Generate as big a list as you can of examples of sex-role stereotyping in these first two chapters." "If you were Lincoln, what would you do?" In giving these instructions, be sure to give the groups a sense of how much time they have to do their work. Second, I believe in varying the ways in which groups are formed in order to create different-sized groups with different constituencies. Pair off ("with someone you don't

know") one day; count off by fives around the room another; form groups of "about eight" around clumps of students sitting near one another on a third day. And third, vary the ways in which groups report out when reassembled. Variations include:

• each group reports orally, with the teacher recording results (if appropriate) on the board
• each group is given a piece of newsprint and felt-pen upon which to record its decision, which are then posted around the room
• space is provided for each group, when ready, to write their results on the blackboard
• each group keeps notes on a ditto master, which the teacher runs off and distributes to everyone for continuing discussion the next meeting
• no reporting out is necessary or reactions are invited from the several groups, but not necessarily from all of them.

Further possibilities for small groups are described in the suggestions that follow:

(6) GENERATING TRUTH STATEMENTS: This exercise develops critical skills and generates a good deal of friendly rivalry among groups. The instructions to each group are to decide upon three statements known to be true about some particular issue. "It is true about slavery that. . . ." "We have agreed that it is true about the welfare system that. . . ." "It is true about international politics in the 1950s that. . . ." "We know it to be true about the theory of relativity that. . . ." And so on. I have found this strategy useful in introducing a new topic—slavery, for example—where students may think they already know a great deal but the veracity of their assumptions demands examination. The complexity and ambiguity of knowledge is clearly revealed as students present their truth statements and other students raise questions about or refute them. The purpose of the exercise is to develop some true statements, perhaps, but mostly to generate a list of questions and of issues demanding further study. This provides an agenda for the unit. Sending students to the library is the usual next step, and they are quite charged up for research after the process of trying to generate truth statements.

(7) FORCED DEBATE: Although neither one of two polar sides of an issue obviously contains the whole truth, it is often desirable to force students to select one or the other of two opposite sides and to defend their choice. "Burke or Paine?" "Booker T. Washington or W. E. B. Du Bois?" "Are you for or against achieving racial balance in the schools?" "Should Nora have left or stayed?" "Who had the better argument: Creon or Antigone?" "Capitalism or Socialism for developing nations?" Once students have made their choice, which may be required prior to entering the room for class that day, I ask them to sit on one side of the table or room or the other to represent their decision. Physical movement is important and sides need to face each other. Once the students have actually, as it were, put their bodies on the line, they are more receptive to answering the question: "Why have you chosen to sit where you are?" Inevitably, there may be some few students who absolutely refuse (quite rightly) to choose one side or the other. If they persist, with reasons, create a space for a middle position. This adds a dimension to the debate and, as in the case of deciding between Burke and Paine on whether or not to support the French Revolution, those in the middle find out what it is like to attempt to remain neutral or undecided in heated, revolutionary times. I also invite students to feel free to change their place during a debate if they are so persuaded, which adds still another real (and sometimes chaotic) aspect to the experience.

(8) ROLE PLAYING: This is a powerful learning strategy, guaranteed to motivate and animate most students and to confuse and make nervous many. Role playing is tricky. It can be as simple (deceptively so) as asking two members of the class to volunteer to adopt the roles of two characters from a novel at a crucial point in their relationship, discussing how they feel about it or what they should do next. Or two students can act out the President and an advisor debating some decision, or two slaves in the quarters at night discussing whether or not to attempt to run away, or a male and female (perhaps with reversed roles) discussing affirmative action or birth control. Issues involving value conflicts, moral choices, and timeless human dilemmas related to the students' world usually work best, but role playing need not be so personal. A colleague of mine in biology creates a student panel of foundation grant evaluators, before whom other students present papers and make research proposals. Or, as students walk into class and sit down, they find a card in front of them which indicates

214

the name of a character from a novel, or an historical personage, or even a concept. For the discussion that follows they are to *be* the role indicated on their card. Knowing this might happen is not a bad motivator to make sure students get their reading done.

Any situation involving multiple group conflicts is appropriate for role playing. There are many simulation games for contemporary issues in the social sciences. But for history, I like to create my own somewhat less elaborate "games," putting students into the many roles represented in some historical event or period. One of my favorites is a New England town meeting in 1779, in which a variety of groups (landed elite, yeoman farmers, Tory sympathizers, soldiers and riff-raff, artisans, lawyers and ministers, etc.) are charged with drafting instructions for delegates to a state constitutional convention. Another is to challenge several groups in 1866—defeated Confederates, southern Unionists, northern Radical Republicans, northern moderates, and Black freedmen—to develop lists of goals and strategies for accomplishing them. I play an active role, as moderator of the town meeting or as President Johnson, organizing and monitoring the interactions that follow group caucuses. Our imagination can create many appropriate examples for role playing. You have, I am sure, your own.

But because role playing can be traumatic for some students and because a poorly planned or poorly monitored role play can get out of control, I want to make a few cautionary suggestions that I have found helpful, if not crucial. First, except for finding the cards at the beginning of class which compel playing a role, in most role playing activities students should have some choice in how much to participate, either by deciding whether or not to volunteer or by being part of a group large enough to reduce the pressures on any one individual. Teachers should monitor carefully the unspoken signals of students who may find their role uncomfortable, and intervene, often by skillfully pursuing their own role, to extricate or reduce the pressures on an actor. Generally, however, I have found role playing to be an effective way for the normally shy student, who has said little or nothing in class, to unblock in the new role and participate more readily in conventional discussions afterwards. Second, give students some time (how much depends upon the nature of the particular role play) to prepare themselves for their role. This might mean two days

or more in order to do some research, or fifteen minutes in groups to pool information, or five minutes to refresh one's memory about a character in a novel, or a couple of minutes simply to get in touch with the feelings of a character and situation. Third, in giving instructions the definition of roles to be played should be concrete and clear enough for students to get a handle on who they are playing, yet open enough for the expression of their own personality and interpretation. If the roles are prescribed too clearly, students merely imitate the character described (although sometimes this is the requirement) and have difficulty going beyond it with anything of themselves. If the roles are described too loosely, without a clear context, students will stray too far from the actual situation to be experienced and learned. And finally—and most importantly—in any role play experience, as much (if not more) time should be devoted to debriefing afterwards as for the exercise itself. This is when the substantive lessons of the experience are discovered, explored, and confirmed. This is when those students who may have served as observers will offer their insights and analysis on what happened. Above all, this is when the actors will need an opportunity to talk about how they felt in their roles and what they learned, both about themselves and about the substantive issues involved.

(9) NONSTRUCTURED SCENE SETTING: Most of the ways of starting a discussion described thus far involve a great deal of structure and direction. But inevitably, when teachers suspect that they have been dominating too much ("I blew it again—talked most of the hour!"), it is clearly time to give students an opportunity to take a discussion in *their* directions, and to do most, if not all, of the talking. The teacher, however, has a responsibility for setting the scene and getting class started. There are a variety of ways to do this, some more directive than others. Put some slides on a carousel and, without a word, show them at the beginning of class. Or, as the students walk into the classroom, the teacher plays a piece of music or a speech on a tape recorder. Or, on the board before class the teacher writes a quotation or two, or two or three questions, or a list of words or phrases or names, or even an agenda of issues to be explored. The only necessary verbal instructions are to make it clear to the students that until a defined time (perhaps the last five minutes) you, the teacher, intend to stay out of the discussion

entirely. Even having said that, I have still found that I am capable of breaking my own contract and intervening or, more likely, affecting the class by nonverbal signals. I tell my students that I find it extremely difficult to stay uninvolved, and that I need their help in making sure I stay out of the discussion. They are usually happy to oblige. If possible, adopt an utterly nonevaluative observer role and take descriptive notes on the course of the discussion. To read your notes back to the students may be the most helpful feedback you can give them.

(10) A TENTH WAY TO START: As the term progresses students will have experienced many different exciting ways to start a discussion, most of which, we hope, enhance their understanding of a text or issue. Once the expectation of variety has been established, there is even a legitimate place for the following strategy: stroll into class with your book, sit on the edge of the table, hold the book up, and ask: "How'd you like it?"

Although it has not been my primary purpose in this article to extol the many values of discussion, I assume that my bias has been implicitly clear. The key to effective retention of learning, I believe, is in owning the discovery. Emerson wrote in his journals that a wise person "must feel and teach that the best wisdom cannot be communicated [but] must be acquired by every soul for itself." My primary strategy as a teacher is to structure situations in which students have as many opportunities as possible to acquire wisdom for themselves; that is, to own the discovery of a new learning insight or connection and to express that discovery to others. In this way their substantive learning is increased and their self-esteem is enhanced. How we plan the start of class is crucial in achieving this goal. "Hey, roomie, I now know what Emerson meant by self-reliance. What I said in class about it today was that. . . ." Which translated means: "Hey, I'm OK, I understand this stuff. I said something today others found helpful." Which translated means: "Class was good today: he let me talk."

Section 6. Summary

I 'll never forget that class on world hunger," Bob Clarkson told the researcher. "I've never been taken by surprise like that before."

Bob Clarkson was an assistant professor at the Bay Area Graduate School of Business Administration (called Bay by most students). Bay was a well-known institution of management education and used the case method of instruction. Bob's primary academic assignment was teaching Sections I and II of a required two-term first-year course called Comparative Political Economy (CPE) that dealt with business-government issues in both a national and international framework. Instructors taught their assigned sections for both terms, with an interim grade given at the end of the first unit. (There were 10 sections, each composed of 80 first-year MBA students drawn from the United States and foreign countries.)

All classes, held in an amphitheater-shaped area with instructors moving from one to another of their own sections, were one hour and twenty minutes in length and met at 8:30 A.M., 10:10 A.M., and 1:00 P.M., Monday through Friday.

Bob Clarkson

Bob Clarkson, now in his second year of teaching at Bay, had taught economics for two years as a teaching fellow at Berkeley. He received his Ph.D. in comparative political economy halfway through his first year at Bay. With that degree came an automatic promotion from instructor to assistant professor, which, he said, made him feel more comfortable in his new professional role. Bob, a young-looking, slim, 30-year-old of medium height, was married, with two children. Experiencing the anxiety typical of younger professors, he asked himself: Confronted by students who are in many cases older than oneself, how does one maintain one's authority in the classroom?

Bob commented:

Students at Bay can be very forceful. In my first year there was a disturbing situation in which a group of them petitioned the dean to remove an instructor they thought incompetent. I determined then and there that no such thing would ever happen to me. Fortunately, I had no trouble of that kind, but I felt quite defensive the first year, especially since I had begun the year as an instructor rather than as an assistant professor. Since then, my teaching style has relaxed quite a bit. I've learned to become less direc-

---

CASE

Class on World Hunger (A)

This case was written by **Abby Hansen** in collaboration with **C. Roland Christensen** for the Developing Discussion Leadership Skills Seminar. While the case is based on data supplied by participants involved, all names and some peripheral facts have been disguised.

tive; and I'm able to relinquish the reins of discussion to the students. I guess I'm feeling more secure, and [he smiled] maybe being a year older has something to do with it too.

I felt a need to maintain my distance from the students because of our close proximity in age. If I became overly familiar, the teacher/student line might be crossed. The next youngest professor teaching this course is 35; another is 38; others, 40 and over.

Bob also learned that teaching at a professionally oriented school like Bay demanded from its instructors perspectives very different from those he had gained in graduate school. He commented:

It's quite a contrast with my past experience. For example, in graduate school in economics, when we studied barriers to entry, it was from the other side. Here, it's how to raise and maintain them; in the economics department at Berkeley, the question was how to get rid of them. I was always interested in the interaction among management, economics, and public policy formulation and implementation, but from the public management point of view. I thought I'd be teaching in a school of public policy, so at first I was surprised when a professor at Bay I'd worked with said, "Why not come here?" The CPE course, once I learned about it, seemed a natural for me to teach.

I've since decided to try to make my career at Bay, although I realize it's unrealistic to be overconfident. Even in my two years here, I've seen faces come and go among the faculty. Fortunately, the case method style of teaching is excellent preparation for many other things, like testifying before Congress, delivering presentations to boards of directors, and handling all sorts of conferences. But, as for the difference between an academic graduate school like Berkeley and a professional, practical institution like Bay, I'm still trying to figure that out.

Bob's Second Year

I found my second year of teaching CPE much more enjoyable. I had gained familiarity with the material and felt more at ease teaching students older than I. A few extracurricular executive training programs and bank training seminars I taught the first year helped build my confidence.

Bob taught CPE to Sections I and II of the first-year MBA program. Teaching Section I had turned out to be a real pleasure. "For some reason," he commented, "I got on their wave length quite early in the first semester."

They were well prepared and eager to contribute, the keenest, most engaged section I had taught so far. By comparison, Section II lagged behind. They were eager to play pranks, prone to lateness, and tended to waste valuable class time with elaborate jokes. Section I, while lively, was generally issue oriented and energetic.

Interestingly enough, at the end of the year, when the students evaluated the teachers, I learned that Section I had rated me a 4.3 out of a possible 5, while II had rated me 3.5. I still wonder whether the whole educational experience—for me and the students— would have been better if I had somehow forged a better rapport with Section II; perhaps they might have performed better. Certainly, I tried to grade objectively, but it seemed that there really was a qualitative difference between the two groups. Perhaps my display of annoyance once at Section II's widespread lateness alienated the group and impaired my relationship with them. To me, effective teaching means keeping one's negative emotions in check for the sake of good class dynamics.

That isn't to say that you can or should avoid emotion in teaching. I don't think you can. In fact, case discussions at Bay are alive with all sorts of emotions—tension, excitement, humor, discovery, fear of failure, intimidation, sometimes resentment—I could go on. And this emotion emanates both from the students and from the instructor. A large part of the instructor's task is managing this emotion. That's probably the most difficult part of teaching here, especially for a young instructor. I think I still have a lot to learn in this regard. But one thing that I have learned is that it just does not pay to get angry at a section of Bay students. I care a great deal about running a demanding, but not unpleasant or humorless, class.

Bay is a school where news about a teacher's performance in the classroom seems to travel fast. Students pass on a lot of information, and so do professors. Once I actually got a note from a senior colleague saying, "Got a super report on your class on so and so. Whatever you're doing, keep doing it!" Negative news can get around just as fast—perhaps faster.

To Bob, teaching was not merely a matter of obligation ("one of certain necessary conditions for advancement at Bay," as he put it). It was also a pleasure, and he felt he had a serious moral responsibility to help prepare leaders of world industry and government for extremely influential positions.

Bob's Teaching Style

Bob described his typical opening:

At the beginning of each case, I usually laid out the three main areas I had worked out according to my teaching plan. In the beginning of the year I tended to stick fairly close to my plan and also to intervene on particulars. When a student simply offered a fact without a hypothesis, or an unsupported conclusion, I would zero in and try to expose the fallacy either by pointing out a contradictory set of facts, or by suggesting an alternative hypothesis to explain the phenomenon in question. As the academic year progressed, however, I tended to avoid that for two reasons. Some of the students were offended by that approach—they seemed to take it personally—and it also robbed other students of an opportunity to correct their colleagues on their own initiative.

I also decided that it was better to let the students talk than to deliver material myself. "Air time," as they call the opportunity to speak in class, is an important factor in students' grades at Bay, and they compete for it. The opportunity cost of an instructor's intervention is lost time for student contribution. If it's managed properly, the students will do all the teacher's work in a lively discussion—bring up his points, expose each other's reasoning. As obvious as this is to me now, I didn't learn this until about 80 percent of the way through my first year here. There are many ways whereby you can have students intervene. Instead of correcting a student, I'd turn to someone else and say, "Joe, tell me why you don't agree with that," or I'd look for someone on whom I thought I might depend to supply a supporting remark to that argument, let the thing build, and then call on someone I knew would present a totally opposite position. I might simply refuse to let anyone take the opposite side until I thought the erroneous argument had been fully laid out.

When asked to describe how he currently ran his classes, Bob replied:

At the beginning of each class I'd go out to the center of the pit and—exactly at the appointed hour—open with introductory comments and describe the class agenda. Then I'd turn to a student and ask him

or her to address the first study question. This was a standard beginning early in the course. We would discuss the economic situation confronting the government of x. Students would have a critical list of economic variables and we'd compare GNP growth rate, inflation, unemployment, productivity, and balance of payments data. At the beginning of the year I wouldn't typically warn the first student contributor beforehand.

I called on people to start off the class and didn't accept volunteers. But about 40 percent of the way through my second year of teaching I stopped this. Section dynamics had gotten more casual and, besides, it was a signal to them that I was satisfied with their general level of performance and didn't need to spur them. It signaled confidence. During the first year I taught I never took volunteers to open the class, and frankly, I don't think that worked out well.

The Incident

That Friday, Bob arrived about 10 minutes early for his session of CPE with Section I. It was 12:50 P.M. No teacher has a predictable year-long schedule at Bay, and Bob had drawn an unusual number of Friday afternoon sessions, but he didn't mind teaching that particular Friday afternoon class. He found the material fascinating because it was close to his own interests, and he also enjoyed Section I.

Bob recalled:

I was on my way to my desk in the pit [the center of the amphitheater] when one of my best students, Ian Kahn, stopped me. I was in a hurry to review a few points before the class started but I paused. "Did anyone tell you what's planned for today?" Ian asked. I said, "No, why?" Ian looked around, shrugged, and said, "Oh, nothing, except that the section's a bit rowdy, that's all." I didn't realize it then, but Ian's words were a warning.

As a few students began to straggle into the classroom, Bob carefully spread out his class notes on the desk and chatted with some of them as they entered the classroom. Amanda Brown paused to greet him on the way to her seat. He asked her how the class play had gone the night before. She responded that it had been a resounding success.

"One of the cast members [and a section member], Alec O'Reilly," she said, "did such a marvelous job last night that he got a standing ovation. Best of all for me, though, was the break the play gave us all from the grind of preparing cases. A whole bunch of us went out drinking afterwards."

As Amanda was speaking, a young man in a three-piece suit presented himself to Bob.

"Professor Clarkson," he said, "I'm Ken Call. Professor Friedman suggested I attend your class. I'm a prospective student. Would it be all right?"

Bob recalled:

> I couldn't imagine why Professor Friedman, a senior colleague I hardly knew, had singled me out, but I told Mr. Call he was certainly welcome to sit in. Call asked if I'd mind if he left at 2:00 for an appointment. Normally, I don't appreciate people coming late or leaving early but I decided to make an exception in this case and said, "I don't think it will be a problem. Maybe you can talk one of these guys into letting you sit near the back door so you can leave inconspicuously."

Then Bob walked up to the back row of seats to chat with Jack Law, the section's social director, who was usually an active participant in CPE discussion. He had invited the professor and his wife to join the section for a baseball outing May 9. Bob wanted to get the details straight and see if Jack had tickets for his youngsters, ages 6 and 4, as well.

"Sure," Jack replied. He seemed to be in a festive mood. "Bring the whole family. We've invited the dean, and he's bringing his kids, too. By the way"—Jack put on a baseball hat—"why don't you play softball with us this afternoon?"

Bob usually devoted his afternoons to work and student conferences. He smiled but shook his head. "Like to, but can't," he said. "Student appointments."

Bob's social interaction with Section I had been pleasant but usually limited to a fairly formal arrangement whereby eight students would sign up with the educational representative of the section for a lunch with Bob. The lunches were friendly and casual, and over half of the section took advantage of the opportunity. They had often invited Bob to their regular Friday afternoon beer busts as well, but he hadn't gone, nor had he played in the section's first Friday afternoon baseball game the previous week. At that time he had had other things to do, but, he explained, "I'm not sure I would have played even if I had been free. I wanted to maintain a little distance."

After speaking with Jack, Bob passed Ian and—

to his subsequent chagrin—ignored his cryptic warning.

"How did you get stuck teaching a tough course like CPE on a Friday afternoon, anyway?" Ian asked.

"Just the luck of the draw," Bob replied.

"Well," Ian continued, "I don't think people really have their minds on the case today, what with the play last night. Eighteen people missed Finance this morning."

"Eighteen?" Bob raised his eyebrows with mock incredulity. "There'd better not be eighteen gone from class this afternoon!"

The Section's Mood

The second term was well under way, but the end from the students' point of view was nowhere in sight. The world hunger case was #36 in a syllabus that ran from #31 through #54. The CPE course had just completed a module on oil with a case on U.S. energy planning. The class discussion had been particularly encouraging to Bob. Students had grappled seriously with the important issues and political constraints that face a U.S. president who attempts to forge an energy strategy. In fact, the discussion had gone even better than Bob expected, given that it had taken place on his first day back in the classroom after the faculty had returned midterm exams and grades.

Bob considered the day's case, World Food Prospects and Policies, especially crucial, because it introduced a new module and therefore set the stage for the level of performance of the next three sessions and because he believed its underlying issue—widespread starvation in the Third World in the face of prosperity in the highly industrialized nations—to be morally significant.

Many first-year students were under substantial pressure at that point in the term because of a slightly unusual circumstance. Not only had they just received the results of their midterm exams in Finance, a subject many found quite difficult, but also, for some reason, the instructors of the Marketing area had delayed returning the March final exam grades until April. They had, in fact, just released the grades, along with an unusually high number of warning letters—30 percent. Normally, only the bottom 10 percent to 15 percent of a class received Low Pass grades, seven of which (out of a possible 15) would force a review of the student's record by the Academic Performance Committee. Receiving a warning letter was always a disturbing event; the student faced the danger of being flunked out of the program ("hitting the screen" in Bay slang). In the opinion of the first-year students, however, it was particularly upsetting for warning letters to be sent *after* the course was completely over and there was no longer any chance of improving one's performance.

"The first-year students," Bob commented, "had reached a peak of frustration, concern, and anxiety. Emotionally, they were exhausted. Like long-distance racers, they were hitting 'runner's wall' [near-paralyzing fatigue], but they knew it wasn't downhill yet. They couldn't quit. I had given my midterm after case #30. World hunger was #36, and my sections had just received their grades. Their performance on the exam was rather good, but some students discovered that they had fared far better in class participation than written work; that meant they had a lot of hard work ahead."

Section I Membership

Bob recalled:

Section I had shown itself to be gifted and mature, even by Bay standards. In discussions with other section instructors, I confirmed my judgment that this was an unusually capable group. Their discussions were almost always vital, with most of the section members participating. I had, in fact, found it difficult to award 10 percent Low Passes on the exam, along with only 20 percent Excellents. I respected the section as a whole and felt that they respected and liked me as well. There had been no crises and no particular tensions in our work together.

Among the students, Jack Law, the social director, was the most gregarious. It says something about him that he was the social director. He didn't like to be seen taking Bay too seriously; he didn't want to lose his personality to the school. Jack often wore a baseball hat in class, was very talkative, organized section athletic events, and tended to make jokes in class although he certainly wasn't a clown. His midterm grade was a Sat+.

Ian, a foreign student, had been a businessman in Japan, dealing with government agencies there. His performance in class had been outstanding. Another of my students, Frank Williams, had been in the Foreign Service, and he approached the material with a point of view similar to mine. Peter Barnes, an Oklahoman, had run for Congress and lost the Democratic primary by 100 votes.

Cynthia Andrews was the educational representative, a young woman Bob described as having "impressive maturity and the ability to understand both the social and intellectual aspects of the class." He found her to be "very motivated. She had come to me, for example, for outside reading on this particular case."

Elliott Farmer, who had participated adequately in class discussions, nonetheless had been given a Low Pass on the midterm. He had, Bob subsequently learned, a special interest in problems of world food distribution and famine relief. Just as some students study nuclear energy or the environment, Elliott made something of an intellectual hobby of the study of the world food situation. His interest in the case, therefore, was high. Martin Harkness was an active Libertarian, prominent in the National Taxpayers' Union.

Amanda Brown was a bright, lively young woman who threw herself enthusiastically into the many social activities of the first-year class. She had mentioned to Clarkson a day or two before the world hunger case that she was working hard on the class play and therefore might not be as well prepared as usual.

As the Class Began

When Bob returned to the pit to review his notes, it was nearly time to start. Neil Salman waited by the desk with two more guests. "This is my wife Ellen and our friend Sara, who is thinking of applying here next year."

"Delighted to meet you," Bob said. "Neil, have you introduced your guests to the section?"

"Yes, I have."

"Fine, then. Why don't you take a seat in the top row?"

Bob turned to start the class as the second hand swept past 1:00. When he walked to the center of the pit he saw that Ian's prediction had been right. There were an unusually large number of students absent, including some of the section's best. And many students were not sitting in their usual places, a major departure from custom. Bob motioned to a student at the back to close the door.

The rest of this case is told in Bob's own words as he recalls how this particular class began.

I began with some irony, and said, "Well, I'm glad to see you all could make it." The section laughed. "We have a visitor," I said. "I'd like him to introduce himself."

The nicely dressed visitor in the back stood up and again it flashed through my mind to wonder why Professor Friedman had steered him to my class rather than someone else's. I hoped it might be because Friedman had heard something good about my teaching.

The class welcomed the visitor with a round of applause, and just then six more students came through the door at the back of class and waved at me on the way to their seats. The class attendance was turning out to be fairly normal after all.

I waved back to them. "Glad you could make it," I said, and they laughed a little sheepishly. "In a moment" I went on, "I'd like our friend Larry Quirk to start the class." I gestured to Larry's empty seat and the section laughed. Then, after a pause, I turned to face the class and began my usual sort of introduction. "Today, we begin our three-day module on the world food problem. . . . "

Food Fight

Before I could finish my sentence, Jack leapt to his feet, bellowed "FOOD FIGHT!" and fired a roll directly at Larry Quirk's empty seat. The roll narrowly missed me. Immediately, students on all sides of the classroom began throwing rolls at each other. Bread materialized, it seemed, from every pocket and purse. The air was full of rolls. It must have been a carefully orchestrated prank. Students picked up rolls that fell near them and flung them out across the room and into the pit again, in several volleys. I retreated in shock and huddled behind the desk among the "breadcrumbs" to avoid the rolls that were still flying.

It was one of those times where you almost see your whole life passing before your eyes. I thought about the visitor, Ken Call. What would Friedman think when he told him about this? What would the other guests think? What should I do to uphold the reputation of the school—this supposed training ground for the future leaders of the world? On this of all days, when we're about to discuss famine and starvation, how can the section dare stage a food fight? What does this mean about their attitude toward the less developed world, those who go without nourishment while we in a place of power fling bread at each other?

A food fight at any time is bad enough, but here we were studying hunger, people who don't have enough to eat, and the students were throwing bread on the ground and at each other. There were rolls all over. The place looked like a pigsty. It seemed like an offense against the poor.

I was upset because I hadn't read Ian's signal, but most important, the symbolism also offended me. It looked as if everybody was involved. People had obviously brought a lot of rolls to toss. All you could see was rolls everywhere. I was so stunned I couldn't see individual faces. I wondered, what sort of a cabal have I stumbled onto? I also thought about Jack, who had heaved the first roll right at the seat to which I had pointed.

There I was, behind the desk with my blood pressure rising. I had been caught unawares. I was bothered by the surprise. I was bothered by the symbolism. I was bothered by the awful embarrassment in front of guests, and I wondered how to manage this process. Should I get really mad and blow my stack, rap their knuckles? I happen to believe that it's always bad to get angry, but should I end the class and send everybody home? Should I excuse the section because it's Friday afternoon and they're under pressure, or take it as the tasteless joke it was and react? If I were to get upset it might do everyone damage, but is one sometimes, nevertheless, compelled to show anger at unacceptable student behavior? The answers just didn't come very easily or quickly, yet I knew that I was going to have to do something and soon.

"Is It Safe to Come Out Now?"

I came out from behind the desk where I had retreated to avoid the rolls. I didn't have a simmering, steaming look on my face. In fact, I appeared stunned—partly on purpose, but also because I really felt uncertain. It was an honest response, but I emphasized my shock, played upon it by shrugging broadly and looking blank. This must have seemed pretty comical, because my body language got a laugh. I felt good about that, since it meant that the roll-throwing had not been a personal insult to me. I had always had a good relationship with this section, and their laughter reinforced this. Still I wondered: should I point out that this section's behavior constitutes an extraordinarily tasteless and immature joke?

How to handle the situation? That was the question. I looked around, then looked directly at

Jack Law, who had started it all, and asked, "Is it safe to come out now?" That got another laugh. I got the feeling that my classroom had turned into a Sigma Chi setting. We were all in a fraternity together. "Frankly," I went on, "I really don't know how to respond to this." I was fishing for a lifeline. I began slowly to focus on individuals, trying to pick out facial expressions that would give me some clues. Some faces, I noticed, were not laughing. Cynthia, for example, looked a little worried. Others appeared to be apprehensive, maybe even offended. Not everybody, it seemed, had been involved in the plot after all. I was still pretty upset, but I recalled a time when I had bawled out Section II, and I didn't want to engage in that sort of negative feedback again. "Can someone suggest where we should go from here?" I asked.

I wasn't even certain myself what I meant by the question, but hands shot up. The section had interpreted my words as a new beginning to the case. Immediately, people looked prepared for a discussion—notably Elliott, who had received a Low Pass on the exam. He had been one of those who looked concerned.

Lots of thoughts rushed through my mind. What I was about to do had implications for the people in the group who hadn't partied the night before or even gone to the play. They hadn't been out drinking; they'd prepared this case. I realized I had a responsibility to them. The students who hadn't prepared would be only too happy if I were to say something like, "Oh what the heck, it's Friday—let's go play ball," and dismiss the section. They would have blown off their anxiety about their other classes and simultaneously avoided doing their work in my class. And I would, in effect, have joined the fraternity.

I saw on Elliott's face a look of "I want to avoid a Low Pass in this class; I have worked hard on this case, and I'm prepared. Give me an opportunity to show it." If I were to dismiss the class, I thought, it wouldn't be fair to him and others. Besides, I wanted to find out what Elliott had on his mind. He looked safe, and he had a very earnest look about him.

So I called on Elliott, and he gave the most beautiful evaluation of the case. He talked for 15 minutes, which was unusual. Typically, the lead-off person talks for a couple of minutes. Every word was a gem. He didn't refer to the food fight

at all. He spoke of the obligation of those with place and power, raising the issue indirectly by saying, "World hunger is a problem for the rich as well as the poor." By the time he was done talking, people were ready to concentrate on the case.

It was the last class of a long week, but as Elliott spoke it might just as well have been Tuesday morning at 8:30. It turned out to be one of the best discussions we had had all year. We did go into the ethical issues relating to world hunger. People became very much involved—even those who hadn't prepared carefully. We talked about ideas rather than numbers; we got personally involved in the matter, really identifying with the involved participants and being genuinely committed in our thinking.

When Elliott gave me his super response, I essentially forgave the section. His excellent presentation blocked the issue. All my anxiety dissipated. I didn't have to halt the class or deliver a tirade. I was lucky. I had called on Elliott because he looked serious and eager. Fortunately, he turned out really to have been the most prepared student in the section. The very case issues that were bothering me were bothering him. I ended up enjoying the class, thinking, "This is the most improbable discussion I have ever had!"

Jack then raised his hand but I ignored him for a good long while, until I thought he was ready for serious contribution. I also noticed Cynthia looking very concerned. Afterwards she came over to me and asked, "Did you really think we were going to hit you?"

As the class ended, I considered making some joking reference to what had happened—"I was sort of worried about finishing the case today" or some such remark— but I concluded instead by thanking Elliott for his careful preparation. I passed out one or two other individual bouquets and then summarized the issues, being quite honestly complimentary. It was no longer "Animal House," it was the Bay Area Graduate School of Business Administration again.

As the students left the room a few came over to thank me for one of the best discussions of the whole year, but mostly they were just saying to each other, "Let's go play ball."

I went away feeling very strange, wondering about this peculiar experience. But I did have a sense of success in having had a good discussion in what had been a potentially disastrous environment. I must have done something right but I still had nagging doubts.

After that, the section went well. The section didn't play any other stunts. It was almost like a trial by fire. Once that critical incident was finessed, we went on to even better discussions. I never heard anything from Friedman nor from any of the guests.

In reflecting on his first two years of teaching at the Bay Area Graduate School of Business Administration, Bob Clarkson gave the following account to the case researcher:

A discussion leader has a problem of balancing discipline and order with the need for student freedom. You recall I spoke with you about my problem of late arrivals for Section II classes, which occurred the same year as Section I's food fight. The way I handled my annoyance at them, and what subsequently happened, taught me something. One 8:30 A.M. session with Section II—the morning before an exam in Managerial Economics—was particularly bad, and I was quite upset with them. Nearly half the class was absent when the discussion was supposed to begin. I remember turning to one of my better students and asking, "Where is everybody?"

"You might want to give it a minute or two," he replied. "At this time yesterday in the Manufacturing class, quite a few students were absent, but they came in a minute or two late."

I decided, based on his comment, to wait. One minute passed, then two. Only one or two additional students arrived. Then I started to get angry. I pursed my lips, put on a troubled look—furrowed brow, folded arms—and stared into space until five full minutes of silence had passed. You could feel the tension in the room.

Then I said, "I really want to address these remarks to those who aren't here, but perhaps you will be the conduits of my message." I spoke in measured tones. "An exam the next day in Managerial Economics is not a sufficient excuse to miss CPE," I said. "At the beginning of the term we talked about a contract. Your part is to be here, to be prepared, and to be on time, and if you can't do one or all of those things, to let me know about it in advance."

[Later, Bob told the researcher, he had second thoughts about that speech.]

It occurred to me, as I thought about that incident, that it was really a one-way sort of contract. I enunciated my terms at the beginning of the course, but I simply assumed they implicitly subscribed to the contract by having come to Bay. I realized all this later and decided it isn't a good idea to berate students for not living up to a one-

CASE

Class on World Hunger (B)

*This case was written by **Abby Hansen** in collaboration with **C. Roland Christensen** for the Developing Discussion Leadership Skills Seminar. While the case is based on data supplied by participants involved, all names and some peripheral facts have been disguised.*

sided contract. After all, a student could say, "I'm paying thousands of dollars for this, and if I decide I ought to miss a day of Clarkson's class to study for someone else's, that's my affair." In a sense, I now think it was unfair of me to get angry, and besides, the students reacted as if I had bawled them out like children. It was bad for class morale. It was very unpleasant. It showed me the cost side of getting mad and made me afraid of damaging the process of discussion with Section I when they staged that food fight.

Bob's Philosophy

His Teaching Experience

My teaching philosophy and style changed rather substantially from the first to the second year. The first year I was very influenced by Michel Crozier's *The Bureaucratic Phenomenon*. Crozier's theory of individual and group behavior in organizations holds that there is a relationship between power and uncertainty. Each group (or person) in an organization seeks to enlarge its discretionary area, and would retreat rather than submit. Being unpredictable can enhance one's power and one's hold on a discretionary area. During my first year, when I felt especially vulnerable—I hadn't yet completed my dissertation or attained professorial rank—I sought to maintain my authority in class by being unpredictable.

I tried to implement Crozier's theory so that the students wouldn't think they had my number, but I now think I was confused then about the proper role of an instructor at Bay.

In my second year at Bay, I started to run a less authoritarian-seeming class. I didn't time the agenda of my classes precisely, although I always started promptly, on the dot of the hour. I would introduce the case by saying that certain aspects seemed to be worth, say, 10 or 15 minutes, but I would let a discussion wander if it was good. When the discussion got too far from the point, I would sometimes stop the class 10 minutes early to make sure that something I thought was vital received coverage.

I did lecture at times like that, but I didn't do it often. Once, for example, I knew that a certain political analysis I had prepared would be very important on an exam. The students in Section II,

however, got off on a tangent talking about terrorism. I decided not to strong-arm them into following my prescribed pattern, and I let the discussion go on. But I did stop the class early and say, "Now this is pretty important, and I want to share my analysis with you." I then put my own diagram on the board and explained it.

I guess both my teaching philosophy and style have evolved over the past two years, too. My central theme now is that I want to manage a discussion rather than deliver my own thoughts. With an eager section you can just call on volunteers to bring out most points in a case. At Bay, we use the metaphor "discussion pastures" in talking about the case method. The instructor polices the fences of a pasture, but lets the cattle graze as they will, without letting the grass become grazed too closely in any one area. You can't cover more than three major areas per class. The teacher becomes a discussion manager, intervening only to move the fences and keep the pasture defined.

In graduate school, I was familiar with professors who had years of expertise to deliver, but that model, I found, didn't apply to the case method of teaching. I came to feel that a professor should be tinder for *discovery*, and that rapport with students was essential. As I gained confidence, I discarded Crozier's model and slowly came to seek consistency instead of inconsistency.

In a discussion of economic performance, for example, someone might say, "GNP is going up, but I think the crucial issue is moral." I'd say, "Fascinating observation, but let's lay out the facts first and then move in that direction." I would try to persuade the class that there's a logic to the agenda.

In a class where you simply lecture, the students' reactions to you are less important than in the case method. You could deliver a sermonette in a lecture class without negative impact, I suppose, but in a discussion class the students' attitude toward you can make or break the whole enterprise. The question that keeps coming back to me is: how do you uphold the standards of your school and the intellectual enterprise without becoming obnoxiously authoritarian so that you destroy or interrupt a delicate rapport?

The narrow path from Uvarovka village to the school had been completely covered with snow during the night, and only the barely perceptible pattern of light and shadow on its uneven surface revealed its course. The young schoolteacher stepped cautiously, ready to draw back her foot at once if the shadows proved treacherous.

It was no more than half a kilometer to the school, and the teacher had merely tied a woolen kerchief round her head and thrown her short fur coat over her shoulders. The cold was fierce, however, and fitful gusts of wind showered her with snow from head to foot. But the twenty-four-year-old teacher did not mind it. She even enjoyed the stinging sensation in her cheeks and the momentary cold touch of the wind. Averting her face from the gusts, she was amused to see the small imprints her pointed overshoes left behind, like the tracks of some forest creature.

The fresh, sunlit January morning filled her with happy thoughts. She had come here only two years ago, straight out of college, and already she was considered the district's best teacher of Russian. In Uvarovka itself, in Kuzminki, in Black Gully village, in the peat settlement, and at the stud farm, everywhere they knew her and called her Anna Vasilyevna, adding the patronymic to show their respect.

The sun rose over the serrated outline of the distant woods and the long shadows on the snow grew a deeper blue, making faraway objects merge with those nearby—the top of the church belfry reached up to the porch of the village soviet, the pines across the river came up the slope of the nearer bank, the wind gauge at the school meteorological station whirled in the middle of the field, right at Anna's feet.

A man was coming across the field. What if he won't step off the path? Anna thought with mock apprehension. The path was too narrow for two people, and stepping aside meant sinking knee-deep into the snow. She knew, of course, that there wasn't a man in the district who would not go out of his way to let the Uvarovka schoolteacher pass.

As they drew closer Anna recognized the man as Frolov, one of the workers at the stud farm.

"Good morning, Anna Vasilyevna," said Frolov, and he raised his fur hat over his shapely, short-cropped head.

"Come on now, put that hat on! What are you thinking in this cold!"

READING

Winter Oak

YURI NAGIBIN

Yuri Nagibin, a Soviet writer, was born in Moscow in 1920 and began his literary career in 1939. During World War II he served as a war correspondent; since that time he has concentrated on writing stories.

Reprinted from the Atlantic Monthly, September 1979, with the permission of Am-Rus Literary Agency representing the copyright agency in the U.S.S.R.

Probably Frolov had no intention of keeping his hat off, but after the teacher's words he took his time about putting it on again. A short sheepskin coat fitted his trim, muscular body. In one hand he held a thin, snakelike whip, which he kept smacking against his high felt boots.

"How is my Lyosha behaving? Up to any mischief?" he asked conversationally.

"All my children are up to mischief; it's quite normal as long as they don't overdo it," replied Anna, savoring her pedagogical wisdom.

Frolov smiled.

"No fear of him overdoing it. He's a quiet one. Takes after his father."

He stepped off the path and immediately sank up to his knees, which made him look no taller than a twelve-year-old boy. Anna nodded to him graciously and hurried on.

The school, a two-story brick building with wide, frost-painted windows, stood a little off the highway, behind a low fence. In the morning light its walls threw a reddish tint on the surrounding snow. Children from all over the district came to it—from nearby villages, from the stud farm, the oil workers' sanatorium, and even the far-off peat settlement. Caps, kerchiefs, hats, hoods, and bonnets flocked to the school along the highway from both directions.

"Good morning, Anna Vasilyevna!"

From some the familiar greeting sounded in clear and ringing voices, from others it was muffled and barely audible, coming through thick scarves and shawls that swathed the young faces up to the eyes.

* * *

Anna's first lesson was to the twelve- and thirteen-year-olds in five-A form. She entered the classroom as the last peal of the bell was announcing the beginning of the class. The children rose, greeted her, and sat down at their desks. But it took some time for them to quiet down. Desk tops banged, benches creaked, somebody sighed heavily, evidently unwilling to switch off the carefree morning mood.

"We shall continue to study parts of speech today."

Now they became perfectly quiet. The sounds of a truck slowly rumbling along the slippery highway could distinctly be heard in the room.

Anna remembered how nervous she had been about this lesson last year. She had kept repeating to herself, like a schoolgirl before an exam, the textbook definition of a noun. And how foolishly afraid she had been that they would not understand!

She smiled at those memories, adjusted a pin in her heavy knot of hair, and sensing confidence coursing like blood itself through her body, she began speaking in a calm, even voice: "A noun is a word that denotes a subject—that is, a person, thing, or quality. A subject in grammar is anything about which you can ask the question What is it? or Who is it? For instance: Who is it?—a pupil. What is it?—a book."

"May I come in?"

A small figure in battered felt boots covered with melting snowflakes stood in the open doorway. The round, wind-reddened face glowed as if it would burst; the eyebrows were white with frost.

"Late again, Savushkin." Like most young teachers, Anna enjoyed being strict, but now an almost plaintive note sounded in her voice.

Considering the matter settled, Savushkin quickly slid into his place. Anna saw him shove his oilcloth schoolbag into the desk and, without turning his head, ask something of the boy next to him.

Savushkin's unpunctuality annoyed Anna; it somehow spoiled the fine opening of the day for her. The geography teacher, a small, dried-up old woman, very much like a night moth, had once complained to Anna about Savushkin's often being late to lessons. She complained about other things, too—the children's inattentiveness, their much too boisterous behavior. "Those first morning lessons are so trying," she said. They may be, for incompetent teachers who don't know how to hold the interest of their pupils, thought Anna disdainfully, and offered to change hours with the older woman. She felt a prick of conscience now: the old teacher had doubtless sensed the challenge in Anna's magnanimous offer.

"Is everything clear?" she asked the class.

"Yes!" chorused the children.

"Very well. Then give me some examples."

There was a short silence and then someone said haltingly, "Cat."

"Correct," said Anna, recalling that last year, too, "cat" had been the first example.

After that examples poured in like a stream: window . . . table . . . house . . . highway. . . .

"Correct," Anna assured them. The children were excited.

It amazed Anna to see such joy at the discovery

of a new aspect in long-familiar words. At first the choice of examples embraced only the most everyday, tangible things: cart, tractor, pail, nest. . . . From the back desk a fat boy called Vasya kept repeating in his thin voice, "Chicken, chicken, chicken."

But then someone said hesitantly, "Town."

"Good," encouraged Anna.

"Street . . . victory . . . poem . . . play. . . ."

"Well, that's enough," said Anna. "I can see you understand it."

The voices died down reluctantly; only fat Vasya's "chicken" still came from the back of the room. And then suddenly, as if awakened out of his sleep, Savushkin stood up behind his desk and shouted eagerly, "Winter oak!"

The children laughed.

"Quiet, please!" Anna brought her palm down hard on the table.

"Winter oak!" repeated Savushkin, heedless of the laughter around him or of Anna's order. There was something peculiar in his manner. The words seemed to have burst out like a confession, like some glorious secret which could not remain unshared.

Annoyed and uncomprehending, Anna asked, barely controlling her irritation, "Why 'winter oak'? 'Oak' is enough."

"An oak is nothing. A winter oak, there's a noun for you."

"Sit down, Savushkin. That's what coming in late leads to. Oak is a noun, and what the word 'winter' is in this case we have not studied yet. You will come to the teachers' room during the long recess."

"Now you'll catch it," whispered somebody behind Savushkin.

Savushkin sat down smiling to himself, not in the least put out by the teacher's strict tone. A difficult boy, thought Anna.

The lesson continued.

* * *

"Sit down," said Anna when Savushkin entered the teachers' room. With evident pleasure the boy sank into a soft armchair and rocked a few times on its springs.

"Will you please tell me why you are always late for school?"

"I really don't know, Anna Vasilyevna," he said with a gesture of surprise. "I leave home an hour before school."

It seemed that even in trifling matters like this, truth was not easily to be established. There were many children who lived much farther away from school, yet none of them needed more than an hour to get there on time.

"You live in Kuzminki, don't you?"

"No, I live on the sanatorium premises."

"Aren't you ashamed, then, to tell me you leave home an hour before school? Why, it's fifteen minutes from the sanatorium to the highway, and no more than half an hour's walk down the highway!"

"But I don't never go down the highway. I take a shortcut through the forest," Savushkin said earnestly.

"Don't ever go," Anna corrected him mechanically. Why did children have to lie? she thought unhappily. Why couldn't Savushkin tell her simply, "I'm sorry, Anna Vasilyevna, I stopped to play snowballs with the kids," or something else equally straightforward. But the boy said no more and just looked at her out of his large gray eyes, as if wondering what else she would want of him.

"That's not very good, Savushkin. I'll have to talk to your parents about it."

"There's only my mother, Anna Vasilyevna," Savushkin said softly.

Anna blushed. She remembered the boy's mother, the "shower nurse," as her son called her. A withered, tired-looking woman who worked at the sanatorium's hydrotherapy section. From continuous contact with hot water, her hands, limp and white, looked as if they were made of cotton. After her husband had been killed in the war, she remained alone to bring up four children as best she could. She certainly had enough worry without being bothered about her son's conduct. But all the same they had to meet.

"I'll have to see your mother, then," said Anna.

"Please do, Anna Vasilyevna. She'll be so glad to see you."

"I doubt that. What shift does she work on?"

"The second. She goes to work at three."

"Very well then. I finish at two. We'll go together right after school is over."

* * *

Savushkin led Anna Vasilyevna along the path that started at the back of the school. As soon as they entered the forest and the heavy, snowladen spruce branches closed behind them, they found themselves in a different, enchanted world of peace and quiet. Now and then magpies and crows flew from tree to tree, shaking the spreading branches, knocking off dry pine cones, and occasionally breaking off a brittle twig. But the sounds were short-lived and muffled.

Everything around was white. Only high up against the blue sky the dainty lacework of the tall birch trees stood out as if sketched in with India ink.

The path followed a frozen brook, sometimes right down along the bank, sometimes climbing up a steep rise. Occasionally the trees fell back, revealing a sunlit clearing crisscrossed with hares' tracks that looked like a watch chain pattern. There were larger tracks too, shaped like clover. They led away into the densest part of the woods.

"Elks' tracks," said Savushkin, following the direction of Anna's gaze. "Don't be afraid," he added, reading an unspoken question in her eyes.

"Have you ever seen one?" asked Anna.

"An elk? No. No such luck," sighed Savushkin, "I've seen elk droppings, though."

"What?"

"Dung," Savushkin explained, embarrassed.

Diving under a twisted willow, the path ran down to the brook again. Parts of the brook's surface were covered with a thick layer of snow; in other parts, its icy armor lay clear and sparkling, and there were spots where unfrozen water stood out in dark blotches like evil eyes.

"Why hasn't it frozen there?" Anna asked.

"Warm springs. Look, you can see one coming up right there."

Bending over the clear water, Anna saw a thin, quivering thread which rose up from the bottom of the stream and burst into tiny bubbles before reaching the surface. It looked like a lily of the valley with a fragile stem and tiny white flowers.

"Plenty of these springs here," Savushkin explained eagerly; "that's why the brook never freezes over completely."

They came to another unfrozen stretch, with pitch-black but transparent water.

Anna threw a handful of snow into it. The snow did not melt, but grew bulkier at once and sank, spreading out in the water like some jellied greenish weeds. This pleased her so much that she started knocking the snow into the water, trying to push off bigger lumps which took on especially fancy shapes. Carried away by the game, she did not notice Savushkin go on ahead. He perched up on a low tree branch hanging right over the brook and sat waiting for her. A thin layer of ice covered the surface of the brook there, and light, fleeting shadows kept moving over it.

"Look how thin the ice is; you can see the water flowing underneath," said Anna, coming up to the boy.

"Oh, no, Anna Vasilyevna, it's the branch I'm sitting on. It sways and the shadows it throws over the ice sway with it."

Anna blushed. It looked as if she had better hold her tongue here, in the woods.

Savushkin trod on ahead, bending slightly and throwing keen glances around. Anna followed behind.

The winding path led them on and on. There seemed to be no end to all those trees and huge snowdrifts, to that enchanted silence and sun-speckled twilight.

Suddenly a bluish-white patch gleamed ahead. The trees grew sparser. The path rounded a nut bush, and a vast clearing flooded with sunlight opened up before their eyes. In the middle of the clearing, in sparkling white raiment, stood an old oak, tall and majestic like a cathedral. Its branches spread far out over the clearing, and snow nestling in the cracks of the bark made its gigantic trunk look as if inlaid with silver. It had not shed its dried foliage and was now covered to the very crown with snow-capped leaves.

"The winter oak!" gasped Anna. She reverently approached the tree and halted under its glittering branches.

Unaware of the tumult in his teacher's heart, Savushkin busied himself with something at the foot of the trunk, treating the magnificent tree with the familiarity of a long-standing friendship.

"Come here, Anna Vasilyevna," he called. "Look!"

He pushed aside a large clump of snow with earth and old grass clinging to its underside. A little ball plastered with decayed leaves lay in the hollow below. The skeleton-like remnants of the leaves were pierced with sharply pointed needles.

"A hedgehog!" cried Anna.

"See how well he hid himself?" And Savushkin carefully restored the protective covering of earth and snow over the immobile hedgehog. Then he dug at another spot and revealed a tiny cave with icicles hanging at its opening. It was occupied by a brown frog, its tightly stretched skin shiny as if lacquered.

Savushkin touched the frog. It made no movement.

"Isn't he a sly one?" remarked Savushkin. "Pretending he's dead. But just watch him leap as soon as the sun warms him up a bit."

He guided Anna on through the world he knew so well. There were numerous other tenants in and around the oak: bugs, lizards, insects. Some hid among the roots, others in the deep cracks of the bark. Thin, withered, apparently lifeless, they hibernated there all through the winter. The powerful tree accumulated in itself a store of vital warmth, and those poor creatures could not wish for a better shelter. Fascinated, Anna watched this hidden forest life, so little known to her.

"Oh, oh, Mother'll be at work by now!" came Savushkin's anxious voice.

Anna looked at her watch. A quarter past three. She felt trapped. Ashamed for her human frailties and inwardly begging forgiveness of the oak, she said, "Well, Savushkin, this only proves that a shortcut is not always the best way to choose. You'll have to go along the highway from now on."

Savushkin looked down and did not reply.

Heavens! thought Anna, isn't this the clearest proof of my incompetence!

The morning lesson flashed through her mind. How dull and lifeless her explanations were, how utterly devoid of feeling. And she was teaching the children their native language, so beautiful, so rich in shades, color, and meaning! An experienced teacher, indeed! She'd taken no more than a few faltering steps along the path that might well require a whole lifetime to cover. And how is one not to swerve aside but follow the correct path? Yet the joy with which her pupils shouted familiar words, a joy she had not fully appreciated or shared, told her now that she had not strayed too hopelessly after all.

"Thank you, Savushkin, for the lovely walk," she said. "I didn't mean what I just told you. Of course you can take the forest path to school."

"Thank you, Anna Vasilyevna." Savushkin blushed with pleasure. He wanted to promise his teacher then and there that he would never be late again, but hesitated, because he was afraid he might not keep his promise. He only raised his collar and, pulling down his hat, said, "I'll walk you back to school."

"No, don't, I can find the way myself."

He looked at her in some doubt, then picked up a long stick, broke off its thinner end, and offered it to Anna. "Take this," he said. "If an elk comes your way, just hit him on the back and he'll run for all he's worth. Though better not hit him, just wave the stick at him. He might get angry, you know, and leave the woods for good."

"Don't worry, I shan't hit him," she promised.

She took a few steps back, then stopped and turned to take one last look at the winter oak, tinged with pink by the setting sun. A small dark figure stood at the foot of the trunk. Savushkin did not go home. He stayed to guard his teacher's way, even if from a distance.

And suddenly Anna knew that the most wonderful being in that forest was not the winter oak but this small boy in battered felt boots and patched clothes, the son of a "shower nurse" and a soldier killed in the war.

She waved to him and went on her way.

PART IV

Supplementary Materials for Seminar Participants

Section 1. Reappraisal and Reflection

I n the Harvard Business School's seminar on Case Method Teaching, we learned in two different ways. The more overt way is a unique kind of textual analysis, which is performed on a "case": a pedagogic problem that is phrased as an incomplete narrative. The assigned task is to propose and justify a solution or ending. A class, however, typically produces more than one solution or ending, so a debate ensues: Which is better? Why? The answers are perhaps conclusive, perhaps not. What matters is not the achievement of a single or "right" reading but rather the generation of readings and the communal judgment of those readings.

But we also learned by watching this performance, by observing Professor C. Roland Christensen teach and ourselves learn. Each member of the seminar is thus both performer and observer—as is the leader himself. Such duality seems difficult but, with practice, we found ourselves shifting roles and perspectives with surprising facility. And the more proficient we became at this back-and-forth movement, the more we learned. Among other things, we learned that observation is not a passive or neutral state. Like the more overt performances of the seminar—the reading, discussing, and judging of cases—the watching of these performances is itself an act: an event that has consequences and, moreover, that can itself be discussed. The heuristic form of the seminar thus became part of its content, its methodology one of its recurrent topics. In other words, we learned that it is not only possible, but instructive to be of two minds at once. The built-in self-consciousness of teaching ourselves how to teach kept our minds both open and critical, equally ready to entertain alternatives and to analyze those alternatives.

* * *

The leader would begin each class with a five- to ten-minute reassessment of the last class—a mini lecture that transformed us from disparate individuals back into the communal organism that we were when we last met. Then two members of the seminar would lead off, presenting their analyses of the assigned case. General discussion would follow. Because we did not know in advance who would be called on, we all came prepared. The leader, however, would choose the two before he began his reassessment: five to ten minutes is sufficient to gather one's thoughts if one is prepared, but not

The Art of Leading a Discussion

ADENA ROSMARIN

Adena Rosmarin is an associate professor of English at the University of Texas at Austin. In 1980–1981 she was an Andrew W. Mellon Faculty Fellow at Harvard University and in 1984–1985 an Ethel Wattis Kimball Fellow at the Stanford Humanities Center.

enough if one has walked in "cold." We learned to be ready to be surprised. Class would end with the leader summing up his reactions both to the case *and* to the class. He would also anticipate the next case. These openings and closings framed and linked our classes, making them at once self-contained and part of a sequence. Put otherwise, the "story" of our seminar had a structure or plot. It possessed the formal dynamics of beginning and ending as well as the affective dynamics of anticipation and surprise.

Between the beginning and end, however, lies the elusive middle: the endlessly variable discussion that is at once the primary topic of the seminar and its primary event. Despite this variability, however, we were always asking one question: What makes a discussion "good"? One answer that stands out in my mind is Christensen's emphasis on emotional control. He taught, both by statement and by act, that each class (meaning each group of people as well as each of their meetings) has an emotional tone that is not only not incidental and random, but instead, is always consequential and potentially designed. For example, to "heat up" a class: be particular rather than general; call on individuals who face each other in the discussion circle; call on students who tend to make personal and opinionated statements rather than analytic or reflexive ones. In general, the greater the abstraction and the fewer the adjectives, the cooler the tone. Moreover, the timing of this emotional peak is as important as its actual happening. If it comes too soon, the rest of the class period will seem anticlimactic, a time for looking at the watch and out the window. If it comes too late, the chance to make sense of it, to reflect upon the strategies that make it happen, is lost. The class ends without concluding, and we walk out without the very lesson we gathered to learn.

Another answer to the question of what makes a discussion good is the seminar's reiterated and dramatized lesson that students and statements are not only what they seem. As in life, statements in class often carry many messages in addition to the obvious or denotative. A statement, in other words, is not only a statement, but also an act. We learned to look for this performative "content," for all the reasons that—in addition to truth-saying—impel people to say what they do. For example: because hostile statements, especially those made early in the semester, usually enact hostility not to you but rather to your role, your statements should perform

your awareness of and response to this fact. Indeed, the hostile student is an invaluable if not always entirely manageable catalyst. Such students can and should be used to dramatize your classes, not allowed to ruin them. The idea is to let their energy bounce off you onto the rest of the class, to turn their pointed antagonism into a communal agon, the pedagogic triumph we call a lively debate.

The seminar also taught that physical things are important. Your movements and gestures can focus a discussion, reveal or conceal your attitude, give you time to think, give your class time to think, break or build tension, and, in sum, create or alter any mood. Moving toward one student and away from another, sitting on the desk, standing up, taking off your jacket and rolling up your sleeves, walking to the window and looking out, making notes as a student talks, checking your watch—all can shift the mood, pace, and even the conclusions of the class. Once again, we learned that things are neither as incidental nor as random as they seem; that, in particular, every physical act is part of the always-developing contract a teacher makes with the class, a contract that at once resists change and makes any change significant. Dress and address are also part of this contract. Christensen, for example, would set the "discussion group" atmosphere by removing his jacket (I sometimes wondered if he put it on when leaving his office just so he could take it off in class), by seating us in a circle, by putting everyone on a first-name basis.

Of course, the driving and directional energy of any good discussion class comes from the teacher's questions. And the best questions are those that seem as spontaneous as they are probing, that seem to be spur-of-the-moment responses to the classroom drama. In other words, they are the very questions that seem most immune to pedagogic analysis. Our seminar leader, however, showed us that this spontaneity can itself be conceptualized and planned—hence, his *typology of questions*. First, the exploratory questions: What are the "facts"? What went wrong? What can be done? Then, the challenge or testing questions: Are these solutions or interpretations adequate to the problem? Are others possible? Where might these plans go wrong? Next, the contextual and relational questions, the weaving devices that at once broaden the perspective of the class and begin the process of tying things together: How is this solution like that solution? How is it different? What *kinds* of solutions do we have? (This last question is especially effective when schematized on the board.) Then come the priority questions: Which is the best solution? Why? And finally, the concluding and conceptualizing questions: What have we learned? What are the principles involved in the choices we made? How do they relate to choices we've made in previous classes? The most important thing to remember about questions, however, is this: "A good question is never answered." It always has offspring. It always engenders more questions and thus more thought.

Good questions are undeniably hard to come by. But good responses are even trickier—harder to plan out in advance and more difficult to predict in the midst. The cardinal rule here is that *some* response is inevitable: no matter what you do or don't do, say or don't say, *you are responding.* Still, you do have several basic choices. Will you respond to stated content or performed content? Will you respond by passing the question or statement on to the class? Or will you answer it yourself? In the last instance you may: (1) restate neutrally—a neutrality that is itself a kind of comment; (2) restate but also add or qualify; (3) noticeably reword, in order to turn the discussion; (4) put your response on the board. This last act, of course, always involves at least one of the previous three. But whatever you do, always keep in mind that *any* verbal response slows down the class. Thus, the less you say in the early stages of discussion the better. The idea is to build momentum.

Speaking of momentum, don't call on the student who has had his or her hand up for a long time. Unfair as this may seem to the individual in question, it is eminently fair to the class, for when the hand goes up, the brain goes off. Students mentally stop the discussion at the moment they think of their comment, and discussions—like conversations—are sensitive to the ongoing moment. In our seminar, Christensen would often solve the problem of unfairness and at the same time teach us how to notice and handle the problem: when he called upon a student who had been waiting for an unusually long time to speak, he would ask, "Have we gone past your comment?" This dramatized insight into the radical temporality and organization of all "talk" characterizes both his attention to practical detail and his power to generalize such details, making them teachable.

Finally, the case method. The case is the text, the topic, the *sine qua non* of this seminar. But cases,

like students and their comments, are more complex than they seem. On the one hand, a case needs to be read naively, as a "slice of life." It must seem to be real in order for its reader to take it seriously and make the analogy to life. On the other hand, a case is not a slice of life. It is a pedagogic, manifestly rhetorical, and often devious instrument: an interpretation of life that is designed to instruct its readers. The difficult status of case/text can be expressed theoretically, either as an ontological ambivalence— it is at once what it seems and more than it seems— or as a heuristic complexity. In practice, however, this difficulty means that the reader of a case/text must understand it as the coincident speech of two narrators: one who tells it like it is, and one who tells this telling for a reason.

The doubleness is frequently encountered in literary texts. The narration of Nelly in *Wuthering Heights,* for example, is not simply a means of representing the Cathy-Heathcliff story. It is also meant to be understood as Nelly's attempt to argue the importance of her role in that story and, at the same time, as her attempt to displace onto others the guilt she incurred by playing that role. Parables and fables even more obviously exemplify this narratorial doubleness: they are meant to be taken as real *and* as designed. They mirror the world, but they also point a moral or, as we might say, make a case.

Reading with an eye to this narratorial doubleness, then, is not unusual per se. We are simply not used to reading nonliterary texts in this way. Nevertheless, the most important interpretive lesson taught in the seminar was precisely the importance of this double vision. If we see only naively, attend only to appearances, we never learn how to *see* the performative complexity of texts or, for that matter, of events. Because the fact that something is true is never sufficient reason for saying or writing it, and because there is always a purpose, a full understanding of a case requires that we not only solve the particular problem it poses, but also that we attend to the case author's reasons for posing this problem. What, in sum, is the problem-solving lesson we are meant to learn?

We end, then, where we began: with a complex, perhaps paradoxical act. Just as in teaching ourselves how to teach we were always both performing and watching that performance (trying to analyze and conceptualize it), so in reading a case we are always both encountering life and watching that encounter, trying to discover its *raison d'etre*. This juxtaposition, of course, suggests a more-than-incidental relationship between our reflexive activity as members of a teaching seminar and the reflexive act of reading a case. Indeed, I would posit their virtual identity as self-conscious, interpretive acts and, further, suggest that in this identity lies the deepest art of the seminar. Just as discussing what we were doing as students and teachers taught us how to do it better, so discussing the heuristic purposefulness of cases taught us how to read them better. These were the discussions, then, that taught the largest lesson of the discussion seminar: whether reading an event or reading a text, the goal is never simply a "knowing that," but always also a "knowing how."[1]

* * *

Such was the experience of the Harvard seminar. But I am writing this from a distance—four years later, at the Stanford Humanities Center—and this distance raises questions. How does looking back on an experience affect that experience? And how has that experience affected the intervening years? In what ways has it shaped the present?

We can best answer such questions by reminding ourselves that, like all questions, they largely dictate their possible answers. In particular, whether they are asked by Romantic poets or contemporary historians or each of us in conversations, classrooms, and private meditations, these questions all presuppose and perpetuate a basic distinction between the past and the present. Thus, to talk in terms of effect and relationships is necessarily to assume not only the sought-for connection between times and experiences, but also their essential difference and separateness. We seek only to connect what we think is apart.

Yet this separation is only a loose or commonsensical distinction, for, in general, it is impossible to say exactly where an experience or event ends and our understanding of or writing about it begins. In the case of the seminar, it is true that it happened at a particular time and place, but it is also true that the seminar continues to happen as long as it is written about—and as long as those writings are read. Evidence of this continuity can be found in the fact that, as with any event, there are multiple ways of telling its story. This multiplicity has led to the distinction—well known in literary studies—between *story* (the event as it "really" happened) and *discourse* (our writing about or textualization of that event). Recently, however, this distinction has been questioned: Is there ever really a story that exists apart from and independent of its telling—an experience apart from its narratized understanding? We can turn to the seminar itself for answers, the case itself exemplifying the inseparability of story and discourse: it seeks to convince us that its discourse is the "real" story, even as it also invites us to seek a rhetorical story, the pedagogical lesson that is deviously, if instructively, concealed. Yet if we find this story, where is it found but in the discourse? It has, if we think about it, no separate existence. But let us consider another example as well—the stories that framed each class. Christensen, as observed earlier, characteristically opened a class meeting by telling us the story of the previous meeting. And he characteristically closed a class by telling another story, his desired "plot" for the next class. Did either story ever exactly correspond to the experience it narrated? The disparity in time alone—the time it takes an event to happen versus the time it takes to narrate that happening—tells us that story and discourse coincide only by rare chance or peculiar design.

Like the cases that functioned as the formal texts of the seminar, the retrospective stories were always true. That is, they contained no false information—although much, of necessity, was left out, and emphases, again of necessity, were added. The anticipatory stories, however, did not always "come true." The class not infrequently took off in unplanned directions, often to everyone's benefit. But did these anticipatory stories then become bad stories? Not necessarily or even probably. These stories are strategic and therefore should be judged as strategies, as instruments for affecting an audience in a certain way. Their value lies in their purpose, which, in this situation, is to inspire a certain kind of debate. Put in pragmatist terms, these stories become "true" when they work—even if they don't come true in the more usual or correspondent sense. And the retrospective stories are also, if less obviously, true or valuable for the same strategic reason. Both kinds of framing stories are properly

---

1. The distinction between "knowing that" and "knowing how" can be traced back to Gilbert Ryle, *The Concept of Mind* (London: Hutchinson, 1949), pp. 25–61.

valued as complex instruments of understanding and action rather than as simple mirrors of either what was or what was to be.

Analogously, the act of writing—for me, the act of writing about the seminar and, also, of writing the case "Sheila Lund"—refuses the distinction between then and now, between story and discourse. It teaches that the writer's looking back is less a recovery than a creation, and what is created is an experience that, like all written experience, is neither distant nor lost but, rather, permanently present tense: I took the seminar in 1980 but in this essay I say that the experience of the seminar is like this. The event of taking the seminar and the event of writing about it are two different experiences, and if all the seminar members were to write essays, there would be that many more experiences. Many of these would, of course, be similar but each would also be distinct. The same story would have engendered many different discourses. All of which is to say that the experience of the seminar lies not in the simple historical fact of its occurrence, but in its complexly continuing recurrence through the subsequent acts of its participants. The seminar is less like something recollected than like a living and thus changing organism, remade anew with each act of writing and rewriting.

And, of course, with each act of teaching. It is impossible, having taken the seminar, to return naively to a classroom. You have learned the import of gestures and the importance of design. But, once again, questions are raised. What does it mean to have learned a lesson? Is it, for example, when you have memorized the grammar and vocabulary of a language, or when you can speak that language—saying sentences that, in the strict sense, have not been learned *until* they are said? One must, I think, answer in favor of the latter. Similarly, learning *in* the seminar is, once again, something that cannot be distinguished from learning *outside* the seminar. The lesson learned *is* the lesson as it is performed or, more exactly, as it is reperformed—one year later, four years later. Each performance is different, yet all are also continuations of the seminar, extended in time and place and personality.

For me, this last year at the Stanford Humanities Center was the most interesting of these performances—the one that, in fact, led to the writing of this essay. I had organized a faculty seminar, composed of fellows of the Center and members of various Stanford departments. There were about fifteen participants—a group that, like the earlier seminar, was interdisciplinary. The benefit of this disparate mix, which in the Harvard seminar included not only assorted humanists but business school faculty as well, is, most obviously, that one hears viewpoints and acquires otherwise inaccessible information. But more important is the fact that one's discourse, whether spoken or written, assumes greater suasive burdens when directed at a nonspecialist audience. The locutions, allusions, patterns of reasoning, and genres of "evidence" that normally lie all too readily at hand must be questioned. And the effort of this questioning can prove catalytic if—and this is a necessary though not a sufficient condition—these disparate minds have convened to work on a common problem.

What brought the Stanford participants together was a common interest in narrative. We asked a question: "What role does narrative play in history, anthropology, and literary criticism?" We answered ourselves by discussing the work of not only practicing historians, anthropologists, and critics, but also of theorists in those disciplines. We began with Herbert Lindenberger's "Toward a New History in Literary Studies," an essay that maps the multiple historical impulses that increasingly inform literary studies. Following this overview, we looked into the use of narrative in anthropology, reading works of Clifford Geertz and Renato Rosaldo. Historiography was the next step: we read Hayden White on "The Question of Narrative in Contemporary Historical Theory," and Louis Mink on the same question. We concluded in two ways: first, by reading Paul Ricoeur's *Time and Narrative*, a densely theoretical inquiry, and—in a separate session—John Felstiner's "'Ziv, that light': Translation and Tradition in Paul Celan." This last session had the character of a workshop. Like Lindenberger and Rosaldo, Felstiner is at Stanford and was a member of the seminar. He presented his (at that time) in-progress essay, and discussion focused on the actual practice of constructing narratives—in this case, a biographical narrative—as modes of explanation and suasion.

At three of the six sessions, then, an author was present, and this presence, of course, made a difference. The lead-off questions were different: when the author was present, we began by asking him how he came to write his essay; otherwise, we began by asking ourselves why we were reading it and what consequences the argument had in our different disciplines. Further, the author's presence meant that attention was focused on a person as well as a text. And this person was also an interpreter, albeit privileged, of the text he had written. The resulting debate was a complex admixture: self-interpretation, retrospection, and tentative proposals complicated our discussion of the text and, looking at the seminar as a whole, gave a lateral pattern to our linear progression.

Finally, my self-defined role was not to teach this group, but to lead it. It was, I thought, important that the imposition of form be minimal, and yet I knew it was equally important that there be a form—that the readings build upon each other, that the meetings (both individually and taken together) describe an ascending curve of involvement and difficulty, that the group conclude, not simply end. These desiderata, of course, are endemic to all discussion teaching, but because this was a faculty group, it more closely approximated the Harvard seminar—specifically in this problem of devising minimal form—than had any intervening class. Yet, if the Stanford gathering is clearly the progeny of that earlier gathering, it is no less clear that the reverse is also the case: that the teaching seminar *is*, in large part, what my and the other participants' writing and teaching have become. The argument of this postcript, in sum, is that no rigorous distinction can ultimately be made between script and postscript, between lesson and performance. The Harvard seminar, by overtly refusing such seemingly intuitive distinctions, prefigured its own future power, its persistence in time. It is, in what I would argue is a quite literal sense, still meeting.

The Crisis of Confidence in Professional Knowledge

Although our society has become thoroughly dependent on professionals, so much so that the conduct of business, industry, government, education, and everyday life would be unthinkable without them, there are signs of a growing crisis of confidence in the professions. In many well-publicized scandals, professionals have been found willing to use their special positions for private gain. Professionally designed solutions to public problems have had unanticipated consequences, sometimes worse than the problem they were intended to solve. The public has shown an increasing readiness to call for external regulations of professional practice. Laymen have been increasingly disposed to turn to the courts for defense against professional incompetence or venality. The professional's traditional claims to privileged social position and autonomy of practice have come into question as the public has begun to have doubts about professional ethics and expertise.[1] And in recent years, professionals themselves have shown signs of a loss of confidence in professional knowledge.

Not very long ago, in 1963, the editors of *Daedalus* could introduce a special volume on the professions with the sentence, "Everywhere in American life the professions are triumphant."[2] They noted the apparently limitless demand for professional services, the "shortages" of teachers and physicians, the difficulty of coordinating the proliferating technical specializations, the problem of managing the burgeoning mass of technical data. In the further essays which made up the volume, doctors, lawyers, scientists, educators, military men, and politicians articulated variations on the themes of professional triumph, overload, and growth. There were only two discordant voices. The representative of the clergy complained of declining influence and the "problem of relevance,"[3] and the city planner commented ruefully on his profession's lagging un-

The Crisis of Professional Knowledge and the Pursuit of an Epistemology of Practice

DONALD A. SCHÖN

Donald A. Schön, *Ford Professor of Urban Studies and Planning, Massachusetts Institute of Technology, prepared this article for the Harvard Business School's 75th Anniversary Colloquium on Teaching by the Case Method. The material in this essay is a condensation and recasting of material from his book,* The Reflective Practitioner *(New York: Basic Books, 1983).*

1. Everett Hughes, "The Study of Occupations," in Merton and Broom, eds., *Sociology Today* (New York: Basic Books, 1959).
2. Kenneth Lynn, Introduction to "The Professions." *Daedalus* 92, no. 4 (Fall 1963): 649.
3. James Gustafson, "The Clergy in the Unites States." *Daedalus* 92, no. 4 (Fall 1963): 743.

derstandings of the changing ills of urban areas.[4] Yet in less than a decade the discordant notes had become the dominant ones and the themes of professional triumph had virtually disappeared.

In 1972 a colloquium on professional education was held at the Massachusetts Institute of Technology. Participants included distinguished representatives of the fields of medicine, engineering, architecture, planning, psychiatry, law, divinity, education, and management. These individuals disagreed about many things, but they held one sentiment in common—a profound uneasiness about their own professions. They questioned whether professionals would effectively police themselves. They wondered whether professionals were instruments of individual well-being and social reform or were mainly interested in the preservation of their own status and privilege, caught up in the very problems they might have been expected to solve. They allowed themselves to express doubts about the relevance and remedial power of professional expertise.

It is perhaps not very difficult to account for this dramatic shift, over a single decade, in the tone of professional self-reflection. Between 1963 and 1972 there had been a disturbing sequence of events, painful for professionals and lay public alike. A professionally instrumented war had been disastrous. Social movements for peace and civil rights had begun to see the professions as elitest servants of established interests. The much-proclaimed shortages of scientists, teachers, and physicians seemed to have evaporated. Professionals seemed powerless to relieve the rapidly shifting "crises" of the cities—poverty, environmental pollution, and energy. There were scandals of Medicare and, at the end of the decade, Watergate. Cumulatively, these events created doubts about professionally conceived strategies of diagnosis and cure. They pointed to the overwhelming complexity of the phenomena with which professionals were trying to cope. They led to skepticism about the adequacy of professional knowledge, with its theories and techniques, to cure the deeper causes of societal distress.

Sharing, in greater or lesser degree, these sentiments of doubt and unease, the participants in the MIT colloquium tried to analyze their predicament.

4. William Alonso, "Cities and City Planners." *Daedalus* 92, no. 4 (Fall 1963): 838.

Some of them believed that social change had created problems ill-suited to the traditional division of labor. A noted engineer observed that "education no longer fits the niche, or the niche no longer fits education." The dean of a medical school spoke of the complexity of a huge health care system only marginally susceptible to the interventions of the medical profession. The dean of a school of management referred to the puzzle of educating managers for judgment and action under conditions of uncertainty.

Some were troubled by the existence of an irreducible residue of art in professional practice. The art deemed indispensable even to scientific research and engineering design seemed resistant to codification. As one participant observed, "If it's invariant and known, it can be taught; but it isn't invariant."

Professional education emphasized problem solving, but the most urgent and intractable issues of professional practice were those of problem finding. "Our interest," as one participant put it, "is not only how to pour the concrete for the highway, but what highway to build? When it comes to designing a ship, the question we have to ask is, which ship makes sense in terms of the problem of transportation?"

And representatives of architecture, planning, social work, and psychiatry spoke of the pluralism of their schools. Different schools held different and conflicting views of the competences to be acquired, [of] the problem to be solved, even of the nature of the professions themselves. A leading professor of psychiatry described his field as a "babble of voices."

Finally, there was a call for the liberation of the professions from the tyranny of the university-based professional schools. Everett Hughes, one of the founders of the sociology of the professions, declared that "American universities are products of the late nineteenth and early twentieth centuries. The question is, how do you break them up in some way—at least get some group of young people who are free of them? How do you make them free to do something new and different?"

The years that have passed since the 1972 colloquium have tended to reinforce its conclusions. In the early 1980s, no profession could celebrate itself in triumphant tones. In spite of the continuing eagerness of the young to embark on apparently secure and remunerative professional careers, professionals were still criticized, and criticized themselves, for failing both to adapt to a changing social reality and to live up to their own standards of practice. There was widespread recognition of the absence or loss of a stable institutional framework of purpose and knowledge within which professions can live out their roles and confidently exercise their skills.

In retrospect, then, it is not difficult to see why participants in the 1972 colloquium should have puzzled over the troubles of their professions. They were beginning to become aware of the indeterminate zones of practice—the situations of complexity and uncertainty, the unique cases that require artistry, the elusive task of problem setting, the multiplicity of professional identities—that have since become increasingly visible and problematic. Nevertheless, there is something strange about their disquiet. For professionals in many different fields do sometimes find ways of coping effectively, even wisely, with situations of complexity and uncertainty. If the element of art in professional practice is not invariant, known, and teachable, it does appear occasionally to be learnable. Problem setting is an activity in which some professionals engage with recognizable skill. And students and practitioners do occasionally make thoughtful choices from among the multiple views of professional identity.

Why, then, should a group of eminent professionals have been so troubled by the evidence of indeterminacy in professional practice?

It is not, I think, that they were unaware of the ways in which some practitioners cope reasonably well with situations of indeterminacy. Indeed, they might easily have counted themselves among those who do so. Rather, I suspect, they were troubled because they could not readily account for the coping process. Complexity and uncertainty are sometimes dissolved, but not by applying specialized knowledge to well-defined tasks. Artistry is not reducible to the exercise of describable routines. Problem finding has no place in a body of knowledge concerned exclusively with problem solving. In order to choose among competing paradigms of professional practice, one cannot rely on professional expertise. The eminent professionals were disturbed, I think, to discover that the competences they were beginning to see as central to professional practice had no place in their underlying model of professional knowledge.

In the following pages, I shall describe this underlying model—this implicit epistemology of prac-

tice—and I shall outline a fundamental dilemma of practice and teaching to which it leads. I shall propose that we seek an alternative epistemology of practice grounded in observation and analysis of the artistry competent practitioners sometimes bring to the indeterminate zones of their practice. I shall attempt a preliminary description and illustration of the "reflection-in-action" essential to professional artistry, and I shall suggest some of its implications for professional education.

The Dominant Model of Professional Knowledge

The epistemology of professional practice which dominates most thinking and writing about the professions, and which is built into the very structure of professional schools and research institutions, has been clearly set forth in two recent essays on professional education. Both of these treat rigorous professional practice as an exercise of technical rationality, that is, as an application of research-based knowledge to the solution of problems of instrumental choice.

Edgar Schein, in his *Professional Education*,[5] proposes a threefold division of professional knowledge:

1. An *underlying discipline* or *basic science* component upon which the practice rests or from which it is developed.
2. An *applied science* or *"engineering"* component from which many of the day-to-day diagnostic procedures and problem-solutions are derived.
3. A *skills and attitudinal* component that concerns the actual performance of services to the client, using the underlying basic and applied knowledge.

In Schein's view, these components constitute a hierarchy which may be read in terms of application, justification, and status. The application of basic science yields engineering, which in turn provides models, rules, and techniques applicable to the instrumental choices of everyday practice. The actual performance of services "rests on" applied science, which rests, in turn, on the foundation of basic science. In the epistemological pecking order, basic science is highest in methodological rigor and

5. Edgar Schein, *Professional Education*, (New York: McGraw-Hill) p. 43.

purity, its practitioners superior in status to those who practice applied science, problem solving, or service delivery.

Nathan Glazer, in a much-quoted article, argues that the schools of such professions as social work, education, divinity, and town planning are caught in a hopeless predicament.[6] These "minor" professions, beguiled by the success of the "major" professions of law, medicine, and business, have tried to substitute a basis in scientific knowledge for their traditional reliance on experienced practice. In this spirit, they have placed their schools within universities. Glazer believes, however, that their aspirations are doomed to failure. The "minor" professions lack the essential conditions of the "major" ones. They lack stable institutional contexts of practice, fixed and unambiguous ends which "settle men's minds,"[7] and a basis in systematic scientific knowledge. They cannot apply scientific knowledge to the solving of instrumental problems, and they are, therefore, unable to produce a rigorous curriculum of professional education.

> Can these fields (education, city planning, social work, and divinity) settle on a fixed form of training, a fixed content of professional knowledge, and follow the models of medicine, law, and business? I suspect not because the discipline of a fixed and unambiguous end in a fixed institutional setting is not given to them. And *thus* [my emphasis] the base of knowledge which is unambiguously indicated as relevant for professional education is also not given.[8]

Glazer and Schein share an epistemology of professional practice rooted historically in the positivist philosophy which so powerfully shaped both the modern university and the modern conception of the proper relationship of theory and practice.[9] Rigorous professional practice is conceived as essentially technical. Its rigor depends on the use of describable, testable, replicable techniques derived from scientific research, based on knowledge that is objective, consensual, cumulative, and convergent. On this view, for example, engineering is an application of engineering science; rigorous management depends on the use of management science; and policymaking can become rigorous when it is based on policy science.

Practice can be construed as technical, in this sense, only when certain things are kept clearly separate from one another. Deciding must be kept separate from doing. The rigorous practitioner uses his professional knowledge to *decide* on the means best-suited to his ends, his *action* serving to "implement" technically sound decisions. Means must be clearly separated from ends. Technical means are variable, appropriate, or inappropriate, according to the situation. But the ends of practice must be "fixed and unambiguous," like Glazer's examples of profit, health, and success in litigation; how is it possible, otherwise, to evolve a base of applicable professional knowledge? And finally research must be kept separate from practice. For research can yield new knowledge only in the protected setting of the scholar's study or in the carefully controlled environment of a scientific laboratory, whereas the world of practice is notoriously unprotected and uncontrollable.

These tenets of the positivist epistemology of practice are still built into our institutions, even when their inhabitants no longer espouse them. Just as Thorstein Veblen propounded some seventy years ago,[10] the university and the research institute are sheltered from the troublesome world of practice. Research and practice are presumed to be linked by an exchange in which researchers offer theories and techniques applicable to practice problems, and practitioners, in return, give researchers new problems to work on and practical tests of the utility of research results. The normative curriculum of professional education, as Schein describes it, still follows the hierarchy of professional knowledge. First, students are exposed to the relevant basic science, then to the relevant applied science, and finally to a practicum in which they are presumed to learn to apply classroom knowledge to the problems of practice. Medical education offers the

6. Nathan Glazer, "The Schools of the Minor Professions," in *Minerva* 12, no. 3 (1974): 362.

7. Ibid., p. 363.

8. Ibid., p. 363.

9. For a discussion of positivism and its influence on prevailing epistemological views, see Jergen Habermas, *Knowledge and Human Interests* (Boston, Mass.: Beacon Press, 1968). And for a discussion of the influence of positivist doctrines on the shaping of the modern university, see Edward Shils, "The Order of Learning in the United States from 1865 to 1920: The Ascendancy of the Universities," *Minerva* 16, no. 2, (1978).

10. See Thorstein Veblen, *The Higher Learning in America*, reprint of the 1918 edition. (New York City: August M. Kelley, 1965).

prototype for such a curriculum, and its language of "diagnosis," "cure," "laboratory," and "clinic" have long since diffused to other professions.

From the perspective of this model of professional knowledge, it is not difficult to understand why practitioners should be puzzled by their own performance in the indeterminate zones of practice. Their performance does not fit the criteria of technical rationality; it cuts across the dichotomies built into the positivist epistemology of practice. Artistry, for example, is not only in the deciding but also in the doing. When planners or managers convert an uncertain situation into a solvable problem, they construct—as John Dewey pointed out long ago—not only the means to be deployed but the ends-in-view to be achieved. In such problem setting, ends and means are reciprocally determined. And often, in the unstable world of practice—where methods and theories developed in one context are unsuited to another—practitioners function as researchers, inventing the techniques and models appropriate to the situation at hand.

The Dilemma of Rigor and Relevance

For practitioners, educators, and students of the professions, the positivist epistemology of practice contributes to an urgent dilemma of rigor or relevance.

Given the dominant view of professional rigor—the view which prevails in the intellectual climate of the universities and is embedded in the institutional arrangements of professional education and research—rigorous practice depends on well-formed problems[11] of instrumental choice to whose solutions research-based theory and technique are applicable. But real-world problems do not come well formed. They tend to present themselves, in the contrary, as messy, indeterminate, problematic situations. When a civil engineer worries about what road to build, for example, he does not have a problem he can solve by an application of locational techniques or decision theory. He confronts a complex and ill-defined situation in which geographic, financial, economic, and political factors are usually mixed up together. If he is to arrive at a well-formed problem, he must construct it from the materials of the problematic situation. And the

problem of problem setting is not a well-formed problem.[12]

When a practitioner sets a problem, he chooses what he will treat as the "things" of the situation. He decides what he will attend to and what he will ignore. He names the objects of his attention and frames them in an appreciative context which sets a direction for action. A vague worry about hunger or malnourishment may be framed, for example, as a problem of selecting an optimal diet. But situations of malnourishment may also be framed in many different ways.[13] Economists, environmental scientists, nutrition scientists, agronomists, planners, engineers, and political scientists debate over the nature of the malnourishment problem, and their discussions have given rise to a multiplicity of problem settings worthy of *Rashomon*. Indeed, the practice of malnourishment planning is largely taken up with the task of constructing the problem to be solved.

When practitioners succeed in converting a problematic situation to a well-formed problem, or in resolving a conflict over the proper framing of a practitioner's role in a situation, they engage in a kind of inquiry which cannot be subsumed under a model of technical problem solving. Rather, it is through the work of naming and framing that the exercise of technical rationality becomes possible.

Similarly, the artistic processes by which practitioners sometimes make sense of unique cases, and the art they sometimes bring to everyday practice, do not meet the prevailing criteria of rigorous practice. Often, when a competent practitioner recognizes in a maze of symptoms the pattern of a disease, constructs a basis for coherent design in the peculiarities of a building site, or discerns an understandable structure in a jumble of materials, he does something for which he cannot give a complete or even a reasonably accurate description. Practitioners make judgments of quality for which they cannot state adequate criteria, display skills for which they cannot describe procedures or rules.

---

11. I have taken this term from Herbert Simon, who gives a particularly useful example of a well-formed problem in *The Science of the Artificial* (Cambridge, Mass.: MIT Press, 1972).

12. Martin Rein and I have written about problem setting in "Problem Setting in Policy Research," in Carol Weiss, ed., *Using Social Research in Public Policy Making* (Lexington, Mass.: D. C. Heath, 1977).

13. For an example of multiple views of the malnourishment problem, see Berg, Scrimshaw and Call, eds., *Nutrition, National Development, and Planning* (Cambridge, Mass.: MIT Press, 1973).

By defining rigor only in terms of technical rationality, we exclude as nonrigorous much of what competent practitioners actually do, including the skillful performance of problem setting and judgment on which technical problem solving depends. Indeed, we exclude the most important components of competent practice.

In the varied topography of professional practice, there is a high, hard ground which overlooks a swamp. On the high ground, manageable problems lend themselves to solution through the use of research-based theory and technique. In the swampy lowlands, problems are messy and confusing and incapable of technical solution. The irony of this situation is that the problems of the high ground tend to be relatively unimportant to individuals or to society at large—however great their technical interest may be—while in the swamp lie the problems of greatest human concern. The practitioner is confronted with a choice. Shall he remain on the high ground where he can solve relatively unimportant problems according to his standards of rigor, or shall he descend to the swamp of important problems and nonrigorous inquiry?

Consider medicine, engineering, and agronomy—three of Glazer's major or near-major professions. In these fields, there are areas in which problems are clearly defined, goals are relatively fixed, and phenomena lend themselves to the categories of available theory and technique. Here, practitioners can function effectively as technical experts. But when one or more of these conditions is lacking, competent performance is no longer a matter of exclusively technical expertise. Medical technologies like kidney dialysis or tomography have created demands which stretch the nation's willingness to invest in medical care. How should physicians behave? How should they try to influence or accommodate to health policy? Engineering solutions which seem powerful and elegant when judged from a relatively narrow perspective may have a wider range of consequences which degrade the environment, generate unacceptable risk, or put excessive demands on scarce resources. How should engineers take these factors into account in their actual designing? When agronomists recommend efficient methods of soil cultivation that favor the use of large landholdings, they may undermine the viability of the small family farms on which peasant economies depend. How should the practice of

agronomy take such considerations into account? These are not problems, properly speaking, but problematic situations from which problems must be constructed. If practitioners choose not to ignore them they must approach them through kinds of inquiry which are, according to the dominant model of technical rationality, unrigorous.

The doctrine of technical rationality, promulgated and maintained in the universities and especially in the professional schools, infects the young professional-in-training with a hunger for technique. Many students of urban planning, for example, are impatient with anything other than "hard skills." In schools of management, students often chafe under the discipline of endless case analysis; they want to learn the techniques and algorithms which are, as they see it, the key to high starting salaries. Yet a professional who really tried to confine his practice to the rigorous applications of research-based technique would find not only that he could not work on the most important problems but that he could not practice in the real world at all.

Nearly all professional practitioners experience a version of the dilemma of rigor or relevance, and they respond to it in one of several ways. Some of them choose the swampy lowland, deliberately immersing themselves in confusing but crucially important situations. When they are asked to describe their methods of inquiry, they speak of experience, trial and error, intuition or muddling through. When teachers, social workers, or planners operate in this vein, they tend to be afflicted with a nagging sense of inferiority in relation to those who present themselves as models of technical rigor. When physicians or engineers do so, they tend to be troubled by the discrepancy between the technical rigor of the "hard" zones of their practice and the apparent sloppiness of the "soft" ones.

Practitioners who opt for the high ground confine themselves to a narrowly technical practice and pay a price for doing so. Operations research, systems analysis, policy analysis, and some management science are examples of practices built around the use of formal, analytical models. In the early years of the development of these professions, following World War II, there was a climate of optimism about the power of formal models to solve real-world problems. In subsequent decades, however, there was increasing recognition of the limited applicability of formal models, especially in situations of high complexity and uncertainty.[14] Some practitioners have responded by confining themselves to a narrow class of well-formed problems—in inventory control for example. Some researchers have continued to develop formal models for use in problems of high complexity and uncertainty, quite undeterred by the troubles incurred whenever a serious attempt is made to put such models into practice. They pursue an agenda driven by evolving questions of modeling theory and techniques, increasingly divergent from the contexts of actual practice.

Practitioners may try, on the other hand, to cut the situations of practice to fit their models, employing for this purpose one of several procrustean strategies. They may become selectively inattentive to data incongruent with their theories,[15] as some educators preserve their confidence in "competency testing" by ignoring the kinds of competence that competency testing fails to detect. Physicians or therapists may use junk categories like "patient resistance" to explain away the cases in which an indicated treatment fails to lead to cure.[16] And social workers may try to make their technical expertise effective by exerting unilateral control over the practice situation—for example, by removing "unworthy" clients from the case rolls.

Those who confine themselves to a limited range of technical problems on the high ground, or cut the situations of practice to fit available techniques, seek a world in which technical rationality works. Even those who choose the swamp tend to pay homage to prevailing models of rigor. What they know how to do, they have no way of describing as rigorous.

Writers about the professions tend to follow similar paths. Both Glazer and Schein, for example, recognize the indeterminate zones of professional practice. But Glazer relegates them to the "minor" professions, of which he despairs. And Schein locates what he calls "divergent" phenomena of uncertainty, complexity, and uniqueness in concrete practice situations, while at the same time regarding professional knowledge as increasingly "convergent." He thinks convergent knowledge may be ap-

plied to divergent practice through the exercise of "divergent skills"[17]—about which, however, he is able to say very little. For if divergent skills were treated in terms of theory or technique, they would belong to convergent professional knowledge; and if they are neither theory nor technique, they cannot be described as knowledge at all. Rather, they function as a kind of junk category which serves to protect an underlying model of technical rationality.

Yet the epistemology of practice embedded in our universities and research institutions—ingrained in our habits of thought about professional knowledge, and at the root of the dilemma of rigor or relevance—has lost its hold on the field that nurtured it. Among philosophers of science, no one wants any longer to be called a positivist.[18] There is a rebirth of interest in the ancient topics of craft, artistry, and myth—topics whose fate positivism seemed once to have finally sealed. Positivism and the positivist epistemology of practice now seem to rest on a particular *view* of science, one now largely discredited.

It is timely, then, to reconsider the question of professional knowledge. Perhaps there is an epistemology of practice which takes full account of the competence practitioners sometimes display in situations of uncertainty, complexity, and uniqueness. Perhaps there is a way of looking at problem setting and intuitive artistry which presents these activities as describable and susceptible to a kind of rigor that falls outside the boundaries of technical rationality.

Reflection-in-Action

When we go about the spontaneous, intuitive performance of the actions of everyday life, we show ourselves to be knowledgeable in a special way. Often, we cannot say what we know. When

14. See Russell Ackoff, "The Future of Operational Research is Past," *Journal of Operational Research Soc.* 30 (1979): 93–104.

15. I have taken this phrase from the work of the psychiatrist, Harry Stack Sullivan.

16. The term is Clifford Geertz's. See *The Interpretation of Cultures: Selected Essays* by Clifford Geertz (New York: Basic Books, 1973).

17. Schein, *Professional Education*, p. 44.

18. As Richard Bernstein has written in *The Restructuring of Social and Political Theory* (New York: Harcourt, Brace, Jovanovich, 1976), "There is not a single major thesis advanced by either nineteenth century Positivists or the Vienna Circle that has not been devastatingly criticized when measured by the Positivists' own standards for philosophical argument. The original formulations of the analytic-synthetic dichotomy and the verifiability criterion on meaning have been abandoned. It has been effectively shown that the Positivists' understanding of the natural sciences and the formal disciplines is grossly oversimplified. Whatever one's final judgment about the current disputes in the post-empiricist philosophy and history of science . . . there is rational agreement about the inadequacy of the original Positivist understanding of science, knowledge, and meaning."

we try to describe it, we find ourselves at a loss, or we produce descriptions that are obviously inappropriate. Our knowing is ordinarily tacit, implicit in our patterns of action and in our feel for the stuff with which we are dealing. It seems right to say that our knowing is *in* our action. And similarly, the workaday life of the professional practitioner reveals, in its recognitions, judgments and skills—a pattern of tacit knowing-in-action.

Once we put technical rationality aside, thereby giving up our view of competent practice as an *application* of knowledge to instrumental decisions, there is nothing strange about the idea that a kind of knowing is inherent in intelligent action. Common sense admits the category of know-how, and it does not stretch common sense very much to say that the know-how is *in* the action—that a tightrope walker's know-how, for example, lies in, and is revealed by, the way he takes his trip across the wire; or that a big-league pitcher's know-how is in his way of pitching to a batter's weakness, changing his pace, or distributing his energies over the course of a game. There is nothing in common sense to make us say that know-how consists in rules or plans which we entertain in the mind prior to action. Although we sometimes think before acting, it is also true that in much of the spontaneous behavior of skillful practice we reveal a kind of knowing which does not stem from a prior intellectual operation.

As Gilbert Ryle puts it:

> What distinguishes sensible from silly operations is not their parentage but their procedure, and this holds no less for intellectual than for practical performances. "Intelligent" cannot be defined in terms of "intellectual" or "knowing-*how*" in terms of "knowing *that*"; "thinking what I am doing" does not connote "both thinking what to do and doing it." When I do something intelligently . . . I am doing one thing and not two. My performance has a special procedure or manner, not special antecedents.[19]

Andrew Harrison has expressed a similar thought by saying that when someone acts intellectually, he "acts his mind."[20]

Examples of intelligence in action include acts of recognition and judgment, as well as the exercise of ordinary physical skills.

Michael Polanyi has written about our ability to recognize a face in a crowd.[21] The experience of recognition can be immediate and holistic. We simply see, all of a sudden, the face of someone we know. We are aware of no antecedent reasoning and we are often unable to list the features that distinguish this face from the hundreds of others present in the crowd.

When the thing we recognize is "something wrong" or "something right," then recognition takes the form of judgment. Chris Alexander has called attention to the innumerable judgments of "mismatch"—deviations from a tacit norm—that are involved in the making of a design.[22] And Geoffrey Vickers has gone on to note that not only in artistic judgment but in all our ordinary judgments of quality, we "can recognize and describe deviations from a norm very much more clearly than we can describe the norm itself."[23] A young friend of mine who teaches tennis observes that his students have to be able to feel when they're hitting the ball right, and they have to like that feeling, as compared to the feeling of hitting it wrong; but they need not, and usually cannot, describe either the feeling of hitting it right or what they do to get that feeling. A skilled physician can sometimes recognize "a case of . . ." the moment a person walks into his office. The act of recognition comes immediately and as a whole; the physician may not be able to say, subsequently, just what led to his initial judgment.

Polanyi has described our ordinary tactile appreciation of the surface of materials. If you ask a person what he feels when he explores the surface of a table with his hand, he is apt to say that the table feels rough or smooth, sticky or slippery, but he is unlikely to say that he feels a certain compression and abrasion of his fingertips—though it must be from this kind of feeling that he gets to his appreciation of the table's surface. Polanyi speaks of perceiving *from* these fingertip sensations *to* the qualities of the surface. Similarly, when we use a stick to probe a hidden place, we focus not on the impressions of the stick on our hand but on the qualities

19. Gilbert Ryle, "On Knowing How and Knowing That," in *The Concept of Mind* (London: Hutchinson, 1949), p. 32.
20. Andrew Harrison, *Making and Thinking* (Indianapolis: Hacket, 1978).
21. Michael Polanyi, *The Tacit Dimension* (New York: Doubleday Publishing Co., 1967), p. 12.
22. Chris Alexander, *Notes Toward the Synthesis of Forum*, (Cambridge, Mass.: Harvard University Press, 1964).
23. Geoffrey Vickers, unpublished memorandum, MIT, 1978.

of the place which we apprehend through these tacit impressions. To become skillful in the use of a tool is to learn to appreciate, as it were, directly, the qualities of materials that we apprehend *through* the tacit sensations of the tool in our hand.

Chester Barnard has written of "non-logical processes" that we cannot express in words as a process of reasoning, but evince only by a judgment, decision, or action.[24] A child who has learned to throw a ball makes immediate judgments of distance, which he coordinates, tacitly, with the feeling of bodily movement involved in the act of throwing. A high-school boy, solving quadratic equations, has learned spontaneously to carry out a program of operations that he cannot describe. A practiced accountant of Barnard's acquaintance could take a balance sheet of considerable complexity and within minutes or even seconds get a significant set of facts from it, though he could not describe in words the recognitions and calculations that entered into his performance. Similarly, we are able to execute spontaneously such complex activities as crawling, walking, riding a bicycle, or juggling, without having to think, in any conscious way, what we are doing, and often without being able to give a verbal description even approximately faithful to our performance.

In spite of their tacit complexity and virtuosity, however, our spontaneous responses to the phenomena of everyday life do not always work. Sometimes our knowing-in-action yields surprises. And we often react to the unexpected by a kind of on-the-spot inquiry which I shall call *reflection-in-action*.

Sometimes this process takes the form of ordinary, on-line problem solving. It need not even be associated with a high degree of skill but may consist in an amateur's effort to acquire skill. Recently, for example, I built a wooden gate. The gate was made of wooden pickets and strapping. I had made a drawing of it, and figured out the dimensions I wanted, but I had not reckoned with the problem of keeping the structure square. I noticed, as I began to nail the strapping to the pickets, that the whole think wobbled. I knew that when I nailed in a diagonal piece, the structure would become rigid. But how would I be sure that, at that moment, the structure would be square? I stopped to think.

24. Chester Barnard, *The Functions of the Executive* (Cambridge, Mass: Harvard University Press, 1968), p. 306; first published in 1938.

There came to mind a vague memory about diagonals—that in a square, the diagonals are equal. I took a yardstick, intending to measure the diagonals, but I found it difficult to make these measurements without disturbing the structure. It occurred to me to use a piece of string. Then it became apparent that I needed precise locations from which to measure the diagonal from corner to corner. After several frustrating trials, I decided to locate the center point at each of the corners (by crossing diagonals at each corner), hammered in a nail at each of the four center points, and used the nails as anchors for the measurement string. It took several moments to figure out how to adjust the structure so as to correct the errors I found by measuring; and when I had the diagonals equal, I nailed in the piece of strapping that made the structure rigid.

Here—in an example that must have its analogues in the experience of amateur carpenters the world over—my intuitive way of going about the task led me to a surprise (the discovery of the wobble) which I interpreted as a problem. Stopping to think, I invented procedures to solve the problem, discovered further unpleasant surprises, and made further corrective inventions, including the several minor inventions necessary to make the idea of string-measurement of diagonals work.

Ordinarily, we might call such a process "trial and error." But it is not a series of random trials continued until a desired result has been produced. The process has a form—an inner logic according to which reflection on the unexpected consequences of one action influences the design of the next one. The "moments" of such a process may be described as follows:

- In the context of the performance of some task, the performer spontaneously initiates a routine of action that produces an unexpected outcome.
- The performer notices the unexpected result which he construes as a surprise—an error to be corrected, an anomaly to be made sense of, an opportunity to be exploited.
- Surprise triggers reflection, directed both to the surprising outcome and to the knowing-in-action that led to it. It is as though the performer asked himself, "What *is* this?" and at the same time, "What understandings and strategies of mine have led me to produce this?"
- The performer restructures his understanding of the situation—his framing of the problem he has

been trying to solve, his picture of what is going on, or the strategy of action he has been employing.

- On the basis of the restructuring, he invents a new strategy of action.
- He tries out the new action he has invented, running an on-the-spot experiment whose results he interprets, in turn, as a "solution"—an outcome on the whole satisfactory—or else as a new surprise that calls for a new round of reflection and experiment.

In the course of such a process, the performer *reflects*, not only in the sense of thinking about the action he has undertaken and the result he has achieved, but in the more precise sense of turning his thought back on the knowing-in-action implicit in his action. He reflects *in action*, in the sense that his thinking occurs within the boundaries of what I call an action-present—a stretch of time within which it is still possible to make a difference to the outcomes of action.

EXAMPLES: These are examples of reflection-in-action drawn from some of the familiar contexts of professional practice:

- A designer, hard at work on the design of a school, has been exploring the possible configurations of small, classroom units. Having tried a number of these, dissatisfied with the formal results, she decides that these units are "too small to do much with." She tries combining the classrooms in L-shaped pairs and discovers that these are "formally much more significant" and that they have the additional, unexpected educational advantage of putting grade one next to grade two and grade three next to grade four.
- A teacher has a young student, Joey, who disturbs her by insisting that an eclipse of the sun did not take place because "it was snowing and we didn't see it." It occurs to the teacher that Joey does not know that the sun is there, even if he can't see it, and she asks him, "Where was the sun yesterday?" Joey answers, "I don't know; I didn't see it." Later, it occurs to her that his answer may have reflected not his ignorance of the sun remaining in the sky but his interpretation of her question. She thinks that he may have read her as asking, "*Where* in the sky was the sun?" With this in mind, she tries a new question: "What hap-

pened to the sun yesterday?"—to which Joey answers, "It was in the sky."

In such examples as these, reflection-in-action involves a "stop-and-think." It is close to conscious awareness and is easily put into words. Often, however, reflection-in-action is smoothly embedded in performance; there is no stop-and-think, no conscious attention to the process, and no verbalization. In this way, for example, a baseball pitcher adapts his pitching style to the peculiarities of a batter; a tennis player executes split-second variations in play in order to counter the strategies of his opponent. In such cases, we are close to processes we might recognize as examples of artistry.

When good jazz musicians improvise together, they display a feel for the performance. Listening to one another and to themselves, they feel where the music is going and adjust their playing accordingly. They are inventing on-line, and they are also responding to surprises provided by the inventions of the others. A figure announced by one performer will be taken up by another, elaborated, and perhaps integrated with a new melody. The collective process of musical invention is not usually undertaken at random, however. It is organized around an underlying structure—a shared schema of meter, melody, and harmony that gives the piece a predictable order. In addition, each of the musicians has ready a repertoire of musical figures that he can play, weaving variations of them as the opportunity arises. Improvisation consists in varying, combining, and recombining a set of figures within the schema that gives coherence to the whole performance. As the musicians feel the direction in which the music is developing out of their interwoven contributions, they make new sense of it and adjust their performances to the sense they make. They are reflecting-in-action on the music they are collectively making, though not, of course, in the medium of words.

Their process is not unlike the familiar improvisation of everyday conversation, which does occur in the medium of words. A good conversation is both predictable and, in some respects, unpredictable. The participants may pick up themes suggested by others, developing them through the associations they provoke. Each participant seems to have a readily available repertoire of kinds of things to say, around which we can develop variations suited to the present occasion. Conversation is collective verbal improvisation which tends to fall into conventional routines—for example, the anecdote (with appropriate side comments and reactions) or the debate—and it develops according to a pace and rhythm of interaction that the participants seem, without conscious attention, to work out in common. At the same time, there are surprises—in the form of unexpected turns of phrase or directions of development. Participants make on-the-spot responses to surprise, often in conformity to the kind of conversational role they have adopted. Central to the other forms of improvisation, there is a conversational division of labor that gradually establishes itself, often without conscious awareness on the part of those who work it out.

In the on-the-spot improvisation of a musical piece or a conversation, spontaneous reflection-in-action takes the form of a kind of production. The participants are involved in a collective *making* process. Out of the "stuff" of this musical performance, or this talk, they make a piece of music, or a conversation—in either case, an artifact that has, in some degree, order, meaning, development, coherence. Their reflection-in-action becomes a reflective conversation—this time, in a metaphorical sense—with the materials of the situation in which they are engaged. Each person, carrying out his own evolving role in the collective performance, *listens* to the things that happen—including the surprises that result from earlier moves—and responds, on-line, through new moves that give new directions to the development of the artifact. The process is reminiscent of Carpenter's description of the Eskimo sculptor who, patiently carving a reindeer bone and examining the gradually changing shape, finally exclaims "Ah, seal!"

That one can engage in spontaneous reflection-in-action without being able to give a good description of it is evident from experience. Typically, when a performer is asked to talk about the reflection and on-the-spot experimenting he has just carried out, he gives at first a description which is obviously incomplete or inaccurate. And by comparing what he says to what he has just done, he can often discover this for himself.

Clearly, it is one thing to engage spontaneously in a performance that involves reflection-in-action, and quite another thing to reflect on that reflection-in-action through an act of description. Indeed, these several, distinct kinds of reflection can play important roles in the process by which an individ-

ual learns a new kind of performance. A tennis coach (Galloway) reports his use of an exercise in which he repeatedly asks his students to say where their racket was when they hit the ball; he intends to help them get more precisely in touch with what they are doing when they hit the ball, so that they will *know* what they are doing when they try to correct their errors. Seymour Papert used to teach juggling by informing would-be jugglers that they are susceptible to a variety of kinds of *bugs*—that is, to typical mistakes ("bugs" by analogy with computer programming) such as "throwing too far forward" or "overcorrecting" an error. He would ask them from time to time to describe the "bug" they had just enacted.

Professional practitioners, such as physicians, managers, and teachers, also reflect-in-action—but their reflection is of a kind particular to the special features of professional practice. *Practice* has a double meaning. A lawyer's practice includes the kinds of activities he carries out, the clients he serves, the cases he is called upon to handle. When we speak of practicing the performance, on the other hand, we refer to the repetitive yet experimental process by which one learns, for example, to play a musical instrument. The two senses of *practice*, although quite distinct, relate to one another in an interesting way. Professional practice also includes repetition. A professional is, at least in some measure, a specialist. He deals with certain types of situations, examples, images, and techniques. Working his way through many variations of a limited number of cases, he "practices" his practice. His know-how tends to become increasingly rich, efficient, tacit, and automatic, thereby conferring on him and his clients the benefits of specialization. On the other hand, specialization can make him narrow and parochial, inducing a kind of overlearning which takes the form of a tacit pattern of error to which he becomes selectively inattentive.

Reflection *on* spontaneous reflection-in-action can serve as a corrective to overlearning. As a practitioner surfaces the tacit understandings that have grown up around the repetitive experiences of a specialized practice, he may allow himself to notice and make new sense of confusing and unique phenomena.

A skillful physician, lawyer, manager, or architect continually engages in a process of appreciating, probing, modeling, experimenting, diagnosing, psyching out, evaluating—which he can describe imperfectly if at all. His knowing-in-action is revealed and presented by his feel for the stuff with which he deals. When he tries, on rare occasions, to say what he knows—when he tries to put his know*ing* into the form of know*ledge*—his formulations of principles, theories, maxims, and rules of thumb are often incongruent with the understanding and know-how implicit in his pattern of practice.

On the other hand—contrary to Hannah Arendt's observation that reflection is out of place in action—skillful practitioners sometimes respond to a situation that is puzzling, unique, or conflicted, by reflecting at one and the same time on the situation before them and on the reflection-in-action they spontaneously bring to it. In the midst of action, they are able to turn thought back upon itself—surfacing, criticizing, and restructuring the thinking by which they have spontaneously tried to make the situation intelligible to themselves. There are, for example:

- managers who respond to turbulent situations by constructing and testing a model of the situation and experimenting with alternative strategies for dealing with it;
- physicians who, finding that "80% of the cases seen in the office are not found in the book," treat each patient as a unique case—constructing and testing diagnoses, inventing and evaluating lines of treatment through processes of on-the-spot experiment;
- engineers who discover that they cannot apply their rules of thumb to a situation because it is anomalous or peculiarly constrained (like the shattering of windows on the John Hancock building in Boston), and proceed to devise and test theories and procedures unique to the situation at hand;
- lawyers who construct new ways to assimilate a puzzling case to a body of judicial precedent;
- bankers who feel uneasy about a prospective credit risk—even though his "operating numbers" are all in order—and try to discover and test the implicit judgments underlying their uneasiness;
- planners who treat their plans as tentative programs for inquiry, alert to discovering the unanticipated meanings their interventions turn out to have for those affected by them.

Kinds and Levels of Reflection

Many such examples of reflection on reflection-in-action occur in the indeterminate zones of practice—uncertain, unique, or value-conflicted. Depending on the context and the practitioner, such inquiry may take the form of on-the-spot problem solving, or it may take the form of theory building, or reappreciation of the problem of the situation. When the problem at hand proves resistant to readily accessible solutions, the practitioner may rethink the approach he has been taking and invent new strategies of action. When he encounters a situation that falls outside his usual range of descriptive categories, he may surface and criticize his initial understandings and proceed to construct a new, situation-specific theory of the phenomena before him. (The best theories, Kevin Lynch observed, are those we make up in the situation.) When he finds himself stuck, he may decide that he has been working on the wrong problem, and evolve a new way of setting the problem.

The objects of reflection may lie anywhere in the system of understanding and know-how that a practitioner brings to his practice. Depending on the centrality of the elements he chooses to surface and rethink, more or less of that system may become vulnerable to change. But, systems of intuitive knowing are dynamically conservative, actively defended, highly resistant to change. They tend not to go quietly to their demise, and reflection-in-action often takes on a quality of struggle. In the early minutes and hours of the "accident" at the Three Mile Island nuclear power plant, for example, operators and managers found themselves confronted with combinations of signals they could only regard as "weird"—unprecedented, unlike anything they had ever seen before.[25] Yet they persisted in attempting to assimilate these strange and perplexing signals to a situation of normalcy—"not wanting to believe," as one manager put it, that the nuclear core had been uncovered and damaged. Only after twelve hours of fruitless attempts to construe the situation as a minor problem—a breach in a steam line, a buildup of steam in the primary circulatory system—did one anonymous key manager insist, against the wishes of others in the plant, that "future actions be based on the assumption that the core has been uncovered, the fuel severely damaged."

Many practitioners, locked into a view of themselves as technical experts, find little in the world of practice to occasion reflection. For them, uncer-

25. Transcript of *Nova*, March 29, 1983: "60 Minutes to Meltdown."

tainty is a threat; its admission, a sign of weakness. They have become proficient at techniques of selective inattention—the use of junk categories to dismiss anomalous data, procrustean treatment of troublesome situations—all aimed at preserving the constancy of their knowing-in-action. Yet reflection-in-action is not a rare event. There are teachers, managers, engineers, and artists for whom reflection-in-action is the "prose" they speak as they display and develop the ordinary artistry of their everyday lives. Such individuals are willing to embrace error, accept confusion, and reflect critically on their previously unexamined assumptions. Nevertheless, in a world where professionalism is still mainly identified with technical expertise, even such practitioners as these may feel profoundly uneasy because they cannot describe what they know how to do, cannot justify it as a legitimate form of professional knowledge, cannot increase its scope or depth or quality, cannot with confidence help others to learn it.

For all of these reasons, the study of professional artistry is of critical importance. We should be turning the puzzle of professional knowledge on its head, not seeking only to build up a science applicable to practice but also to reflect on the reflection-in-action already embedded in competent practice.

We should be exploring, for example, how the on-the-spot experimentation carried out by practicing architects, physicians, engineers, and managers is like—and unlike—the controlled experimentation of laboratory scientists. We should be analyzing the ways in which skilled practitioners build up repertoires of exemplars, images, and strategies of description in terms of which they learn to see novel, one-of-a-kind phenomena. We should be attentive to differences in the framing of problematic situations and to the rare episodes of frame-reflective discourse in which practitioners sometimes coordinate and transform their conflicting ways of making sense of confusing predicaments. We should investigate the conventions and notations through which practitioners create virtual worlds—as diverse as sketchpads, simulations, role-plays and rehearsals—in which they are able to slow down the pace of action, go back and try again, and reduce the cost and risk of experimentation. In such explorations as these, grounded in collaborative reflection on everyday artistry, we will be pursuing the description of a new epistemology of practice.

We should also investigate how it is that some people learn the kinds and levels of reflection-in-action essential to professional artistry. In apprenticeships and clinical experiences, how are textbook descriptions of symptons and procedures translated into the acts of recognition and judgment and the readiness for action characteristic of professional competence? Under what conditions do aspiring practitioners learn to see, in the unfamiliar phenomena of practice, similarities to the canonical problems they may have learned in the classroom? What are the processes by which some people learn to internalize, criticize, and reproduce the demonstrated competence of acknowledged masters? What, in short, is the nature of the complex process we are accustomed to dismiss with the term *imitation?* And what must practitioners know already—what kinds of competences, what features of stance toward practice must they already have acquired in order to learn to construe their practice as a continuing process of reflection-in-action?

Clearly, just as some people learn to reflect-in-action, so do others learn to help them do so. These rare individuals are not so much *teachers* as *coaches* of reflection-in-action. Their artistry consists in an ability to have on the tip of their tongue—or to invent on-the-spot—the method peculiarly suited to the difficulties experienced by the student before them. And, just as professional artistry demands a capacity for reflection-in-action, so does the coach's artistry demand a capacity for reflection-in-action on the student's intuitive understanding of the problem at hand, the intervention that might enable her to become fruitfully confused, the proposal that might enable her to take the next useful step.

The development of forms of professional education conducive to reflection-in-action requires reflection on the artistry of coaching—a kind of reflection very nicely illustrated by the studies of case teaching conducted over the past many years at the Harvard Business School. If educators hope to contribute to the development of reflective practitioners, they must become adept at such reflection on their own teaching practice.

In this way, perhaps, we will be heeding Everett Hughes's call for a way of undoing the bonds that have tied the professional schools to the traditions of the late nineteenth-century university. At least, and at last, we will be getting some group of young people who are free of those bonds, making them free to do something new and different.

Have You Done Your Best?

PAUL HAMILTON

*This profile was prepared by **Paul Hamilton** under the direction of **Katherine K. Merseth**, director for the Mid-Career Math and Science Program at the Graduate School of Education, Harvard University.*

She wasn't particularly attractive, this middle-aged schoolmarm. She wouldn't be noticed sitting among a busload of people or standing on the street corner. In fact, she was really rather plain, now that I think of it. She was sturdily constructed without being fat, and she wore her fine black-and-silver hair cut short with a single wave on the right side. Or was it the left side? That further details of her physical makeup elude me is ample testimony to the strength of her character and the influence she exerted upon a young man still very much in his formative years.

The Stadium High School class of 1953 knew her as Miss Forbes—that form of address had not yet been discredited—but her name was Evelyn Forbes. She was a mathematics teacher. I suppose she had been at Stadium High for many years, but because I had come there only to complete my senior year, I don't know how long she had been on the faculty. One of the courses she taught was solid geometry. If one wanted to take solid geometry, then one had Evelyn Forbes for a teacher.

When the students filed into her class, they would find the theorem for that day up on the chalkboard—not scribbled haphazardly with criss-crossing white chalklines so that its essential three-dimensional nature would be obscured, but in a neat hand and in color! She would ask each of several students to work out one of the homework problems on the chalkboard, then she would go over each one before covering the new theorem. During the final ten or fifteen minutes of class, she would give a "miniquiz." She always had a reserve of additional problems for those who completed the quiz early, and she awarded extra points for correct solutions.

When any of her students completed an assignment or a test and handed it in to her, she would ask, "Is it your best?" More often than not, students would return to their desks, paper in hand, and go over it one more time until at last it would indeed become their best. She took great pains to see that the students understood the theorems, and could derive the proofs. She showed enthusiasm for mathematics, and transferred this enthusiasm to the class.

What made Evelyn Forbes unique? Was it her patience, thoroughness, and attention to detail? Was it her cool logic and her insistence that her students learn by thinking and not by rote? I have struggled to find that single word or phrase that best describes this magnificent teacher as I remember her now, thirty-one years later. Why does she alone stand out in my memory, among all of my teachers, through all the years? My own experience has provided me with the answer that I could not have expressed before. Evelyn Forbes was a professional. She knew what she wanted to do. She knew how to do it. She did it, and she did it every day.

The Uses of Videotape Replay

CATHERINE G. KRUPNICK

Catherine G. Krupnick, deputy director of BRIDGES, an international educational development program at Harvard's Institute for International Development and the Graduate School of Education, directed the Video Laboratory from its inception in 1975 until 1985.

Our traditional regime for preparing college-level teachers is curiously empty at its center. College and university teachers are carefully trained in research skills, in the arts of writing books and articles, and even in the folkways of academic administration. Paradoxically, however, they seldom receive instruction in the one activity that is at the core of their profession, namely, classroom teaching.

Beginners at the craft of college teaching usually face three problems: they lack experience, training for classroom communication, and a source of reliable feedback on their performance. Moreover, these problems are not restricted to beginners. Even experienced teachers face the same difficulties whenever they switch from one course or student population to another. Closely examined, the causes of these difficulties appear rooted in the current traditions of higher education. But before proceeding to discuss causes, it is important to state the good news first. There is a quick and fairly easy solution available, which takes the form of establishing a video-replay-based service for teachers.

Such a service is simple to understand and implement. It employs an advisor (sometimes a professional who is a veteran college teacher—often a peer volunteer) and a videotape of the subject-teacher's own classroom situation. Its strengths are that it provides reliable and detailed data for teachers who wish to work on their teaching, and it provides a situation conducive to the serious discussion of classroom teaching. Taken in combination, these factors ameliorate many of the causes of ineffective teaching.

Insufficient training in classroom communication, lack of closely examined experience, and a paucity of feedback have several causes. One is that teachers are appointed to be professional "experts," and thus often find it hard to ask their colleagues for fundamental advice. Even when they do request help, the specialization of college and university teachers by discipline obscures the common features of effective teaching that extends across fields. In addition, because college teachers spend relatively little time in the classroom (compared, for instance, with primary or secondary schoolteachers who gain a minimum of thirty hours of classroom experience per week), the rate at which college teachers learn their craft is comparatively slow. Finally, a third obstacle to acquiring the craft of college teaching is the sporadic and almost random quality of feedback on one's own performance.

Most colleges and universities provide instructors little if any support or supervision by veteran teachers. Instructors are left, instead, to rely on end-of-semester evaluations which praise or denounce (too frequently with such vague phrases as "boring" or "interesting") after it is impossible to adjust one's teaching. And because their teacher-student contact hours are limited, most teachers feel they have very little opportunity to monitor students' progress. It is difficult, in general, to develop any skill without feedback, and teaching is no exception. What videotape replay services do—in teaching as in sports—is help teachers learn to monitor their environment and their performance within that environment.

Helping College and University Teachers in Classroom-Teaching Skills

Most of the comments that follow are based on my ten years as an advisor at the Harvard-Danforth Video Laboratory. This faculty development institution was established in 1975 to help Harvard University instructors (of all levels) become informed experts in their own craft, and to work toward excellence in their teaching. The Lab's primary program consists of one-on-one consultations, which will be described later.

Advisors at the Harvard-Danforth Lab are all veteran university teachers and inveterate listeners. Indeed, these traits were our only initial qualifications, although we believe that subsequent years of work with clients have added to our store of knowledge. Our facilities, which were originally one and a half small rooms, have since tripled in size. Our equipment—originally a single ancient camera, video deck, and a monitor—has been expanded and modernized over the years. But facilities and hardware are relatively unimportant compared with the provisions of an *in situ* tape and a listening ear; hence the latter will be discussed first.

The Video Solution: Facilitating the Process of Learning from Oneself

To learn classroom skills, teachers must have accurate data on what they do with students and on how individual students react. Often, teachers see the effects of subject matter on only the most active students; however, even instructors with very keen

memories find that videotape replays provide a highly informative account of classroom dynamics.

Providing Tapes

Providing instructors with a videotape record of their teaching is quite simple. The most basic equipment—a portable camera, omnidirectional microphone, and playback unit—are inexpensive and widely available at colleges and universities. Even amateurs can make useful tapes, as long as they remember three basic rules: first, *tape teachers and students in actual classroom settings;* second, *show teachers and students reacting to one another;* and third, *focus on students' reactions to each other.* Beyond these simple taping rules, any refinements that one can add should be regarded as extras. Of course, a zoom lens adds useful detail, a color camera adds moments of beauty, and a sound equalizer makes voices sound more pleasant. But nothing is as important as capturing the actual classroom interaction, for that is the record which makes learning from tapes possible.

Providing Counseling; Framing the Consulting Session

Although videotape can be a wonderful tool, it also has the potential to do harm. The greatest danger attending videotape replay is that teachers who watch themselves on tape may come away from the experience feeling worse about themselves *and* their students.

We have found, however, that this disappointment seldom arises from the teacher's performance per se, since teachers already expect the worst on this count. Rather, video-induced despair is more likely to stem from the cosmetic distortions produced by the medium itself. Tapes made *in situ* usually exaggerate a person's weight and age, make receding hairlines recede further back, make voices sound somewhat high and flat, and magnify regional accents. Never mind how "objective" tape is supposed to be, it will never be totally realistic. Worse still, it's never as slick as television! The importance of warning clients about cosmetic disappointments before you even turn on the viewing monitor cannot be overestimated. Regardless of how sincere your clients are about examining their teaching, you must prepare them for the physical aspects of their image before you can get down to the business of analyzing their teaching. The first thing to keep in mind is this: *Never* let clients watch their own tapes by themselves! Without a trained professional to keep them focused away from their distorted cosmetic appearance, even the most sincerely intentioned instructor is likely to come away having learned more about video images than about teaching.

Ordinarily, it takes twice as long to view a class tape as it does to tape it. This means that you will want to schedule a two-hour session for viewing a one-hour class. Usually, the best way to begin is by having the teacher state his or her objectives and concerns about a taped class, and then move on from the necessary preliminary warnings to actual plans—for example: "I'd like to warn you that videotape has 20/20 vision—it is capable of adding 20 pounds and 20 years to the average teacher. Moreover, it distorts voices and accents, so please don't expect a totally realistic depiction of your body or voice. What we will be watching is a kind of home movie; it is not television! Unless I warn you about this, it would be natural for you to wonder why your class lacks the technical liveliness of studio broadcast television, and I don't want you to have to spend the next couple of hours wondering why your class lacks a certain undefinable something. . . . Most teachers find they get used to it. Do you have any questions? . . . All right then, let's get an opening shot of you and your class starting up, and then you can introduce me to your students."

By focusing away from the teacher's physical person, the advisor helps the client focus on the classroom environment. In most cases, the teacher will make this transition smoothly, although many will need to pause and bemoan their poor posture or ask you if they are moving their hands "too much." Questions like this need not be an impediment; as long as you remember that the tape itself is the primary data base, a response such as "How would we be able to decide what 'too much' is?" will come naturally.

Beyond Framing: Seeing and Concluding

In most cases, teachers who watch their tapes closely will identify both the problems in their teaching and the requisite solutions, with only occasional prompting from their advisor. Given two hours to review sixty minutes of tape, both teacher and advisor will usually begin by discussing the objectives of an individual class session, then progress to the challenges posed by individual students, and end with a clearly delineated set of behavioral goals. Examples of such goals might include facing the class while lecturing, looking around the class purposively, to encourage unlikely contributors, or intervening when a long-winded, dominant student begins to lecture the class.

The advisor should let the teacher take the conversational lead. Occasionally, silence may result. (Of course, silence is easiest when two people feel at ease with each other. Happily, this ease will usually come naturally if you let the teacher take the conversational lead.) If, however, you find that a silence between you seems to be lasting forever, check your watch and count the minutes of silence. Most teachers will be eager to discuss their teaching with you, so you needn't worry about keeping a conversation going. After all, your job is to keep the teacher's attention focused on the content of the tape, or on issues arising directly out of tape watching.

Perhaps the hardest part of an advisor's job is maintaining a focused and nonjudgmental attitude. Keep in mind that it's far easier to give very general advice or to get drawn into a conversation about subject matter than to refrain and let the tape provide evidence. Remember also that teachers feel this temptation too, and it often gets in the way of their students' learning. Finally, keep in mind, also, Disraeli's maxim that "it's easier to criticize than to create."

There will be many times during the course of a tape-viewing session when you will have strong opinions about how a teacher should have behaved or refrained from behaving. Again, your job is to maintain your silence until the teacher has asked for your opinion—or until the tape has demonstrated your point conclusively. For example, your observation that a given teacher speaks quickly and avoids eye contact with students is merely a criticism *until* the teacher has noticed the same thing and asked for confirmation, or *until* the tape shows several students losing the battle with rapid note taking. The creation of a worthwhile advising period lies in being willing to confirm observations and to help the teacher focus into a realistic plan of action. There are, however, a few additional tips—role-modeling pointers, really—which you will want to keep in mind as well. The first of these is to refer to students by name whenever possible. Since the teacher has already introduced you to the students at the beginning ("framing") of the session, names are focal pieces of knowledge which you and your client share. If you refer to students by name, the teacher will feel comfortable in doing so too; the value of your tape-watching session will be doubled if this behavior is encouraged in the classroom.

Speak as specifically as possible; avoid generalizations. Also, rather than answering an inquiry (about, for example, whether a teacher is talking too fast and avoiding eye contact) with a simple "yes" or "no" or "compared with most teachers . . . ," direct your client's question to the evidence on tape. You might say, for instance, "Let's look to the tape and see what evidence we can find. . . . It does seem that Doris and Mike look as if they're relaxed and keeping up, but the others *do* seem to be tensed up over their notebooks. . . . Also, I notice those three in the back row in sweatshirts—Elizabeth and Lou and Toby—looking at each others' notebooks. Do you think *they're* behind?"

Third—and this has already been implied—keep your eyes on the tape at all times. When you and your client want to discuss a point, *put the tape on pause* and hold it there. (Video technicians will tell you this is bad for the equipment, and it is, but this is one of those cases where the end justifies the means. Anything advisors do that underscores an interest in seeing the whole class imparts a feeling of respect for the teacher's endeavors.)

Finally, remember that one of videotape's main advantages is its instant-replay-feature capability. Many problems that arise during the class are rooted in events that happened earlier in the hour. You as the advisor should try to find those events which triggered the problem you're discussing. Sudden inattentiveness on the part of diligent students, for example, is frequently the result of something that the teacher or another student has said; find out if this is the case. And urge your teacher-client to suggest parts of the tape that should be reviewed in order to examine the roots of puzzling classroom behaviors.

Such diagnostic and prescriptive work, however, is not the whole story of a first two-hour session. The first session should also be considered an opportunity to accomplish something equally important—namely, to identify and reinforce the most positive aspects of the teacher's instructional behavior. Novice teachers, in particular, often have unrealistically low opinions of their own skills. Thus, your first viewing session should be aimed at realistic assessment. For example, many beginning math teachers discover to their surprise and pleasure that they really do give clear answers to student questions, convey enthusiasm for elegant mathematical solutions, and outline class material effectively. The professional pride that beginning instructors can justifiably take in these areas of competence is a powerful inducement for them to invest in changing the less-satisfactory aspects of their classroom performance, such as an overly rapid pace of delivery, or infrequent use of students' names. By the end of your first viewing session with a teacher, the two of you should be able to state both the teacher's strengths and long-term improvement objectives as well as that teacher's immediate goals for change in the classroom.

Repeat the Experience

As important as these critical and reinforcing experiences of the first two-hour session are, however, they do not exhaust the potential of video-based consultation. Ideally, teachers will view themselves at least three times in the course of a year. If they do, the review of a second classroom tape, made within a few weeks of the first one, will provide an opportunity to assess progress toward the teacher's target objectives, and to elaborate a second set of immediate goals. This is also an integral part of motivating the teacher to remain attentive to the lessons of the first tape-viewing session. Ordinarily, teachers leave the second session with a firm understanding of their professional assets, an informed self-evaluaton of their progress, and an expanded list of target objectives for future work. In addition, the second session also broadens the scope of the inquiry beyond the characteristics of the teacher's behavior to the fairly predictable behaviors of individual students in the classroom. It is at this time that many teachers consider the various ways in which particular students or classroom dynamics work to shape the presentation of material.

If a third or fourth viewing session can be arranged, it can complete the shift in focus from teacher's behavior to interaction between the teacher and the dynamics of the class. The third session may confirm earlier findings or provide new, sometimes contradictory, data. Either way, it will provide a new text for the analysis of classroom behaviors.

A third session is often scheduled after the

teacher has shifted to new students and subject matter at the outset of a new semester. Such changes in class and subject matter provide a special challenge in that they require the instructor to summarize the methodological lessons learned during the first two sessions, and generalize from them. By this time teachers are usually fairly fluent at articulating classroom problems and at generating lists of target objectives with minimal assistance from their advisors. Nevertheless, the opportunity to do so aloud is important because it builds self-confidence. In addition, the third session also gives teachers the opportunity to reflect for the first time upon all of the major variables in the craft of self-disciplined teaching, and all at once: teacher behavior, class dynamics, and subject matter. This permits teachers and advisors to explore more subtle craft issues, such as how to direct discussion by drawing on the strengths of individual students or how to assess the evolution of learning among various groups of students.

Three Examples

The following three examples[1] should help clarify the objectives and accomplishments of videotape replay sessions.

EXAMPLE NO. 1: Jesse Jensen, a teaching fellow with two years' previous experience, responding to the question "How can I help you with your classroom teaching?"

I like teaching my sociology class, but I don't think I will by the end of the semester. I feel like things are about to go out of control. I worry about what part I should play in getting students to talk. Things go pretty well in the sense that we cover material during the hour—but it's October, we've been meeting for a month, and I'm beginning to realize that there are some smart people in the section of twenty students who hardly ever say anything. I don't want to call on people who don't have their hands raised, because that doesn't seem to be a good way to get the best answers; but I don't want the shyer students to get short-changed just because there are a couple of highly verbal pre-law types in the section. What should I do?

The advisor turned the question around by asking Jesse if he could see anything on the tape which

1. All three examples are disguised to protect the identity of involved participants.

suggested a solution. Jesse, however, still found it hard to address the issue of imbalanced participation directly:

Well, what I immediately think about is whether or not people can learn when they're intimidated. . . . I mean there have been many situations in graduate school where I've had nothing at all to contribute. I always hate being called on in a time like that.

The advisor's objective in this case was to direct the conversation to allow Jesse to realize that his confusion about teaching strategies was due—at least in part—to having insufficient information. (Usually a question like "Do you remember your response last time one of the shy students responded?" shifts the teacher's focus away from the immediate need for a solution to a broadly defined teaching problem toward a desire for more information.) At this juncture, the advisor suggested they continue playing the tape to see what new information could be gained.

Within minutes, Jesse noticed something about his teaching style that contributed to the uneven patterns of participation: when the highly verbal pre-law types talked, he listened silently and intently, even picking up a pencil to jot down notes on their contributions. But when more retiring students talked, they received a far different response. Almost as soon as they opened their mouths to talk, Jesse got to work "encouraging them" with short interruptions of "uh-huh, uh-huh, very good." Just as invariably, they took this as a signal to be brief; their contributions were shorter, and Jesse did not take notes on them. The teacher and advisor noticed another thing, as well: the students who sat directly flanking him *never* talked.

From these observations Jesse derived two hypotheses. First, the students who were interrupted by the teacher (regardless of how these interruptions were intended) were less likely to volunteer comments. And, second, there seemed to be an inverse relationship between being "out of sight" and a tendency toward participation. The happy thing about having hypotheses based on solid evidence is that they suggest possibilities for experimentation. In this case, the experiment was simple: Jesse, the teacher, would change his seating so that he would sit directly across the table from the quieter students, and he would attempt to maintain fairly regular eye contact with each speaker. Also, the teacher would make no verbal interruptions at all while any student was speaking. If these hunches proved to be correct, participation would even out.

Jesse and the advisor allowed a week to pass, taped another class, and—upon review—found that the experiment had succeeded. In the second viewing of the class, not only did two of the retiring students talk, but also, a third shy person (one who had formerly sat next to Jesse) contributed thoughtfully and at considerable length toward the end of the class.

Of course these conversational techniques were specifically suggested for one context—Jesse's sociology section. A sensitive teaching advisor will approach each new tape with the idea that a unique procedure might be necessary for this particular admixture of client and teaching situation.

It is often assumed that viewing tapes is a "hard business" and damaging to the ego, but that is rarely true. Recall that the teacher (Jesse) came to us with an uncomfortable dilemma: should he go against his instincts and put students on the spot? The viewing sessions resolved the dilemma and gave genuine cause for satisfaction. Of course, not all cases are so simple.

EXAMPLE NO. 2: Sara, a pleasant, lively young woman teaching Biochemistry at the medical school, asked to be taped because she was "just curious." According to her account, "I get pretty average ratings, but there are one or two complaints from students. Some of them say I'm boring and that I kill their interest. One of them even wrote [on an end-of-semester evaluation] that I reminded him—or her—of a corpse."

The tape-viewing session revealed a nearsighted teacher holding a single-spaced typed text close to her face, and reading it in the kind of flat voice that's usually possible only when one is cut off from all human contact. Watching the videotape of herself made Sara visibly uncomfortable, and after several minutes she stared into her lap as the camera panned the students' bored faces. (Here was a client who needed careful handling.) Finally Sara turned to the advisor: "I do sound pretty deadly, don't I?"

ADVISOR: What do you mean by *deadly?*
TEACHER: [*with exasperation, but also more clarity*] Well, it sounds like I'm putting them to sleep, doesn't it?

ADVISOR: Do the students, in fact, ever fall asleep in class?
TEACHER: No—I mean yes—a few, the ones in the back row. But that's not the point. The point is that they all look dead to me, and I seem deadly to them. I don't know what to *do*. It's hard to think of reading my notes any other way, but the way things are going, the harder I prepare my notes, the less they seem to listen; they don't even answer my questions when I do try to get some reaction.
ADVISOR: Sara, let's find a spot on the tape where you do ask a question. [*The tape runs for several minutes.*]
TEACHER ON TAPE: In 1959 Janssen searching for a better analgesic agent developed the *butyrophenones.* Can anyone tell me the other name for butyrophenones? No? [*5-second pause*] All asleep? The other name—and this may be in the test, so you'd better listen—is *phenylbutylpiperidines.* I don't have time to spell it now, but you'll find it in the book.
TEACHER: I guess I didn't wait very long for that answer, but I was running late. That's the trouble with these classes. Too short to get through all my notes. Of course, now that I listen to myself, I'm not too fond of my note reading either. A lot of that stuff could be on a handout. The really interesting questions about clinical uses and side effects should be getting more attention.
ADVISOR: Would you consider lecturing from an outline instead of a full set of notes, Sara?
TEACHER: I'd lose the precision. Hmmm. . . . What's the point of messing around with an outline?
ADVISOR: Well, for one thing your voice would probably sound more like it does now, so students wouldn't be tempted to, as you say, fall asleep. Secondly, you'd get a chance to walk around and look at students in the room. Eye contact has a number of advantages.
TEACHER: For instance?
ADVISOR: For instance, you could see if people were engaged in finding an answer to your question. Also, if you continue looking at a silent audience for four or more seconds, you *almost always* get an answer.
TEACHER: Yeh, I guess I know the answer to that. The real truth is that it's hard for me to do anything less than perfectly. But now that I see this lecture isn't working—I mean the students are

right; I look like a corpse and I sound agressive. But reading will be hard to give up. Perhaps I could try a phased withdrawal?

ADVISOR: Why not, Sara? Many teachers find it useful to try to change their classroom behavior in small increments.

The teacher and advisor then worked out a plan which involved a phased withdrawal from dependence on notes. During the next class Sara spoke from an outline for the first five minutes, and her outline included several probing clinical questions. A favorable student response could be seen on the second tape, and even more so on the third one. Sara pronounced herself "enormously cheered." By the end of the semester the mood of the class had changed dramatically; student evaluations placed Sara in the upper 20 percentile. Sara herself had this to say:

> You know, I admit I enjoy my class a lot more now. I feel good when they come up to me after class with questions—which hardly ever happened before—and when they say 'hi' in the halls. But you know [laughs], perfectionist that I am, I just can't shake my habit of going for quality, so I guess what I like best is that I'm . . . I can see that I'm teaching far more effectively. The students have totally changed. I can see they're really getting into the material!

EXAMPLE NO. 3: A 55-year-old senior professor in the social sciences called up the video lab one day to see if he could be taped. "My students have always responded well," he said. "But this semester they tell me that I should see myself on tape. I think something's up!"

That week he was taped during his seminar. Several days later he arrived for his viewing appointment. He was ten minutes late and—uncharacteristically—puffing on a cigarette. Within minutes of watching his tape, his face was beaming proudly: "By golly, I'm good!" he exclaimed. "No wonder they say all those great things about me. Those kids are really participating. I'm going to recommend this to all my teaching fellows. Young people need to feel good, too!"

Each of these cases illustrates a broad problem or situation that can be tackled efficiently through a video consultation, be it conversational dynamics,

preparation of outlines vs. notes, or the banishment of haunting self-doubts. All are grist for self-reflection; all are aided by reviewing a whole class episode on videotape.

Setting Up a Video Program

Establishing Counselor Credibility

The most difficult thing about setting up a video program is establishing your credibility. What people—all of us—commonly fear about video is that it will reveal some dark, Ingmar Bergman-like "truth" about ourselves: a confused unconscious, perhaps, or a frightened or fraudulent front. Such revelations occur no more often in watching video than they do in real life, and watching oneself on video can almost always bring pleasant surprises. Still, the initial offer to do video analysis will probably be met with apparent indifference.

Besides the fears attending self-confrontation, potential clients will probably worry that their tapes will not be treated as "confidential." This fear has many expressions, none of which are frivolous. No scholar wants to be held up to ridicule. No scholar wants to be evaluated behind his or her back. It is important to develop a firm policy: *Never show a teacher's tapes to anyone who was not in the class at the time of the taping, unless you have the teacher's written consent.* Publicize this policy before each taping, by announcing to the students:

> Hello, my name is _____ _____. I will be taping your class today so your teacher can have a chance to see himself [herself] teach. These tapes are the joint property of your teacher and the lab. They will not be used for an evaluation of your teacher or yourselves. If you would like to review today's class, please give us a call and we will make an appointment for you to see the tape.

Even if such fears were not a problem, clients would probably not beat down your doors during the first semester of your operation. Every new institution needs time to gain acceptance. But have patience; there's plenty to do while you wait to develop your client base.

Getting Your Equipment Ready

First, you need to get your equipment together. You will want to get a recording deck, a camera, one or more omnidirectional microphones (capable of picking up students' as well as teachers' voices clearly), and a playback unit. The playback unit includes a deck (you can actually use your recording deck for this function) and a monitor (a monitor is like a TV without channels). As mentioned previously, these need not be fancy, and they need not belong to you. As long as you can borrow functioning equipment and a private room for viewing on a regular basis, you will be in business. There's no need to worry about a permanent location until your operation shows signs of performing a necessary service.

Sponsoring Faculty Development Activities

It may seem impossible to establish a reputation for being helpful while you're waiting for people to get their classes taped, but it is not. There are several kinds of popular faculty development activities that will involve teachers in discussing their own teaching, and you can sponsor any or all of them. The first of these, which we call *microteaching*, is ideally suited for videotaping. It enlists a group of five or six teachers to deliver and critique a few minutes of a class lesson with their colleagues. Not only is this experience a good learning activity for instructors, but it also provides you, the advisor, with taping experience and an excellent vantage point from which to observe how various critical styles affect individual teachers. Though microteaching has a hypothetical and transitory quality that makes it inferior to real-class viewing, it can be a tremendously powerful tool if you insist that participants tape at least twice and then compare their "before" and "after" performances.

Another service that draws potential clients is a *teaching workshop.* Ordinarily these are seminar discussions targeted toward a single group, such as new faculty members or writing instructors who are interested in getting methodological tips on various aspects of the teacher's craft. Since workshop participants do not require a promise of confidentiality, you can get administrators' help to target the potentially interested teachers. By calling people from this list, you will learn of topics that need addressing. Don't worry about being an expert. Think of yourself as an organizer or a conversational facilitator and your session will go well. Most teachers enjoy the chance to learn from colleagues almost as much as they appreciate having the advice itself. If you *do* have permission to show tapes of a real class or of a microteaching session, your workshop will have an immediate focus, but tapes are by no means necessary to lively and productive conversation.

A third service that you may want to offer is the *individual taping of a lecture practice session.* This activity, which consists of working through a lecture or a series of lectures until the client is totally satisfied with the finished product, is an excellent way for you to expose yourself to the various ways teachers plan their classes, and an equally good way for clients to ease into an enthusiasm for a live class taping.

Conclusion

Video-replay-based faculty consulting programs provide clients with the opportunity to gain a closer experience of, and insight into, their own teaching. Given the chance to watch a replay of one or more whole classes, college and university instructors can learn to become competent experts on their own classroom teaching. Although the technical details of setting up a classroom taping laboratory are relatively simple, adjunct professional activities should be planned while the constituency for taping services grows and the advisors gain experience in being creative and nonjudgmental observers of teaching in many contexts. Within several semesters, advisors and faculty will be learning together about teaching, in the best way possible: unbiased reflection on experience.

Reflections of a Casewriter: Writing Teaching Cases

ABBY J. HANSEN

The peculiar thing about writing teaching cases—as opposed, for example, to government or management cases—is that contemplating the process can be like getting lost in a carnival fun house. The raw material is the teaching process; the goal of the enterprise is to aid the teaching process; the major case characters are usually teachers; the audience for the case consists of teachers; the discussion leader will probably also be a teacher. Since I, a writer of teaching cases, am also a sometime teacher, the attempt to capture and elucidate the process of writing teaching cases makes me feel like Alice beyond the looking glass: a teacher writing about teachers to help other teachers teach teachers to teach—help!

Let the prospective writer of teaching cases be reassured, however: despite the unavoidable circularity that occasionally confuses the issue, the purpose of a teaching case is not to settle some vexed question forever, but simply to provide fodder for a rich discussion. The researcher need not understand the workings of every molecule of a case to write well and usefully. In fact, most people familiar with case method study agree: "There are no answers." The casewriter's challenge is to coax informants into providing vivid recollections, and then organize and present these so that readers may find them challenging and interesting enough to draw their own conclusions.

During the past five years of writing teaching cases about instructors in professional schools and in liberal arts institutions, I have found that the centrality of the discussion leader's art links pedagogy in many apparently unrelated disciplines and specialties. Holding content to one side, one notices that the task of guiding a group through a complex issue in ancient Chinese law bears more similarity than difference to that of shepherding a first-year MBA class through a case on marketing baby food in Guatemala. The central elements are a teacher, some discussion participants, and a document subject to varieties of interpretation. The imponderable—and all-important—element is the discussion process itself: the quicksilver essence of human relationships that makes each case discussion a new adventure. The secret of good casewriting is equally elusive. It involves recognizing the teachable moments in a series of events, encouraging informants to recollect them honestly—often in tragicomic detail—and then presenting them, as clearly and vividly as possible, in writing. Experience shows that metaphors—which can function almost as minidramas—make the greatest impression on the mind. In moments of frustration, for example, this writer finds more comfort in the adage "sometimes you eat the bear; sometimes the bear eats you" than in reflecting, "Some projects are more difficult than others."

This essay is not prescriptive; it is merely my attempt to describe how I have written teaching cases. It will also, by the way, ventilate a few of my prejudices about writing in general and, I hope, demonstrate that the teaching case can be a creative literary form. For me, much of the fun has been in meeting and interviewing teachers from fields vastly different from my own scholarly background (English Renaissance Literature) and observing discussions in which participants found far more in my cases than I had ever consciously put into them. One of my greatest satisfactions, however, has been the process of writing itself, the essence of which is *re*writing. It's a little like topiary. You start with a bush (a first draft) which you clip and trim. Then you step back and size it up, and clip and trim some more. If you do it right, the reward lies in finally producing something with real form: a document your readers will find accessible and possibly even exciting. Writing is one of the toughest jobs I know, so there's no point pretending it's all fun. But its satisfactions can be solid. There's a certain power in touching people's minds and emotions through your words, and casewriting gives one the added pleasure of knowing that the product is actually going to be read and discussed. How many scholars can be sure of such an audience?

Let me reiterate: there are no answers. Every case is as different as the people to whom it happened. Its events will fall into segments whose proportions may not be obvious until the project has gone through many drafts; and each discussion it produces will be a unique result of the chemistry of some particular discussion group. The process of creation is mysterious, but in this instance, it has a clear goal: a published case whose ultimate effect on its readers is unforeseeable. By writing and publishing a teaching case, you are starting a potentially infinite chain reaction.

What Is a Case?

It is said that the king of a small European principality once conducted interviews for the post of minister of economics for his realm by asking each

of three candidates to propose a price for bread. One man suggested a high price—10 crowns per loaf—to stimulate production. The second disagreed and proposed 1 crown per loaf to increase demand. The king scratched his beard and turned to the third candidate, who replied, "It depends. If we're buying, I like the second fellow's price, but if we're selling, I hold with the first candidate." He got the job—which demonstrates a point I cherish: the "right" answer to most questions has a lot to do with your point of view.

To a harried student, a case is often a bunch of stapled papers perched on a huge stack of similar bunches that all demand attention before bedtime. To a teacher, it can be discussion fuel, a means to spark a group of people into brilliant, heartfelt intellectual exchange (or, perhaps, an opportunity to show off, which is less helpful to the student). To a writer, it can mean weeks, even months, of gathering, analyzing, and refining data, writing and editing drafts, and then trying to view the product from yet another perspective in order to write a teaching note. It's a complex process, but exhilarating when it really clicks—partly because it involves getting people to open up, reexperience, and really communicate striking events, and that is the stuff of life. (Besides, the interviewer's role confers a delightful freedom to be nosy.)

From the writer's point of view, I would describe a case as an account of real events that seem to include enough intriguing decision points and provocative undercurrents to make a discussion group want to think and argue about them.

How Are Cases Used?

Just as a piece of music exists only partially when it isn't being sung or played, a case comes fully to life only when it's being discussed. Generally, case discussions begin with about an hour's conversation based on the (A) case, starting with "action questions": "What should Case Character Smith do at the first decision point?" Then they go to analysis: "How did he or she get into this pickle? If you were a friend of the case character, what advice might you have furnished at various sensitive points in the train of events?" The discussion group chews on the details, tries to psych out all the characters and assess the process at work in the events, and then formulates some sort of recommendation for action. Most instructors ask for fearless predictions at the end of (A) cases. "What did Case Character

Smith probably do, and how did it work?" Then the (B) case is distributed, and this reveals what *did* happen (a satisfying moment for those who predicted correctly, and a welcome break for all). The (B) cases are usually fairly short. Their discussions last another half hour or so, and often focus on trying to extract some general principles from the whole chain of events. If (B) happens to end with another decision point, there may be a second call for predictions, followed by a (C) case. Or the (B) case may conclude the events while (C) presents the case characters' reflections on what they learned from their experience. It is usually interesting to see if they drew the same lessons the seminar group perceived; often they did not.

As a casewriter, you should be aware—if only subliminally—of the natural breaks that will probably occur in the class discussions. During interviews, listen for points that seem to signal these breaks. Remember, the case will furnish raw material for discussion. This is comforting, because the task of listening for decision points or mentally tagging some of your informants' reflections for (B) and others for (C) is far less formidable than, say, trying to choose the three most significant causes of the Franco-Prussian War. Casewriting is a craft. Like any craft, it can aspire to artistry, but it is accessible to the journeyman through certain rules and guidelines. Paramount among these are: try to write clearly; try to write vividly; remember, your work will be *read*.

Gathering Data

In my experience, case discussion groups are the most fertile breeding grounds for cases. When it really catches on, case method study can be so exhilarating that participants begin to see cases everywhere in their own professional histories. Sometimes they write these cases themselves—as I and most casewriters I know have done. If you choose to write about yourself, your principal advantage will be easy access to your informant, but your disadvantage will be subjectivity. It is extraordinarily hard, for example, to describe yourself objectively on paper. Writing cases about *other* people presents a different, intriguing set of challenges because not only must you ascertain what sort of information is useful for the case, you must figure out how to get the informants to reveal some of their true emotions, not just some glossy, intellectualized, predigested version of what occurred.

Most people propose cases in the form of written sketches and consider these nearly complete. They are wrong, and the casewriter will probably have to interview them a few times to get enough material. Fortunately, most informants are willing to appear in less-than-flattering lights in the finished cases. If they hadn't felt perplexed they wouldn't have proposed the case in the first place. Interviewing these people is usually quite a lot of fun—and hard work. I do not happen to like tape recorders because the transcriptions force me to relive every "um," "ah," and "harummph," second for second. When I take notes I edit as I listen, noting (in my own improvised speedwriting) only those remarks that really seem to count. I try to get informants beyond abstractions, into graspable specifics. The objective of the interviews is to get some "juice," as well as thoroughness and coherence, for the case. A great source of vividness is *classroom dialogue*. This is the closest the reader can get to firsthand observation of the whole event, complete with complex personal interaction, as it occurred. And that interaction—the *process*—is the true subject of our analysis and source of our learning. Try, therefore to get your informant to reconstitute a few "scenes" as he or she recalls them.

Over the years, I have learned how difficult it is for case informants to recall actual classroom dialogue. Most teachers are far more comfortable analyzing than simply recounting events. But the game is worth the candle because dialogue is tremendously effective in cases. Professor Z will probably say, "X was disruptive." You should counter, "Professor Z, could you give me a sample of just what the class might have been saying and the words X would have used to interrupt?" Or your might request. "Reenact a typical opening for one of your classes." Or ask for physical description: "When X shot his hand up, was he tense-looking, oddly dressed, sitting in an unusual posture . . . what?" The object of such close questioning is to pull out as many graspable details as possible. A good case will seem almost like a short story. The most vivid cases—those that stimulate the best discussions—are those in which readers almost feel they were spectators who heard, saw, and felt the drama of the case events. As I ask questions, I also try to note details of the informant's environment, stance, dress, and general body language. These details can provide handles for interpretation when you write the case. A reader has something to work with when he reads, "'I didn't dislike X for his interruptions,' said Professor Z, breaking his pencil in half."

When I complete an interview—right hand aching from an hour's frantic jottings—I type up my notes as soon as possible (mostly because my shorthand is so quirky that even I have trouble deciphering it if I wait too long). Then I try to comprehend the notes, order them, put the informant's reminiscences in chronological sequence, and find the first *break* for the (A) case. Let's say the case deals with a group of students who start out wildly enthusiastic, bungle the midterm, and then take a collective slither into the abyss. The first decision point would probably be right after midterm grades. How might the instructor bail this sinking ship as the water level rises? Whom should he or she blame? Where might help be found? Each "break" should involve potential action for the main case character: there must be something one might constructively *do*. In the best of all possible worlds, there is also some underlying dynamic to be discerned—a dynamic that the reader, with benefit of hindsight, can analyze and (one hopes) recognize again should it materialize in his or her professional life.

When the material is organized, I usually submit it to a knowledgeable and sympathetic reader (my senior colleague) and also send it to the informant, requesting a *written release of the information*, and often adding a disguise for the characters' names, institution, location, course, and date. (Protecting your informants and the people they describe should be a fundamental concern. You should assure informants of this at the outset.)

Reassessing and Reworking the Material

Submitting a case-in-progress to an experienced, helpful reader can make a huge difference in the final product. The reader can find incoherences in organization, point out the holes in the material itself, and suggest other avenues to pursue. In the intensity of interviewing I may, for example, have neglected to ask the informant about *other students* in the class besides the obvious "sore thumb." If so, this is an oversight to be corrected in further interviews because what goes on in the classroom affects everyone; the teacher must consider the group as a whole. It may be that I have forgotten to include enough physical details and my reader is having trouble picturing the people in the case. If so, this is another deficiency to remedy. It may be that I haven't gotten the informant to speak with the ring

of truth: most people initially overintellectualize their experience, and the result is flat. A case reader empathizes more with "and then I felt like braining the little squirt, but I just stalked from the room" than "as I recall, the anger level in the room was elevated that day."

When possible, it is a good idea to ask the principal informant not only to check your data and furnish a release, but also to suggest other people in the case that you may approach for interviews. For example, if student X was a giant millstone around Professor Z's neck all second semester, it would be very useful to talk to X and find out what he thought Z was doing to *him* during that time. You might also try to speak to the teacher's colleagues: what sort of reputation does this teacher have? Or you might speak to other students who witnessed the principal events. Did this so-called "crisis" really upset the whole class? Include as many perspectives as you can without confusing the reader. Discussions thrive on diversity.

Think of all the pedagogical techniques you know and try to furnish footholds for them in the case materials. The instructor might ask participants to size up case characters, do a little role playing and reenact scenes from the case, attempt philosophical analyses of the underlying dynamic, or theorize about how things might have been different if one of the characters had behaved differently, for example. Have you included data in the case that would make all these—and more—techniques possible? The interviews are the occasions for gathering these data. (By the way, telephone interviews, though less desirable than actual meetings, are a practical solution to many people's time constraints.)

Writing the Case

Style

The English poet Percy Bysshe Shelley wrote, "Poets are the unacknowledged legislators of the world." I don't go that far, but I think that the written word can permanently etch a reader's mind. Every time I overwrite, ghostly echoes from Willard Strunk and E. B. White's *The Elements of Style* and George Orwell's "Politics and the English Language" command me to prune and weed my prose. Like Joan of Arc, I think my voices are right. In writing, especially narrative prose, less is more; pomposity is boring; and incoherence is a complete disaster. Orwell left me hypersensitive to the power of language to bamboozle and benumb as well as enlighten. Strunk and White left me terrified of being fuzzy or dull, and morbidly averse to the passive voice. It *hurts* me to read sentences like "Measures are being taken against the crime wave in our city." *What* measures, I want to know. And who is taking them? What does this mean? Another study in progress? More squad cars in the streets? A raise for the police commissioner?

To me, one hallmark of good writing is that it involves *all* the senses, even when its purpose is intellectual. T. S. Eliot said the first way to get to know a new city is to smell it. I think of this remark every time I get a whiff of strong diesel exhaust and, for a flash of time, find myself crossing the Euston Road to the tube stop I always used on the way to the British Museum when I was doing my thesis research. If I were writing about London I would include that diesel exhaust to convey the "feel" of the place. The same technique holds for casewriting. I try to convey details of characters' personalities by their actions, the sounds they make, the environments they inhabit. If a case informant smiled or offered the researcher half of a tunafish sandwich when making a particular remark, I may refer to these details in the case. If, on the other hand, his or her eyebrows knit, jaw clenched, fingernails clicked, or nostrils flared . . . you get the picture.

The point here is to include suggestive detail without overt editorializing. Let your reader draw conclusions. I think that a teacher who sits ramrod-straight, keeps jacket buttoned up on a warm day, and taps a ruler on a squared-off pile of typed notes while describing a student's classroom outburst conveys quite a lot of nonverbal information, but my task as a casewriter is neither to judge nor analyze, but to notice these details and present them to my readers. Which would you rather read, a summary judgment like "Professor Sylvia Mangrove was an unconventional, creative person who claimed to welcome spontaneity in the classroom but actually feared it," or "Professor Sylvia Mangrove disentangled her orange serape from her 'Down with Authority' button and turned in the direction of the cheerful whistle that had rent the stillness of her Economics 243 classroom, but her anticipatory smile froze when she read the crudely lettered political slogan Lawrence Wingford waved. She had warned her students not to depart from

the syllabus. The rest of the class began to cough with embarrassment."?

Models

The best advice I can give about writing is to pick out a few cases that work for you and try to emulate them. How do they portray characters and present information? How long are their sections? What sort of language do they use? How much background material do they provide, and in what order? Certainly, no case will be very appealing if it is just one thick desert of prose with no oases. Break your material into units and give each some sort of title. See how your favorite cases approach these tasks.

Openings: Grabbing the Reader and Hanging On

Many of our cases begin with a "teaser":

Sally Gerrity, a 26-year-old Princeton Ph.D., sighed deeply as she contemplated the tatters of Biff Gripshaw's final exam in Statistics U., where Sally had come to teach after her Rhodes Scholarship year at Oxford. She thought her tutoring had truly helped him grasp the rudiments of Bernoulli's Law, but even as she wondered how to grade his bizarre performance, she could still picture the poor fellow screaming, weeping, and tearing his bluebook in the middle of the packed exam room that morning. Could this debacle somehow be her fault?

After an opening like that, you can circle back to the less immediately interesting material—the name, geographical location, and demographics of the institution, a brief biography and description of the teacher, a description of the course and the other students, sketch of the problem student. (Check your favorite cases for the way they present these facts.) Then you can go back and retell the story more fully, in chronological order. How did the course start? How did Biff do initially? When did Sally notice he was in trouble? When and how did she try to help him? How did he react? In short, how did things go, up to this point? Put in as much concrete detail and reconstructed dialogue as you can.

Closings: Summarizing the Options

End the case with a summary of Sally's options, as she might have seen them. These will probably be the point of departure for a class discussion that will attempt to see the situation in its totality, figure out how it developed, and draw some practical pointers from the analysis. Is the real issue how to grade Biff, or how to help untalented or shy students in general? Has Sally killed Biff with kindness by walking him through homework assignments through the term? Has he exploited her? Is she afraid to flunk him? Why? What are Sally's (or any teacher's) real responsibilities?

If, as you go through these questions in your mind, you decide that Sally's most crucial decision point occurred back at the midterm when she suspected but could not prove that Biff got his A– by means of equations scribbled on his wrist in disappearing ink, try breaking the (A) case there. Don't worry if you find two, three, or four decision points. You can extend the case to several segments (B's, C's and so forth, maybe only a paragraph or two long). Or you can combine a couple of brief episodes into one segment. The point is, let the material fall into its natural clusters and try to imagine how you would teach each unit.

The Writing Process as a Whole: Overview

To my way of thinking, casewriting bears a closer relationship to journalism, short-story writing, and drama than to the bare sequential logic of, say, a scientific report. A case has characters, like a story or play, and it describes real—though disguised—events, like a news story. But its uniqueness lies in its special mission: to stimulate discussion. Unlike an editorial or scholarly essay, where the author hopes to persuade, the case tries to present an actual episode or series of episodes objectively, without analyzing them. Like life, cases throb with ambiguity. I have said elsewhere that a case is like a kaleidoscope: what you see in it depends on how you shake it. Its purpose is to intrigue readers and let them form hypotheses to present to their peers. (As a casewriter, I have embraced the opportunity to deal in ambiguity partly because it lets me off the hook. I'll bet the court reporter has more fun during a juicy trial than the judge or jury.) The readers will have to do the really hard work: absorb the events, assess their significance, and then present and defend their analyses.

Because cases are usually assigned readings, the question of audience is paramount in their design. Before you begin to gather data, consider *for whom you are writing.* How much time should you ask these people to devote to this material? What do you, the writer, hope they find worthy of discussion

here? What will they underline in that first, harried skim-through to decide whether there's any point in going back for a closer look? How long are your readers' attention spans likely to be? Should you write long paragraphs or short ones? How should you label each section—with rubrics? quotations? rhetorical questions? What skills are your readers likely to bring to interpreting the case? If you, the writer, hold strong views about its *meaning*, should you expose these at the outset, conceal them in the form of clues, extirpate them entirely? Finally, how are you going to grab your readers and keep hold of their lapels until you're done with them?

Like all writing, casewriting is a complex process: The writer gathers data, tries to organize the heap of impressions in his or her mind, and attempts to convey that tentative structure to the page. Many writers stop at this point, and the result is usually a burden to read. We have all struggled with reports, memoranda, business letters, even articles and books written by this partial process. My point is: everybody writes like that at first. The trick is to recognize the thudding passages in one's own early drafts, and either throw them out or impove them. This is why soliciting a colleague's opinion at this point can make the difference between good, readable writing and alphabet soup.

One further—and essential—step in the process of writing is to reconsider the material *from a reader's point of view.* I recommend assuming that the reader is every bit as intelligent, sophisticated, humorous, overcommitted, fatigued, irritable, emotional, and generally *human* as you are. In other words, write for *yourself*, in the role of a discussion group member who has just picked up this case and started thumbing through the pages the night before (the hour before?) a discussion in which you hope to participate and maybe even distinguish yourself by the insight and grace of your contributions. What do you need to see—quickly—in the pages of this case?

There are many tricks to lively writing. One is to involve the reader's five senses, rather than simply the intellect, with imagery that stimulates fantasy. Another is to use alliteration and assonance. No one can forget a title like *Pride and Prejudice.* But what if Jane Austen had called her novel *Inflated Social Self-Perception and Biased Assessment of One's Peers?* Another is to vary the length and syntax of sentences, using first a short one, then a long one, then perhaps, a fragment. Like this. Put the most important details at the beginning or end of paragraphs (many people automatically skim all the middles). Check to see if too many of your paragraphs begin with participial phrases, or the word *He*, or whatever. Repetition dulls the mind. I have found that focusing on my *students'* need to come to grips with whatever I'm teaching—rather than my own urge to show off—has enormously improved my teaching. The same insight holds true for writing, which is, like teaching, a kind of performance. Both are forms of communication—means to impress and move people. I think all discursive writers should think, compassionately, of their readers. In preparing teaching cases, imagine your words being read and studied by people like you—people interested in teaching, anxious to do a better job, constrained to read and absorb fast. Don't give these decent folks a hard time.

R ough day," was about all Nick Maitland could think to say to Professor Rowe when he caught up with him at the water fountain. Quite surprised by Rowe's abrupt exit from class, Nick (a Ph.D. candidate at Farwestern and observer in the class) had followed him out of the classroom and down the hall.

"Yeah! If a bar were around, I'd buy us a drink." Professor Rowe was really "dragging," shaking his head as they continued to walk down the hall. "I just don't understand it. Here it is, almost the middle of the year, and this class is terrible." The frustration so evident a few moments before in class was returning to his voice. "They don't prepare, don't show any interest. As a class they just don't seem to have developed any effectiveness in discussing a case. I don't know, Nick. What do you think? What do I do?"

"Well, the last few classes before the holiday didn't go well and there certainly wasn't much happening there today," Nick replied. "But I have a hard time assessing the situation. The cases are long, the subject matter is complicated and difficult, and perhaps many of the students just don't have enough analytical background to handle it. On the other hand, those students who do have strong backgrounds don't seem to be helping much." Nick felt he wasn't shedding much light on the problem.

Rowe's shoulders were still drooping and he seemed more discouraged now than angry. "Look, every year there are students who have to struggle with this stuff because their analytical backgrounds aren't that strong. I think it's an important and exciting part of my job to work with them, but what bothers me most here is that this group just doesn't seem to be making an honest effort."

The Incident on December 1

It was Wednesday, the third day of classes after the four-day Thanksgiving break, but the first post-holiday meeting of Planning in Complex Systems (PCS). Professor Douglas Rowe was teaching the International Trading Co. (D) case to his first-year section at one o'clock. (The (A), (B), and (C) cases had been taught during the three preceding classes.) It was not long before it became obvious that this class was not going well. Professor Rowe surveyed the room at the beginning of class and noted that a dozen students were absent. As he began the class, members of the section seemed restless and uninvolved. One of the first students

CASE

We're Just Wasting Our Time

Here is a sample case followed by a sample teaching note. These are provided for members of any institution interested in trying the case method of teaching.

*This case was written by **Gale D. Merseth** under the supervision of **C. Roland Christensen** for the Developing Discussion Leadership Skills Seminar. While the case is based on data supplied by participants involved, all names and some peripheral facts have been disguised.*

he called on declined to participate, acknowledging that he was unprepared. No one was volunteering, and Rowe tried several lines of questioning without results.

"How does this company's strategy compare with that of Northstar?" (Northstar was a case they had studied earlier in this course.) Several students tried to respond, but their comments were obviously shallow and most missed the point.

It was like pulling teeth. In another attempt to get things going, Rowe moved to the chalkboard and talked briefly about several key elements in the case. He returned to the center of the amphitheater classroom and said, "This company's strategy represented a great economic success story. How did they do it? What's their comparative advantage?" Still no one volunteered. He stood facing the right-hand side of the class. "Dave, do you understand comparative advantage?" Dave shook his head. The professor started working his way down the row. "Marie?" "No, I'm afraid I really don't." Rowe tried again, "How about you, Jack?" Still nothing.

By now, Doug Rowe was angry. "In all the years I've been teaching, I've never seen a class as poorly prepared as this one. We're just wasting our time. If you can't do better than this you'll have to get somebody else to teach this section." With that Professor Rowe gathered up his papers, threw his coat over his shoulder, and left the classroom. It was 1:20 P.M.

MBA Core Program

Following are excerpts from the Farwestern's *Bulletin* describing the first year of the MBA Program.

The purpose of the MBA Program is to train and develop professionals who possess the ability and understanding to deal effectively with issues and complex problems of the contemporary business world. The successful MBA graduate must possess a solid foundation in all the fundamentals of business and must be professional in personal conduct. Most important, the skills to apply that knowledge as well as the personal versatility and flexibility to respond to new and unexpected situations must be developed.

The MBA Core Program, which is the first year of the MBA Program, provides the educational base tomorrow's business managers must have. Each student receives a thorough grounding in the behavioral and quantitative sciences as well as a rigorous exposure to the functional areas of business: marketing management; financial management; business and managerial economics; decision making and communication. Not only do students acquire a sound knowledge base in these disciplines but they also receive an opportunity to apply knowledge and develop skills.

A seasoned, professional faculty team works closely with students on an individual, small-group and class-wide basis. A varied mix of proven teaching approaches such as case discussions, lectures, team projects, exercises, workshops, and simulations are utilized.

Students in the integrated program enroll in one section and remain together for class work and study throughout the year.

Three aspects of the first-year program at Farwestern's Graduate School of Business (GSB) are worthy of special mention: pedagogy, scheduling, and the importance of the sections. While the *Bulletin* mentions a variety of teaching approaches, the use of cases dominates the pedagogy of the program. Readings, exercises, lectures (really lecturettes), and other forms of teaching would best be thought of as supplementary to the case method rather than as equal partners with it. Despite a predictable amount of frustration, students soon come to have a respect for and enjoyment of the case method even in subjects that are often considered poor candidates for such an approach.

Courses in the Core Program are scheduled in free-form fashion so that their content relates to and builds upon one another rather than being fitted into a more rigid quarter or semester system. The effect of this scheduling arrangement is that some courses begin in September and others at various times from November to March. Some courses are compressed into two months while others extend to five. In fact, some courses run for a few months, stop for a time, and finish up later in the year. Students typically have three 80-minute classes per day.

Each of the sections mentioned in the *Bulletin* has an enrollment of approximately 65–70 students. Because sectionmates take all of their classes together for a year, the section becomes the dominant social, as well as educational, unit in Farwestern's GSB. Members of a section tend to develop strong relationships with one another, and the section develops distinctive behavior norms. For example, some sections might be characterized as quite competitive and others as more supportive. Some tend to be hard-working, some playful. Being a part of such a group for an entire school year is an important learning experience in itself. Students tend to become quite conscious of the behavior and norms of their section and think of it as unique and having its own "personality." Each section elects a representative to the programwide Education Committee of the Graduate Student Council. Elections are held at the beginning and middle of the year.

Courses comprising the Core Program during 1976–77 were: Management Control and Reporting, Financial Management, Management of Operations, Behavioral Psychology, Planning in Complex Systems, Marketing Management, Business and World Economics, Statistical Analysis for Business, and Business Information Systems.

The Course

Planning in Complex Systems was considered by all to be a difficult course. It dealt with complicated problems, and few students had had experience in the field prior to enrolling at Farwestern. Several earlier versions of the course had proved unsuccessful and were scrapped. The current course had been significantly revised several years earlier by some of Professor Rowe's colleagues. According to a statement of course goals by the teaching group, they felt that they were now at a point where they had a course concept and a set of teaching materials which allowed them to help their students effectively develop "basic technical skills . . . (and) . . . minimum levels of knowledge, skills and attitudes for generalists in this field." The course relied heavily on cases in planning developed for the course and a set of readings that gave students necessary background in the techniques, models, and theory of planning. Cases and readings tended to be long compared with those assigned in other first-year courses. For example, the cases in the International Trading series averaged about 30 pages of text and 10 pages of exhibits each. The (D) case, assigned for the first class after Thanksgiving, contained 33 pages of text and 8 pages of exhibits.

The Professor

Douglas Rowe had been a member of the Farwestern faculty for approximately 20 years. He had taught both first- and second-year courses in the MBA Program and had studied planning problems extensively. Since joining the PCS teaching group,

he had contributed significantly to the thinking of his colleagues concerning the course content and presentation. This year in particular he had looked forward to his teaching assignment because he felt confident about the current state of the course; the teaching materials were in good shape and the pieces of the course seemed to fit together well. Beyond that, he had noted from the information provided to the faculty by members of their sections that several Section IIIers seemed to have strong backgrounds in planning, and he hoped they would be good resource people for the class.

By the time PCS began in November, Professor Rowe had talked with two colleagues teaching other courses to Section III, and they had both expressed their disappointment with the preparation level of the section. However, these instructors had not expressed their displeasure directly to the section.

At the beginning of the course, Professor Rowe had talked with Section III about the goals of the course and what he hoped they would learn. He noted the importance of effort on their part because the materials tended to be long and the subject complicated. In the early classes, he took great care to go slowly over points that were especially important or difficult, pausing often to ask students if they understood. He emphasized the importance of understanding case facts, relating them to one another, and developing an integrated understanding.

During the second week of the course, he had returned to the matter of his expectations for the class: "Your part of the bargain is to be prepared; my part of the bargain is to make a useful learning experience out of it."

By the time the Thanksgiving break rolled around he was particularly disappointed in the work of the section. Discussions in class were going badly, and it appeared that most students were not putting in sufficient effort to be adequately prepared. Another problem was also apparent: in the second class before the holiday break, 15 students were absent and the day before Thanksgiving, attendance had dropped to 40 out of 65.

Nick Maitland's Interview with Jim Catterson

As a part of his doctoral program, Nick Maitland was sitting in on classes taught by experienced case-method teachers. He had spent some time discussing with Professor Rowe the outline of the course and how Rowe would approach the teaching.

Several months after the December 1 incident, Nick talked with Jim Catterson, one of the student leaders in Section III. (A few weeks after the December 1 incident, Catterson had been elected the section's representative to the Education Committee.)

Maitland began by explaining his reason for the interview: "As you know, Jim, I'm a doctoral candidate here in Management Planning and Theory. Part of our work focuses on the teaching process itself, and that is why I've been sitting in on your class. Professor Rowe has agreed that the incident with your section might make a good case for use with people studying case-method teaching. You know—what really happened? What did Rowe do and why? Might he have handled it differently? The standard case-method approach. So, if you could give me some of your impressions, it would be a big help. Could you tell me some of the things going on in Section III at the time, and your impressions of the incident?"

Jim Catterson was thoughtful, but animated and eager to talk about "the incident."

JIM: I'll never forget that day. It was incredible. I can still see Doug Rowe standing in front of the right-hand section of the class. He had asked several people the same question, and they all said they weren't able to comment on it. He was furious; he threw his papers on the desk. He said people weren't prepared. He said he would not teach another class like that one and, in fact, he said somebody else would have to teach the class if we couldn't do better. Then he stormed out of the room.

We all sort of sat there stunned for a minute; then people started getting really angry. You know—saying "What right does he have to just walk out?" and that sort of thing. Some people turned to the ed rep and he said, "Well, Rowe's probably right." Then people were really mad.

NICK: What things were going on in Section III at that time?

JIM: Lots of things. First of all other teachers we had at the time were terrible! We had—I'm going to be very candid with you and I'll use names—Professor Roger Williams for Business Information Systems. He's very famous, but he never prepared the cases. If you asked him a question, he couldn't answer it. He talked all the time. He never wrote on the chalkboard. He just looked for particular words, not for your ideas. That's not the way you teach here.

In Finance, we had Irv Kincaid who is still at the school but not teaching in the MBA Program anymore. He's a very nice guy and, as a matter of fact, he's brilliant. But he just could not teach by the case method. He couldn't get it into his head how to approach people. He was too far above everybody; he assumed he knew everything and we didn't know anything.

Then we had Francis Gress for Marketing Management. He had just been informed that he was not being rehired—didn't get tenure.

So the day that Doug Rowe walked out, all of these things were happening at once. One teacher didn't care because he wasn't rehired, another teacher couldn't teach, and a third teacher was terrible. That particular day, December 1, we had Finance and Marketing in the morning, and they were just terrible classes. No one was participating anymore. Everyone was saying, "Why are we spending *thousands* of dollars to come here? We're getting crap right now." It was just terrible! Doug didn't understand that and he walked out. He thought it was that we weren't preparing for his class, but it was actually a much, much larger problem than that. It was that the whole case method wasn't working. Our group had just fallen apart.

NICK: Had it been working better earlier in the year?

JIM [*his face brightening up*]: Oh, it was great. In the beginning of the year we were a tremendous section. In fact we were said by some instructors to be "too rambunctious." People wouldn't raise their hands, they'd just jump right in. Everybody had something to say. There'd be 20 hands up at a time.

What happened was that our faculty coordinator[1] in the fall, Professor Bob Waggonier, said that we were too rambunctious and that we had to be more rigorous. He really clobbered somebody in class. The person said a really dumb thing in class and Waggonier said members of the section should have jumped in and criticized him for the statement. That quieted things down a lot.

Also, earlier in the year we had Professor Richard Hagey, who is an excellent professor but a bit of a manipulator. So, a lot of people in

1. A senior faculty member who offered informal, administrative, and academic leadership for a section's teaching group.

the class didn't like him—a majority didn't. I did, but a lot of people really didn't like him at all. They felt he was manipulating the class.

Little by little, these teachers began to pull out of us a lot of the real zip that we came in with. So, by the time Doug Rowe started teaching, things had fallen apart. And by the time the Thanksgiving break came around, people were just dead. There was no interest. Does that answer the question?

NICK: Do you have any feeling as to why as experienced a teacher as Doug Rowe, starting to teach his course several months into the school year, could get nearly a month into his course without being sensitive to the things you've described?

JIM: The reasons are somewhat . . . well they're very interesting. First of all, Doug Rowe is an extremely sensitive individual. He's probably the most perceptive individual I've met here. So, the fact that it took *him* a month to get into it was very interesting. The reasons? One, his course had some fairly serious problems, not our year but the year before. He had played such a major role in designing the course that he was very heavily invested in it personally. He felt he was on the line. So this year he was very sensitive to what was happening to the course as a whole but not very sensitive to what was happening in our section.

Then, he came in the first day of class in November and he didn't really go through a synopsis of what the course was about. He said something like, "We're going to have some hard cases in the beginning of the course but it will even up. You can take a look at the syllabus—the list of cases—and see what we'll be covering. I think that's all I want to say about the course for right now, so let's just start with the first case." He didn't go through what we would have considered the basics of what the course was to be built on, didn't really give us any background. We expected some sort of an outline. Then he could have said, "Even if you don't understand it right now, as we go along you'll see it fit together."

He was very sensitive to what was going on in other first-year sections, was very "into" what was going on with other teachers teaching the same course: What was going on? How were new teachers doing? That sort of thing. He spent lots of time with teachers in other sections who were having a particularly hard time of it. It's a hard course to teach. Consequently, he simply must not have had time to ask the other teachers of Section III about their perceptions of how we were doing. Plus, when he first started teaching us, our section was still decent. It wasn't until the end of the month that we went right down the tubes.

TEACHING NOTE

We're Just Wasting Our Time

W e're Just Wasting Our Time" is a case that concerns a nearly universal problem in teaching: how to deal with apathy and students' failure to prepare for class. In addition, it highlights the difficulty of accurately "reading" a section so as to stay in touch with its process of learning and development.

This case is usually used near the end of our seminar on case method teaching, after the major themes of the course (e.g., rapport, the teacher-student learning contract, questioning, listening, and responding) have been introduced. During this latter phase, we consider a variety of special but recurrent problems of teaching, while reviewing and further exploring the central themes of the course.

Course Summary

"We're Just Wasting Our Time" is a moderately long case, and thus lends itself best to seminars in which participants are able to prepare the case in advance. It includes information about the evolution of a section during the semester—from the perspectives of both the instructor and a student leader in the section—and thus provides material for a discussion on how various factors can combine, over time, to produce a problem situation. In addition, because the case contains background information on the MBA program at Farwestern Graduate School of Business, it is relatively easy to use with seminar members who are not familiar with the school or with business education in general. (For more information on the school for which "Farwestern," "Bay," "New Dominion," and "Metropolitan" are pseudonyms, see Abby Hansen's "Background Information on a Graduate School of Business Administration" in Part III of this book.)

The Institutional Context

"We're Just Wasting Our Time" takes place in a required course in Farwestern's first-year MBA core program, which covers most aspects of business practice. Courses are scheduled in free form, rather than in the conventional semester or quarter format, and build upon each other in terms of content. For example, courses vary in length from two to five months, and may begin anywhere from September to March.

All students are assigned to sections of 60 to 70 members. Sections take all of their classes together for the year and tend to become important social as

This teaching note was written by Dr. **James F. Moore**, in collaboration with Professor **C. Roland Christensen**, as an aid to instructors in the classroom use of the case We're Just Wasting Our Time, *HBS Case No. 9-378-035*.

well as educational units. The group process varies from section to section, and both students and faculty members typically sense distinctive characteristics—"personality traits"—in particular sections.

Teaching at Farwestern is conducted primarily by the case method, with which most students are initially unfamiliar. They normally take some time to learn to learn in this mode. Though the method was developed and used for many years at Farwestern, it is still somewhat controversial, and new students sometimes wonder if it is working. However, most adjust well and find this form of instruction both productive and enjoyable.

MBA students typically have three 80-minute classes each day, taught by different instructors. Since all sections take the same course during the same period, each course is taught by a number of faculty members. This course "teaching group" is normally overseen by a "course head" who teaches a section as well as managing the group.

The Course

Planning in Complex Systems (PCS), the case text reports, is "considered by all to be a difficult course" for which few students are prepared by their previous experience. The cases in the course tend to be longer than those assigned in other first-year courses. PCS begins in November and runs for several months.

In response to difficulties encountered in previous versions of Planning in Complex Systems, the course design has been substantially revised in recent years. The instructors now believe the course will be effective in helping students develop "basic technical skills . . . [and] minimum levels of knowledge, skills and attitudes for generalists in this field."

Douglas Rowe is a senior faculty member who has been at Farwestern for 20 years. He is experienced with both first- and second-year MBA courses, and has studied planning problems extensively.

Rowe has contributed a great deal to the content and presentation of the current version of Planning in Complex Systems. He looks forward to teaching the course this year both because he believes the course design to be in good shape, and because several students in his section have some planning background and he hopes they will contribute a great deal to the discussions.

Nick Maitland, a doctoral student, has been sit-

ting in to observe case method classes, and witnesses the pivotal incident on December 1. Several months later he interviews Jim Catterson, a student leader in the section.

The Section

Section III consists of first-year, first-semester MBA students. Though the names of several students are mentioned in the description of the incident with Rowe, only one student is described—and he only briefly. This is Jim Catterson. It is through his eyes that the reader is given the students' view of the situation in Section III. We learn little else about Catterson, except that a few weeks after the December 1 incident he was elected the section's representative to the Education Committee.

The Teacher-Student Relationship

The case first describes the teacher-student relationship from the faculty perspective. By the time Professor Rowe began his course, two other instructors had reported feeling disappointed with the section's preparation level. They had not expressed their feelings directly to the section, however.

Rowe begins his teaching (in early November) by stressing his expectations for the section: "Your part of the bargain is to be prepared; my part of the bargain is to make a useful learning experience of it." Note that while he makes clear his view of the contract, he does not ask for input from the students.

By Thanksgiving Rowe is disappointed in the section's performance. Discussions are described as going badly, and Rowe believes most students are not putting enough effort into preparing for class. Further, absenteeism is becoming a problem.

Rowe's view of the situation contrasts with that of the students, as reported by Jim Catterson. Catterson emphasizes that although Rowe contributed to the section's problems, they were due largely to events that happened before PCS began and to concurrent events beyond Rowe's direct control.

Catterson reports that Rowe did not give the students a clear overview of his course at the beginning—which the students expected. Further, although he mentioned that some of the cases would be quite difficult, he did little to reassure the students that they would eventually come to understand the material.

Moreover, students did not think Rowe was particularly sensitive to what was going on in Section III. Rather, he seemed to be putting his energy into the teaching group, trying to keep track of progress in the other sections of his course. Ordinarily this orientation would not have been a serious problem. Section III, however, was having a variety of difficulties unrelated to Rowe's teaching, but inevitably affecting its performance in his classes.

Jim Catterson reports that at the beginning of the year the section was "tremendous"—lively and described by some instructors as "too rambunctious." Jim describes a class section early in the term when the section's faculty coordinator, Professor Bob Waggonier, rebuked the section for its exuberance and urged them to be more critical of each other's contributions to the discussion. This "quieted things down a lot."

Another of the early instructors, Professor Richard Hagey, was seen by the section members as a "manipulator." Though this term is not defined by Jim Catterson, the implication is that the professor was not trusted, and maintained an uncomfortably one-sided and controlling contract with the section.

Jim Catterson reports that by the time Rowe took over, "things had fallen apart." Moreover, the section was not responding well to the other teachers to whom it was exposed during Rowe's tenure. Professor Roger Williams talks to the class rather than leading discussions, and the students feel he has not prepared the cases. Irv Kincaid is described as a brilliant person who is also very nice but cannot relate well to people—and therefore can't teach. Finally, Francis Gress has just been informed that he will not get tenure; the implication is that this bad news has had a decidedly negative impact on his teaching.

Finally, on the day of the incident, the two classes preceding Rowe's have been "terrible"; the section as a whole has stopped participating and is spending its energy questioning the value of the educational experience at Farwestern. It is this situation that Doug Rowe walks into on December 1.

The Incident

The case incident occurs during the fourth class in a series concerning the problems of International Trading Company. Students are to discuss "International Trading Co. (D)," having worked through the (A), (B), and (C) cases in the three preceding class sections. Though this point is not made explicitly in the text, four class sessions in a row is an

unusually long time to spend on one case series—and such sequences can become quite tedious. Moreover, the case sequence has been interrupted by the Thanksgiving break. The December 1 discussion is the first PCS class after Thanksgiving. Attendance and interest often slack off just before vacations, and in this course both declined greatly. While the December 1 discussion presumably assumes a familiarity with the earlier cases in the series, many students have probably not digested them. The previous case discussion occurred seven days earlier and was poorly attended.

On the day of the incident, Rowe finds a dozen students absent, and those present seem unengaged. No students volunteer to speak, and one of the students called upon earlier passes, saying he is not prepared. Rowe can elicit only mediocre contributions. He tries lecturing briefly, hoping to stimulate some thinking, but in the moments following, no one volunteers. Finally he becomes visibly angry (according to Jim Catterson), and asks several students in a row the same simple question. No one answers.

At this point, Rowe explodes: "In all the years I've been teaching, I've never seen a class as poorly prepared as this one. We're just wasting our time. If you can't do better than this, you'll have to get somebody else to teach this section." He then collects his notes, throws his coat over his shoulder, and leaves the room. Only 20 minutes have elapsed since the beginning of the class session.

Jim Catterson reports the students' reactions: "We all sort of sat there stunned for a minute; then people started getting really angry: you know—saying, 'What right does he have to just walk out?' and that sort of thing. Some people turned to the ed rep and he said, 'Well, Rowe's probably right.' Then people were really mad."

A Note on Study and Discussion Questions

Typically we prepare at least two sets of questions for use with each case. The first consists of study questions (see *Exhibit 1*); these can be handed out with the case for participants' use in preparing for class. The second set is a series of discussion questions (see *Exhibit 2*), to be used by the seminar leader in preparing for the case discussion and in guiding the case discussion when appropriate. For all discussion questions, but not for study questions, we have provided detailed usage and analytical notes.

Exhibit 1

WE'RE JUST WASTING OUR TIME

Study Questions (for distribution with case)

1. What is your diagnosis of the situation? Of Rowe's action?
2. What should Professor Rowe do now?
3. As a section instructor, how do you evaluate the overall section's progress toward becoming a learning group? How do you evaluate *section* performance?
4. What are the key techniques for tracking the performance of individual students in a section? What constitutes a positive contribution? What constitutes grounds for a poorer evaluation?

Exhibit 2

WE'RE JUST WASTING OUR TIME

Discussion Questions (for use by seminar leader)

1. From your own experience as a student, what are some of the reasons that students don't prepare for class sessions?
2. Summarize, as a friend of Rowe's: How and why did Rowe get into trouble?

The following questions can be used to deepen the diagnostic discussion:

3. What questions does the case pose for you?
4. What are the significant factors that contribute to this situation?
5. Why was Rowe so angry? What is going on for him? What was his perception of the situation?
6. Jim Catterson, the student section's leader, says that it took Rowe a month to become fully aware of the section's problems. Why didn't Rowe, a sensitive and seasoned professor, read his section better?

The next two questions move the discussion to a consideration of action:

7. What are the pros and cons of Doug Rowe's action—chastising the section and walking out?
8. What is the situation now? What are his alternatives for following up?

The following questions now shift to generalization:

9. What questions does this case raise for you?
10. What, in general, can an instructor do to counter apathy and poor preparation when those problems first appear?

A Suggested Process Plan for the Case

In discussing this case, we emphasize ways to deal with classroom apathy and lack of preparation. We ordinarily combine a standard case discussion (developing diagnoses, action plans, and conclusions/generalizations) with a working session on how to increase classroom involvement and student preparation.

In the working session, we first raise the issues, then ask participants to think about the underlying causes of these problems and to suggest ways to deal with them. The working-session approach is particularly valuable because apathy and lack of preparation are among the most perplexing and complex difficulties instructors face. Moreover, most participants have directly experienced these difficulties and have already given them serious thought.

Our first question, "From your experience as a student, why don't students prepare?" and our third question, "What questions does this case raise for you?" encourage seminar members to define the issues presented by the case. Typically, a cluster of concerns will be raised, all related to the general topics on involvement and student preparation. Opening the session with these concerns stimulates participants to generalize from the case and consider their own experiences, thus setting the stage for the later working session.

The effect of these opening questions is also to make the case itself somewhat less central than it is in most discussions. Instead of being an all-important, perplexing mystery, this case is made subordinate to the complexity of the participants' own experiences with similar problems.

After this initial foray into generalization, we use Questions 2, 4, 5, and 6 to move the seminar's attention to the case situation. Our overall plan is first to examine the facts of the situation, and then to highlight the professor's understanding of it. We then move to a consideration of the section's perspective, building up to a discussion of why its understanding of the situation is so different from Rowe's.

We hope in this discussion not only to emphasize the complexity of the situation facing Rowe, but also to suggest that most instances of sustained apathy and lack of preparation involve a mesh of intertwined factors that are difficult to understand. We underscore the risks of jumping to conclusions, as well as the need to create ways to "listen in" on the learning process of one's sections.

Questions 7 and 8 move the seminar to an examination of Rowe's actions, and thus set the stage for a discussion of both tactics appropriate to his particular situation and more general approaches to dealing with apathy and lack of participation. The seminar often moves into what we have called the working-session mode at this point. Questions 9 and 10 then encourage a broad discussion of means for creating involvement at the section level.

Notes for Discussion Questions

We have briefly indicated the pedagogical intent and use of the suggested discussion questions in *Exhibit 2*. In addition, we have provided our best attempt at a reasoned response to each question. These analytical responses are provided primarily to aid the instructor in preparing for class and are intended to sensitize him or her to key issues in the case. These responses represent our current thinking on the questions raised by the case—not a definitive solution. "We're Just Wasting Our Time," like other cases, can be profitably analyzed from a variety of viewpoints—and a variety of actions could be usefully taken in situations similar to those described in the case. We hope each new discussion of the case will provide new insights of value to both the discussion participants and the discussion leader—and we can say with gratitude that this has been our experience in leading discussions of this case and others in the seminar.

Question No. 1. From your own experience as a student, what are some of the reasons that people don't prepare for class sessions?

USAGE NOTE. This opening question asks participants to probe their own experiences, thus identifying more deeply with the students in the case and perhaps becoming more appreciative of the complex variety of reasons that may lie behind lack of preparations and/or apathy.

ANALYSIS. There are many, many possible reasons for lack of preparation. Individual students have a variety of commitments competing for their attention. A student under pressure from other quarters may decide to risk not preparing for a particular class on a given day. Personal problems may also interfere. Individuals may find the class work overwhelmingly difficult, and give up in frustration. Students may become angry or discouraged with the professor, with what is going on in the course, and/or with their school experience—and some may express their frustration by consciously or unconsciously withdrawing commitment and preparing less.

When an entire class ceases to prepare, the causes most likely lie in the experiences they share—often within the particular class, and sometimes within their overall school program. Possible explanations of apathy are still myriad, however. For example, the course material may be discouragingly difficult, and the students may not be able to find ways to communicate their problem and get adequate help. The process of the class sessions may also be discouraging. Some instructors are unduly severe with students, often without being aware of it. Students may react by resisting participating in class. Other instructors are themselves apathetic, withdrawn, and uninterested in the daily dynamics of the classes—and students soon realize this and find it hard to stay engaged.

Moreover, what goes on in any given classroom plays only a small part in the students' overall experiences. Students must cope with the substantive and process demands of several separate courses while also dealing with the human dynamics of their overall educational program group and the school or university as a whole. Sometimes societywide conditions—for example, wars and economic recessions—may lead students to see their educations as relatively useless and result in apathy and lack of participation.

Question No. 2. Summarize, as a friend of Rowe's: How and why did Rowe get into trouble?

USAGE NOTE. This question provides four levels of direction to participants. First, it asks them to examine the factors that led up to the incident on

December 1, thus beginning the discussion with analysis rather than action planning, and suggesting a temporal perspective (by asking how he got into trouble rather than what the trouble is).

Second, by implying that Rowe, rather than the section, is "in trouble," the question invites the seminar to look for aspects of Rowe's behavior that could have contributed to the problems with the section. Third, it asks participants to take the stance of a friend of Rowe's, thus encouraging collegiality and identification with his plight. Fourth, it asks participants to summarize their answers and be succinct. This last directive is not always used, but is an option to consider if the particular seminar group tends toward wordiness and lack of focus.

ANALYSIS. In the opinion of most seminar participants, Rowe got into trouble primarily by not taking Section III's problem more seriously earlier, when he still had time to try to discover its nature and to respond more gradually and perhaps less dramatically.

Though colleagues had alerted Rowe to a potential problem in Section III, his only response was a one-way communication of his expectations. There is no evidence that he tried to speak with section members, including the educational representative, about the reports of difficulty. Nor did he take any measures to increase preparation over the first few weeks—for example, asking students to work in groups and present panel reports, or assigning students specific preparation tasks in advance.

Questions 3 through 6 can be used to deepen the diagnostic discussion.

Question No. 3. What questions does the case pose for you?

USAGE NOTE. This very broad query encourages generalization and typically brings a number of issues out on the table for consideration. By following it with probes about what specific items in the case stimulated these questions, one can encourage the seminar to consider the complex set of factors that contributed to apathy in Section III.

ANALYSIS. This case raises a variety of issues, including but not limited to the following: How can one encourage preparation for class? How can one create involvement during discussions? When an entire section is "going downhill," how can it be turned around? How can an instructor read and respond to conditions in the section that he or she has not created—for example, problems apparently caused by other instructors? How can one help a collection of individual students become a learning community?

Question No. 4. What were the significant factors that contributed to this situation?

USAGE NOTE. This question is similar in effect to Question 3 but promotes less generalization. It encourages an understanding of the many intertwined factors that may have contributed to the problems of the section.

ANALYSIS. Participants usually identify a wide variety of factors that apparently contributed to Section III's apathy and lack of preparation. One issue is the relationship that has evolved between the section and its instructors (other than Doug Rowe). The group's early energy, which might have been harnessed to productive purposes, was apparently killed by the faculty coordinator who verbally chastised the section and followed up by punishing a student for a poor contribution. The section's feeling of powerlessness was then apparently reinforced by Professor Richard Hagey's style of teaching, which the section members experienced as manipulative. Finally, Professors Roger Williams, Irv Kincaid, and Francis Gress added to the problem in that none was able to create rapport and excitement in his classes—rather, these instructors taught over students' heads or missed them completely, thus making the section even more discouraged.

Doug Rowe began his course in a way that ran counter to the expectations of the students, did not meet their needs, and was more or less unilaterally imposed. The students, according to Jim Catterson, expected and felt they needed a conceptual overview of Rowe's course. Their anxiety at not getting one was probably magnified by the course's reputation for difficulty—a reputation reinforced by Rowe's early remarks. Rowe seemed unaware of the section's anxiety and did not respond to it in a way that the students perceived as helpful. He laid out what he expected of students, pointing out the need to be prepared. He did not ask what they expected of him, either informally out of class or in the classroom. This relatively one-way mode of communication did little to mitigate the alienation that had been developing in their other courses.

During the following weeks, Rowe seems to have been preoccupied with the progress in the other sections and not to have worked consciously enough to build a good relationship with Section III. Thus, a bad situation deteriorated further.

Splitting a long and probably difficult case around the Thanksgiving vacation probably added to the apathy. Students have enough trouble recalling case facts and discussion points from one class to another. After six days, the problem is much worse. Further, many of the students had been absent just before the vacation, and thus were probably lost in the (D) case discussion, which built on work in the previous sessions.

Rowe's handling of the class on December 1 did not include any special response to either the previous absenteeism or the long break. For example, he could have begun with a review of the earlier case segments, or asked students who had actively participated in those discussions to provide such a briefing for the section. Instead, he seems to have called upon students without considering how well prepared they might be. The result in retrospect probably was predictable: many ill-prepared contributions. At this, Doug Rowe became angry. Turning to the class, he asked a relatively simple question and, getting unsatisfactory responses, went down a row asking the same question to each person in the series. The students, already turned off and feeling hostile toward the school and their instructors, may have experienced this action as punitive and insulting—and showed their consequent resentment and anger by not cooperating.

Question No. 5. Why was Rowe so angry? What is going on for him? What was his perception of the situation?

USAGE NOTE. The question shifts the focus from the development of the situation to Rowe's perceptions and motivations. Our hope is first to help the seminar understand how complex a problem apathy can be, and then to examine the difficulty that even experienced instructors—like Rowe—may have in reading such situations accurately. Concurrently, this question moves consideration from the background of the crisis to the current situation.

ANALYSIS. Rowe seems to see the problem as a lack of effort on the part of the students. Not knowing

what has happened in their relationships with other instructors, and not sensing his own contributions, Rowe cannot find an explanation for their apathy and lack of participation. This is frustrating, especially for an experienced "teacher's teacher" like Rowe. Many people in such a situation would wonder whether the section were just being perverse, lazy, or "bad." If Rowe sees things in this light, he may feel let down by the section, and may think that students are challenging his authority and competence. Either conclusion could be insulting and angering for a dedicated teacher.

More than other PCS instructors, Rowe has strong personal reasons for wanting the section to perform well. He takes pride in his work on the content and presentation of the course. Further, as the course head, with responsibility to supervise other instructors, he could find it embarrassing if his section did poorly.

Question No. 6. Jim Catterson, the student section's leader, says that it took Rowe a month to become fully aware of the section's problems. Why didn't Rowe, a sensitive and seasoned professor, read his section better?

USAGE NOTE. This question continues the line initiated in Question 4, encouraging participants to appreciate the factors that kept Rowe from understanding his section—factors like those which participants may encounter in their own teaching.

ANALYSIS. Rowe's wider responsibilities as course head apparently distracted him from his own section. The apathy in Section III, although recognized as a problem from the first, perhaps did not, on balance, seem serious enough to warrant extensive attention—until the December 1 incident.

Rowe's problem was complicated by the fact that the section was responding not only to his actions, but to the present and past actions of five other instructors. Though Rowe was keeping abreast of developments in other sections of *his course*, he was not attending to Section III's experiences in *their* other courses. Rowe could probably have learned about such circumstances through exceptionally candid discussions with students such as the educational representative, as well as by discussing the section's progress in detail with the other instructors. Because Rowe did not cultivate the sorts of relationships that would promote such candid communication, he remained unaware of important factors bearing on his own in-class situation.

The next two questions move the discussion to a consideration of action:

Question No. 7. What are the pros and cons of Doug Rowe's action—chastising the section and walking out?

USAGE NOTE. This question shifts the focus from analysis to a consideration of action alternatives, while encouraging participants to take a broad, evaluative approach to the case.

ANALYSIS. Many participants believe Rowe's response may shake up the section and turn it around. Such an outcome is possible if Rowe's assertion that he has never seen a class so poorly prepared succeeds in mobilizing the section's collective self-esteem. Students' liking and respect for Rowe will also be an important ingredient, perhaps motivating them to work hard so that he will be willing to continue teaching them. Finally, the section members may make an effort to avoid the schoolwide scandal that might be associated with an instructor's refusal to teach them.

Rowe's action could backfire, however. If enough section members do not like his teaching, they might welcome his departure and resist his further leadership in either subtle or overt ways. Rowe would then face a very difficult situation. It is unlikely that he could carry through his threat to quit teaching the section, and thus he would be left with his bluff called and a section that felt rejected and rejecting.

In addition, seminar participants often point out that Rowe's denunciation of the class's poor preparation misses the true nature of their situation. It may shake them up, forcing them to realize that even if they have valid reasons for not liking the way they are being taught, they must continue to prepare for class. But it does nothing to address their underlying concern that their instructors cannot understand and relate to them, and continue to impose unilateral teacher-student contracts. Thus, though this intervention may force compliance from the section, it is unlikely to produce, in itself, a renewal of the personal engagement that is central to effective learning.

Question No. 8. What is the situation as a result of his speech and walking out? What are his alternatives for following up?

USAGE NOTE. This question asks participants to consider the important issue of monitoring and following up on interventions. Whatever one believes about Rowe's action, it is important to consider what to do next.

ANALYSIS. The case text tells very little about students' reaction to Rowe's intervention, except that they became very angry. It is not clear what sorts of collective and individual conclusions they came to, or how these were expressed in their actions following the incident.

Participants in the seminar usually suggest a broad range of options for follow-up; which one is best would depend on the section's response to Rowe's intervention and on his preferred style of leadership. To begin with, most participants suggest that he should try to learn more about the section, perhaps talking with the educational representative (who the text suggests is sympathethic to Rowe's aims), or with other students with whom he can develop some rapport.

If the intervention seems to have shaken students out of their lethargy, Rowe can continue the next class without changing his basic approach, hoping that the class will be better prepared and more involved. The disadvantage of this strategy is that it does nothing to help the section members with their substantive problems with the course material. Moreover, leaving a major, four-part case poorly analyzed may put them at a further disadvantage.

To address students' substantive needs, Rowe could ask the students to reconsider the International Trading Company case in the next class. He could go further and analyze the case himself for the section. To show the level of discussion expected, he could provide tips on preparation, as well as review the course outline and goals, in order to help the students become oriented to the central aims of the course. These interventions would begin to respond to the students' learning needs and might be well received, since the ultimate underlying goal of most students is to learn the course content.

Such an approach, however, would still represent a unilaterally imposed contract. Even though it responds to some of the students' needs, they may still feel angry and alienated. If Rowe's intelligence gathering suggests that such feelings are running high, he might call a meeting, perhaps outside of class time, to discuss the overall situation in Section III and to work collaboratively toward a better learning process. Though this session could prove very difficult to manage, it would restore a two-way contracting process. Alternatively, if Rowe is not confident that his group leadership skills would ensure a happy outcome in such a session, he could meet informally with small groups of students from the section, listening to their views, creating rapport, and signaling that he intends to stay in closer touch with them and respond more sensitively to the needs of the section.

The last two questions help us shift now to generalization:

Question No. 9. What questions does this case raise for you?

USAGE NOTE. This broad question encourages generalization while allowing the seminar members virtually complete freedom to follow whatever lines of discussion they find important. The same question was asked earlier as Question 3, and it can be interesting to compare participants' original responses with those made after the discussion. This slant can be emphasized by asking participants, "Now that we have discussed the case, what new questions does it raise for you?"

ANALYSIS. This question allows seminar members to bring in a wide range of concerns. In addition to the questions typically mentioned at the beginning of the discussion (see the analysis of Question 2), participants sometimes wonder how instructors can set up channels of communication to their students and other instructors, and how instructors can remain sensitive to the subtle signals of the classes when they are under a variety of other pressures. Usually, seminar members return to the difficult questions of how to encourage students to prepare well for class and how to create involvement with course material. Finally, they often focus on the instructor's role in creating an involved community of students (i.e., the section as a whole) rather than simply engaging individual students.

Question No. 10. What, in general, can an instructor do to counter apathy and poor preparation when these problems first appear?

USAGE NOTE. Following the very broad discussion of Question 9, we now return to the specifics of responding to apathy and lack of preparation. This

question can be a springboard for turning the seminar into a brief session in which participants can share insights and techniques for handling these two recurring problems.

ANALYSIS. One of the *least* helpful approaches to an apathetic class, many experienced instructors suggest, is to discuss the situation directly with the students as a problem of poor preparation. This labels the situation in a way that gives students only two options: either they can continue as they are, thus doing something now defined as "bad," or they can "shape up" and comply with the instructor's standards. At best, the students are likely to feel that they are succumbing to pressure, rather than becoming genuinely engaged in learning. Further, any special teaching techniques that the instructor uses after raising the problem explicitly will be readily identified as "ways to manipulate the section into participating more." Section members may not recognize that, while the instructor has some effect, it is their genuine response to those interventions that makes the difference. Their involvement is real, and they can be proud of it. Students will find it more difficult to achieve this recognition if the section has been explicitly labeled a problem group.

Seminar members usually offer a wealth of suggestions for creating involvement. Most of these techniques work best when used subtly, so that students are more aware of their own improving performance than of the instructor's interventions.

Instructors can use their questioning style to increase involvement in the classroom, in ways that have been described in earlier teaching notes. For example, one can ask students for increased personal commitments to their arguments by personalizing discussion questions (e.g., "Jane, what would you do if you were Doug Rowe?"). One can create excitement and potential conflict by beginning discussions with action planning rather than analysis. By the way that the instructor bridges between comments and summarizes discussion, he or she can highlight conflict and differences of opinion, thus sharpening the dialogue between groups of participants.

Competition within the classroom can be heightened even more by creating formal, though temporary, competing groups. For example, the instructor can assign one role to the left half of the class, and another to the right, and pose questions to each side. Students sitting in the middle can then be asked which group did better and why.

Section performance can be improved by inviting guests to be present, and announcing their visits in advance. It is especially useful to invite guests whom students see as having some potential impact on their futures. For example, one can mention in passing that "the dean of the graduate program is interested in Monday's case and will be sitting in with us." To avoid looking bad before such guests, students are likely to invest a good deal of extra effort in these sessions.

If the students seem to be frustrated with the difficulty of the materials, a variety of approaches may be helpful. At the beginning of class each day, the instructor can summarize the previous session's case in order to create a better sense of continuity and to give students a map of where they have been. This practice can be continued for several weeks.

In addition, one can create success experiences by addressing discussion questions to individuals with relevant strengths. For example, a student who is a good lead-off person should be used in that role. Another student who is clearly effective in summmarizing might be asked to provide integration and direction when it seems appropriate. And the instructor can provide opportunities for students with background in particular areas to share their experience through their comments in class.

One can also make the section more attentive to its own process, and offer instructive guidance, by providing fast and frequent—but unobstrusive—process feedback. This approach is often most effective when used to signal something done well. For example, "Our discussion of the case so far has been most productive, because we have been able to highlight . . . and get a clearer understanding of the issues of. . . ."

In addition, it is often possible to insert into the course schedule a substitute case that is known to be both exciting and relatively easy for students to analyze. When the section does a truly excellent job on a case, students know it; often their morale rises and they become enthusiastic to tackle bigger challenges.

The instructor can approach particular students in advance and ask them to be the opening speakers in class, thus giving them an opportunity to prepare carefully. Students can be assigned such roles as much as a week in advance. To provide further

structure, the instructor might ask each of several students to take a different position, or to describe the case from a particular point of view. The class can then be asked questions about these presentations.

These techniques can be used with small groups as well as individuals. Several students can be asked to work together and report to the class as a panel. (Groups can be self-selected or chosen by the instructor.) Other students can then question the panel members about their remarks.

One can also make it a regular practice to meet outside of class with subgroups of section members—discussing the forthcoming case and/or other aspects of the course material. Held shortly before a class session, such a meeting provides a warm-up for the following discussion. In addition to stimulating the students and signaling concern about their learning, these informal sessions allow the instructor to learn more about how the students are doing and how they are experiencing the course. These meetings can be regularly scheduled, perhaps over breakfast or lunch before class. In another case in our syllabus, "Class on World Hunger," the instructor made excellent use of such sessions. Students participated on a voluntary, rotating basis, with scheduling handled by the section's educational representative.

Suggestions for Building the Seminar Group

"We're Just Wasting Our Time" is generally used late in the semester, and plays a part in our "end game" for the seminar. The quintessential case discussion begins with analysis, moves to a consideration of action, and concludes with an opportunity to generalize from the case. The teaching seminar follows a broadly parallel pattern. The last cases, while continuing to introduce new material, provide the participants with occasions for reflecting on what has come before, thinking about educational philosophy, and exploring the connections between the seminar material and their own teaching.

As instructors, we help create these moments for reflection. For example, we no longer press the participants to stick with the case material. Instead, we use bridging, selective attention, and summarizing to highlight the seminar's efforts at generalization. Our questions also contribute to the shift of focus. We are more likely now to ask, "What issues does this case raise for you?" or "What questions does this discussion leave you with?" We might also ask people to talk about similar experiences they have had, comparing and contrasting them with the case situation. Finally, by asking participants to discuss *apathy* or *lack of preparation* in the generic sense, we encourage them to make direct connections between their own experiences and those described in the case.

Bibliography

CYNTHIA INGOLS

KAREN MALONEY

This bibliography is intended to be a tool for those who are interested in doing further reading on issues which emerge from the preceding cases. We have organized the list to proceed from general to specific topics. Section I contains books and articles on education and teaching in general; these have been selected to give a representation of the many different approaches to, and philosophies in, education and teaching. Section II is more specific, focusing on case method and discussion teaching. Section III addresses operating problems of the case method teacher. Beginning with a list of problems identified by practitioners in these teaching seminars, we searched the literature, finding that some of these problems, though frequently discussed, are seldom written about. Section III includes issues on which we did find valuable material. Our selection has been based on the clarity, soundness, and usefulness of the material, and on its appropriateness to undergraduate, graduate, and professional school teaching.

I. Education and Teaching in General

Axelrod, J. *The University Teacher as Artist.* San Francisco: Jossey-Bass, 1976.

Barrows, H. S. and R. M. Tamblyn. *Problem-Based Learnings: An Approach to Medical Education.* New York: Springer, 1980.

Barzun, J. *Teacher in America.* Boston: Little, Brown, 1944.

Bruner, J. S. *The Process of Education.* Cambridge: Harvard University Press, 1961.

————. *Toward a Theory of Instruction.* Cambridge: Harvard University Press, 1966.

Cross, K. P. *Adults as Learners.* San Francisco: Jossey-Bass, 1981.

Dewey, J. *How We Think.* Boston: D. C. Heath, 1933.

————. *Human Nature and Conduct.* New York: Random House, 1922, 1957.

Dressel, P. L. and D. Marcus. *On Teaching and Learning in College.* San Francisco: Jossey-Bass, 1982.

Eble, K. E. *The Craft of Teaching: A Guide to Mastering the Professor's Art.* San Francisco: Jossey-Bass, 1976.

————, ed. *Improving Teaching Styles. New Directions for Teaching and Learning,* No. 1. San Francisco: Jossey-Bass, 1980.

Eisner, E. N. "On the Art of Teaching." In *The Educational Imagination* by E. N. Eisner. New York: Macmillan, 1979.

Epstein, J., ed. *Masters: Portraits of Great Teachers.* New York: Basic, 1981.

Fuhrmann, B. S. and A. F. Grasha. *A Practical Handbook for College Teachers.* Boston: Little, Brown, 1983.

Gullette, M. M., ed. *The Art and Craft of Teaching.* Cambridge: Harvard-Danforth Center for Teaching and Learning, 1982.

Hamachek, D. E., ed. *Human Dynamics in Psychology and Education,* 3rd ed. Boston: Allyn and Bacon, 1977.

Hawkins, D. "Human Nature and the Scope of Education." In *The Informed Vision* by D. Hawkins. New York: Agathon, 1974.

Jackson, P. W. *Life in Classrooms.* New York: Holt, Rinehart, and Winston, 1968.

James, W. *Talks to Teachers: On Psychology; and to Students on Some of Life's Ideals.* New York: Norton, 1958.

Katz, J. and R. T. Hartnett. *Scholars in the Making.* Cambridge, Mass.: Ballinger, 1976.

Lowman, J. *Mastering the Techniques of Teaching.* San Francisco: Jossey-Bass, 1984.

McKeachie, W. J. *Teaching Tips: A Guidebook for the Beginning College Teacher.* Lexington, Mass.: D.C. Heath, 1978.

Parker, J. C. and L. J. Rubin. *Process as Content: Curriculum Design and the Application of Knowledge.* Chicago: Rand McNally, 1966.

Perry, W. G., Jr. "Cognitive and Ethical Growth: The Making of Meaning." In *The Modern American College,* by A. W. Chickering and Associates. San Francisco: Jossey-Bass, 1981.

——. *Forms of Intellectual and Ethical Development in the College Years: A Scheme.* New York: Holt, Rinehart and Winston, 1970.

Peters, R. S. "Must An Educator Have An Aim?" In *Concepts of Teaching: Philosophical Essays,* ed. C. J. B. MacMillan and T. W. Nelson. Chicago: Rand McNally, 1968.

Peterson, H. *Great Teachers.* New Brunswick, N.J.: Rutgers University Press, 1946.

Raths, L. E., S. Wassermann, A. Jonas, and M. Rothstein. *Teaching for Thinking: Theory and Application.* Columbus, Ohio: Merrill, 1967.

Roethlisberger, F. J. *The Elusive Phenomena,* ed. G. F. F. Lombard. Boston: Division of Research, Harvard University Graduate School of Business Administration, 1977.

Rogers, C. R. *Freedom to Learn.* Columbus, Ohio: Merrill, 1969.

——. "Student-Centered Teaching." In *Client-Centered Therapy: Its Current Practice, Implications, and Theory* by C. R. Rogers. Boston: Houghton Mifflin, 1965.

Scheffler, I. "The Concept of Teaching." In *Concepts of Teaching: Philosophical Essays,* ed. C. J. B. MacMillan and T. W. Nelson. Chicago: Rand McNally, 1968.

Schön, D. A. *The Reflective Practitioner: How Professionals Think in Action.* New York: Basic, 1983.

Schwartz, L. L. "Criteria for Effective University Teaching." *Improving College and University Teaching* 28 (1980): 120–121.

Weitz, S., ed. *Nonverbal Communication: Readings with Commentary.* New York: Oxford University Press, 1974.

Whitehead, A. N. *The Aims of Education and Other Essays.* New York: Macmillan, 1929, 1957.

Wilson, J. D. *Student Learning in Higher Education.* New York: Wiley, 1981.

II. Case Method and Discussion Teaching

Andrews, K. R., ed. *The Case Method of Teaching Human Relations and Administration.* Cambridge: Harvard University Press, 1953.

Argyris, C. "Some Limitations of the Case Method: Experience in a Management Development Program." *Academy of Management Review* 5 (1980): 291–298.

Berger, M. "In Defense of the Case Method: A Reply to Argyris." *Academy of Management Review* 8 (1983): 329–333.

Copeland, M. T. "The Case Method of Instruction." In *And Mark an Era: The Story of the Harvard Business School.* Boston: Little, Brown, 1958.

Corey, E. R. "Case Method Teaching." HBS Publishing Division, Harvard Business School, Boston, Mass. HBS Case No. 9-581-058.

Erskine, J. A., M. R. Leenders and L. A. Mauffette-Leenders. *Teaching with Cases.* London, Canada: Research and Publications Division, School of Business Administration, The University of Western Ontario, 1981.

Fraser, C. E., ed. *The Case Method of Instruction: A Related Series of Articles.* New York: McGraw-Hill, 1931.

Frederick, P. "The Dreaded Discussion: Ten Ways to Start." *Improving College and University Teaching* 29 (1981): 109–114.

Glover, J. D. and R. M. Hower. "Some Notes on the Use of *The Administrator: Cases on Human Relations in Business.*" Chicago: Irwin, 1950.

Gragg, C. I. "Because Wisdom Can't Be Told." In *The Case Method at the Harvard Business School,* ed. M. P. McNair with Anita C. Hersum. New York: McGraw-Hill, 1954. Available as reprint from HBS Publishing Division, Harvard Business School, Boston, Mass. HBS Case No. 9-451-005.

Hunt, P. "The Case Method of Instruction." *Harvard Educational Review* 21 (1951): 2–19.

Lawrence, P. R. "The Preparation of Case Material." In *The Case Method of Teaching Human Relations and Ad-*

ministration, ed. K. R. Andrews. Cambridge: Harvard University Press, 1953. Available as reprint from HBS Publishing Division, Harvard Business School, Boston, Mass. HBS Case No. 9-451-006.

McNair, M. P. "Tough-Mindedness and the Case Method." In *The Case Method at the Harvard Business School*, ed. M. P. McNair with A. C. Hersum. New York: McGraw-Hill, 1954. Available as reprint from HBS Publishing Division, Harvard Business School, Boston, Mass. HBS Case No. 9-379-090.

———, with A. C. Hersum. *The Case Method at the Harvard Business School*. New York: McGraw-Hill, 1954.

Merry, R. W. "Preparation to Teach a Case." In *The Case Method at the Harvard Business School*, ed. M. P. McNair with A. C. Hersum. New York: McGraw-Hill, 1954. Available as reprint from HBS Publishing Division, Harvard Business School, Boston, Mass. HBS Case No. 9-354-021.

———. "Use of Case Material in the Classroom." In *The Case Method at the Harvard Business School*, ed. M. P. McNair with A. C. Hersum. New York: McGraw-Hill, 1954. Available as reprint from HBS Publishing Division, Harvard Business School, Boston, Mass. HBS Case No. 9-354-019.

Miner, F. C. "An Approach for Increasing Participation in Case Discussions." *Exchange: The Organizational Behavior Teaching Journal* 3 (1978): 41–42.

Reynolds, J. I. *Case Method in Management Development: Guide for Effective Use*. Geneva, Switzerland: Management Development Series No. 17, International Labour Office, 1980.

———. "There Is Method in Cases." *The Academy of Management Review* 3 (1978): 129–133.

Roethlisberger, F. J. "Teaching by the Case Method." In *The Elusive Phenomena*, ed. G. F. F. Lombard. Boston: Division of Research, Harvard University Graduate School of Business Administration, 1977.

Sargent, C. G. and E. L. Belisle. "Section One: Some Aspects of Administrative Situations and Cases." In *Educational Administration: Cases and Concepts*. Boston: Houghton Mifflin, 1955.

Shapiro, Benson P. "Hints for Case Teaching." HBS Publishing Division, Harvard Business School, Boston, Mass. HBS Case No. 9-585-012.

Tagiuri, R. "Miscellaneous Thoughts on the Case Method." In *On Teaching Money and Banking by Cases*, ed. L. E. Davids. Homewood, Ill.: Irwin, 1966.

Tedesco, P. H. *Teaching with Case Studies*. Boston, Mass.: Public Information Center, Federal Reserve Bank of Boston, 1974.

III. Operating Problems

1. The Role of the Teacher

Athos, A. G. "Contingencies Beyond Reasoning." *Exchange: The Organizational Behavior Teaching Journal* 4 (Spring 1979): 7–12.

Bailey, J. C. "Memo on a Session with Section E." HBS Publishing Division, Harvard Business School, Boston, Mass. HBS Case No. 9-462-001.

Fraher, R. "Learning a New Art: Suggestions for Beginning Teachers." In *The Art and Craft of Teaching*, ed. M. M. Gullette. Cambridge: Harvard-Danforth Center for Teaching and Learning, 1982.

Peltier, G. L. and J. A. Bailey. "When Neophyte Teachers Face Themselves." *Improving College and University Teaching* 25 (1977): 119–121.

Purkey, W. W. "The Task of the Teacher." In *The Helping Relationship Sourcebook*, ed. D. L. Avila, A. W. Combs, and W. W. Purkey. Boston: Allyn and Bacon, 1971.

Seldin, P. "Self-Assessment of College Teaching." *Improving College and University Teaching* 30 (1982): 70–74.

Wolcowitz, J. "The First Day of Class." In *The Art and Craft of Teaching*, ed. M. M. Gullette. Cambridge: Harvard-Danforth Center for Teaching and Learning, 1982.

2. Questioning, Responding, and Listening

Brammer, L. M. "Helping Skills for Understanding." Chapter 4 of *The Helping Relationship* by L. M. Brammer, 2nd ed. Englewood Cliffs, N.J.: Prentice-Hall, 1979.

Hyman, R. T. *Strategic Questioning*. Englewood Cliffs, N.J.: Prentice-Hall, 1979.

Kasules, T. P. "Questioning." In *The Art and Craft of Teaching*, ed. M. M. Gullette. Cambridge: Harvard-Danforth Center for Teaching and Learning, 1982.

Rogers, C. R. and R. E. Farsen. "Active Listening." Reprinted in *Effective Behavior in Organizations* by A. R. Cohen, S. L. Fink, H. Gadon, and R. S. Willits. Homewood, Ill. Irwin, 1976.

3. Leadership Issues in Class Discussions

Dearborn, D. C. "Observer's Report on the Role of the Instructor in Case Discussions." In *The Case Method at the Harvard Business School*, ed. M. P. McNair with A. C. Hersum. New York: McGraw-Hill, 1954.

Finkel, D. P. and G. S. Monk. "Teachers and Learning Groups: Dissolution of the Atlas Complex." In *Learning in Groups*, eds. C. Bouton and R. Y. Garth. San Francisco: Jossey-Bass, 1983.

Gordon, T. "Group-Centered Leadership and Administration." Chapter 8 of *Client-Centered Therapy: Its*

Current Practice, Implications, and Theory by C. R. Rogers. Boston: Houghton Mifflin, 1965.

Nyaman, R. T. *Improving Discussion Leadership.* New York: Teachers College Press, 1980.

4. Group Process in the Classroom

Bouton, C. and R. Y. Garth, eds. *Learning in Groups: New Directions for Teaching and Learning,* No. 14. San Francisco: Jossey-Bass, 1983.

DuJardin, P. and C. F. Gibson with M. Lawrence. "Managing Workgroups." HBS Publishing Division, Harvard Business School, Boston Mass. HBS Case No. 9-477-097.

Gadlen, H. and R. Rosenwein. "Process Issues in the Discussion Group." *Improving College and University Teaching* 16 (1968): 250–257.

Hargreaves, D. N. *Interpersonal Relations and Education.* London: Routledge and Kegan Paul, 1972.

Schein, E. H. "The Structure and Function of Groups." In *Organizational Psychology* by E. H. Schein, 3rd ed. Englewood Cliffs, N.J.: Prentice-Hall, 1980.

Schmuck, R. A. and P. A. Schmuck. *Group Processes in the Classroom,* 2nd ed. Dubuque, Iowa: Brown, 1975.

Tuckman, B. W. "Developmental sequence in small groups." *Psychological Bulletin* 63 (1965): 384–399.

5. Grading

Cahn, S. M. "The Uses and Abuses of Grades and Examinations." *In Scholars Who Teach: The Art of College Teaching* by S. M. Cahn. Chicago: Nelson-Hall, 1978.

Entwistle, N. J. and J. D. Wilson. *Degrees of Excellence: The Academic Achievement Game.* London: Hodder and Stoughton, 1977.

Fuller, S. H. "What Is an Unsatisfactory Examination Paper?" In *The Case Method of Teaching Human Relations and Administration,* ed. K. R. Andrews. Cambridge: Harvard University Press, 1953.

Jedrey, C. M. "Grading and Evaluation." In *The Art and Craft of Teaching,* ed. M. M. Gullette. Cambridge: Harvard-Danforth Center for Teaching and Learning, 1982.

Rowntree, D. *Assessing Students: How Shall We Know Them?* New York: Harper & Row, 1977.

6. Enhancing Student Involvement

Altmaier, E. M., ed. *Helping Students Manage Stress.* San Francisco: Jossey-Bass, 1983.

Bowers, W. J. *Student Dishonesty and Its Control in College.* New York: Bureau of Applied Social Research, Columbia University, 1964.

Hawley, C. S. "The Thieves of Academe: Plagiarism in the University System." *Improving College and University Teaching* 32 (Winter 1984): 35–39.

Lanig, M. "Student Apathy." *Improving College and University Teaching* 15 (Winter 1967): 33–37.

Shaftel, F. R. and G. Shaftel. *Role Playing in the Curriculum.* Englewood Cliffs, N.J.: Prentice-Hall, 1982.

7. Gender and Minority Issues in the Classroom

Adler, N. E. "Women Students." In *Scholars in the Making,* ed. J. Katz and R. T. Hartnett. Cambridge, Mass.: Ballinger, 1976.

Austin, A. W. *Minorities in American Higher Education.* San Francisco: Jossey-Bass, 1982.

Duncan, B. L. "Minority Students." In *Scholars in the Making,* ed. J. Katz and R. T. Hartnett. Cambridge, Mass.: Ballinger, 1976.

Forisha, B. L. "The Inside and the Outsider: Women in Organizations." In *Outsiders on the Inside,* ed. B. L. Forisha and B. H. Goldman. Englewood Cliffs, N. J.: Prentice-Hall, 1981.

Gibbs, J. T. "Black Students at Integrated Colleges: Problems and Prospects." In *Black/Brown/White Relations,* ed. C. V. Willie. New Brunswick, N. J.: Transaction Books, 1977.

Hall, R. B. and B. R. Sandler. *The Classroom Climate: A Chilly One for Women?* Washington, D.C.: Project on the Status and Education of Women, Association of American Colleges, 1982.

Heller, T. *Women and Men as Leaders.* New York: Praeger, 1982.

Hennig, M. and M. Jardim. *The Managerial Woman.* New York: Doubleday, 1976.

Miller, S. B. *Toward a New Psychology of Women.* Boston: Beacon Press, 1976.

Rossi, A. and A. Calderwood, eds. *Academic Women on the Move.* New York: Russell-Sage, 1973.

Tagiuri, R. "The Foreign Student and the Case Method in Business Administration: Some Remarks Regarding the Learning Process." *The Journal of Social Psychology* 53 (1961): 105–111.

Willie, C. V. and A. S. McCord. *Black Students at White Colleges.* New York: Praeger, 1973.